Optimal Enterprise

Complex and Enterprise Systems Engineering

Series Editor

Paul E. Garvey & Brian E. White

PUBLISHED

Optimal Enterprise

Structures, Processes and Mathematics of Knowledge, Technology and Human Capital

By Mikhail V. Belov and Dmitry A. Novikov

CRC Press
Taylor & Francis Group
Boca Raton London New York

CRC Press is an imprint of the
Taylor & Francis Group, an **informa** business

First edition published [2021]
by CRC Press
6000 Broken Sound Parkway NW, Suite 300, Boca Raton, FL 33487-2742

and by CRC Press
2 Park Square, Milton Park, Abingdon, Oxon, OX14 4RN

ISBN: 9780367652432 (hbk)
ISBN: 9780367541750 (pbk)
ISBN: 9781003128564 (ebk)

Typeset in Times
by Deanta Global Publishing Services, Chennai, India

Contents

PART II   Mathematics: Mathematical Models and Methods of Enterprise Control

PART III   Practice: Business Tools and Applications

Foreword

In the modern world, most of the gross product resulting from human activity is created within companies; organizations; institutions; projects; project programs; state, regional, and municipal agencies; and transnational corporations and their divisions, as well as various associations and compositions of all of the above entities. Such entities are usually considered a special class of complex systems – the *Enterprise* (see, for example, Gorod et al. 2015, Martin et al. 2012, Rebovich and White 2011).

The concept and term Enterprise is widespread and has a long, centuries-old history, accompanying almost all the contemporary development of humankind, starting with the period of great geographical discoveries and the subsequent expansion of world trade. Enterprises, being, on the one hand, complex, and, on the other hand, widespread systems, are the subject matter of various knowledge domains, such as cybernetics, system theory, systems engineering, operations research, game theory, sociology, economics, business and management sciences, and many other fields of fundamental and applied science.

To date, significant success has been achieved in these branches of knowledge, and many methods and approaches to managing firms, their divisions and associations, projects, and project programs have been developed – these are Enterprises.

However, due to the complexity of the subject matter, the formalization of the Enterprise has not yet been advanced to the development of a unified mathematical model (or harmonized system of such models) of the Enterprise as a managed object or its control process. The absence of such models, in turn, does not allow us to formulate mathematically rigorous foundations for Enterprise control.

The employment of such models and foundations seems to be extremely important, not only for fundamental science, but also in practice, since the use of fundamental – mathematically rigorous – foundations allows us to evaluate

- the optimality of Enterprise management systems and decisions made;
- the maximum possible (under certain conditions) efficiency of the Enterprise (firms, projects, project programs).

The use of heuristics, practical experience (including the case studies method), patterns based on actual data (including intensively developing Machine Learning), and other widely used approaches as basics of control systems does not allow drawing conclusions about the optimality of control, nor does it even correctly judge the management efficiency of any new Enterprise based on information about even a huge number of other Enterprises studied. Moreover, operations research and related sciences, widely used in practice, provide optimization of the constituents of an Enterprise without modeling it as a whole system. However, the optimization of parts does not lead to the optimality of the whole, while the absence of top-down and holistic mathematical models (or an integrated system of models) of an Enterprise contradicts the principle of holism and the system approach.

Following the system approach, in turn, an Enterprise is considered to be a complex system in the presented research. Along with the *Enterprise*, its *complex activity* (CA) that implements the main purpose of the Enterprise – creating value for stakeholders – is studied. The complexity of the Enterprise gives rise to various classifications and relations of an Enterprise with more general and more specific categories; they are fixed below to determine the subject matter of the study more accurately. First and foremost, among all kinds of systems, we distinguish artificial, humanmade and engineered systems (see Figure f.1).

In addition, an Enterprise belongs to the class of *sociotechnical systems* (STSs), consisting of people and technical components.

Complex systems (see Section Definitions) form a very important subclass of systems and unite not only STSs but also other systems with the property of emergence and with continuously interacting and competing elements. For example, biological systems like biocenoses are not STSs but belong to Complex Systems (Figure f.1).

In general, an Enterprise consists of more or less autonomous units, each of which, in turn, is an enterprise; thus, an Enterprise constitutes a *System of Systems* (Figure f.1). However, an Enterprise is not necessarily a System of Systems: a small family business, although definitely an Enterprise (albeit possibly a trivial one) should not be considered a System of Systems.

Being an STS, an Enterprise includes people as constituents. In turn, the basic property of people that distinguishes us from all other objects of the real world is activity, including free will, goal-setting, intent, motive, and purposeful choice. Therefore, the Enterprise is an *Active system* (Figure f.2) in terms of the theory of organizational systems (Burkov 1977, Novikov 2013). An organization or *Organizational system* – an organized group of people that jointly implements a certain program or reaches a goal and acts following certain procedures and rules – is a special case of an active system (Figure f.2); and a human is a "trivial" organizational system.

Another point of view exists: an Enterprise definitely should be considered a system of an organizational system and a technical system, each of which is a system in itself. As an organizational system, an Enterprise includes people; as a technical system (*Technical system* – one, including only inanimate elements, some of them possibly being humanmade), it includes material objects, energy, financial resources, and information/knowledge (Figure f.3).

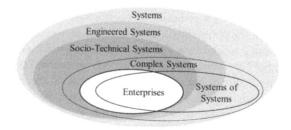

FIGURE F.1   Classes of systems – 1.

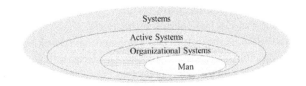

FIGURE F.2   Classes of systems – 2.

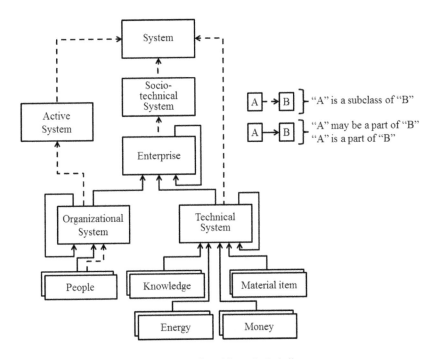

FIGURE F.3   Systems – "class I subclass" and "part I whole."

The multidisciplinarity of the subject matter of this research also requires terminology clarifications of the categories of control, management, and other related categories, which are paramount, as are the categories of the Enterprise and the sociotechnical system.

In general, there might be only two ways to reach any goal[*] or to get any value: (a) doing something that leads to the goal; (b) influencing somebody/something else to do something that leads to the goal. The first one is an execution of CA, while the second one is *control* in a broad sense (in the sense of classical *cybernetics* (Wiener 1948) and second order cybernetics (Foerster 1995), as well as its numerous branches – see surveys in Umpleby (1990) and Novikov (2016). Both approaches are realized

---

[*] Goal-setting and purposefulness issues are discussed in Section 2.1 in more detail.

through a complex system or Enterprise (or an individual as a trivial case of an Enterprise) as the actor of CA and control, respectively.

In the 1940s and 1950s, at the time of the appearance and development of cybernetics and *systems theory*, the term control could be considered sufficient and adequate to mean the targeted influence on the controlled subject (system). But with the progress of the world economic system and advance of knowledge of complex systems and business management, as well as psychology and sociology, the term control, as applied to an Enterprise or a complex system or STS, does not seem adequate enough. Now, different means of influencing an Enterprise and/or STS, first of all a participating human, by various stakeholders are considered: organization, leadership, management, governance, corporate culture, guidance, mentoring, coaching, involvement, and others. Significantly different from the practical and business point of view, all these categories have a fundamental methodological commonality: all of them are implemented as a CA by which the actor (leader, manager, organizer, governor, etc.) influences the behavior of the Enterprise or STS to reach the actor's goals or objectives. Therefore, for the purpose of methodological analysis, we unite all these types of activities into a single set and we will refer to it as *management in a broad sense*. Hereinafter, the term *management*, unless otherwise specified, denotes this set of types of CA (which are methodologically similar but different from the practical and business points of view). These various kinds of managerial* complex activity and their specifics – commonalities and differences – are studied from the methodological point of view as well as from the business and practical points of view in Sections 1.5.1 and 8.1.1.

In addition, the term *control* is used as an equivalent to *management*, and the verbs *to manage* and *to control* are used as synonyms, relying on the fact that the Merriam–Webster's Collegiate Dictionary defines the verbs to manage and to control as synonyms in the following case: "to use one's powers to lead, guide, or dominate," while "manage implies direct handling and manipulating or maneuvering toward a desired result" and "control implies a regulating or restraining in order to keep within bounds or on a course." Following the traditions prevailing in the relevant branches of science, when considering the methodological foundations (Chapters 1 and 2) and business practice (Chapter 8), we will mainly use the terms management and to manage, while in chapters representing mathematical models and methods (Chapters 3–7), we use control and to control.

Thus, following a system approach and the principle of holism, an attempt is made in this book to pose and solve the *Enterprise Control Problem* as a holistic and top-down mathematical optimization problem. The general scheme for solving the problem follows the common methodological scheme of cognition:

First, a ***methodological analysis*** is made (Part I, Chapters 1 and 2) and a qualitative formalism is developed in the form of an integrated set of structural and process models describing the Enterprise and its complex activity.

---

* The authors chose the term management to mean a set of all these, generally speaking, considerably different categories, given the fact that the term management is always present in various denominations of the domains of theoretical and applied knowledge that involve the study of these categories.

Furthermore, based on this formalism, a ***generalization*** of the analysis output is performed, and a formal and holistic mathematical optimization problem – the Enterprise Control Problem – is formulated (Part II, Chapter 3). As a result, a harmonized set of mathematical models and methods is proposed that not only models the essential features of the Enterprise as a complex sociotechnical system but also allows us to analytically study and obtain a solution to the Enterprise Control Problem (Part II, Chapters 4–7).

Constructive synthesis (Part III, Chapter 8) is carried out on the basis of the fundamental results obtained above: the principles of development of Enterprise management systems in the form of the *Optimal Enterprise Control Framework* are formulated; the practical application of the developed models and methods is illustrated by business cases.

The distinctive features of the Optimal Enterprise Control Framework are, first, that it integrates, generalizes, and constructively concretizes well-known managerial and economic approaches and methods:

- value chain (Porter 1985),
- management by the objectives approach – from foundation (Druker 1954) to contemporary studies (for example, Gotteiner 2016),
- lifecycle concepts (Adizes 1999),
- PDCA (Tague 2005), Fayol (Fayol 1917) and other managerial cycles,
- quality management, process approach, and continual improvement process (ISO 9004:2018),
- business process reengineering (Hammer and Champy 1993),
- leadership, corporate culture and related concepts (Cole 2018, Kotter and Heskett 1992),
- project management (PMBOK 2017),
- risk management (ISO 31000:2018),
- Agile and Scrum approaches (Sims and Johnson 2012),
- concepts of the theory of the firm (Coase 1937, Foss et al. 2000), industrial economy (Williamson 2009), business economics (Moschandreas 2000), managerial economics (Allen et al. 2009, Png and Lehman 2007),
- and many other well-known and widely useful features.

Second, the framework is focused not only on activity directly aimed at achieving the ultimate goals, but also on "preparatory" activity – the development of technology – thus examining the entire lifecycle of the Enterprise and its activity. Moreover, a uniform formalism is proposed to describe and analyze heterogeneous elements of the CA of an Enterprise.

The contents of the book are as follows:

First, **Chapter 1**, the Enterprise, paired with its CA, is considered as a complex sociotechnical system and formally represented as a hierarchical fractal aggregate of interconnected elements of CA.

Furthermore, in **Chapter 2**, the *methodological factors of Enterprise management* are researched, including an analysis of the interrelated lifecycles of the following constituents of CA: actors (also playing the role of key stakeholders and being a part of the Enterprise), subject matter, the results of activity, CA technologies, and resources; based on this analysis, Enterprise Control Subproblems are formulated.

Next, the Enterprise Control Problem is formulated in **Chapter 3**. Based on the results of Chapters 1 and 2, a uniform description of all the heterogeneous fields of activity of the modern Enterprise (marketing, sales, manufacturing, HR, finance, etc.) is made and the control problem is posed as a top-down and holistic mathematical optimization problem. At the same time, all the essential features of the Enterprise as a complex STS throughout the entire lifecycle* are considered in the statement of the problem (first and foremost, the uncertainty generated by various sources and, in particular, the behavior of people participating in the system).

Chapter 4 is devoted to the development of original models and methods of contract theory, the application of which allowed for the first time the following results to be obtained:

- formulating sufficient conditions for optimal control of the Enterprise as mathematically rigorous foundations for developing a management system;
- correctly decomposing the optimization problem into a number of mathematical tasks; methods to carry out these tasks are presented in Chapters 5–7.

Chapter 5 presents a new class of mathematical models and methods – models of processes for the development and implementation of the technology of CA.

In **Chapter 6**, mathematical models of human behavior – human capital that is a core element of an Enterprise – are developed. The importance of the proposed models lies in the fact that, on the one hand, they reflect the specifics of people's active choice, their creative abilities, and on the other hand, they model people as resources of the Enterprise.

Chapter 7 is devoted to the development of mathematical models and methods for CA planning and resource planning in the Enterprise. These models fall under well-known areas of operations research, and their novelty lies in taking into account the combination of specific Enterprise features.

The Optimal Enterprise Control Framework is introduced and examples of the practical implementation of the developed mathematical models and methods are presented in **Chapter 8**.

---

* Lifecycles of CA and its constituents are defined and studied in Section 1.4.

Basic Notation and Abbreviations

AE	active element;
AS	active system;
CA	complex activity;
IM	informational model;
LC	lifecycle;
MCA	the methodology of complex activity;
OR	operations research;
SEA	structural element of activity;
SoS	system of systems;
STS	sociotechnical system;
TCOr	theory of control in organizations.

Definitions

Activity (Novikov and Novikov 2013, p. 4) – meaningful human work or actions; – the process through which an actor purposefully impacts objects in the outside world and/or themselves.

Active system – one whose elements demonstrate the property of activity – free will, goal-setting, intent, motive, and purposeful choice.

Actor of the activity (Belov and Novikov 2020) – a sociotechnical system or an individual, who executes the activity.

Behavior of system, of object (Belov and Novikov 2020) – a successive (in time), at least partially observable, responsive, measurable objective fixation of its state changes. For an individual, behavior is a sequence of his/her actions, an interaction with the environment, mediated by his/her external (motor) or internal (mental) actions.

Complex activity (Belov and Novikov 2020, Belov and Novikov 2020a) – an activity with a non-trivial internal structure and with multiple and/or changing actors/players, methods, and roles of the subject matter of activity in its relevant context.

Complex system (White 2006) – a system with the property of emergence; an open system with continuously interacting and competing elements. Openness is understood as free and unlimited by artificial factors of participation and interaction of elements with each other and the environment.

Complex Adaptive System (SEBoK 2019) – system where the individual elements act independently but jointly behave according to common constraints and goals.

To control – to exercise restraining or directing influence over: regulate (Merriam–Webster's Collegiate Dictionary).

Engineered System (SEBoK 2019) – a system designed or adapted to interact with an anticipated operational environment to achieve one or more intended purposes while complying with applicable constraints.

Enterprise (SEBoK 2019) – a complex, (adaptive) sociotechnical system that comprises interdependent resources of people, processes, information, and technology that must interact with each other and their environment in support of a common mission.

Enterprise (Merriam–Webster's Collegiate Dictionary) – 1: a project or undertaking that is especially difficult, complicated, or risky. 2a: a unit of economic organization or activity especially: a business organization; b: a systematic purposeful activity. 3: readiness to engage in daring or difficult action.

Extended Enterprise (Extended Enterprise 2019) – wider organization representing all associated entities, customers, employees, suppliers, distributors, etc. who directly or indirectly, formally or informally, collaborate in the design, development, production, and delivery of a product to the end user.

Emergence – the principle that whole entities exhibit properties which are meaningful only when attributed to the whole, not to its parts. Every model of a human activity system exhibits properties as a whole entity which derives from its component activities and their structure, but cannot be reduced to them (Checkland 1999).

Lifecycle (ISO/IEC/IEEE 2015) – evolution of a system, product, service, project or other human-made entity from conception through retirement.

Management (Belov and Novikov 2020-a) – a means (complex activity) by which the manager (actor) influences the behavior of the managed system (managed object) to reach the goals or objectives of the manager (actor).

Management (Merriam–Webster's Collegiate Dictionary) – judicious use of means to accomplish an end.

Organization (Belov and Novikov 2020) – as a process is a means (complex activity) by which internal orderliness and coherence of interaction among more or less differentiated and autonomous elements of the organized system (organized object) are established (by establishing and maintaining the specified interrelations among elements).

Organizational system – an association of people that jointly implements a specific program or goal and acts on the basis of certain procedures and rules.

Sociotechnical system, STS (SEBoK 2019) – an engineered system which includes a combination of technical and human or natural elements.

System (ISO/IEC/IEEE 2015) – combination of interacting elements organized to achieve one or more stated purposes.

System (SEBoK 2019) – an arrangement of parts or elements that together exhibit behavior or meaning that the individual constituents do not.

Technology (Belov and Novikov 2020) – a system of conditions, criteria, forms, methods and means of successive achievement of a stated goal.

Technology management – complex activity aimed at creation of technology components in the form of information models and their integration, testing, use, and maintenance in an adequate state depending on the environment during the entire lifecycle of the CA.

Uncertainty in complex activity (Belov and Novikov 2020) – possible occurrence of some events that affect the implementation of the complex activity and the outcome. *Measurable uncertainty* in a CA is defined as the possibility of the occurrence of events described by certain laws. *True uncertainty* in a CA is the possibility of the occurrence of unique (or rarely repeated) events, which are not explained by any existing fundamental laws, and for which there are no a priori observations or adequate specification.

REFERENCES

Adizes, I. 1999. *Managing Corporate Lifecycles: An Updated and Expanded Look at the Corporate Lifecycles*. First edition. First printing. Paramus: Prentice Hall Press.

Belov, M. and Novikov, D. 2020. *Methodology of Complex Activity - Foundations of Understanding and Modelling*. Heidelberg: Springer.

Belov, M. and Novikov, D. 2020a. *Methodology of Complex Activity / Handbook of Systems Sciences*. Ed. by Gary S. Metcalf, Kyoichi Kijima and Hiroshi Deguchi. Singapore: Springer.

Allen, W., Weigelt, B. and Doherty, N. 2009. *Edwin Mansfield Managerial Economics: Theory, Applications, and Cases*. Seventh edition. W. W. Norton & Company.

Burkov, V. 1977. *Foundations of Mathematical Theory of Active Systems*. Moscow: Nauka (in Russian).

Coase, R. 1937. The Nature of the Firm. *Economica* 4(16), 386–405.

Cole, K. 2018. *Leadership and Management: Theory and Practice*. Seventh edition. Cengage Learning: Australia.

Drucker, P. 1954. *The Practice of Management*. New York: Harper, Butterworth-Heinemann, 2007.

Extended Enterprise. 2019. *Business Dictionary*. Definition: Extended Enterprise. http://www.businessdictionary.com/definition/extended-Enterprise.html Accessed September 20, 2019.

Fayol, H. 1917. *Administration industrielle et générale*. Paris: Dunod et Pinat.

Foerster, H. 1995. *The Cybernetics of Cybernetics*. Second edition. Minneapolis: Future Systems.

Foss, N., Lando, H. and Thomsen, S. 2000. The Theory of the Firm. In B. Bouckaert, G. De Geest (Eds.), *Encyclopedia of Law and Economics: Volume III. The Regulation of Contracts*. Cheltenham: Edward Elgar Publishing, 631–658.

Gorod, A., White, B., Ireland, V., Gandhi, J. and Sauser, B. eds. 2015. *Case Studies in System of Systems, Enterprise Systems, and Complex Systems Engineering*. Boca Raton: CRC Press.

Gotteiner, S. 2016. The OPTIMAL MBO. *European Accounting and Management Review* 2(2), 42–56.

Hammer, M. and Champy, J. 1993. *Reengineering the Corporation: A Manifesto for Business Revolution*. New York: Harper Business Books.

ISO 31000:2018, *Risk management – Guidelines*.

ISO 9004:2018, *Quality Management – Quality of an Organization – Guidance to Achieve Sustained Success*.

Kotter, J. and Heskett, J. 1992. *Corporate Culture and Performance*. New York: Free Press.

Martin, J., White, B. et al. November 30, 2012. *Enterprise Systems Engineering*. http://www.sebokwiki.org/1.0.1/index.php?title = Enterprise_Systems_Engineering / A. Pyster et al., eds., *Guide to the Systems Engineering Body of Knowledge (SEBoK) v. 1.0.1*. http://www.sebokwiki.org/1.0.1/index.php?title=Main_Page. Accessed September 19, 2019.

MEDES. 2019. *International Conference on Management of Digital EcoSystems*. http://medes.sigappfr.org/ Accessed September 19, 2019.

Moschandreas, M. 2000. *Business Economics*. Second edition. London: Business Press.

Nachira, F., Nicolai, A., Dini, P., Le Louarn, M. and Leon, L. 2007. *Digital Business Ecosystems*. European Commission, Publication Office.

Northouse, P. 2015. *Leadership: Theory and Practice*. New York: SAGE Publishing.

Novikov, D. 2013. *Theory of Control in Organizations*. N.-Y.: Nova Science Publishers.

Novikov, D. 2016. *Cybernetics: From Past to Future*. Heidelberg: Springer.

PMBOK guide. 2017. *A Guide to the Project Management Body of Knowledge*. Sixth edition. Newtown Square: Project Management Institute.

Png, I. and Lehman, D. 2007. *Managerial Economics*. London: Blackwell Pub.

Porter, M. 1985. *Competitive Advantage: Creating and Sustaining Superior Performance*. New York: Simon and Schuster.

Rebovich, G. and White, B. eds. 2011. *Enterprise Systems Engineering - Advances in the Theory and Practice*. Complex and Enterprise Systems Engineering Series. Boca Raton: CRC Press.

SEBoK Glossary. 2019. https://www.sebokwiki.org/wiki/Category:Glossary_of_Terms. In A. Pyster et al., eds., *Guide to the Systems Engineering Body of Knowledge* (SEBoK) v. 1.0.1. http://www.sebokwiki.org/1.0.1/index.php?title=Main_Page. Accessed September 19, 2019.

Sims, C. and Johnson H. 2012. *Scrum: a Breathtakingly Brief and Agile Introduction*. Menlo Park, CA: Dymax.

Tague, N. 2005. *Plan–Do–Study–Act Cycle. The Quality Toolbox*. Second edition. Milwaukee: ASQ Quality Press.

Umpleby, S. 1990. The Science of Cybernetics and the Cybernetics of Science. *Cybernetics and Systems* 21(1), 109–121.

White, B. 2015. On Leadership in the Complex Adaptive Systems Engineering of Enterprise Transformation. *Journal of Enterprise Transformation* 5(3), 192–217.

Wiener, N. 1948. *Cybernetics: or the Control and Communication in the Animal and the Machine*. Cambridge: The Technology.

Williamson, O. 2010. Transaction Cost Economics: The Natural Progression. Nobel Lecture. *American Economic Review* 100(3), 673–690.

Part I

Methodology
Foundations of Enterprise Control

1 Enterprise and Complex Activity
Qualitative Models

1.1 INTRODUCTION

As a *complex sociotechnical system*, an *Enterprise* is not created merely to exist in and of itself. The value of any system does not lie in the system itself: the system itself only consumes resources to be supported and maintained. But valuable output is produced exactly by functions, operations, and the *activity* of the system. If nontrivial, complex output is needed (which is always or nearly always the case), it is necessary that, in turn, *complex activity* be carried out. So, precisely, CA is a primary source of value in general, while an Enterprise is secondary, executing CA as an actor.

In Chapter 1, an Enterprise is modeled and studied based on the concepts of the methodology of complex activity (Belov and Novikov 2020), where "complex activity" is defined as activity (activity means meaningful human work or actions (Novikov and Novikov 2007), p. 4) with a non-trivial internal structure and with multiple and/or changing actors/players, methods, and roles of the subject matter of the activity in its relevant context. In view of the distinctiveness of CA, it is taken into consideration here along with the implementing entity – an Enterprise or any STS within the framework of *systems science* (see the foundations in Bertalanffy 1968 and the review in Novikov 2016). In other words, the subject matter of this study is CA, and the research topic is the general principles underlying its organization and management.

Consequently, a series of assertions and an integrated system of structural and process models that represent all significant aspects of CA (including management) and Enterprise through the whole lifecycle has been developed. The proposed models provide a systematic basis for solving *Enterprise Control Problem*, which is the core subject matter of the book.

The developed models are diverse and quite numerous, which reflects the natural complexity of CA as a system, so modeling a large number of concrete elements of a CA is rather time-consuming and requires a great amount of effort. However, the system of models is constructed in such a way that it does not require an obligatory description of the "entire" CA of the whole Enterprise each time. Such a system allows one to abstract and focus on the elements of interest and to model exactly these elements in detail, leaving the rest of the abstract as "black boxes" without losing the expressive properties of the models and without worsening the quality of the presentation.

1.1.1 Complex Activity and an Actor: an Enterprise

Activity as meaningful human work and actions is just as universal a part of human existence as the satisfaction of basic needs. However, unlike the latter, CA is quite intricate, as are the actors involved in it. In the modern world, the bulk of the gross product (as a *result* of human activity) is created in Enterprises (in firms and companies; within projects; in state, regional, and municipal agencies and entities; and in transnational corporations and their subsidiaries; as well as in various associations and groupings of all of the above entities and operations, along with all kinds of information and technical assets, systems, and equipment associated with them). All these entities tie together several fundamental notions. First, they constitute complex systems; second, they include people as elements; and third, a significant number of their constituent parts are artificial, that is, they are human made. By combining similar entities according to a specific rationale, they are considered to be an Enterprise, defined as a complex STS that comprises interdependent resources of people, processes, information, and technology that must interact with each other and their environment in support of a common mission.

The concept of an Enterprise encompasses almost all kinds of STS used and created as a result of human activity and which are made up of people. On the one hand, Enterprise is the results and subject matter of human activity; on the other hand, human activity is carried out within the framework of Enterprises: Enterprises function as complex actors in activity, that is, Enterprises are the actors, subject matter, and/or means of CA, Figure 1.1.

Let us clarify this statement.

First, being organized and purposeful, practically all human activity is carried out within the framework of one Enterprise or another, each of which has its own behavior concerning existence and development.

Second, Enterprises do not represent value in and of themselves; they do not bring benefits simply through their existence. Moreover, as material objects, they always require expenditures to maintain them. Value and utility arise from their implementing objectives, from their carrying out activity, from their functions, see Figure 1.2. In addition, productive activity cannot be implemented without some preliminary preparation – the development of methods and the creation of resources, conditions, and means to achieve the goal. Therefore, the Enterprise and its CA should be considered during the entire time of their existence, the entire lifecycle, despite the fact that value and utility are developed only during one productive phase of the lifecycle.

In this regard, Enterprises play the role of the *actors* involved in activity, for which they are actually created. Likewise, neither management in and of itself nor management systems are intrinsically valuable: from the point of view of the end result, they are not needed, nor is even the management impact on the object, but the

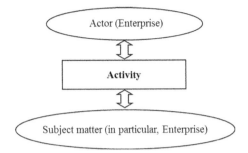

FIGURE 1.1 Activity and its actors and subject matter.

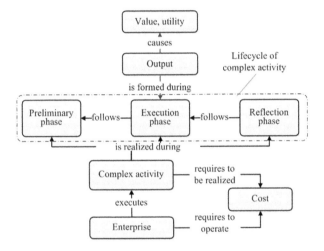

FIGURE 1.2 Enterprise, complex activity, and value creation.

value represents the state of the object being managed which was achieved as a result of a management exercise. That is, both Enterprises and their management constitute unavoidable "costs" when achieving the ultimate goals.

Third, Enterprises are the results and/or subject matter of another activity, and, being complex, they require a suitable CA from which to come forth. To correctly and completely describe such an activity, it is necessary to expand the concept of activity as currently accepted in philosophy, psychology, and methodology and to introduce a definition of CA. Here, we merely note that the complexity of the activity (especially a non-routine one) is usually no less than that of its subject matter.

Thus, CA and the STS together form a system of systems, a complex dialectical pair with each opposing the other (see Figure 1.1): "the actor (Enterprise) vs. the activity" and "the activity vs. the subject matter (in particular, Enterprise)."

This chapter is devoted to the study of this pair: the CA and the Enterprise.

Let us consider how the activity and its actor correspond. Without question, the following dialectical dualism is valid: without an actor, an activity cannot exist (or be carried out) and, at the same time, an individual or Enterprise cannot be an actor outside an activity ("without an activity"). It is undoubtedly expedient to be guided by the following principle: there is at least a short initial period during which the CA exists in an informational form of a desire for a solution, an idea "in the head" of one (!) individual (for now an individual, not artificial intelligence and, that being so, the individual "creator" of a primary idea can always be unambiguously identified); we will call them the "initiator." In this period, after the initiator has formulated the internal desire for a solution but has not yet involved anyone in the discussion or implementation of the CA, the actor involved in the activity, as an example of an STS, consists of that person alone.

It is important to note that the "initiator's" idea (*need*) did not appear when he/she was already carrying out a new activity, but namely when they were implementing some other activity (or were "inactive": the lack of activity can be regarded as its particular case).

With further implementation, the activity becomes more complicated; it has a substantial internal structure, and other actors with their own know-how vis-à-vis the activity are drawn in. Accordingly, the generalized actor of this activity becomes more complicated: they actually become an STS.

Therefore, it can be said that activity in the form of intention–need arises no later than its actor (the activity's actor!) in the form of a single individual, an elementary Enterprise. In other words, the actor as an individual (elementary Enterprise) and activity, as a minimum, "emerged equally early on." But activity in a more complex form is primary with respect to a non-elementary Enterprise, since a complex system – Enterprise – is formed in response to the need to implement the activity.

Another argument in favor of the primacy of CA with respect to the actor and Enterprise is that it is exactly the activity that provides the desired benefit, while the STS accumulates the costs to maintain it.

A significant practical conclusion follows from the theoretical observation about the primacy of the CA with respect to the non-elementary Enterprise: in analyzing, creating, and managing sociotechnical systems, the focus must not be on the Enterprise itself, but on the CA implemented by the Enterprise. That is, the kind of "secondary" firms, organizations, project teams, and – even more so – productive and non-productive assets in relation to the activity (goals, results) that they are called upon to carry out must be kept in mind. In fact, a CA establishes requirements for the Enterprise, which is its actor.

For many modern Enterprises, activity is a system-forming factor. It is no secret that some organizations have functioned – both previously and currently – for the sake of self-existence, carrying out, for example, the search for business in order to "feed" employees, utilize equipment, etc. A more striking example is bureaucracy, which itself often "dreams up" activity for itself and others (subordinates, the population, etc.) in order to justify its existence and ensure its own growth.

The thesis on the priority of CA agrees with the recommendations of international standards of quality management systems (ISO 9000:2015): "Consistent and predictable results are achieved more effectively and efficiently when activities are understood and managed as interrelated processes that function as a coherent system." However, this ISO 9000-approach does not solve the problems of organization and management of activity or take into account such essential aspects of activity as uncertainty or the active behavior of the actor (and sometimes even the subject matter) of activity, which are key points of approaches and models developed in this book.

1.1.2 MANAGEMENT OF ENTERPRISE AND ITS COMPLEX ACTIVITY

The vast majorities of artificial systems have purpose and therefore require management in a wide sense or control (see Section Foreword). Purposefulness means result-oriented, aiming to obtain the desired result, achieving certain goals. The source or root cause of any result is activity, with its components and elements, and, above all, people as the actors involved in activity, the most important component of the activity. Management represents methods of influencing a managed object to achieve defined goals. Insomuch as the "fountainhead" of any result is the corresponding activity, influence must be exerted on the activity and its components.

To lay out the subject matter of this study, it is necessary to analyze the categories of management and CA and consider how they relate to each other and to the categories of Enterprise and STS.

The general *methodology* considers *activity* in the form of a set of *procedural components* (Figure 1.3), generalizing and structuring A. Leontiev's model (Leontiev 1979). The procedural components of the activity (Novikov 2007) are as follows: the *need*, *goal*, *tasks*, and *technology* (including the forms, resources, and methods involved in the activity); and the impact and *results* of the activity (the "process" links among them are shown in bold arrows in Figure 1.3).

The following characteristics of the activity are external to this set: special features, *principles*, *criteria*, *conditions*, and *norms*. This understanding and the design of the methodology made it possible to create and lay out methodologies for scientific research (Novikov 2013), utilitarian and artistic activity, educational and communicative activity (Novikov 2007), and management (Novikov 2013b) from a single

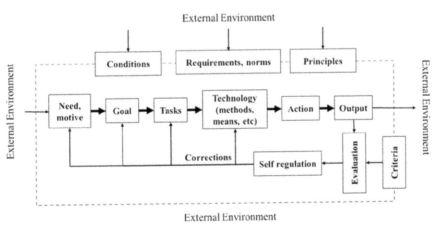

FIGURE 1.3 Procedural components of activity (Novikov 2007).

standpoint using a uniform logic. The actors involved in the activity (who carry out the activity) and the subject matter of the activity (which changes throughout the course of the activity) are the key categories without which a description of the activity is undoubtedly incomplete.

It's reasonable to mention that further research (Novikov 2020) extends the activity components concept identifying three groups of internal and one group of external components of activity:

- The *procedural components*, considered above.
- The *psychic components* are the components of the personality structure, need, motive, reflection (more precisely, auto-reflection), assessment, and self-regulation.
- The *behavioral components* are action, the state of the subject of activity, and result.
- The *external components* are criteria, norms, principles, requirements, and conditions.

Let us consider how the categories of activity and management relate.

In managing a CA and/or Enterprise, the subject matter is complex and includes a complex interacting and interrelated pair: "CA ⇔ Enterprise."

CA is the primary subject matter of management, and the Enterprise itself is an intermediary, playing the roles of the actor involved in the CA and/or its subject matter.

A detailed consideration of management problems requires a more detailed analysis of the management category and its correlation with related.

The definition of *management* as a CA that ensures the impact of a manager (the actor involved in this CA) on the system being managed (management goal) designed to ensure his/her behavior leading to the attainment of the goals of the manager highlights several aspects.

First, it is stated that there is an actor making an impact. STS plays the role of *complex actor* of CA; therefore, the impact on the management target is the result of the activity of these STS. Management is a special case of activity (just as in the framework of the management methodology, management is a special case of practical activity (Novikov 2013b)). In view of the complexity of the actor and the target, management, as a rule, constitutes a CA.

Second, by virtue of the specifics of sociotechnical systems, the actor involved in managerial activity is a complex one. It is important that the management impact be directed toward a system that is organized and focused, meaning the management subject matter (as an activity) is also generally complex and includes a pair (Enterprise and CA).

Third, both the definition itself and the first of these noted aspects (management is activity, and activity is always purposeful) emphasize the *purposefulness* of management.

Fourth, the definition refers to the direction of the impact on the management target, which in turn ensures that the result required by the manager is obtained. Put another way, management activity affects the final result indirectly and implicitly through the management target.

Fifth, the emphasis is on "ensuring the *behavior*" of the management target, i.e., managerial activity is aimed at changing the sequence of states of the management target (see the definition of behavior of an object and/or a system).

From the point of view of an "*external observer*," the state of any real-world object can change over time for two reasons. The first is derived from some internal properties of the object and under the influence of the (possibly un-targeted) external environment; we will call this change "*inherent behavior*." Second, the change in the state of the object can occur under the influence of this observer, who has their own goals and tries to influence the object. However, the observer's influence on the object is activity of the first one, meaning that the reasons for any changes to the state of the object from the viewpoint of the observer are the inherent behavior of the object (naturally, including changes in the behavior of the object under the influence of results of activity by other actors apart from itself) and/or the activity of the observer himself or herself.

The above aspects of management categories, considered to be activity, allow it to be correlated with the category of *organization* (as a process), which is also considered to be an activity. According to the Webster Dictionary, organization is defined as "the act or process of organizing or of being organized," in turn, to organize means "to form into a coherent unity or functioning whole: integrate." To organize activity means to arrange it into a coherent system with clearly defined characteristics.

In this book, the following definition is employed: an organization is a CA aimed at creating internal order and co-ordination among the interactions of more or less differentiated and autonomous elements of the actor involved in this activity (including through the formation and maintenance of interrelationships with given characteristics among these elements).

It makes sense to highlight the similarities and differences between organization and management as kinds of activity in relation to the case considered in this book, where the actor involved in the activity is an Enterprise.

The first three aspects highlighted above are inherent in both management and organization, and represent an activity (usually complex), the subject matter of which is a complex dialectic pair (Enterprise and CA), and which is purposeful.

The fourth aspect, the indirectness and obliqueness of influence on the final result (the result of the activity of the management target) through the subject matter of this activity (the management target) constitutes the distinguishing feature of *management in wide sense* (and organization as well) and allows it to be identified from among all the elements of the "complex activity" array.

Analogously, the goal in the form of a change in internal order – the co-ordination of interacting parts – unambiguously singles out organization from among other forms of activity; therefore, it is the distinguishing feature of organization.

Essence of organization and management may be formulated as follows:

Both management and organization as processes are kinds of activity, usually complex ones, the subject matter of which is the CA and the corresponding Enterprise. At the same time, the indirectness and obliqueness of the influence on the final result through the subject matter of management activity is a distinctive feature of management in the wide sense, and the goal in the form of a change in internal order and coordination of interacting parts is a distinctive feature of "organization."

A more detailed understanding of organization and management is discussed in Section 1.5, where it is shown that organization being a specific form of management includes such kinds of activity as analysis, synthesis, and concretization, while management includes organization, as a special case, *regulation*, and *evaluation*.

An investigation of the management of CAs and Enterprises allows the assertion that, in comparison with general methodology (Novikov 2007), which is for the most part descriptive in nature and investigates how an activity is organized, the next step in this research below is normative, i.e., the issues of management are studied and it is determined how to manage activity.

The definitions of management as "activity overseeing activity" possess a recursiveness (Figure 1.4) and, as a result, there is the potential for an infinite expansion of the subject matter.

Management, looked at as kinds of activity, is inherent in the actors and, in either case, the activity along with the corresponding actors can also be considered as a matter of "superior" activity – management (strictly speaking, they must be considered, since any activity has to be also organized). In addition, this superior activity has an actor and so on. No activity subject matter can be so in the absence of activity, while activity cannot exist without its subject matter. An equivalent assertion also holds for the actor involved in the activity. Therefore, "*activity overseeing activity*" – being recursive and nested – is potentially infinite. Consequently, attempting to include the "entire superior" recursive chain of subject matter and actors in the subject matter is not constructive.

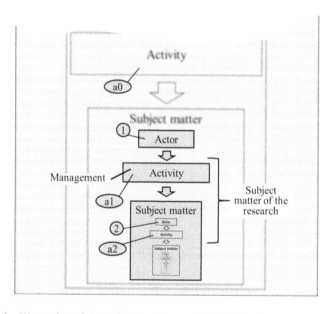

FIGURE 1.4   Illustration of the definition of research subject matter.

However, the subject matter of our study – and of every specific study of CAs – is naturally limited, due to the following considerations. It was noted above that either the behavior of the object itself or the activity of the very observer constitutes the reason behind any changes in the state of an object from an observer's point of view. Therefore, the condition for inclusion of the actor – who is superior in the recursion – into the research topic framework can be determined by the answer to the question, "Is the given actor considered to be changing, following only from their own behavior, or does the researcher also intend to study the influence on the superior actor's behavior?" If the researcher does not plan to study the effects on the actor (in the figure, this actor is indicated by the number 1), higher conceivable or existing activity (number a0 in Figure 1.4) is not included in the subject matter of the study, and the change in the state of such an actor over time is considered only within the scope of their own behavior (in particular, it is considered to be unchangeable). Conversely, when the researcher influences the actor (number 2 in Figure 1.4), the activity–impact on the actor must be included in the subject matter of the research (number a1 in Figure 1.4).

Thus, the subject matter of this study is complex activity (a1) carried out by the Enterprise/actor (1) for the management of CA (a2) implemented by the Enterprise/actor (2). A change in the state of the actor (1) is taken into account within the scope of his/her own behavior; the diagram in Figure 1.5 illustrates relations between key categories.

1.1.3 RELATED DISCIPLINES AND KNOWLEDGE DOMAINS

The subject matter of Enterprise management is a part of the domain of managing complex organizational and technical systems in general, which has long been a research topic (see the review and references in Novikov 2013b). First and foremost have been philosophers, since this issue is interdisciplinary, and this was realized from the very first attempts to resolve it, simply because it "did not belong to" (in the era of post-differentiation of the sciences) the scope of interests of any of the "mono-disciplines." Later, problems concerning sociotechnical systems management

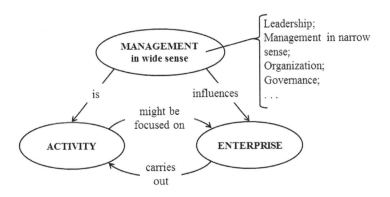

FIGURE 1.5 Key categories.

continued to be dealt with by philosophers and cybernetics experts (sometimes together with "sectoral" experts) (Novikov 2016) – see the brief review of *management philosophy* in (Novikov 2013b).

Problems concerning sociotechnical systems management began to be discussed particularly intensively at the beginning of the 20th century, because sociotechnical systems developed and became complicated and massive. The key factor is that they became massive (!), because, throughout the entire development of humankind, there have always been individuals who "worked," "balanced," and explored at the edge of a *recognized complexity* (at that historical time), for example, the managers overseeing the construction of the pyramids in ancient Egypt or the Great Wall of China. But they were isolated. With the waves of industrial revolutions, first, sociotechnical systems and Enterprises became massive and, second, not just systems, but systems of systems – systems comprising both systems and Enterprises (Ackoff 1971) – began to take shape. The realization that a system of systems requires special approaches came much later, only in the 1990s.

Society began to feel the need to manage sociotechnical systems and Enterprises – their creation and application – based on scientific approaches, i.e., the need arose to move from the art of management to "mass" management. Therefore, at the beginning of the 20th century, attempts were begun to understand the general patterns of the *organization* of biological, social, and other systems (Bogdanov 1926). In the middle of the 20th century, highly complex technical systems began to be intensively created and developed (along with organizational ones). Naturally, they were included in the sociotechnical systems management research topic. Then came the formulation of Norbert Wiener's *cybernetics* and Ludwig von Bertalanffy's *general systems theory* as "a logico-mathematical field, the subject matter of which is the formulation and deduction of those principles which are valid for 'systems' in general" (von Bertalanffy 1950, see also the review and discussion in Novikov 2016).

However, the main thrust (mainly because of the Second World War and the Cold War that followed) quickly came to focus on technical systems and the most pressing problems that could be described by suitable mathematical models; approaches like *operations research* (Wagner 1975) – which, using mathematical methods, examined individual fields and applied management tasks via both technical and organizational systems – quickly emerged and were thoroughly developed, but did not solve the sociotechnical system and Enterprise management question as a whole.

In parallel, *system engineering* was institutionalized. Applied approaches, methods, and tools for the mass (!) resolution of problems involved in creating and applying complex technical systems were developed (Haskins 2012, ISO/IEC/IEEE 2015, Pyster and Olwell 2013). Within the framework of systems engineering, areas related to *systems of systems* (System of Systems Engineering), Enterprises as a system (Enterprise Systems Engineering) (see the historical review in Gorod 2014), etc., stood out.

At the same time, mathematical methods for researching organizational systems and Enterprises began to be developed: the *theory of active systems* and the *theory of organizational systems control* (Burkov et al. 2015, Novikov 2013d), *contract theory*

(Hart and Holström 1987), the *theory of hierarchical systems* (Mesarović et al. 1970, Germeier 1986) and others appeared.

Business is a very particular application of the Enterprise, so, since the beginning of the 20th century, theoretical and applied management has developed intensively (and since the second half of that century it has developed very intensively), and in the second half of the 20th century the theory of business processes likewise advanced. The following are used as research methods (specification tools) related to the analysis and description of business processes (i.e., *"business process theory"*) and *project management*, which includes both theoretical foundations and Hoare's theory of communicating sequential processes (Hoare 1985), Milner's calculus of communicating systems (Milner 1980), multi-agent models (Holland 2006, Rzevski and Skobelev 2014), the algebra of interacting processes (Bergstra 1984), the Petri net theory, discrete-event systems, partial order theory, temporal logic, synchronously and asynchronously interacting automation, process theory, system standards for quality management and quality assurance (ISO 9000:2000 standards system), etc.

Economics* also considers Enterprise as an agent which directly executes the processes of production, distribution of goods and services. Various fields of economic sciences as the *theory of the firm* (Coase 1937, Foss et al. 2000), *industrial economy* (Williamson 2009), *business economics* (Moschandreas 2000), *managerial economics* (Allen et al. 2009, Png and Lehman 2007) have been developed to study different characteristics of Enterprise, its lifecycle and its operations.

Separate, known attempts have been made to create unified models and to develop integrated approaches to the description of various aspects of STS (see, for example, Dori and Sharon 2012). For instance, the classical study by M. Porter (Porter 1985) is based on a representation of the firm as a collection of various types of activities that make up a chain to create value (*Value Chain*). The section, devoted to Enterprises (Enterprise Systems Engineering (Gorod 2014, Pyster and Olwell 2013, Rebovich and White 2011)), appeared in the system engineering domain.

As noted above, Enterprises constitute the source and basis of the existence of humankind and its development. Thus, in a broad sense, the Enterprise management theme is to some extent currently being examined in various fields of knowledge: general systems theory and systems engineering, theories of organizational systems control, firms, organizations, projects, etc. (Novikov 2013c), management (Mescon 1988), organization theory (Bogdanov 1926), methodology (Novikov 2007), cybernetics and automatic control theory (Bubnicki 2005, Dorf 2011, Levine 2010), and many other areas of modern fundamental and applied science, each of which involves dozens or hundreds of various approaches and methods.

However, existing theories focus mainly on the elements of the Enterprise; for example, a great number of results have been obtained from the theory of organizational systems, and many tools have been developed to describe business processes.

---

* Economics: the branch of knowledge concerned with the production, consumption, and transfer of wealth (Oxford University Press); a social science concerned chiefly with description and analysis of the production, distribution, and consumption of goods and services (Merriam-Webster).

In spite of all this, a unified theory of Enterprise management or control has not yet been created. The Enterprise as a subject matter of study is an extremely complex one. Therefore, the formalization of the Enterprise as a managed entity and the process of management have not yet led to the development of a unified mathematical model of Enterprises (or a harmonized system of such models). The absence of such models, in turn, obstructs the development of mathematically rigorous foundations for Enterprise management or control.

In this book, an attempt is made to pose and solve the Enterprise management problem as a complex mathematical optimization task.

In Chapter 1, a methodological analysis is made and a qualitative formalism of the Enterprise in the form of sets of general and universal models is developed. The analysis expands the methodological direction presented in the works by A. Novikov and D. Novikov (Novikov 2007, Novikov 2013, Novikov 2013b) and their colleagues. On the other hand, CA is viewed as a complex system, so the research relies on and develops approaches and methods for systems theory (Systems Science) and its applied expansion of engineering systems (Systems Engineering) (Haskins 2015, ISO/IEC/IEEE 2015).

1.2 STRUCTURAL MODELS OF COMPLEX ACTIVITY AND ENTERPRISE

The *structure* is one of core general properties of complex activity: its elements might be broken down into other elements, each of which, in turn, is CA, so elements of CA form multi-level "fractal" hierarchies. Thus, two kinds of model tools must be developed to represent, study, and synthesize CA: (a) a model of elements of CA and (b) models of the structure of CA.

1.2.1 STRUCTURAL ELEMENT OF ACTIVITY

Consider the model describing an element of CA based on a known scheme of *procedural components* (Novikov 2013) of CA exhibiting an "elementary cycle of activity": certain *actions* are taken in accordance with the *technology* to reach a definite *output* (which, in general, may not comply with the *goal* defined by *demand* and *needs*). Sequential transition through this cycle (position 1 in Figure 1.6) from demand to output might be called the implementation of the activity (or the element of activity).

The core components of CA (1) should be supplemented with the *actor* (2) and *subject matter* (1) of the CA to reflect very close links among activity, actor, and subject matter (discussed in Section 1.1 above). In this way, "triad 1-2-3" forms a *"structural element of activity"* (SEA) which is used as a basic model of CA and is presented in Figure 1.6.

The SEA models an item:

- which is established to achieve a definite goal/to get a definite output: to transform the subject matter of activity;

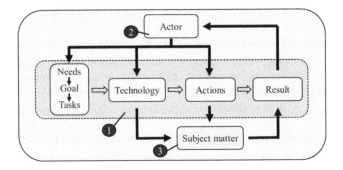

FIGURE 1.6   Model of structural element of activity.

- which represents the CA (aimed at obtaining a result) in accordance with a definite technology executed with a certain subject matter;
- the actor of which is a certain STS.

In system engineering terms (ISO/IEC/IEEE 2015, Pyster and Olwell 2013), the elements of SEA (Figure 1.6) might be considered in the following manner:

- activity (1) – as a *system-of-interest*,
- the subject matter of CA (3) – as a system reflecting the characteristics of the *operational environment*,
- the actor (2) – as an enabling system,
- all elements (1–3) – as a whole system associated with the element of CA.

In general, each of the constituents of "triad 1–2–3" could be a system; therefore, "triad 1–2–3" might be considered a complex system, a system of systems (Ackoff 1971, Gorod 2014), or an Enterprise system (Rebovich and White 2011).

The arrows in Figure 1.6 represent the following:

- the arrow from the actor to the "needs–goal–tasks" aggregate indicates that the actor accepts the demand (and need) and executes the goal-setting;
- the arrows from the actor to technology and to actions mean that the actor executes actions (acts) according to the technology;
- the arrow from the result to the actor presents the evaluation of the output, as well as the self-regulation and reflection of the actor;
- the arrows from technology and actions to the subject matter mean that the subject matter is transformed by the action according to the technology;
- the arrow from the subject matter to the result means that the result is the final state of the transformed subject matter.

The non-trivial, multi-level internal structure of CA should be represented in models of CA, so each SEA will be considered a composition of lower-level elements of CA.

A special case of an element of CA which has a confluent structure (consisting of the only element) is methodologically important for the correct modeling of CA; such an element is designated by the term *elementary operation*. This case corresponds to elementary activity which has a singular goal that does not allow or does not require further itemization and in which all the procedural components should be considered a singular action.

Thus, any SEA is considered a composition of other SEAs and/or elementary operations. Elementary operation is a special case of an element of CA which has a confluent structure "consisting of itself" – consisting of the only element which has a singular goal that does not allow or does not require further itemization and in which all the procedural components should be considered a singular action.

1.2.2 Logical Structure of Complex Activity

Let's analyze the structure of CA. First, it is necessary to choose the basics to define the structure of activity (the structure of a system is the set of stable connections or relations among its elements, so it is necessary to decide what kind of relations are considered to be "primary"). Any activity is launched by *needs*, which generates a *goal*, and concludes with a result, whether for an elementary operation or for an SEA of any level of complexity. The needs, goal, and result are the main "target" components of activity; therefore, the structure of CA should be defined based exactly on their structure, i.e., a *structure of goals* (since the result does not always coincide with the goal and the needs are not always specific or detailed enough, and it is not they but the goal that defines tasks, technology, and actions). *Technology* is secondary to tasks and goals, so the technological structure (being, nevertheless, more detailed) corresponds to the structure of the goals. Tasks are the decomposition of goals and their concretization to specific conditions. *Actions* – being aimed at implementing the tasks within the framework of the technologies used – also follow the structure of the goals. The result obtained is a consequence of actions and technology, so its structure reflects that of the goals (taking into account the uncertainty inherent in the result).

Thus, the structures of other components "repeat" the structure of the goals, so the structure of goals is used as the basis for the structure of CA: the composition of the elements of CA and the "target" connections or relations among them.

The *logical structure of CA* is defined as a finite acyclic graph (Figure 1.7) which represents the fact that each SEA (and CA as a whole) is broken down into a finite number of lower-level SEAs and elementary operations: SEA "G" consists of or is broken down into SEAs* $G_1 \ldots G_J$ and elementary operations $Op_1 \ldots Op_L$.

An actor of the SEA is also the actor of all elementary operations into which the SEA is broken down: the actor of G is also the actor of $Op_1 \ldots Op_L$.

Hierarchical structures created by breaking down some SEA into a set of lower-level (subordinate) SEAs and elementary operations demonstrate the *general system property* of CA; while *specific features* are concentrated in elementary operations,

---

* The notation "SEAs" is used to stress the plural form for multiple "structural elements of activity."

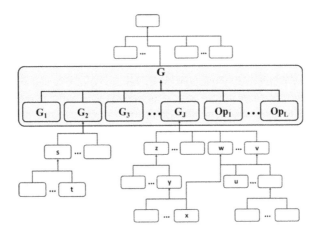

FIGURE 1.7   Example of logical structure of SEA.

their content exactly distinguishes one particular CA from another having the same structure.

Since the logical structure reflects the goal breakdown, its graph has a single root vertex. This means that to achieve the main goal G it is necessary to ensure the achievement of sub-goals $G_1, G_2, ..., G_J$ (the arcs are directed from sub-goals to goal) for which the corresponding SEAs are defined, as well as a number of sub-goals $Op_1 ... Op_L$ achieved by performing elementary operations.

Achieving all sub-goals is not mandatory in all cases (SEAs) to achieve the ultimate goal G due to uncertainty and the creation of new CA elements, which is discussed in Section 1.3.

The logical structure of an elementary operation (Figure 1.8), which has a trivial form, is necessary to complete the formalism developed. The arc–loop is a virtual one; it illustrates the possibility of a further "breakdown" of Op_l only into itself.

The logical structure also reflects the relationship of the source of demand (it is also a consumer of the output of the activity) and the actor of CA: the *superior SEA* (its actor) generates demands from *subordinate SEAs* – it sets the requirements for the outputs of the lower SEAs and later consumes their outputs. In response, lower SEAs, having specific capabilities to fulfill demands, impose restrictions on the capabilities of superior entities. Thus, the connections in the logical structure also reflect the bilateral relations "demand – capabilities (to fulfill demand)" or "needs – capabilities" in the terminology of Pyster and Olwell (2013).

The logical structure, in addition to the structure of goals, represents the "management" hierarchy of SEA subordination and the responsibility of actors for the output –

FIGURE 1.8   Logical structure of an elementary operation.

for achieving goals. Actors of the higher SEAs, together with the responsibility for achieving their "own immediate" goals, are also responsible for the attainment of lower goals and, as a consequence, for actions within the framework of the lower SEA.

The *managerial hierarchy* (responsibility relations) of CA and its logical structure highlight the necessity for the actor to organize the activity, to monitor its implementation, and to resolve all problems that arise in the area of its responsibility. On the other hand, subordinate actors (actors of subordinate SEAs) are obliged to follow the instructions of superiors and provide superiors with full and timely information, including information on emerging issues that require decision-making at higher-level entities, and *escalate problems* to a higher level of the hierarchy. Thus, the management hierarchy defines the responsibility relationship between the SEA actors, the nested relationships, the ownership of areas of responsibility, and areas of escalation of problems.

1.2.3   CAUSE–EFFECT STRUCTURE OF COMPLEX ACTIVITY

All elements of CA are interconnected by cause–effect relations, forming a time or sequential structure determined by technology (taking into account CA uncertainty, discussed below). The cause–effect model of CA has been developed to represent these relations. An example of the cause–effect model of the SEA is presented in the basic BPMN-notation, process diagram (BPMN 2011) in Figure 1.9.

Rounded rectangles denote elements of activity – SEAs (G_1, G_2, ..., G_J) and elementary operations (Op_1, Op_2, ..., Op_L); circles are events of uncertainty occurring during the execution of CA elements and affecting the course of their implementation; diamonds (for example, d, f, and k) are control points – gateways – reflecting forks (parallelization) and mergers in execution of the CA elements. The elements of notation are linked by arrows, which reflect the cause–effect relationships and control the flow of the CA elements.

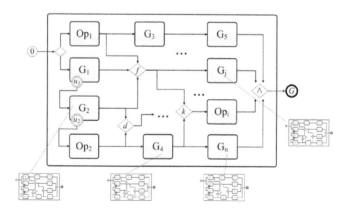

FIGURE 1.9   Example of the cause–effect model of SEA.

The concept of a *"token"* is employed as an attribute of the BPMN approach (BPMN 2011) to represent control flow: the execution of actions is reflected by the generation of abstract items – "tokens" – and their movement from one element of the cause–effect structure to another, following the arrows, or links. The starting point of SEA implementation as a whole is modeled by the generation of a single token in the model element representing the initial event (indicated by "0" in Figure 1.9). The execution of the elements following the initial one (in this example, parallel execution of Op_1 and G_1) corresponds to the disappearance of the token in "event 0" and the generation of two tokens in Op_1 and G_1. Upon termination of Op_1 and G_1, the tokens disappear in them and are generated in the following elements, as if moving along the lines of the arrows, and so on.

The events u_1 and u_2 represent the occurrence of uncertain events during execution of G_1 and G_2 – the appearance of tokens in u_1 and then in G_2 and u_2, and then in Op_2, respectively. Actually it is a fork – the generation and parallel execution of CA elements. The cause–effect model should include a specification of events u_1 and u_2 as well.

The terminal event (indicated by circle G with a thick line) models the final point of the technology of the SEA and the completion of the SEA. This event will occur when all the generated tokens "move" to element G.

Control flow links in the model represent causal and sequential relations among SEAs; for example, the goal of G_3 is a pre-condition for the goal of G_5, so SEAs G_3 and G_5 are presented as a sequence. The conditions for achieving goals that are a combination of several parallel sub-goals might be defined by the corresponding rules (conjunctive–disjunctive forms). For example, goal f is a conjunctive–disjunctive combination of the goals of G_1, Op_1, and G_2, let's say $f = \{\{G_1 \text{ or } Op_1\} \text{ and } G_2\}$. In this case, the sequence of achievement of G_1 and Op_1 is not defined, since they are drawn as "parallel" objects. After one of them and G_2 are fulfilled, the implementation of their successors is launched – the SEA G_j and maybe elementary operation Op_i, depending on the fulfillment of sub-goal k.

The complexity of activity implies the possibility of parallel execution of many of its elements; therefore, within the framework of the SEA, several subordinate SEAs and elementary operations can be executed in parallel. This is reflected in the presence of several outgoing arrow-links from the model elements, and the possibility of uncertain events occurring (for example, u_1, u_2), which can happen during the implementation of the SEA and which leads to a response to uncertainty.

The causal structure reflects the technological relations among elements of the CA, being actually a general system technology, while the elementary operations (their content) and the cause–effect relationships themselves represent a specific domain of the CA.

Several rules might be defined to specify relations between logical and cause–effect models. First of all, all vertices of the logical structure of the SEA, which are goals or sub-goals, should be represented in the cause–effect model to define the technological causal relations among SEAs. Second, the root vertex of the logical structure coincides with the terminal event of the cause–effect model. Third, the arcs of the logical (relations of the breakdown of goals and subordination) and the

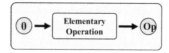

FIGURE 1.10   Cause–effect model of an elementary operation.

cause-and-effect (causality and following relations) structures are independent of each other in general.

The *cause–effect model* of an *elementary operation* must be defined to complete the cause–effect formalism (Figure 1.10).

It makes sense to compare the cause–effect model of CA with similar models and tools from related disciplines and knowledge domains. Such tools include numerous formal models of the *theory of processes*, models of manufacturing and *business processes*, and variations of project schedules, Gant diagrams, etc.

The cause–effect model has similarities to the mentioned tools:

- it is a structural model and reflects the causal relationship among the elements,
- it allows the complex nature of the elements themselves,
- it is based on graph theory tools.

However, it considerably differs from the mentioned models:

1. the SEA formalism is much "richer" (it represents goals, technologies, actions, actors, and subject matter) than the other tools (which describe only actions: work, processes).
2. a general property of the cause–effect model is its adaptability during implementation of the CA which it describes. In fact, it "changes itself" due to the basic properties of CA – uncertainty and the generation of elements and their evolution over time (Next sections).

1.3   UNCERTAINTY AND CREATION OF ELEMENTS OF COMPLEX ACTIVITY

Uncertainty in CA is defined as the possible occurrence of some events that affect the implementation of the CA and the outcome. The consequence of the uncertainty is the impossibility a priori of predicting the characteristics of the output of CA, the completion time, and the efforts (resources) that will be spent to complete the CA.

Following the ideas of F. Knight (Knight 1921), first, measurable uncertainty is separated from true uncertainty, and second, uncertainty is considered to be not only a source of problems, but also an origin of development; in the case of CA, it is the source of demand and, consequently, creation of elements of activity.

Measurable uncertainty in a CA is defined as the possibility of the occurrence of events described by certain laws. Quantitative methods (for example, stochastic) based on previous measurements or fundamental laws (with the assumption of the invariance of external conditions) might be applied to analyze such events.

True uncertainty in a CA is the possibility of the occurrence of unique (or rarely repeated) events, which are not explained by any existing fundamental laws, and for which there are no a priori observations or adequate specification.

The fundamental difference between true and measurable uncertainty is that the events of the former are caused by unknown factors (human active choice is one example), while the events of the latter, although unpredictable, might be described by certain laws.

The category of uncertainty is the subject matter of *systems theory*, along with the categories of *complexity* and *emergence*, which are traditionally considered the key characteristic features of complex systems (Ackoff 1971, Belov 2018, Checkland 1999, Gorod 2014). The factors of complexity and emergence are also inherent in CA, and they operationally manifest themselves as uncertainty (including uncertain properties and uncertain behavior of systems). Consequently, the category of uncertainty can be considered sufficient to adequately account for complexity and emergence, so it is reasonable to operate only with the category of uncertainty.

Uncertainty in a CA can be due to various sources associated with all the procedural components of the CA:

1. Uncertainty in the external environment is the uncertainty of external demand and external conditions, requirements, and norms.
2. Uncertainty of technology and the subject matter is the uncertainty of the means, methods, and factors of CA.
3. Uncertainty of the actor (active behavior and rational choice, including reflection) is the uncertainty of the understanding of the external need, goal-setting, the implementation of actions, the evaluation of the result, and, finally (or primarily) making a fundamental decision on whether to act as an actor in one specific CA or another.

There might be instances of both measurable and true uncertainty in each of the three listed groups, see the examples in Belov and Novikov (2020).

During implementation of a CA, some CA elements are completed by satisfying the demand/needs and do not lead to any a priori unknown consequences in terms of activity. In other cases, during the implementation of some SEAs, new SEAs and hierarchies of SEAs might be generated: new needs might be generated within the execution of some SEA, or the demand might be updated within the execution of another SEA. After an actor identifies needs, he or she executes goal-setting and establishes new activity – he or she organizes a new SEA and the hierarchy of subordinate SEAs in the logical structure. "New activity" can be focused on satisfying the needs or on identifying the feasibility of the CA (for example, checking the profitability of some business). As the elements of activity are completed, the output is formed, and the SEA ceases to exist.

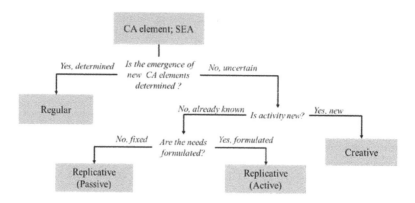

FIGURE 1.11   Classification of CA and SEAs based on the creation of new CA elements.

Demand generation and the creation of new elements of CA might be ascribed to one of two factors:

- the deterministic decomposition of an already existing SEA according to a known technology;
- the occurrence of uncertain events causing the generation of elements of activity.

A classification of CA and the SEA can be developed on a system-wide basis: the creation of new elements of the CA (see Figure 1.11).

1) *"Regular"* CA ("regular" SEA). In this case, new elements of a CA appear only as the result of deterministic decomposition of superior SEAs corresponding to an a priori known technology (a deterministic demand). The structure and technology of regular CA are deterministic. One of the key trends of the current stage of human development is that any activity (especially in an Enterprise!) is purposefully subjected to maximum simplification, standardization, and regulation as much as possible. Standardization and regulation of activity are two of the main ways to improve effectiveness of an Enterprise. Automation and robotics, in turn, continue this trend, replacing activity with machine operations, displacing a person from the field of routine (regulated) operations, and leading to the disappearance of many professions. Over past decades, the professions of telephone operator, typist, typographic worker, and craftspeople in many industries have thus disappeared. Mass production and service operations are examples of regular CA.

   All examples of regular activity can probably be considered potentially *fully automated* (including based on artificial intelligence), and the selected basis of the definition of regular activity can be a criterion for the distinction between potentially automated and non-automated kinds of activity:

deterministic technology and the creation only of the elements known a priori.

In fact, the process of regularization of CA is some kind of "exploration" that fixes and systematizes knowledge about CA.

The technology of regular activity is determinate, stable, and multiply verified and does not require changes, so technological uncertainty can be caused only by an inadequacy of resources, methods, or factors related to CA tasks and the external environment. In practice, such events appear as changes in the external environment, malfunctions and equipment failures, the use of substandard materials and components, and similar causes.

2) *"Replicative (passive)"* CA and "replicative (passive)" SEAs. CA of this type generates new SEAs of a known type (known needs, known goals, and known technologies); the non-trivial aspect of such CA is not to create but to fix an uncertain demand. If the demand has the character of a mass, typical, repetitive phenomenon, it should only be fixed, and the basic uncertainty of such activity is measurable.

Cashier or salesclerk jobs in a supermarket or retail bank branch are examples of passive replicative CA.

3) *"Replicative (active)"* CA and "replicative (active)" SEAs. In the case of such activity, new demand is created, new needs of a known type (perhaps a new consumer is developed) are formulated and, as a consequence, a new activity of a known type is generated. New demand development cannot be considered to be a typical, repetitive, or well-known action, at least at the initial stage. Therefore, the basic uncertainty of an active replicative CA must be considered to be true.

Business development (for an existing line of business) is an example of active replicative CA.

4) *"Creative"* CA and "creative" SEA. Such activity generates an uncertain demand for outputs of a priori unknown activity, the technology of which does not exist and must be created. The uncertainty of the technology is due to the uncertainty of demand and/or the uncertainty in the specification of the desired output of the activity. This is an activity to obtain an output that is not fully defined at the beginning of CA execution. This class of CA includes the examples of activity of chief designers and technologists, researchers, film and stage producers, law firm partners, etc.

An actor of creative CA creates or designs future output of the activity, so her role is very "active"; it is the role of a "designer" or "architect" of future output, and so it is the role of the architect of activity as a system, architects of the technology as a system, and architects of the result as a system.

The fundamental contrast between creative CA and replicative and regular CA is the necessity of developing a new technology of CA. Thus, logical and cause–effect models of creative CA always include at least one CA element which is focused on the development of a new, a priori unknown, technology of CA.

The key specific of creative CA is that the basic uncertainty is true and is due to a composition of uncertainties in the external environment, in the technology, and of the actor.

1.4   LIFECYCLES OF COMPLEX ACTIVITY

1.4.1   CONCEPTUALIZATION OF THE LIFECYCLE OF COMPLEX ACTIVITY

The definition of *lifecycle* of a complex activity (LC of CA) or any of its elements might be established based on a general definition of lifecycle (ISO/IEC/IEEE 2015). The LC of CA is defined as a complete (possibly repeatable) process which starts from the establishing demand and understanding needs and includes goal-setting, structuring goals and objectives, technology creation/development, executing action according to the technology, getting output, output evaluation, and reflection. The LC of CA is actually the "deployment on a timeline" of the *procedural components* of the activity (needs → goal → tasks → technology → action → output (Belov and Novikov 2019)).

Following the *systems engineering* concept (Haskins 2015), the temporal structure of LC of CA (Figure 1.12 and Table 1.1) is represented as *steps*, combining them in *stages*, and merging the amalgamation into *phases*.

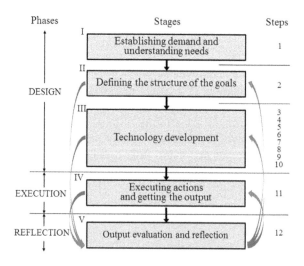

FIGURE 1.12   Lifecycle of CA: phases, stages, steps (Belov 2018).

TABLE 1.1

Phases, Stages, and Steps of LC of CA

Phase	Stage	No	Step	Contents of the Stage
DESIGN	I. Establishing demand and recognizing needs	1	Establishing demand and recognizing needs	The superior SEA or the external environment shapes the demand for the outputs of the CA element. The actor establishes the demand, understands needs, and decides to carry out activity.
	II. Goal-setting and structuring of goals and tasks	2	Synthesis of a logical model	The need is structured and checked as to whether it is already known or new. (2-a) If the need and CA are known, a logical model (goal structure) is not developed but is "extracted from the information store." Otherwise, the goal structure is formulated. Goals are set in terms of the expected characteristics of the output of CA elements. Consistency of goals is checked. Each goal of the SEA is aligned with the role of the actor and the technology – the characteristics of the subject matters and technologies are specified.
	III. Developing the technology	3	Technology readiness verification	The existence of known technology is verified: the cause–effect model, the technologies of all subordinate SEAs and elementary operations, and the availability and sufficiency of the resources. If the technology exists and is ready to use, Step 7 is executed; otherwise, Steps 4, 5, 6 are carried out. The logical consistency of the SEA and resource pools is checked – the availability and sufficiency of resources for the designation of actors of lower-level SEAs and the provision of technologies for subordinate elementary operations, taking into account the use of these resources in parallel when implementing other SEAs.
		4	Synthesis of the cause–effect model	Cause–effect relationships between the goals/results of subordinate SEAs and ElOps are determined and modeled, as are possible events of uncertainty and the rules for responding to them.
		5	Synthesis of the technologies of subordinate elements of the CA	For any elementary operation, the development of technology is specific and does not allow a further breakdown. For any SEA, Steps 1–6 are recursively executed.
		6	Synthesis/ modernization of resources	In the absence of necessary resources, the SEA supporting development or modernization of resource pools is performed.

(Continued)

TABLE 1.1 (CONTINUED)
Phases, Stages, and Steps of LC of CA

Phase	Stage	No	Step	Contents of the Stage
		7	Scheduling and resource planning	The activity progress chart is formulated. The consistency of the key milestones and resource pool is checked, taking into account the use of resources by other elements of activity. If there is inconsistency, a return to Steps 2–4 is made or the problem is escalated to a supervisor (upper-level SEA).
		8	Optimization of resource use	Optimization of resource use (taking into account the possibility of implementing these resources in parallel with other CAs).
		9	Assigning actors and defining responsibilities	A matrix of responsibility (correspondence between actors in the SEA and personnel) is established. In fact, the appointment of actors means the formulation of demand for the results of lower-level SEAs and, thus, a recurrent execution of the LC of subordinate SEAs: all phases of the "Design Phase" must be executed.
		10	Assigning resources	In accordance with the technology of elementary operations, the resources required for the implementation of technologies are assigned.
EXECU-TION	IV. Executing actions and forming the output	11	Executing actions and forming the output	preconditions for initiating subordinate SEAs and ElOps are checked; subordinate ElOps are launched and carried out; subordinate SEAs are launched and monitored.
REFLEC-TION	V. Evaluation of the output and reflection	12	Evaluation of the output and reflection	The characteristics of the output are compared with the required ones, and the number of resources is compared with those given. Requirements for adjustments to goals, technology, etc. are designed.

In parallel with the main steps of the LC of CA (1–12), the actor also detects, monitors, and reacts to uncertain events, which indicate that technology is not consistent with current conditions. The reaction in general means that other SEAs should be launched (sometimes starting with new technology development).

A model of the LC of CA execution is referred to as a *"process model."*

The universal properties of the LC of CA are formulated below as a description of the steps of the lifecycle. Executing the LC of CA is a complex activity in and of itself, so the phases, stages, and steps also might be represented as elements of CA. In general, the process of realizing the LC of CA might be iterative; its stages can be repeated and overlapped, especially at the stages of technology development and performance of actions.

Iteration of the LC of CA shows the reflexive nature of complex activity, one of its characteristic reflexive cycles.

1.4.2 The Process Model (Model of the Lifecycle of Complex Activity)

The general properties of the lifecycles of CA (inherent in the LC of any SEA) have been summarized in Table 1.1 in the form of phases, stages, and steps of the LC of CA. The implementation of the LC of any SEA is also "a complex activity": phases, stages, and steps might be considered elements of such activity. From this point of view, the implementation of the LC is an SEA consisting of subordinate operations and SEAs, and the model of implementation of the LC is a cause–effect model of the SEA called "Implementation of the LC of CA." Therefore, the BPMN format should be used to represent the model of LC of CA execution, called a *process model*. In fact, the process model is an algorithmic form of the general properties of the lifecycle of CA formulated in Table 1.1 and represented in BPMN format in Figures 1.13–1.17 in an algorithmic form.

The process model and LC execution process are depicted as a whole and in parts in Figures 1.13–1.17 in an algorithmic form;* all elements of the models are enumerated by the numbers of the LC of CA steps in Table 1.1.

The simplest case of the lifecycle is the LC of an elementary operation, but this lifecycle is degenerate: it is not detailed and is presented as a single stage. Its system-wide process model is trivial, consisting of a single specific object, and does not require further description; the formal expression of the process model of an elementary operation coincides with its causal structure (Figure 1.10).

1.5 IMPLEMENTATION OF THE MANAGEMENT PROCESSES

All artificial systems are developed focusing on some expected *output*, aiming to create desired *value*, and achieving certain characteristics of the output. But any *result*, output, or value is generated by the CA – its elements; a complex system is actually created to play the role of the actor of the activity. Since the activity is the initial or core "generator" of any result or value for stakeholders, it is necessary to influence the activity and its constituents to get the desirable result and value, and management – in a broad sense – is exactly such an influencing tool.

1.5.1 A Methodological Analysis of the Category of Management

Management or *control* is defined above as a means (complex activity) by which the manager (actor) influences the *behavior*† of the managed system or object to reach

---

* *Process model* (Figures 1.13–1.17) is, in fact, a "universal algorithm of control" – generalized technology to manage or control any CA or STS.
† The term "influence the *behavior*" is used to designate the result of the corresponding managerial activity and can be interpreted as management in the narrow sense. In the case of automatic control in some technical systems, the "influence" is executed by the control unit ("pseudo-actor") implementing some control algorithm created by a designer.

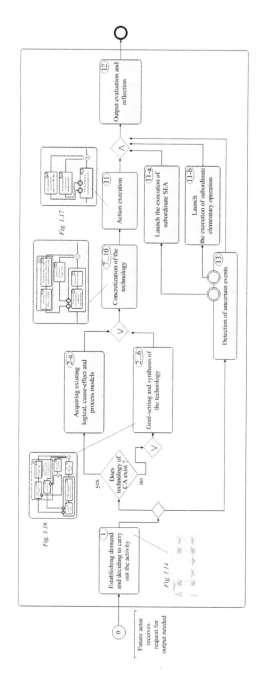

FIGURE 1.13 Lifecycle execution model – process model of the SEA as a whole (Belov 2018).

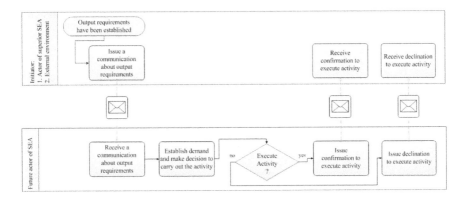

FIGURE 1.14   Establishing demand and making decision to carry out the activity (Belov 2018).

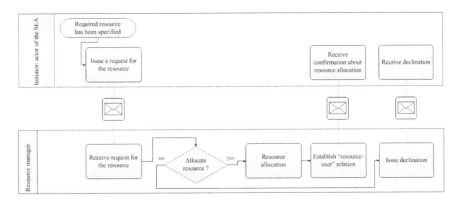

FIGURE 1.15   Requesting and assigning resources (Belov 2018).

the goals or objectives of the manager (actor). Management, on the one hand, is a special case of elements of CA; on the other hand, it is focused on other elements of CA (Belov and Novikov 2020). We'll study from this point of view the activity of the actor during the implementation of an SEA lifecycle in more detail in Section 2.3. Thus, at various phases and stages of the lifecycle, the activity of the actor in the SEA (Table 1.1) is a sequence of *analysis, synthesis, concretization, regulation,* and *reflexion* in parallel with the direct *execution* of elementary operations.

The actor in the SEA actually plays two roles simultaneously:

- As the actor of several subordinate elementary operations, which are constituents of the SEA, it directly implements the actions of these elementary operations, directly formulating outputs.
- As the actor of a complex element of activity, SEA, which includes many subordinate elements – SEAs and elementary operations – it performs analysis, synthesis, concretization, regulation, and reflection.

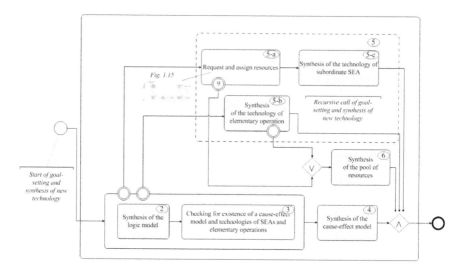

FIGURE 1.16   Goal-setting and new technology development (Belov 2018).

The *concretization* is actually a direct establishing of relations and some order in the set of elements, so concretization is some kind of organization. Similarly, synthesis in general is the creation, arrangement, and ordering of knowledge about future activity in the form of models. The analysis itself is not of value – it is performed as a preliminary phase of synthesis. Thus, analysis, synthesis, and concretization might be considered to be organization in a broad sense. *Organization* as a process is a *means** (CA) by which internal orderliness and coherence of interaction among more or less differentiated and autonomous elements of the organized system (organized object) are established (by establishing and maintaining the specified interrelations among elements).

Regulation is the direct impact on the behavior of the subordinates, so it is management (more precisely, management in a narrow sense). Organization is also the impact on (the future behavior of) the organized system, so organization is a special case of management.

Reflection closes an information *feedback*, which is an extremely important part of the management cycle. Therefore, it makes sense to say that management includes organization, regulation, and reflection. Management in a narrow sense can only be considered to be regulation. The object of management and organization is the SEA and all subordinates in combination with their complex actors: sociotechnical systems or Enterprises.

Thus, a methodological structure of activity might be formulated: **all constituents of complex activity – except the execution of elementary operations – are management in a broad sense, including organization, regulation, and reflection, while analysis, synthesis, and concretization are components of organization.**

This methodological structure is applicable to any management or control process:

---

* As in the case of management, an *organization* in the narrow sense can be interpreted as a result of specific action implemented within the organizational activity.

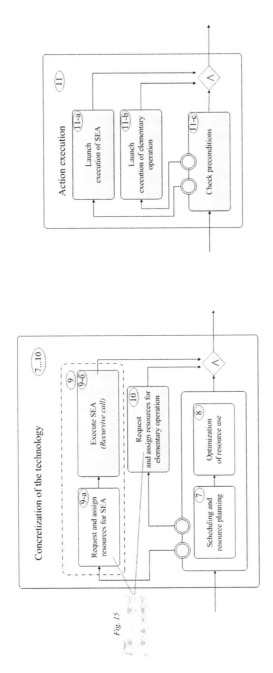

FIGURE 1.17 Parts of lifecycle execution model – concretization and action execution (Belov 2018).

- Management of social and human systems;
- Management of human–machine, ergatic systems, when some STS performs as complex actor of CA;
- Automatic control in technical systems, when control is carried out by an automatic device that does not include any people. This case can be considered an indirect execution of the regulation by the human–actor, who synthesizes the control algorithm at Steps 2–6.

In analyzing the category of "management," it is necessary to study it from the practical and business points of view. Various kinds of managerial activity – organization, leadership, management, guidance, governance, and others – are methodologically similar, but fundamentally different from the practical and business points of view. More precisely, the methodological similarity of these types of CA is that the actor influences not only an Enterprise as a whole, but also its organizational system – organized individuals. At the same time, the business and practical differences are manifested in the same ways as such an impact is.

We study these similarities and differences considering modern concepts and approaches of management theory and practice as they relate to human capital management, i.e. tools to influence employees. These are the concepts of corporate culture (Kotter and Heskett 1992, Sherriton and Stern 1997), employee involvement (Cotton 1993, Heckscher 1996), leadership and influence (Cole 2018, Northouse 2015), soft and hard skills (Klaus 2007, Taylor 2020), and related ones. All of them are based on the opposition of formal, direct, directive (hard) management skills and informal methods of influence – soft skills.

There are many more or less accurate definitions of "*hard and soft skills*"; based on them, we can say that "hard" management skills are teachable and measurable capabilities, such as operational planning or cost control. In contrast, "soft" skills are traits based on personal abilities influencing people, supporting them, and getting along with colleagues and employees.

These definitions split the set of management types of activity into two subsets: those that implement "soft" and those that implement "hard" management skills, respectively; and both kinds of activity are present in any practical management CA but in different shares.

"Hard" methods affect the routine, operational elements of human activity: the execution of CA. Concretization and regulation can mainly be formalized: they correspond to "hard" factors. In contrast, soft methods do not affect CA execution, but people's value systems, their goal-setting; soft methods play a key role at the "early stages" of LC of CA – analysis and synthesis. Almost all researchers who study "soft" and "hard" concepts emphasize the importance and even the priority of "soft" approaches and skills in business practice.

"Hard" management methods are regulatory and directive in nature, so they are implemented as a regular CA (Section 1.3). At the same time, "soft" methods are practically informal, which means that technologies, for example, of leadership, employee involvement, or the formation of a corporate culture, cannot be specified in the form of algorithms or regulations. That is, an actor implementing such CA often creates CA technology ad hoc – practically simultaneously with its implementation – and a priori an actor is hardly able to describe the technology of its activity. This impossibility of "separating" the CA technology from the actor performing it makes the role of the actor as a carrier of key, but implicit, knowledge critically important. As an example, synthesis (the creation of new CA technologies) and the analysis that precedes it (including goal-setting) are of particular importance in the development of a new complex business and/or Enterprise transformation. Thus, "soft" methods, primarily leadership, play a key role in Enterprise systems engineering and complex sociotechnical systems engineering activities (White 2015).

Concluding the analysis of the management category, it can be summarized that, despite the significant practical and business differences among the components, all of them are implemented in the form of CA, which is studied in this research as a universal means of achieving goals. A methodological structure of the category of management in the broad sense, considering practical and business factors, is shown in Figure 1.18.

1.5.2 Enterprise Complex Activity as an Aggregate of Lifecycles of SEAs

Analysis and *synthesis* among all these elements are heuristic and non-routine; the rest of the components are routine and "mechanistic." Analysis and synthesis as elements of CA are creative (Section 1.3); *true uncertainty* is inherent in them. Therefore, on the one hand, they are the most "complex," generate most of the problems, and require the greatest expenditure of resources. On the other hand, analysis and synthesis are exactly the basics for the development of activity in general and our civilization as a whole. Designing activity, especially synthesis, generates new creative SEAs; they also create technologies and pools of resources.

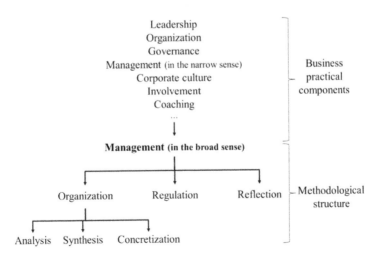

FIGURE 1.18 Systematization of management categories.

The *execution phase* – the regulation (including managerial influence of a superior SEA and the choice of actions by subordinates) – is in many respects "mechanistic," just like concretization; both processes (regulation and concretization) are strongly directed by technology. As a metaphor, analysis and synthesis are the development of a "program" (technology); concretization is the "binding of the program" to calendar time and the allocation of resources and their assignment; and regulation is the "interpretation of the program" – implementation of the technology. Implementation as well as concretization – is "simple and mechanistic." All problems and achievements appear during the creation of technology ("writing programs"). The effectiveness of "the implementation of the program" is determined by the program itself (technology), malfunctions (uncertainty), and the ability to respond effectively to unknown failures (true uncertainty) by generating a new program (new technology).

Diagrams of the process model (Figures 1.13–1.17) represent, in fact, a *"universal algorithm** or program of control"* – generalized technology to manage or control any CA or STS. However, each component of management (analysis, synthesis, concretization, regulation, reflection), in turn, might be represented as one or more elementary operations, ordered by the cause–effect structure.

Based on all of the above, it might be stated that any CA (or any of its elements that is also CA) can be represented as an aggregate of lifecycles of SEAs (Figure 1.19). The lifecycle of each SEA is a combination of (a) actions performed directly by an SEA actor (analyzed above) and (b) all and any subordinate SEAs – elements of activity.

Accordingly, activity performed directly by an SEA actor is defined by the *logical structure* of the SEA and ordered by the *cause–effect structure*. Each lifecycle is executed relatively independently and autonomously, on the one hand, while, on the other hand, all lifecycles are organized and united by a common goal-setting – a logical structure – and by a cause–effect structure. In addition, SEA actors usually share common resources, and such resources impose constraints on the cooperative execution of the SEAs.

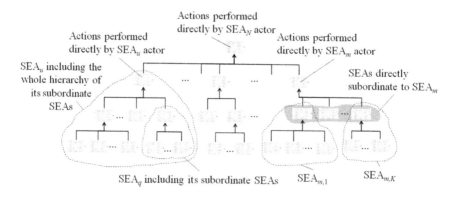

FIGURE 1.19 Complex activity represented as an aggregate of lifecycles of SEAs.

---

* *Universal algorithm* is considered in more detail in Section 8.1.

CONCLUSION

This chapter undertakes a methodological analysis of an Enterprise as the subject of management or control.

An integrated set of formal and unified models is developed to represent and to study a dialectically coupled pair: an Enterprise and its CA of any kind. The primacy of CA relative to the Enterprise follows from the fact that it is exactly an activity that forms the final output (of the Enterprise).

An aggregate of the lifecycles of structural elements of activity representing an Enterprise and its CA is proposed and will be used in the next chapters as an initial model to formalize the Enterprise Control Problem. The proposed representation of an Enterprise as the subject matter of management models the following key aspects of an Enterprise:

- Humans and their active choices as key elements of an Enterprise;
- Nontrivial structure of the subject matter of the management, which is defined by the goal structure;
- Implementation of CA during all phases of its lifecycle;
- Technology of CA – the system of conditions, criteria, forms, methods, and means to successfully achieve a stated goal.

Given the complexity of the subject matter of the research, we consider it necessary to clarify the equivalence of terms which are used in the research and in related disciplines to refer to the same categories (see Table 1.2).

TABLE 1.2
Equivalence of Terms

Business and Practice	Methodology	Systems Theory and Systems Engineering	Theory of Control in Organizations
Business unit; (Cost or profit center); human; employee; working or project group/team; department/division; enterprise; firm; company; corporation.	Complex actor; actor of SEA	System; complex system; sociotechnical system; system of systems; enterprise; subsystem; constituent of system of systems.	Active system; organizational system; active element
work; task; project; (project) program; activity of working or project group/team, department/division, enterprise, firm, company, corporation.	Action; Elementary operation; SEA; hierarchy of SEA	System; complex system; sociotechnical system; system of systems; enterprise; subsystem; constituent of system of systems.	Action

TABLE 1.3
Basic Assertions of the Methodology of CA

Name	Wording
Primacy of CA in relation to the subject (1.1.1)	An activity arises in the form of a concept or need no later than its actor in the form of a single individual – the "elementary Enterprise." At that time, CA is primary in relation to its actor – a non-elementary Enterprise.
Subject matter of organization and management as CA (1.2.1)	When managing CA and/or an Enterprise, the controlled subject is complex and always includes a complex interacting and interconnected pair { CA ⇔ an Enterprise}. CA is the primary controlled subject, but the STS itself is indirect, playing the role of the actor.
Essence of organization and management (1.2.1)	Both management and organization (as processes) constitute activity (see Figure 1.18) and, as a rule, CA, the subject of which is another CA and the corresponding Enterprise. At the same time, the indirectness of influence on the final output through the actor of controlled activity is the hallmark of "management," and the goal in the form of a change in internal ordering, consistency of interaction of the parts, is the hallmark of "organization."
External and usually uncertain nature of demand for output of CA	Activity (its elements), as a rule, is generated as a response to factors or events external to it. These factors and events induce the actor to realize an activity and are often a priori uncertain. Since the activity is generated by external sources, the consumers of the result of the activity are also external persons (in relation to the CA and its actor). At the time of the generation of activity, the future actor/individual actualizes external demand, turning it into their internal demand.
Foundations of the logical structure of CA (1.2.2)	The only constructive basis for the structuring of CA – the allocation of the hierarchy of their elements – is the structure/hierarchy of the goals of the activity (Figure 1.7). The logical structure also reflects the "managerial" hierarchy of subordination and responsibility of subjects of elements of the CA for results – achieving goals. Actors of a higher SEA, along with responsibility for achieving "their" goals, are also responsible for achieving lower goals and, as a consequence, for the activity of a lower-level SEA.
Cause–effect structure of CA (1.2.3)	The cause–effect model of CA represents the specific factors of its technology (Figure 1.9).
Order of creation of elements of integrated activity	The creation of elements of CA is carried out in sequence only from a higher element to lower ones in a logical structure, including the case of self-organization.
Sources of demand for activity	Only the actor of a (higher element of) CA or environmental factors can initiate a demand for the results of a new element of CA.
System description of technology of a CA element	The technology of any element of CA is fully described by logical, cause–effect, and process models, combined with the technologies of subordinate SEA and elementary operations.

(Continued)

TABLE 1.3 (CONTINUED)
Basic Assertions of the Methodology of CA

Name	Wording
Multi-agent representation of CA	Any CA (paired with an Enterprise as an actor) might be represented as an extended multi-agent model (Figure 1.19).
Factors determining the effectiveness and efficiency of CA	Efficiency and effectiveness are completely determined, first, by the characteristics of the technology, and second, by uncertainty characteristics.
Organization and management components (1.5)	Management components are organization, regulation, and reflection. The components of an organization are analysis, synthesis, and concretization (see Figure 1.18).
Components of CA	Any CA (as well as any of its elements, which, in turn, constitute a CA) can be represented as a composition of elements (organized and united by a common goal structure) of the following types: • specific elementary operations (representing elementary activity); • managing elements of activity (SEA or elementary operations) that implement analysis, synthesis, specification, regulation, and assessment of CA. The relations between the elements (their organization) are in the nature of the exchange of information messages and/or the exchange of information through a common resource – the information model of CA. The most "complex" control components are analysis and synthesis. At the same time, concretization (which consists of establishing and maintaining relations between the actors of elements of CA, resources, and actors of subordinate elements) and regulation (multiple or continuous verification of the occurrence of certain conditions and the initiation of the corresponding elements of activity) are "simple" and routine.
Universal algorithm of control of CA (1.4.2)	The managerial algorithm of any element of CA (with its subordinate elements) can be represented by a universal algorithm, which is described by the SEA process model, goal-setting model, technology creation model, and model of resource lifecycle (Section 1.4.2, BPMN diagrams, Figures 1.13–1.17).
Aggregated representation of CA	Any CA (as well as any of its elements, which, in turn, are a CA) can be represented as a composition of elements (organized and united by a common goal structure) of the following types: • specific elementary operations (representing elementary activity) united by a single logical and single cause-effect structures; • the only managing element (of activity) that implements analysis, synthesis, concretization, regulation, and assessment of CA. The actor of the aggregated managing element will be a complex one, combining all the actors of the initial elements of the CA and, similarly, goals, technologies, and other components of the CA.

TABLE 1.4
MCA Requirements and Components of MCA Which Meet Them

Requirement	Component Which Meets the Requirement
a. MCA must include models of both elementary and complex kinds of activity, i.e., both possessing and not possessing an internal structure. Models of the elements of activity and models/tools to integrate them must be developed.	Structural element of activity (1.2.1). Logical structure of CA (1.2.2). Assertion "Foundations of the logical structure of CA."
b. CA has a structure that is, in general, multi-level. Since the elements of CA of different levels themselves are CA, we can say that elements of CA are fractal or self-similar. Structural models of CA should reflect its hierarchy, nesting, and fractality.	
c. CA is purposeful; therefore, MCA should allow describing and analyzing the goal structure of the CA, as well as evaluating the degree of achievement of the goals and creating value/utility as a result of the CA.	
d. Technology of CA defines cause–effect relationships among elements of activity; therefore, MCA should contain cause–effect models of CA.	Cause–effect structure (1.2.3). Assertion "Cause–effect structure of CA."
e. Elements of CA exist over time: needs arise, generate CA elements that are realized, and then cease to exist. Therefore, MCA should describe the lifecycles of the elements of CA.	Models of creation of elements of CA. Model of establishing demand and making decisions to carry out the activity (Figure 1.14).
f. MCA must allow describing and analyzing the uncertainty of CA (measurable and true), realized in the form of the occurrence of a priori unpredictable events. The reaction to uncertainty (the onset of events) is the generation of a new activity (absent before the onset of the event) with known or new (to be developed) technology. MCA should describe the generation of new elements of CA.	Process model of SEA (1.4.2). Assertions "The order of creation of elements of integrated activity," "Sources of demand for activity," "External and usually uncertain nature of demand for output of CA."
g. MCA must describe the creation of new technology (as a consequence of requirement f).	Model of goal-setting and new technology development (Figure 1.16).
h. Resources used, consumed, and accumulated during the implementation of activity are an essential aspect affecting the technology, actor, and subject matter of CA, which should be considered by the MCA.	Model of lifecycle of the resources.
i. MCA must include models of organization and management as kinds of CA.	Assertions "Organization and management components," "The essence of organization and management," "Components of CA," "Aggregated representation of CA."

(Continued)

TABLE 1.4 (CONTINUED)
MCA Requirements and Components of MCA Which Meet Them

Requirement	Component Which Meets the Requirement
j. CA is implemented as a combination of elements, each of which conditionally refers to the process or project types which must be taken into account in the respective models. MCA should combine project and process approaches within a single formalism.	Structural element of activity. Properties of SEA.
k. The methodology of CA should represent all modern forms of organization of activity: (a) elementary operations, (b) complex operations, (c) projects and project programs, (d) lifecycles.	
l. Multiple and complex relationships of the elements of CA and their actors, the emergence of "meta-actors" of CA that make up "meta-systems" (extended Enterprises) are essential aspects of CA that are necessary to model in the framework of MCA.	

In conclusion, it seems valuable to list the basic assertions (Table 1.3) obtained and stated in the *methodology of complex activity*, MCA (Belov and Novikov 2020), and the set of requirements for the MCA with the components of the MCA, which exactly meet the requirements (Table 1.4) – a kind of well-known and widely used tool: "Requirements Verification and Traceability Matrix" (Haskins 2015).

REFERENCES

Ackoff, R. 1971. Towards a Systems of Systems Concepts. *Management Science* 17(11), 661–671.
Allen, B., Weigelt, K., Doherty, N. and Mansfield, E. 2009. *Managerial Economics: Theory, Applications, and Cases.* Seventh edition. New York:W. W. Norton & Company.
Belov, M. 2018. Theory of Complex Activity as a Tool to Analyze and Govern an Enterprise. In *13th Annual Conference on System of Systems Engineering (SoSE 2018).* Paris, France, 19–22 June 2018, 541–548.
Belov, M. and Novikov, D. 2019. *Methodological Foundations of the Digital Economy / Big Data-Driven World: Legislation Issues and Control Technologies.* Springer nature Switzerland, 3–14.
Belov, M. and Novikov, D. 2020. *Methodology of Complex Activity -Foundations of Understanding and Modelling.* Heidelberg: Springer.
Bergstra, J. 1984. Process Algebra for Synchronous Communication. *Information and Control* 60, 109–137.
von Bertalanffy, L. 1950. An Outline of General System Theory. *British Journal for the Philosophy of Science* 1, 139–164.
von Bertalanffy, L. 1968. *General System Theory: Foundations, Development, Applications.* New York: George Braziller.

Bogdanov, A. 1926. *Algemeine Organisationslehre (Tektologie)*. Berlin: Hirzel.

Bogdanov, A. 1980. *Essays in Tektology*. Seaside: Intersystems Publications.

BPMN. 2011. *Business Process Model and Notation*, v2.0.2. http://www.omg.org/spec/BPMN/2.0.

Bubnicki, Z. 2005. *Modern Control Theory*. Berlin: Springer.

Burkov, V., Goubko, M., Korgin, N. and Novikov, D. 2015. *Introduction to Theory of Control in Organizations*. Boca Raton, FL: CRC Press.

Checkland, P. 1999. *Systems Thinking, Systems Practice*. New York: John Wiley & Sons.

Coase, R. 1937. The Nature of the Firm. *Economica* 4(16), 386–405.

Cole, K. 2018. *Leadership and Management: Theory and Practice*. Seventh edition. Sydney: Cengage Learning Australia.

Cotton, J. 1993. *Employee Involvement: Methods for Improving Performance and Work Attitudes*. New York: SAGE Publications.

Dorf, R. and Bishop, R. 2011. *Modern Control Systems*. Upper Saddle River, NJ: Prentice Hall.

Dori, D. and Sharon, A. 2012. Integrating the Project with the Product for Applied Systems Engineering Management. In *14th IFAC Symposium on Information Control Problems in Manufacturing. IFAC Proceedings Volumes* 45(6), 1153–1158.

Foerster, H. 1995. *The Cybernetics of Cybernetics*. Second edition. Minneapolis, MN: Future Systems.

Foss, N., Lando, H. and Thomsen, S. 2000. The Theory of the Firm. B. Bouckaert and G. De Geest (eds.), *Encyclopedia of Law and Economics: Volume III. The Regulation of Contracts*. Cheltenham: Edward Elgar Publishing, 631–658.

Germeier, Yu. 1986. *Non-Antagonistic Games*. Dordrecht: D. Reidel Publishing Company.

Giachetti, R. 2010. *Design of Enterprise Systems: Theory, Architecture, and Methods*. Boca Raton, FL: CRC Press.

Gorod, A., Gandhi, J., White, B., Ireland, V., and Sauser, B. 2014. Modern History of System of Systems, Enterprises, and Complex Systems. In Gorod, A. and White, B. (eds.), *Case Studies in System of Systems, Enterprise Systems, and Complex Systems Engineering*. Boca Raton, FL: CRC Press, 3–32.

Hart, O. and Holström, B. 1987. The Theory of Contracts. In Bewley, T. (ed.), *Advances in Economic Theory*. Fifth World Congress. Cambridge: Cambridge University Press, 1–132.

Haskins, C. (ed.). 2015. *INCOSE Systems Engineering Handbook Version 3.2.2 – A Guide for Life Cycle Processes and Activities*. INCOSE, Fourth edition. San Diego, CA: John Willey & Sons.

Heckscher, C. 1996. *The New Unionism: Employee Involvement in the Changing Corporation with a New Introduction*. Ithaca; London: Cornell University Press.

Hoare, C. 1985. *Communicating Sequential Processes*. New York: Prentice Hall.

Holland, J. 2006. Studying Complex Adaptive Systems. *Journal of Systems Science and Complexity* 19(1), 1–8.

ISO/IEC/IEEE 2015 ISO/IEC/IEEE 15288:2015 *Systems and Software Engineering - System Life Cycle Processes*.

ISO 9000:2015 *Quality Management Systems -Fundamentals and Vocabulary*.

Knight, F. 1921. *Risk, Uncertainty and Profit / Hart Schaffner and Marx Prize Essays*. No. 31. Boston, MA: Houghton Mifflin.

Klaus, P. 2007. *The Hard Truth about Soft Skills: Soft Skills for Succeeding in a Hard World*. New York, NY: HarperCollins e-books.

Kotter, J. and Heskett, J. 1992. *Corporate Culture and Performance*. New York: Free Press.

Leontiev, A. 1979. *Activity, Consciousness and Personality*. Upper Saddle River, NJ: Prentice-Hall.

Levine, W. (ed.). 2010. *The Control Handbook*. Boca Raton, FL: CRC Press.

Mesarović, M., and Mako, D. 1970. *Theory of Hierarchical Multilevel Systems*. New York: Academic.

Mescon, M., Albert, M., Khedouri F. 1988. *Management*. Third edition. New York: Harper & Row College Div.

Milner, R. 1980. *A Calculus of Communicating Systems*. Lecture Notice in Computer Science. Heidelberg: Springer.

Moschandreas, M. 2000. *Business Economics*. Second edition. London: Business Press.

Northouse, P. 2015. *Leadership : Theory and Practice*. New York: SAGE Publishing.

Novikov, A. and Novikov, D. 2007. *Methodology*. Moscow: Sinteg (in Russian).

Novikov, A. and Novikov, D. 2013. *Research Methodology: From Philosophy of Science to Research Design*. Boca Raton, FL: CRC Press.

Novikov, D. 2013a. *Control Methodology*. New York: Nova Science Publishers.

Novikov, D. 2013b. *Theory of Control in Organizations*. New York: Nova Science Publishers.

Novikov, D. (ed). 2013c. *Mechanism Design and Management: Mathematical Methods for Smart Organizations*. New York: Nova Science Publishers.

Novikov, D. 2016. *Cybernetics: From Past to Future*. Heidelberg: Springer.

Novikov, D. 2020. Control, Activity, Personality. *Advances in Systems Science and Applications* 20(3), 113–135.

Png, I. and Lehman, D. 2007. *Managerial Economics*. London: Blackwell Publishing.

Porter, M. 1985. *Competitive Advantage: Creating and Sustaining Superior Performance*. London: Collier Macmillan.

Pyster, A. and Olwell, A. (eds.). 2013. *The Guide to the Systems Engineering Body of Knowledge (SEBoK)*, v. 1.2. Hoboken, NJ: The Trustees of the Stevens Institute of Technology. http://www.sebokwiki.org [Accessed 16 December 2019].

Rebovich, G. and White, B. 2011. *Enterprise Systems Engineering: Advances in the Theory and Practice*. Boca Raton, FL: CRC Press.

Rzevski, G. and Skobelev, P. 2014. *Managing Complexity*. London: WIT Press.

Sherriton, J. and Stern, J. 1997. *Corporate Culture, Team Culture: Removing the Hidden Barriers to Team Success*. New York: Amacom.

Taylor, A. 2020. *Soft Skills Hard Results: A Practical Guide to People Skills for Analytical Leaders*. Tadley: Practical Inspiration Publishing.

Umpleby, S. 1990. The Science of Cybernetics and the Cybernetics of Science. *Cybernetics and Systems* 21(1), 109–121.

Wagner, H. 1975. *Principles of Operations Research*. Second edition. Upper Saddle River, NJ: Prentice Hall.

White, B. 2006. Fostering Intra-Organizational Communication of Enterprise Systems Engineering Practices. MITRE Public Release Case No. 06-0351. National Defense Industrial Association, in *9th Annual Systems Engineering Conference*, San Diego, CA.

White, B. 2015. On Leadership in the Complex Adaptive Systems Engineering of Enterprise Transformation. *Journal of Enterprise Transformation* 5(3), 192–217.

Wiener, N. 1948. *Cybernetics: Or the Control and Communication in the Animal and the Machine*. Cambridge: The Technology.

Williamson, O. 2009. Transaction Cost Economics: The Natural Progression. *American Economic Review* 86(3), 215–226.

2 Enterprise Management and Lifecycles Compatibility

Lifecycles have long been studied from different points of view in many fields of science, primarily in systems engineering (Haskins 2015, ISO 2015) – lifecycles of artificial material objects and in management sciences (Adizes 1999) – lifecycles of organizations. However, the fundamental properties of lifecycles have not yet been considered in sufficient detail. At the same time, lifecycles (those of elements of complex activity, enterprises, and other entities and actors) are essential for the Enterprise Control Problem. Therefore, the interrelated lifecycles of CA constituents are studied applying the approaches and models of MCA (Belov and Novikov 2020). The *methodological factors of Enterprise management* are researched in this chapter by analyzing the compatibility of LCs of the actor (who also plays the role of key stakeholder and is part of the Enterprise), the subject matter, the result, the technology, and the resources of Enterprise CA. Based on the above studies, subproblems of the Enterprise Control Problem are formulated.

2.1 A SOCIOTECHNICAL SYSTEM, COMPLEX ACTIVITY, AND PURPOSEFULNESS

The *structure of goals* is one of the key aspects of CA; therefore, when starting to consider methodological factors of Enterprise management, we should analyze complex activity actors and summarize and highlight their system-wide particular features that relate to goal-setting, on the basis of which we will define principles for their reasonable management.

The definition of *management in a broad sense* given in the Foreword and Chapter 1, first, clearly "separates" an actor from the managed entity; second, it allows the goals of managing actors not to conform with the those of managed entities (of a sociotechnical system as a whole or of elements of its subsystems and/or of individuals involved in the same); third, it declares the obligation to change the states of a managed entity in time (staying in the same state is a special case of dynamics). In addition, the definition implicitly fixes two possible ways for an actor to achieve the goal:

- Directly, when the actor executes actions aimed at achieving the goal by himself/herself;

- Indirectly, by management, by influencing some managed entity or system in such a way that, as a result of the behavior of the entity or system, the initial goal is achieved.

Consideration of a *goal-setting* source allows us to divide all sociotechnical systems (STSs) into two classes (or groups):

Class I. STSs with externally established goals;
Class II. STSs forming goals by themselves.

The first class (group) includes such STSs as firms, organizations, enterprises, state and municipal agencies and bodies, project groups, and similar complex activity actors created and functioning in the interests of external stakeholders (owners/ shareholders, governments, municipalities, etc.).

The second class (group) includes, first of all, people, as individuals, whose lives and activities, in and of themselves, have intrinsic value for them and therefore are determined by their final and internally established goals. In addition, "internal" goals guide such actors as families, tribes, ethnic groups, or states, for which existence and development have intrinsic value. A distinctive feature of class II STSs is the potential to have an independent active choice (including that of a group) of goals; by emphasizing this particular feature, we will conventionally call a *class II STS* an *"active STS."* It is the functioning of the *class I STS*, the activity they execute (generally complex) that produces the result that represents value/usefulness to stakeholders, while such STSs themselves only provide a means to implement their activities and consume resources.

A certain dualism of pair "activity-STS" also allows us to take a different position that is adequate for STSs of class II. Namely, such an STS is a self-sufficient goal-setting actor and performs its activity in a certain way, by reaching a final result to meet its own interests.

It is necessary to stress that among constituents of any class I STS, there are always those whose roles are played by class II STSs. At least, according to the above definition of STS, such an STS must include people who are the "main" particular case of class II STSs. Thus, all class I systems are characterized by the problem of coordinating the "internal" goals, inherent in class II STSs, with the "external" goals that should be achieved by such a system as a constituent of a class I STS. The problem of compatibility of an actor's "external" and "internal" goals should be solved based on an analysis of goal-setting sources or causes, which are the motives and/or preferences of the actor (see Figure 1.3).

Based on this definition,* we consider the *motives* of a CA actor to be the reason for his/her future specific actions leading to the results that he/she requires (these

---

* *Preference* – the power or opportunity to choose; the act, fact, or principle of giving advantages to some over others (Merriam-Webster). *Interest* – a feeling that accompanies or causes special attention to something or someone (Merriam-Webster). *Motive* – something (such as a need or desire) that causes a person to act (Merriam-Webster).

actions are needed just to achieve the results). An actor's *preferences* allow him/her to compare different actions and different results of activity; according to his/her preferences, an actor sets the goal as the anticipated (desired, preferred) result of his/her activity. Then, the problem of coordinating the goals, which is under analysis here, comes down to *coordinating the preferences, interests,* and *motives* of actors.[*]

This problem is studied in such fields of science as decision theory, game theory, the theory of active systems, the theory of management of organizational systems, and the theory of contracts (see a review of the relevant branches of knowledge in (Novikov 2013)), and is considered below to be one of the key Enterprise management tasks.

An Enterprise is just an organizational (and technical) class I system, which is formed or exists to achieve goals or create benefits to meet the interests of external stakeholders. Therefore, in this study, we will focus on class I STSs; however, we will take into account that the roles of some constituents of an STS are always played by active class II STSs.[†] The above considerations allow us to formulate

Thesis 1	The key issue of Enterprise management is the coordination of the externally formulated goals of CA actors, which come down to coordination with the preferences, interests, and motives of these actors.

2.2 SUBJECT MATTER OF ENTERPRISE MANAGEMENT[‡]

While discussing factors of Enterprise or STS management, it is necessary to "stay outside" of the STS, separating the managing actor from the managed entity, i.e., the STS. To manage an STS, i.e., to impact its behavior in order to achieve the goal, it is necessary to study how the state of an STS changes, i.e. how the final (overall) *goals* are achieved.

In the previous section, the primacy of implementing the CA by STS versus STS itself was demonstrated, from which follows

Thesis 2	Since the goal of an Enterprise or STS is implemented through the goal of its activity, in order to manage an Enterprise or STS (as an actor of activity), it is necessary to manage its activity.

[*] Let us illustrate the problem of coordinating goals through an example of two actors, whom we will conventionally name "A" and "B," who play the roles of some elements of class I STS "C." Let subject "B," within their role in STS "C," form a goal for the role performed by subject "A." This goal is "external" for subject "A," who, being an individual case of a class II STS, always has their "internal" goals. Then, in order to coordinate the "external" and "internal" goals of subject "A," it is necessary to coordinate the interests of subject "A" with the interests of subject "B."

[†] In addition, the application of the above definition of management to class II STSs hits upon the methodological complexity of separating a managing actor from a managed entity.

[‡] Hereinafter, in this study, unless otherwise specified, the term management will be used in a broad sense, considering organization as one of the components of management, according to Belov and Novikov (2020) and Figure 1.18.

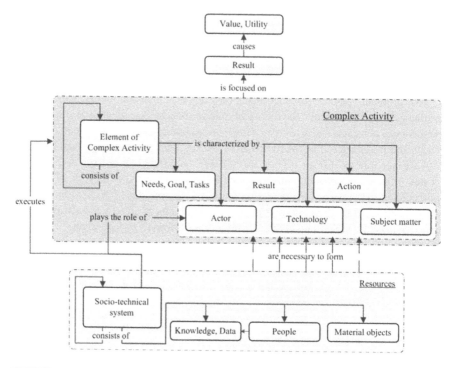

FIGURE 2.1 Structure of terms related to STSs and CA.

The fractal hierarchy of elements, SEAs, (Chapter 1) constitutes a complex activity (Figure 2.1):

- an *actor* who executes a CA element and whose role is played by an STS,
- *needs* (which determine requirements for the result),
- *goals* and *tasks* (defining the desired, anticipated image of an activity result),
- *technology* (a system of conditions, criteria, forms, methods, and means of successive achievement of a stated goal),
- *subject matter* (to which the activity is applied and the role of which can be played by an STS, people, information and knowledge, material objects),
- an *action*,
- a *result*.

Thus, CA implementation needs:

a) an STS (or an individual as a special case) performing the role of a CA actor;
b) material objects and knowledge constituting technology;
c) an STS, or people, or material objects, or knowledge that constitutes the subject-matter of a CA element.

In this sense, STSs, people, material objects, and knowledge constitute *resources* of CA. These considerations allow us to formulate

---

Thesis 3　　CA is the fractal (goal) hierarchy of elements, each of which is directly related to:
1. a superior (in the hierarchy) CA element, the sub-goal of which is implemented by this CA element;
2. subordinate (in the hierarchy) CA elements, which implement the sub-goals of this CA element;
3. resources used to implement this CA element.

Consequently, two types of binary relationships can be defined: "goal/sub-goal" (which is also subordination and responsibility), reflecting the first two connections, and a "consumer/supplier" of resources, reflecting the third connection.

Complex activity and its components must be considered during their lifecycles due to a simple consideration: the period of direct execution of CA, of actually creating utility or value (or direct use of resources for their intended purpose) is always preceded by a period of CA design or preparation (creation of technology, in particular, resources), during which it is necessary to bear costs. At the same time, the period of CA execution (use of resources) is followed by a period of completion/reflection (including recycling or discarding remaining resources and other things), which also requires outlays.

This allows us to distinguish three phases of lifecycles and formulate

---

Thesis 4　　CA, its elements, and resources used to execute CA exist in time during three *phases* (a description of the phases is provided in parallel for both CA elements and resources)
- *Preparatory or design phase*, during which {CA is designed/the resource is created}, because before the start of the LC of CA {CA/the resource} does not exist;
- *Phase of {CA execution/resource use}*, during which utility is derived or value is created;
- *Reflection/final phase*, following phase 2, during which {CA reflection is executed/the resource is recycled or discarded}, because, upon completion of CA, the CA/resource ceases to exist.:

The lifecycle phases can be cyclically repeated, replacing each other, while the phases allow their breakdown into stages and milestones (Belov and Novikov 2020, Belov 2018).

On the one hand, CA has a complex hierarchical fractal structure, and its elements are heterogeneous. On the other hand, elements of both CA and its context exist in time in the form of lifecycles. Therefore, in order to manage the CA of an Enterprise or STS, one needs to consider a significant number of heterogeneous LCs, i.e., elements of activity, their procedural components, and constituents connected to each other (see Table 2.1).

TABLE 2.1
Analysis of Lifecycles

Lifecycles	Comment
1 LC of a resource (STS, or staff, or material object, or knowledge/ information).	LC of a resource generally includes three phases (see Thesis 4). Therefore, LC of a resource is reduced to the sequential implementation of several CA elements: creation, use, disposal; therefore, LC of a resource can be represented as a composition of several CA elements. But a composition of CA elements = CA element. Conclusion: *LC of a resource* can be represented (modeled) as the LCs of a CA element (Figure 2.2).
2 LC of CA	CA as a whole is a special case of a CA element; therefore, *LC of CA* is represented as the LC of a CA element.
3 LC of a structural element of activity (LC of SEA)	Such as used as the main element of CA modeling – LC of a structural element of activity – *LC of SEA*.
4 LC of an actor	An STS, or an individual, as a special case of "resource (see item 1 in this table)," becomes an actor of CA, once having fixed demand and having decided to execute the CA. Therefore, the *lifecycle of an actor* coincides with the phase of use of the lifecycle of the "resource," and there is no need to independently consider the lifecycle of an actor.
5 LC of a need, goals, and tasks	A need is external to and precedes the CA that it initiates: as soon as a future actor fixes a need, he or she executes the LC of CA to satisfy the need. If the formation of the need is of interest to the study itself, it should be modeled. But the process of forming needs is an activity; therefore, the model of the process of forming needs is also an LC of a CA model. If the process of forming a need is not interesting for research, it is presented as the initial event of the LC of CA satisfying this need. Thus, the *LC of a need* can always be represented as LCs of CA. The goals and objectives are formed and achieved in the framework of the LC of the corresponding element of CA; therefore, it is not necessary to consider the *LC of goals* and objectives as a separate model.
6 LC of technology	Technology is an organized set of knowledge/information and material objects. Therefore, by virtue of considerations similar to item 4, it follows that the LC of technology coincides with the phase of use of the LC of the "resource," and there is no need to study the *LC of a technology* as a separate model.
7 LC of subject matter	Any of the "resources " (from the list in item 1 in this table) can play the role of subject matter; therefore, by virtue of reasons similar to item 4, it follows that the *LC of subject matter* coincides with the phase of use of the LC of the "resource," and there is no need to study the LC of subject matter as a separate model.
8 LC of the result	The result is the final state of the subject matter, so its LC should not be studied as a separate model.

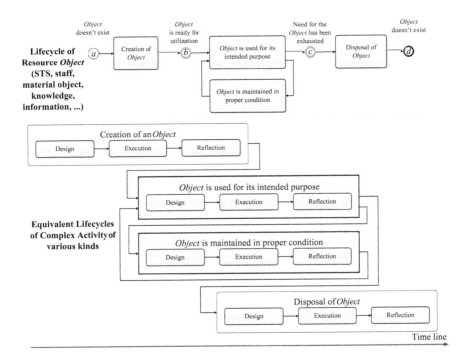

FIGURE 2.2 Representation of LC of a resource by lifecycles of CA.

Table 2.1 identifies a set of LC classes that is minimally necessary for adequate representation (modeling) of CA and STSs by listing the lifecycles of all entities and actors that are more or less related to the CA, including those that are part of or coincide with others. In addition, Table 2.1 demonstrates that the formalism of the LC of SEA, extended by a phase of the formation of the need for results of complex activity, is sufficient for the representation of all aspects of CA and its systemic context (Figure 2.3).

The LCs of all entities dealing with CA in one way or another can be represented in the form of LCs of SEAs or are part of them:

- the existence in time of technology, an actor, and an entity (and result) is modeled as the LCs of resources, which in turn are represented as the LCs of SEAs;
- the existence in time of a need, goals, tasks, and actions is modeled as the LCs of SEAs.

Certain classes can be defined over a set of lifecycles (Table 2.1) based on the following consideration. All entities listed in items 2–8 in Table 2.1 are, in a certain sense, individual and unique: they relate to specific samples of CA elements or their procedural components. Unlike these entities, resources (item 1) can also be unique but can also form groups of samples with equivalent properties – so-called *resource*

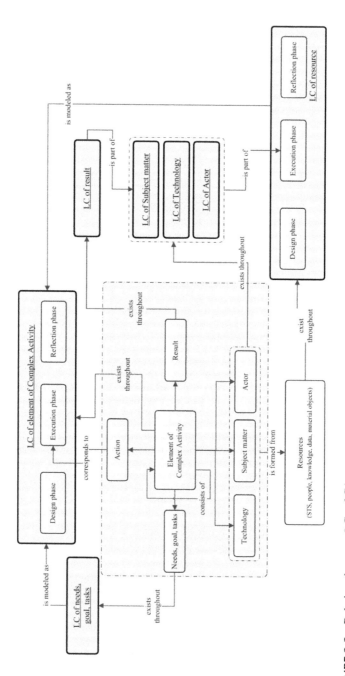

FIGURE 2.3   Relations between LCs of CA components.

pools. Activity applied to them is also homogeneous, so, in order to shorten the presentation, some CA elements applied to equivalent resources can be unified. From a practical standpoint, such CA elements correspond to the *management of the resource pools* (including their creation and use) – human resources, stocks, materials, equipment, energy resources, and others.

The creation and use of resource pools has another, practical, basis, namely as follows: resources of all of the abovementioned types (STSs, staff, and other material objects, as well as technological knowledge and information) are used to form the subject matter and/or components of CA technology; therefore, they are not required constantly, but only during periods of preparation and execution of CA elements. When expenses (first and foremost time) used to attract resources exceed those used to accumulate pools of resources and to subsequently maintain those pools, it turns out to be valuable to create and maintain resource pools perpetually. This allows, if necessary, devoting minimal time and other expenses to resources. These theses illustrate Coase's ideas (Coase 1937) explaining the existence of a firm by transaction costs. The problems of human resource pools, as a key resource of an Enterprise, are considered in detail in Chapter 6. Thus, let us formulate

---

Thesis 5   The lifecycles of CA elements and their components, together with the LCs of STSs and the LCs of resources, can be represented by a set of interconnected LCs of SEAs, some of which execute the management of the resources focused on the pool of resources as the subject matter of such SEAs.

Historically, the concept of lifecycles, originally developed relative to systems, complex products, and software products (Haskins 2015, ISO 2015), has expanded in recent decades to organizations (Adizes 1999), as well as to technology and knowledge. The practical significance of Thesis 5 lies in the fact that it generalizes, at the system level, the concept of lifecycles of all listed entities and reduces them to the LCs of an SEA.

For clarity, we combine Theses 2–5 in a table format (Table 2.2).

Theses 2–5, together with the definition of management given above, allow formulating

---

Thesis 6   Enterprise or STS management should be implemented as the management of a set of interconnected lifecycles of SEAs.

2.3   MEANS OF AND FACTORS INVOLVED IN ENTERPRISE MANAGEMENT

Let us structure Thesis 6 and fix the means of STS/Enterprise management.

STS/Enterprise management is the impact on the behavior of the entire multi-level hierarchy of SEAs in order to achieve a desired output of corresponding CA.

TABLE 2.2
Logic of the Problem of STS Management

Thesis 2	Since the goal of an Enterprise or STS is implemented through the goal of its activity, in order to manage an Enterprise or STS (as an actor of activity), it is necessary to manage its activity.
Thesis 3	CA is a fractal (goal) hierarchy of elements, each of which is directly related to: 1. a superior (in the hierarchy) CA element, the sub-goal of which is implemented by this CA element; 2. subordinate (in the hierarchy) CA elements, which implement the sub-goals of this CA element; 3. resources used to execute the CA element.
Thesis 4	CA, its elements, and the resources used to execute it exist in time during three phases.
Thesis 5	The lifecycles of CA elements and their components, together with the LCs of STSs and the LCs of resources, can be represented by a set of interconnected LCs of SEAs, some of which execute the management of the resources focused on the pool of resources as the subject matter of such SEAs.

Let us analyze the main factors affecting the output of CA, the "determinants of the output."

An *output of activity* (Belov and Novikov 2018, Belov and Novikov 2020) is formed in the process of implementation of complex activity by an actor according to the technology. Therefore, **technology is one of the determinants of the output of activity**.

The multi-level hierarchy of SEAs corresponds to a hierarchy of actors, which is distinctive by the following potential systemic contradiction. It is exactly the possible inconsistency between the interests and the "internal" goals of an actor as an active STS (class II) and goals,* being "external" for him/her and attributed to him/her due to his/her role as an actor of CA, which he or she plays as a constituent of an STS with goals set from the outside (class I). From the point of view of STS management, the incompatibility of the interests of actors causes a violation in the implementation of the lifecycles of CA elements by the actor (first of all, in the form of refusal to fulfill the role of the actor even before the lifecycle of CA begins). This, in turn, gives rise to a trend of a natural mismatch in the lifecycles of various elements of CA, corresponding to the mismatching goals of the actors. A mismatch or, on the contrary, **the compatibility of LCs of SEAs is the second determinant of the output of activity**.

During a CA lifecycle, uncertainty events can occur, affecting the output as well. True uncertainty of CA violates the implementation of technology; therefore, in developing technology, one should provide options for responding to true uncertainty and criteria for identifying true uncertainty events that require a modernization of the technology (since only measurable uncertainty can be eliminated, this elimination is achieved by including scenarios of reactions to measurable uncertainty in the technology). The occurrence of events of true uncertainty makes the CA technology inadequate to the external environment; therefore, the reaction to such events is a change in the technology – modernization of the same kind or development of a new type. It is also obvious that, for the effective operation of an STS (achievement of

---

* Goal-setting and STS classes, as well as the sources of this mismatch were discussed in Section 2.1.

goals), it is necessary to identify an inadequacy of the technology as early as possible, maybe even based on indirect proactive signs. Due to the possibility of the occurrence (at any moment of the lifecycle of any SEA) of true uncertainty events, the development/modernization of technology can be performed many times – initially during synthesis, then during specification and implementation of CA. **Uncertainty events are the third determinant of the output of activity**.

That is, an output of CA is determined by the

1. technology (which should also include response scenarios to measurable uncertainty and procedures for detecting events of true uncertainty);
2. compatibility or non-compatibility of the implementation of CA lifecycles;
3. uncertainty events and their parameters.

Let us consider potential *means of management* – ways to influence the output of activity by influencing its determinants.

1. Let us start with the influence of a type of technology of CA. *Technology* is defined in Belov and Novikov (2020) as a system of conditions, criteria, forms, methods, and means for the consistent achievement of a goal; means are formed from *resources* – material entities, knowledge, and information. Means of influence on technology are such management components as *synthesis* and *concretization* (see a detailed discussion of management components in Section 1.5 of this book and Section 7.2 of the monograph (Belov and Novikov 2020)). Synthesis includes, for example, the creation of methods, algorithms, regulations, and rules for performing actions, as well as tools, equipment, buildings, and hiring and training employees. Concretization impacts both information/knowledge components and the assignment of specific items of resources to the roles of actors and material components of technology (in particular, concretization of a *cause–effect model* in the form of plans and schedules, the appointment of employees to specific roles, the dedication of specific items of equipment, etc.).

Synthesis and concretization are distinguished by the following features:

- synthesis, having been performed once, allows several lifecycles of activity to be implemented,
- concretization must necessarily be performed in each lifecycle.

Procedure of synthesis should be considered to consist of:

a. the creation of information/knowledge components of technology in the form of *information models*;
b. the creation of *pools of material resources* to be assigned to the roles of the actors and material components of the technology (while realizing that their creation is always preceded by the development of an appropriate information model).

This separation is in line with the generally accepted practice, when information technology models (methods, algorithms, rules, regulations, and specifications, including material resources) are first created and optimized, after which material components (pools of material resources) are created.

It is not feasible to structure concretization in a similar way, because, in practice, planning and assigning resources are carried out within the framework of a single iterative process, because plans and schedules should be provided with resources. At the same time, the process itself is in the nature of a strict implementation of relevant regulations violated by an event of uncertainty; the regulations should be specified earlier during the creation of information models (during the synthesis) by taking into account the characteristics of uncertainty.

Thus, the means of influencing the output of CA through an impact on the technology are synthesis (consisting of components (a) and (b)) and concretization.

2. The compatibility of CA lifecycles can be violated due to a mismatch of the goals/interests of actors; therefore, a means to eliminate this violation is coordination of the interests and, consequently, coordination of the goals of the actors. Coordination of interests is the establishment of certain relations among the actors or an ordering of the actors, i.e., coordination of interests is an organization and, therefore, is management. Coordination of interests is carried out during the assignment of specific types of human resources to the roles of actors, i.e., in the course of concretization.* At the same time, network planning and scheduling, resource assignment, and other similar activities are executed. Coordination of interests, as a component of management, is, on the one hand, a particular case of concretization and, on the other hand, a case that affects the consistency of LCs of CA directly and to the greatest extent. Therefore, another means to influence the output of CA is coordination of the interests of actors and other activities that are constituents of concretization.

3. There are no means to influence any *uncertainty events* directly. According to the definition (Section 1.3), the occurrence of uncertainty events leads to the appearance of a priori unknown circumstances that change the progress of CA. Such changes can be attributed to one of two classes: (a) those in which the technology becomes inadequate, which makes the goal of SEA unattainable; (b) those in which the technology remains adequate and that do not impede the achievement of the goal but change the course of action relative to the initial plan (events of uncertainty that do not affect the execution of the action can be ignored).

Hereinafter, we will assume that in the first case the unplanned "attainability" of the goal of an SEA is due to the occurrence of events of *true uncertainty* (Section 1.3).

---

* It is just during the concretization that implementation of consistency of interests takes place, while the consistency mechanism is being developed during synthesis – creation of components of the technology. The same arrangement is true for all other management components. The issue of creating mechanisms during some stages of lifecycle and their implementation during others is discussed in more detail below – while formulating Thesis 7.

True uncertainty is beyond description, accounting, prediction, etc., because of its fundamental properties – the absence of a priori information that allows the creation of formal models. Therefore, such outcomes cannot be predicted, and the only constructive way of acting in this case is to detect, as early as possible, the actuality of the occurrence of true uncertainty events (including doing so by implicit, directly unobservable signs). And after such detection, the technology of CA must be modified in order to bring it in line with the new circumstances. In fact, any revelation of conditions showing technology inadequacy is a revelation of demand for the output of a new CA, i.e., analysis (Figure 1.18).

In the second case, the actor attains the goal. This means that, during the implementation of an SEA, there is not enough time for the occurrence of any of events of true uncertainty that can change the circumstances so that the achievement of the goal becomes impossible. But events of measurable uncertainty can occur, which is manifested in the occurrence of a priori unknown factors that impede (or, vice versa, facilitate) the implementation of the CA and the achievement of its goal. In this case, the achievement of the goal requires a priori uncertain expenses from the actor and an uncertain duration of action. Since the occurrence of such uncertainty changes (but does not violate) the progress of the CA technology, it is in the nature of things to believe that uncertainty can be a priori taken into account and modeled, since it is measurable. Therefore, both duration and expenses can be reasonably predicted, based on knowledge about the properties of measurable uncertainty.

That is to say that the negative impact of uncertainty can only be mitigated by taking into account measurable uncertainty within the framework of synthesis and concretization, as well as by using analysis – the well-timed detection of true uncertainty events leading to inadequacy of the technology and properly responding to them – by bringing the technology to an adequate state and maintaining the same throughout the entire lifecycle of CA.

Analyzing the means of influence on the output of CA, the following factors should be emphasized. In general, the state of the subject-matter of activity at any moment of time can be described by a multidimensional vector of some parameters; then:

- the implementation of activity is a purposeful change to the vector of parameters of the subject matter (at least some of these parameters);
- the output of CA* is described by values of the parameters of the subject matter of CA at the moment the action is completed (terminal conditions are discussed in this section below).

The final values of the parameters of the output may or may not allow the CA to be continued (implementation of a cause–effect model and following the technologies of constituents) without changing the technology. In the first case, we will say that the output (actions of the actor) of the SEA is consistent with the planned goal or

---

* Action by an actor, by definition, always ends with an output; see Figure 1.3, Procedural components of activity, or Figure 1.6, Model of structural element of activity.

that the goal of the SEA is achieved, and in the second case, that the goal of the SEA is not achieved, and therefore the technology must be modified, since it is not consistent with the current environment. Note that, from the point of view of CA implementation, all values of the parameters belonging to the target domain are indistinguishable; as a consequence, they can be replaced by a single aggregated value. One may believe that an SEA can have several options for goals, each of which corresponds to a single target (aggregated) value of the parameters of the output. Moreover, for the implementation of CA, in each case, one of them is chosen as the goal of the SEA.

Thus, from the point of view of continuing the CA and achieving the planned goals, the output of CA is always binary: goal achieved vs goal not achieved.

While considering the creation process of a new CA technology, as well as its further testing and evolution (mathematical models of this process are presented in Chapter 5), it is necessary to note that, during the initial period, uncertainty events of all types occur for the first time. Therefore, they are considered to be events of true uncertainty, and the reaction to them is a modernization of the technology – its development and an increase in its level of maturity and readiness. As the technology is being developed, most uncertainty events occur many times and no longer require changes in technology: their influence on CA results was taken into account earlier. Thus, we define a *"mature technology of CA"*: such technology is characterized by the fact that, first, events of true uncertainty requiring changes in the technology occur extremely rarely; second, upcoming events of measurable uncertainty do not lead to unattainability of the CA goal, their consequence being uncertainty in values of the characteristics of the CA output within the target area, as well as uncertainty about the duration of actions and expenses of the CA actor.

As a result, we formulate

Thesis 7 The Enterprise or STS management (in the form of managing a set of interconnected LCs of SEAs) is executed by the following types of CA (management components):
- synthesis as a part of:
  - creation and modernization of technology components in the form of information models (including resources and mechanisms to coordinate interests);
  - creation and modernization of pools of material resources which are used to form actors and technology components;
- concretization, consisting of mechanisms to coordinate the interests of actors of CA elements and other activities, such as network planning and scheduling and assigning resources;
- analysis, consisting of sequential detection of events of true uncertainty (possibly by indirect signals) throughout the entire lifecycle of CA.

All management components should be developed and implemented taking into account the need to eliminate measurable uncertainty – including scenarios of response to measurable uncertainty, and also allow the possibility of repeated synthesis as a response to the occurrence and detection of events of true uncertainty.

Let us note that Class II STSs (Section 2.1) determine the goals of CA themselves in order to meet their own interests; consequently, they specify requirements for the output of CA themselves, they create the technology of their CA themselves, and, in this sense, they implement self-government. So, the management components and uncertainty affect the compatibility of the lifecycles of CA elements and their components (discussed in detail when formulating Thesis 5 above). Moreover, synthesis and concretization provide consistency based on various foundations, while uncertainty violates consistency.

2.4 ORDERING OF MANAGEMENT ACTIONS ALONG THE LIFECYCLE OF COMPLEX ACTIVITY

Let us consider a process of STS/Enterprise management during the lifecycle of complex activity (see Figure 2.4; see also Table 1.1 and Figs. 1.13–1.17).

Step 1 (Figure 2.4, Table 1.1). The potential *actor* performs an analysis of *demand* – the situation as a whole, experience from a previous activity, the general capacity to meet demand – and makes a decision to execute the activity or not. In fact, the actor compares their "internal" interests with "external" ones, expressed in demand. If the interests turn out to be consistent, they decide to implement the activity and begin the implementation of its lifecycle by analyzing the structure of goals and tasks. In the case of inconsistency of interests, refusal to implement the role of the CA actor occurs.

Steps 2–6 (Figure 2.4, Table 1.1). *Logical* and *cause–effect models*, resources, and technologies of subordinate elements are developed, that is, the actor synthesizes (or acquires if it already exists) the technology of the future activity: "his/her own" SEA and all subordinates, i.e., the future activity is being synthesized – its technology, elements, connections between the elements, etc. The result is described in the

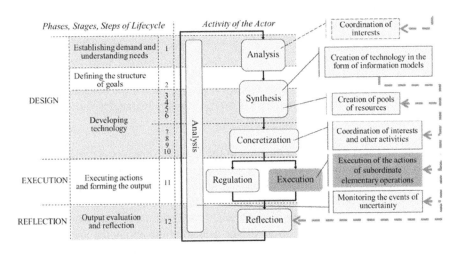

FIGURE 2.4 Activity of an SEA actor during the CA lifecycle (Belov and Novikov 2020).

form of information models. Neither the actors nor the resources of these elements have been assigned yet.

Steps 7–10 (Figure 2.4, Table 1.1). The cause–effect model is concretized in the form of an activity progress chart and schedules, while the resources and actors are being assigned to appropriate roles. In general, the relations among the elements of the CA are established. The actor concretizes and organizes the activity: "his/her own" SEA and all subordinates. The actor then requests and receives the resources for the appointment of actors of subordinate SEAs and the provision of technologies for subordinate operations, filling the roles of actors and resources with specific items. Thus, specific relations between the actors of superior and subordinate SEAs and among the resources are established: first and foremost, the interests of the actors are coordinated.

Step 11 (Figure 2.4, Table 1.1). The actor (also being the actor in subordinate elementary operations) directly performs the actions of the subordinate *elementary operations* (right stream in Figure 2.4). In parallel, the actor also monitors the onset of conditions according to the cause–effect model and initiates the actions of the subordinate SEAs, that is, regulates the activity of the subordinate elements (left stream in Figure 2.4). *Regulation* is a decision-making process within the framework of a given technology, including response to true uncertainty events (technology modernization or new technology development).

Step 12 (Figure 2.4, Table 1.1). The actor *evaluates* the output obtained (as well as that obtained by subordinates), external conditions, technology, resources, etc. This is *reflexion* in the broad sense.

In parallel, the actor carries out analyses detecting true uncertainty events (including by indirect signs), which may lead to the inadequacy of the technology and to the appearance of demand for new complex activity.

The direct arrows in Figure 2.4 reflect the natural sequence of the implementation of components of activity. The reverse arrow from reflection to analysis represents possible cyclical repetitions of activity with "*self-management/self-regulation*" by rethinking needs, targeting and changing technology, etc.

Figure 2.4 emphasizes the dual role of an SEA actor, who carries out:

- management activities of the actor related to the process model (Figs.1.13–1.17), which are shown by rectangles with a lighter fill and black font;
- elementary operations of the SEA itself, shown by rectangles with a darker fill and no border lines.

It should be noted that the coordination of the interests of actors is carried out both during the stage of analysis and during the stage of concretization. In the first case, a potential actor coordinates his/her "internal" interests with the "external" interests of his/her potential role as the actor of a CA element, expressed in the form of demand. In the second case, an actor sets demand and, through the same, sets "external" interests for potential subordinate actors (in the goal structure and in the logical model). In the first case, the actor plays the role of an *agent* and makes an active choice (being, generally speaking, a "managed entity"), and, in the second case, the actor plays the role of a *principal* (in terms of contract theory and the theory of control of organizations), which manages and defines the technology of interests coordination. This duality reflects the *fractal and hierarchical properties* of the structure of CA.

All management components are, of course, important, but the creation of technology in the form of information models (and maintaining them in an adequate state) is of exceptional importance, because, during such a process, technologies of all other components are formed (gray dashed arrows in Figure 2.4). The implementation of actions comes down to the implementation of technology and, possibly, to the occurrence of uncertainty events, which fix the result.

Thus, the result of the implementation of all components and the CA as a whole is actually determined when creating technological components at the synthesis stage (taking into account the occurrence of uncertainty events). The formulated considerations allow us to lay out

---

Thesis 8   STS/Enterprise management is realized during all phases and stages of a CA lifecycle. A critical influence on the effectiveness and efficiency of CA is implemented by the creation and updating of components of the technology (including management components – synthesis and concretization) in the form of information models during the synthesis phase. Management components, being created during the synthesis stage, are "automatically" implemented during other phases of the lifecycle.

In many practically interesting cases, the activity of an STS has a cyclical pattern. Completely naturally, one can see cycles associated, for example, with the repetition of one typical business operation, manufacturing some product, or providing a particular service; a work shift or work day; a reporting/calendar period. Often, after the actor secures the demand and coordinates his interests with the "external interests," he/she realizes there is a need for a new activity and formulates the technology, and then he or she repeatedly does the same in the course of repeating CA cycles.

In particular, when a new business is being created, the output product or service of the business is designed; a company is organized, which implements an activity according to the technology during as many periods as possible. Having been hired, an employee makes a fundamental decision one time to fulfill the duties assigned to him/her or not; thereafter, he or she repeatedly executes them. The technology remains unchanged until a need for its modernization arises, after which the cyclic implementation of CA with a constant technology continues again.

By repeating cycles many times, an actor nevertheless carries out analysis and synthesis (at least in the form of activity planning for the current or next period), as well as reflection (at least by evaluating the output of CA for a period) and the implementation of all phases of an LC of CA (see Figure 2.5).

Synthesis and concretization are performed in this case in parallel with the implementation, and the analytical activities of reflection and analysis actually combine with each other by closing the management cycle. The assumption of repeatability of cycles also corresponds to a generally accepted *principle of a "going concern,"* which is usually applied when considering any business: a company is believed to

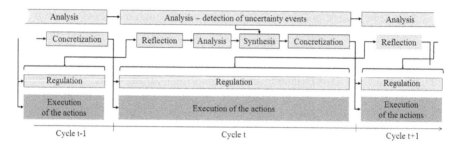

FIGURE 2.5 Cyclical nature of activities of an actor of complex activity.

carry out its activities both in the previous periods and in subsequent periods by continuing to do the same.

The multiple repetition of lifecycles leads to the fact that the components of technology and resource pools, once created in the form of *information models*, are used repeatedly; they are modernized for this purpose and are thereby kept updated. Therefore, to maintain generality, let's not call the management components into which the synthesis is broken down "creation," but "management," namely:

- *technology management* – CA for creating technology components in the form of information models and their integration, testing, use, and maintenance in an adequate state, depending on the environment during the entire lifecycle of the CA;
- *resource management* – CA for creating and maintaining pools of material resources, i.e., for assigning resource items to the roles of actors and technology components.

Management of a set of LCs of interconnected SEAs requires a clarification of the concepts of the managing actor and the managed entity, of the actor of the CA element, as well as of connections among these concepts. In Section 1.5, it is shown that any complex activity, except for an execution of specific elementary operations, is a management one: that is to say, the activity of each SEA actor is:

- management of SEAs that are subordinate and situated lower in the logical/goal structure;
- an execution of specific elementary operations (if elementary operations are parts of this SEA).

The actor of any SEA (for example, SEA_N, Figure 1.19) directly manages the subordinate SEAs and their actors (SEA_u, ..., SEA_m) included in this SEA_N, and, through the actors of other SEAs (for example, through the actor of SEA_m), manages indirectly all subordinate SEAs in the goal hierarchy ($SEA_{m,1}$, ..., $SEA_{m,K}$). In this sense, management of complex activity in the form of a set of SEAs is both hierarchical and distributed.

It should be noted that the actor of any SEA always carries out *"self-management"* in a certain sense: during the synthesis phase, an SEA actor forms logical and cause–effect models of this SEA as well as of the technology of elementary operations (that form parts of this SEA); furthermore, during the concretization phase, he or she assigns resources of elementary operations by significantly affecting, in such a way, his/her future behavior. This actor performs such actions aimed at him/herself that fall under the definition of management. This also reveals a certain duality of *self-management*: the creation of technology, on the one hand, is an activity and, on the other hand, it influences the future behavior of the actor during the period that he/she implements activity according to the technology, i.e. during the period of implementation of his/her mission.

Thus, the management of an entire set of SEAs is carried out by either (a) the actor of the SEA who is superior in the set (actor of SEA_N in Figure 1.19) or (b) the actor of some "external" SEA who is superior with regard to the entire set of SEAs. In fact, this "external" SEA unites the entire managed set and, in such a way, the second alternative (b) is reduced to the first (a). These considerations allow us to formulate

---

Thesis 9   Management of an entire set of SEAs is both hierarchical and distributed and, in general, is carried out by the actor of the SEA who is the highest in the hierarchy (as noted above, they also perform self-management by implementing such actions that fall within the definition of management). In that regard, a direct managerial effect on the actor of each SEA is exerted by the actor of an SEA who is superior in the logical structure.

In relation to STS/Enterprise management, this means that a managing actor of CA as a whole is either some managing subsystem of the initial STS or an STS which is external to the original STS; the actor of the former has formulated the goals of the initial STS, while each particular STS (which collectively form the original STS) is managed by a relevant actor.

From Thesis 9, one can conclude that for *active STSs* (class II STSs; see Section 2.1) there are no managing actors, i.e., active STSs are "unmanageable from the outside"; one can say that they exercise self-management.

2.5 COMPATIBILITY OF COMPLEX ACTIVITY LIFECYCLES

The existence of a set of interconnected lifecycles of SEAs, as a managed entity, imposes an additional requirement on management: it is necessary not only to take into account the connections among elements (of a managed entity), but also to establish them. By emphasizing this particular feature, we consider a coordinated management of lifecycles in the sense of ensuring the *compatibility* of LCs in a broad sense.* Coordination, as the bringing into proper condition and/or the establishment of relations, is a special case of organization. At the same time, the principle of *incentive-compatible control* (an incentive scheme and plans are such that the implementation of plans is beneficial to all actors) is one of the main principles in the

---

* Compatible (Merriam-Webster) – 1: capable of existing together in harmony; ... 5: designed to work with another device or system without modification.

theory of active systems and in the theory of Control in Organizations (TCOr; see (Novikov 2013)).

Compatibility (including that of management activity) requires a choice of foundations on which it is achieved, and such foundations should be as general as possible. Therefore, with regard to a set of LCs of SEAs, it is natural to choose all the constituent parts of an SEA as such a basis, namely (a) the *actor* (see Thesis 1, Section 2.1); (b) *procedural components* of activity (needs, goals, and tasks, technology, action, output: Section 1.1.2); (c) the *subject matter*; and (d) the moment of time to achieve the *goal* of CA.

The grounds listed above can be grouped, which in turn determines a set of management tasks (Table 2.3) and corresponding mathematical models.

At the same time, as noted above, uncertainty events can violate the compatibility of LCs for any foundation. While measurable uncertainty can be considered in a CA model (for example, using statistical or other methods) within the framework of each of the tasks, true uncertainty cannot be eliminated due to the absence of rules describing it. Therefore, it is necessary to carry out an analysis – namely, to detect LC inconsistencies – events of true uncertainty (and/or their signals) leading to inadequacy of the technology.

Coordination of implementation of LCs of CA and coordination of resources are close to each other; in practice, they are performed together and ensure:

a. scheduling and resource planning;
b. formation of managing actions according to the plans;
c. identification of actual deviations from the plans;
d. adjustment of the plans and managing actions if necessary.

TABLE 2.3
Foundations for Compatibility and Management Tasks

Foundations for compatibility		Management tasks	
Actors of CA, their interests (Thesis 1)		Coordination of interests of CA actors	Detection of mismatch of LCs – events of true uncertainty leading to inadequacy of technology
Need, goal, tasks, action, result of CA. Time to achieve goal		Coordination of implementation of the LCs of CA	
Subject matter of CA		Coordination of resources	
CA technology	Means to achieve the goal of CA – Resources		
	Methods, ways, means to achieve the goal of CA	Creating, developing, testing, and using CA technologies	

In that regard, the formation of actions (b) is a "technical" step, the identification of deviations (c) is a special case of the problem of detection of LC mismatches, and the adjustment of plans (d) coincides with planning. Therefore, all these tasks (and the corresponding models and methods) can be combined into one group called CA and resource planning (coordination).

When analyzing CA resources, we can see a very special kind of resource – people. On the one hand, people play a key role in CA implementation as the actors and create value; on the other hand, people are those resources which superiors use to mold subordinate actors. What's more, people have the distinguishing characteristic of *active choice*: they act following their own interests and motives. So we pay special attention to people as *active resources* of Enterprise CA and, following today's trend, we use the term *human capital* to denote them. Quantitative models of human capital are proposed in Chapter 6, and planning methods based on these models are developed in Section 7.4.

Figure 2.6 illustrates lifecycles of procedural components of CA, the compatibility of which is influenced by the solution to some management task or another.

The rounded rectangles present the lifecycles to be coordinated, and arrows demonstrate management components ensuring the compatibility. The following abbreviations are used for management tasks:

- Pl – Complex activity and resource *planning* (coordination), including the detection of mismatches in the LCs of CA;
- TM – *Technology management*: creation, development, testing, and use of CA technologies;
- CoI – *Coordination of the interests* of actors of CA, taking into account the LCs and technology of their activity.

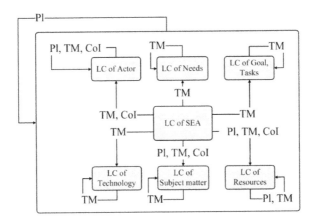

FIGURE 2.6 Effect of management tasks on the compatibility of lifecycles of complex activity.

A diagram of *compatibility of lifecycles* (Figure 2.6) emphasizes two aspects.

The first one is the central role of the lifecycle of a structural element of activity in the sense that, not only are other lifecycles coordinated with the LC of an SEA, but also the compatibility of LCs of the constituents with each other is implemented through the LC of an SEA.

The second one is the central role of technology and of the technology management process in coordinating the LCs, because the TM process impacts all kinds of compatibility of all LCs.

Management tasks significantly affecting all the constituents of Enterprise CA, in turn, are Subproblems of the Enterprise Control Problem.

Thus, the following thesis is formulated:

Thesis 10   The presence of a set of interconnected lifecycles of SEAs as a managed entity requires not only taking into account the relations between managed constituents (LCs), but also establishing them. The compatibility of LCs should be ensured by solving the following Enterprise Control Subproblems: (a) Coordination of the interests of CA actors; (b) Complex activity and resource planning (coordination), including the detection of mismatches of LCs of CA; (c) Technology management.

In concluding this section, we should note that the classes of management tasks defined above and appropriate mathematical models studied below (Chapters 4–7) cover all the procedural components of both elementary and complex activities (Figure 2.7).

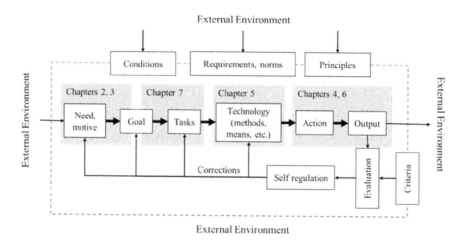

FIGURE 2.7   Procedural components of activity and models of Enterprise management.

CONCLUSION

Let us summarize all the theses formulated in the chapter above (Figure 2.8 illustrates the structure of these theses).

Based on **Theses 2–5**, the key **Thesis 6** is formulated: STS/Enterprise management should be implemented as the management of a set of interconnected lifecycles of the SEAs.

Thesis 6 gave rise to **Thesis 7**, fixing management components as a means of STS/Enterprise management and particular features of their implementation. **Theses 8, 9**, and **10** are stated based on **Theses 1 and 7**.

Thus, we can formulate <u>methodological factors of Enterprise management</u>, specifying the actor, the means, the subject matter, the uncertainty, and the management tasks:

I. Enterprise or sociotechnical system management is carried out in the form of management of a hierarchical set of interconnected lifecycles of structural elements of complex activity implemented by an Enterprise or STS. LCs of SEAs also generalize LCs of all procedural components of activity and resources.

II. Means of STS/Enterprise management are the following management components:
   - analysis (first of all, detection of mismatches of LCs – events of true uncertainty leading to the inadequacy of CA technology),
   - synthesis (technology management; resource management),
   - concretization (first of all, coordination of the interests of actors).

III. STS/Enterprise management should be performed taking into account the need to eliminate measurable uncertainty (by including scenarios of response to measurable uncertainty) and react to true uncertainty events (by the earliest detection of mismatches of LCs of CA and modifying CA technology).

IV. Enterprise or STS management is executed during all phases and stages of the lifecycles of its activities. However, the critical influence on the effectiveness and efficiency of CA is the technology of management during the synthesis phase.

V. Management of an entire set of SEAs is both hierarchical and distributed and, as a whole, is carried out by the actor of the SEA, who is the superior in the hierarchy. In that regard, a direct managerial effect on the actor of each SEA is exerted by the actor of an SEA, being superior in the logical structure.

VI. The presence of a set of interconnected lifecycles of SEAs, as a managed entity, requires not only taking into account the relations between managed constituents, but also establishing them. The compatibility of LCs should be ensured by solving the following Enterprise Control Subproblems:
   a) Coordination of the interests of CA actors;
   b) Complex activity and resource planning (coordination), including the detection of mismatches of LCs of CA;

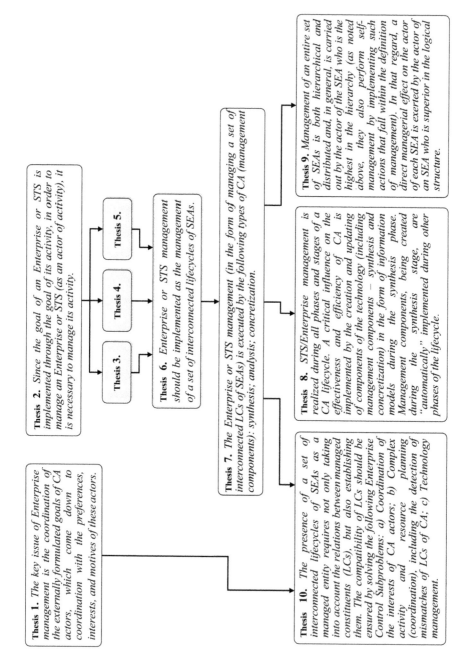

FIGURE 2.8 Structure of theses of Enterprise management.

c) Technology management (including the creation, development, testing, maintenance, and use of CA technologies).

Applicable mathematical models and methods to solve management tasks are described in the following chapters.

REFERENCES

Adizes, I. 1999. *Managing Corporate Lifecycles: An Updated and Expanded Look at the Corporate Lifecycles*. First edition. Paramus, NJ: Prentice Hall Press.

Belov, M. 2018. Theory of Complex Activity as a Tool to Analyze and Govern an Enterprise. In *13th Annual Conference on System of Systems Engineering (SoSE 2018)*. Paris, France, 19–22 June 2018, 541–548.

Belov, M. and Novikov, D. 2019. *Methodological Foundations of the Digital Economy / Big Data-driven World: Legislation Issues and Control Technologies*. Heidelberg: Springer, 3–14.

Belov, M. and Novikov, D. 2020. *Methodology of Complex Activity: Foundations of Understanding and Modelling*. Heidelberg: Springer.

Coase, R. 1937. The Nature of the Firm. *Economica (new series)* 4(16), 386–405.

Haskins, C. (ed.). 2015. *INCOSE Systems Engineering Handbook Version 3.2.2 – A Guide for Life Cycle Processes and Activities*. INCOSE, Fourth edition. San Diego, CA: John Willey & Sons.

ISO/IEC/IEEE 15288: 2015 *Systems and Software Engineering. System Life Cycle Processes*. Internatonal Standard Organisation.

Novikov, D. 2013. *Theory of Control in Organizations*. New York: Nova Science Publishers.

Pyster, A. and Olwell, A. (eds.). 2013. *The Guide to the Systems Engineering Body of Knowledge (SEBoK)*, v. 1.2. Hoboken, NJ: The Trustees of the Stevens Institute of Technology. http://www.sebokwiki.org [Accessed 16 December 2019].

Part II

Mathematics

Mathematical Models and
Methods of Enterprise Control

3 Enterprise Control Problem

The Statement

Turning to the formal statement of the Enterprise Control Problem in the form of a mathematical optimization problem, we will use as a starting point the qualitative models of the Enterprise and CA, developed above in Part I. From this point of view, the methodological foundations of Enterprise control (see conclusions of Chapter 1 and Chapter 2) might be summarized as the following theses, which are illustrated by Figure 3.1:

- Valuable output of any Enterprise is produced exactly by CA (of the Enterprise) but not only by the existence of the Enterprise in and of itself.
- Any kind of CA (or any of its elements that is also CA) is represented as an aggregate of lifecycles of SEAs, and the lifecycle of each SEA is a combination of (a) actions executed directly by an SEA actor and (b) the activity of all subordinate SEAs.
- Actions executed directly by an SEA actor are the behavior of a controlled entity. These actions include, first, elementary operations that are part of an SEA (Section 1.2) and, second, managerial or control activities – constituents of the process model (Figures 1.13–1.17). The behavior of each of the complex actors of SEAs is, in a sense, autonomous and independent of the others and consists of the implementation of a sequence of actions (whose implementation is determined by its technology) ordered by cause–effect and process models. The general goal and cause–effect structures (defined by logical and cause–effect models), as well as commonly shared resources, serve as constraints on the behavior of actors.
- Enterprise management/control is considered a concerted impact on (a) the behavior of each of the complex actors of SEAs and (b) the technologies of SEAs (information models and material resources), taking into account the characteristics of the external environment, in order to obtain the desired output of the Enterprise CA as a whole. Management/control is hierarchical and distributed, and a direct control impact on the actor of each SEA is exerted by the actor of the SEA, being superior in the logical structure.
- Means to solve the Enterprise Control Problem are management components: analysis (first and foremost, detection of mismatches of LCs – events of true uncertainty – leading to the inadequacy of the technology), synthesis (technology management; resource management), and concretization (first of all, coordination of the interests of actors).

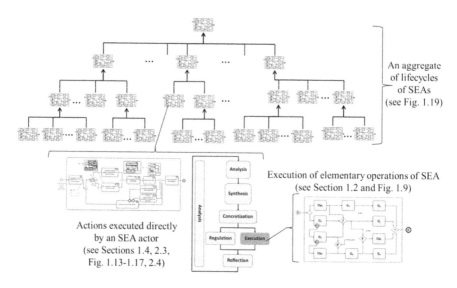

FIGURE 3.1 Methodological foundations of Enterprise control.

3.1 CONCEPT OF OPTIMIZATION

Since this book is devoted to an optimal Enterprise, and namely the possibility of correct optimization is the distinctive feature of the approach proposed, we will briefly consider what the essence of optimization is.

Consider some system. First of all, it should be borne in mind that for *optimization*, i.e., to select the implementation option for the system or its behavior that is characterized by the maximum efficiency under given conditions (with existing constraints), one should have a *model* of the system being optimized – its analogue or "deputy" in cognition (Novikov and Novikov 2013). Indeed, optimization implies a comparison of different options, and this comparison, in most cases, is performed mentally, without implementing each of the options in reality.

The following **stages of model design** can be distinguished (Novikov and Novikov 2013).

1. *Determination of the subject matter and the goal of modeling*, including boundaries of the system being researched and those basic properties that should be reflected in the model.
2. *Choice of modeling language ("apparatus")*. To date, there is no universally accepted classification of methods for modeling. There are several dozen formal "instruments" for modeling (see bibliographic references in Novikov and Novikov (2013)), each of which is a multidivisional branch of applied mathematics.

3. *Choice of variables* describing the state of the system and essential parameters of the external environment, as well as scales of their measurement and evaluation criteria.

4. *Choice of constraints*, that is, sets of acceptable values of the variables and of the *initial conditions* (initial values of the variables).

5. *Determination of connections among the variables*, taking into account all the information about the system being modeled, as well as known laws, rules, etc. that describe the system and its behavior. This stage is sometimes called "model design" in the broad sense.

6. *Research of the model*, or simulation, and/or the application of optimization methods and, perhaps, solving the control problem. This stage is sometimes called "modeling" in the narrow sense.

7. *Study of the stability and adequacy of the model.*

Subsequent stages related to practical implementation of the model and/or implementation of the modeling results are not considered below.

Note that mathematical modeling can be divided into analytical and simulation.

It is characteristic of *analytical modeling* that the processes of functioning of elements of a system are written in the form of some relations (for example, equations – algebraic, differential, integral, etc.) or inequalities or logical conditions:

- analytical when one intends to obtain explicit dependences in a general (analytical) form for goal characteristics in the form of certain formulas;
- numerical when, not being able to solve systems of equations and/or inequalities and/or optimization problems in a general way, one intends to obtain numerical results for some specific initial data (for example, using a computer);
- qualitative when, without having an explicit solution, one is able to find some of its properties. An example is so-called "soft" models, in which analysis of differential equations describing the most diverse processes (economic, environmental, political, etc.) allows qualitative conclusions to be drawn about the properties of their solutions – the existence and type of equilibrium points and attraction sets, areas of possible values of variables, etc.

Simulation is characterized by a research of individual trajectories of the simulated system dynamics. In this case, some initial conditions are fixed (the initial state of the system or model parameters) and one trajectory is calculated. Then other initial conditions are selected, and another trajectory is calculated, etc. That is, analytical relationships among model parameters and future system states are not sought. As a rule, simulation involves numerical methods implemented on a computer. The advantage of simulation is that different *scenarios*, sometimes even for very complicated models, can be analyzed. Its drawback* is that it is impossible to obtain, for

---

* Analytical models are free from this drawback, but they can rarely be constructed and investigated for sufficiently complicated systems.

example, an answer to the question: in what cases (under what values of the initial conditions and model parameters) will the system dynamics satisfy the specified requirements? In addition, analyzing the stability of a simulation model is usually difficult.

Optimization consists of finding, among many possible options (models of a system being designed) the best ones under given conditions – with given constraints – i.e., *optimal alternatives*. In this phrase, every word is important. In saying "the best," we assume that we have *a criterion* (or a number of criteria), a method or methods to compare the options. At the same time, it is important to take into account the existing conditions and constraints, because their change can lead to the fact that, with the same criterion (criteria), other options will turn out to be the best.

The term *optimality* has received a rigorous and accurate representation in various mathematical theories by having firmly entered into the practice of design and operation of technical systems and has played an important role in the development of modern system approaches widely used in administrative and public practice and has become a concept known to almost everyone. This makes sense: the desire to increase the labor efficiency of any purposeful activity, speaking metaphorically, has found its expression: its clear and comprehensive form in the idea of optimization.

In a mathematical sense, the essence of *optimization*, in short, is as follows. Let the state of a modeled system be determined by a set of *indicators*: $x = (x_1, x_2, x_3, ..., x_n)$, which take numerical values. The set of possible states of the system is subject to a *constraint*: $x \in X$, where set X is determined by existing physical, technological, logical, resource, and other constraints.

Next, function $F(x)$ is introduced, which depends on $x_1, x_2, x_3, ..., x_n$, called an *objective function* and taking a numerical value. The objective function defines the *efficiency criterion*: it is assumed that the higher the values taken by function $F(x)$, the higher the efficiency, that is, the "better" the state x of the system.

The optimization problem is to find the *optimal* value x^*, that is, the feasible state of the system ($x \in X$), having the maximum efficiency: $F(x^*) \geq F(x)$ should be fulfilled for all x from set X. Sometimes, *bounded rationality* is considered (see also the approximate solutions below), when such a feasible state of a system is chosen that has an efficiency no less than the given one or differs from the maximum at no more than a given value.

Thus, the indispensable four *components of the optimization* problem are:

1) the state of a system and of the environment (a set of variables and corresponding scales) and maybe of control variables;
2) constraints (sets of feasible values of variables);
3) laws and rules that reflect relationships between variables;
4) the efficiency criterion.

These four components are present in any problem of optimization of a system of any nature, being considered within the framework of models of the optimization theory, of operations research, or of the mathematical theory of control (including sociotechnical systems) or other areas of applied mathematics.

It is interesting to note that the requirement that the four above-mentioned components be present simultaneously is quite tough – any partial description is incomplete. Therefore, there is a very clear "watershed" between mathematical optimization models of Enterprises and, for example, their descriptions in the theory of processes or systems engineering and, moreover, in management, psychology, sociology, etc.

3.2 ENTERPRISE CONTROL PROBLEM: QUALITATIVE MODEL

Creating a qualitative model of the *Enterprise Control Problem* requires clarification of four core constituents:

- controlled entity;
- control means;
- uncertainty;
- objective function and constraints.

3.2.1 CONTROLLED ENTITY

Let us analyze the model of the implementation of an SEA's LC as a constituent of a complex controlled entity – the CA of an Enterprise.

Execution of CA – the implementation of a hierarchical aggregate of LCs of SEAs – is considered in increments of time, each of these increments being called a *period*. The discrete time model is quite natural for human activity in general and Enterprises in particular: both management and reporting by firms, corporations, projects, and enterprises in other forms are almost always performed for time periods (years, quarters, months, work shifts, etc.).

The use of a discrete time scale forces one to abstract from specific moments of the occurrence of events and characterizes a moment of occurrence of any event with an accuracy of the identifier (number) of the period during which it occurred.

The end of one period coincides with the beginning of the next one. Therefore, for definiteness, we assume that an actor makes all decisions – choices of actions – at the initial moments of each period and implements actions during the period. Decisions to start or terminate CA are special cases of the choice of actions, and the decisions are based on the analysis and other actions implemented in previous periods, as well as on information about uncertainty events that occurred earlier.

As emphasized above, the implementation of the LC of each SEA is a combination of actions of the complex actor of the given SEA and complex activity of its subordinates. At the same time, one part of direct actions is related to the implementation of specific elementary operations of the SEA constituting the CA (Section 1.2.1), and the other part is related to the management of the subordinated (in the logical structure) SEAs, i.e., to the formation and implementation of control actions according to the "universal algorithm of control" (Sections 1.4.2, 1.5.2).

Consequently, it can be affirmed that, during each period of time, a complex actor implements several actions (in a particular case, one action), being ordered by a cause–effect structure – the technology of CA. Moreover, the technology of all actions is known at the beginning of a period (possibly as an outcome of the development and implementation of technology obtained during previous periods). For definiteness, we assume* that the duration of any action does not exceed one time period, and all actions implemented during the period start after the beginning of the period and end before the end of the period. An aggregate of these actions is the behavior of a controlled entity – the hierarchy of actors of SEAs.

To summarize, we describe the order of functioning of the actor of an SEA by the following scheme (Figure 3.2), which in aggregated form represents the "universal algorithm of control" (Sections 1.4.2, 1.5.2).

A. *At the beginning of each time period*, an actor makes a decision to start/ continue the implementation of CA (lifecycle of an SEA) or refuse/discontinue this implementation, both decisions having an additional alternative to initiate implementation of new elements of CA.

B. *During a period*, the complex actor of an SEA implements heterogeneous actions that, first, are related to elementary operations of the given SEA (in fact, these are exactly the valuable CA). Second, these are actions to control

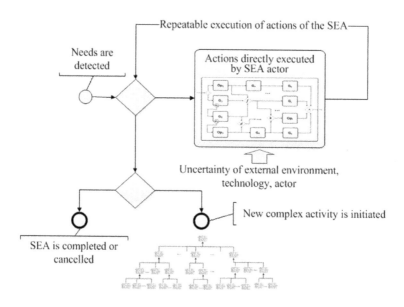

FIGURE 3.2　Scheme of functioning of an SEA actor.

---

* This assumption does not limit the generality of the model, because it is obvious that any long-term action, if necessary, can always be broken down into a sequence of shorter ones, defined as intermediate goals.

the given and subordinate SEAs: analysis, synthesis of technology, concretization, regulation, and reflection. Within the framework of these actions, an actor can carry out information exchange with the actors of subordinate and superior SEAs, including the same within the framework of the organization of coordination of interests of the actors. In addition, during a period, events of true and/or measurable uncertainty can occur and have an impact on the implementation of CA (see Section 2.3).

C. At the *end of the time period*, the actor proceeds to the next period (returns to Step A), making decisions based on the output of this period (and previous ones) at the initial moment of the next period.

3.2.2   CONTROL MEANS

An important property of a controlled entity (a hierarchical aggregate of actors of SEAs) under consideration is the presence of a human in its composition, and therefore the possibility of an active choice (in particular, a group one). When it is important to underline this property in order to designate any formations that include people, we will use the term *active systems*, abbreviated ASs, which include *active elements*, abbreviated AEs (Burkov 1977, Burkov 2013). In particular, actors of SEAs are active elements, as a single or group, and an Enterprise as a whole is also an AS (see Foreword).

The active choice property paves the way to manage active elements in the form of coordination of their interests (Sections 2.1–2.3), carried out by means of organizing their activity, i.e., by ordering, establishing relations or links between them and among the elements of corresponding SEAs.

Relationships between AEs and controlling the connections between them are the subject matter of a knowledge domain that unites the *contract theory* (Bolton and Dewatripont 2005, Laffont and Martimort 2001, Salanie 2005) and the *theory of control in organizations* (Novikov 2013). Hereinafter, we rely on the terminology, axiomatics, approaches, and outcomes of the TCOr by taking into consideration its commonality with the theory of contracts. Traditionally, in the TCOr, a controlling active element is referred to as a *principal*, and a controlled one is referred to as an *agent*, both of them possessing the property of active choice and the eligibility to play the role of actors of SEAs. Therefore, we use these terms when it is necessary to underline the active properties and hierarchical relations between actors of SEAs.

A commonly accepted means of control action in the TCOr is a *contract*, which is offered by a controlling AE, a principal, to a controlled AE, an agent. We define a contract as a relationship between two actors that defines the obligation of one of them, the controlling one (principal), to implement certain actions, depending on the actions implemented by the other, controlled, AE (agent). A contract defines a binary relation to the multiplication of sets of possible actions of the agent and the principal or is defined by the pair <"action by a server, agent"; "incentives from a client, principal">. A contract is a means to incentivize a controlled agent to behave as required, as a consequence of which such an output will be obtained that meets the goals of the principal. A contract is a specification of: (a) the goal of a controlling actor (a *plan for output*) that a controlled actor must achieve (or his behavior directly – a *plan for actions*); (b) technology (methods, ways, and means of achievement of the goal); (c) an incentive system – the principal's response, in particular, remuneration, which will be paid by the principal to the agent if the agent fulfills the terms of the contract.

Therefore, a control action is implemented in the form of one or more contracts offered to actors of SEAs by some controlling entity. In addition, due to the hierarchical structure of an aggregate of SEAs, the actor of a superior SEA may also control subordinate SEAs by means of such contracts that establish relations between superior and subordinate actors of SEAs. At the same time, actors of SEAs play the role of agents in relation to superior actors in the hierarchy and principals in relation to subordinate ones. A hierarchy of actors of SEAs forms an AS, which operates over multiple time periods; it is usually referred to as a *multilevel dynamic active system*.

3.2.3 Uncertainty

In the preceding chapters, *uncertainty* (true or measurable) was considered to be one of the immanent conditions under which any complex activity of an Enterprise is carried out. The nature and sources of uncertainty (Section 1.3), as well as the influence of uncertainty on the implementation of lifecycles and their compatibility (Section 2.3), were considered above.

It has been stated (Section 2.3) that the impact of *measurable uncertainty* events on CA may be reduced to the uncertainty of the duration of actions and/or an actor's expenses required to achieve the goal, but such events do not interrupt the execution of CA. The presence of a priori knowledge of measurable uncertainty allows one to eliminate it; so, let us do this when solving the Enterprise Control Problem. Assume that the technology of activity is mature and well tested; therefore, the duration of an action (under the impact of measurable uncertainty) varies within only one time period, that is, it is negligible in the discrete time model.* For uncertainty of expenses, depending on the availability of enough a priori information, interval or probabilistic models may be used to eliminate the uncertainty by methods of a guaranteed result or expected utility.

At the same time, *true uncertainty* events interrupt CA execution and require a reaction in the form of technology modernization (Section 2.3): they actually change the CA as a whole. The lack of a priori information about such events does not provide constructive reasons for its elimination in the framework of an optimization problem. Therefore, we will not take into account true uncertainty in the formulation of and solution to optimization problems, keeping in mind, however, the potential occurrence of such events. As a constructive way of operating with true uncertainty, the detection of mismatches of LCs of CA must be executed; such detection should be performed independently of solving optimization problems due to a lack of significant reasons to do them in conjunction.

---

* Changes in the number of periods required to complete an action should be considered a change in technology. Therefore, events leading to significant changes in the duration of actions or changes in the number of periods will be attributed to manifestations of *true uncertainty*.

3.2.4 OBJECTIVE FUNCTION AND CONSTRAINTS

The *objective function* of an Enterprise is defined as the difference between a *value*, or *utility*, expressed in unified numerical units, obtained as a result of achievement of the CA goal/fulfillment of the mission of the Enterprise, and *expenses* incurred to achieve this goal, over a certain period of time. An objective function is also conventionally referred to as economic output or simply the output of an Enterprise, and the objective function characterizes the *efficiency* of the Enterprise (Section 3.1).

By following generally accepted practice, we assume the additivity of value/ utility and expenses. Then, the *optimal* solution (with maximum efficiency) in the Enterprise Control Problem is an implementation of such CA that provides the maximum possible value of the economic output for a selected period of time under given constraints, including conditions under which CA is implemented (conditions for the functioning of an Enterprise), as well as resource constraints and external requirements for its outputs.

General conditions surrounding the problem of Enterprise Control include modeling complex activity (Chapter 1) in the form of goal and cause–effect structures, technologies of SEAs, and a process model of CA. These conditions are not restricting – the models have a methodological commonality and describe uniformly any Enterprise and its CA.

Specific conditions, in particular in the form of assumptions about the properties of the structure of a multi-level dynamic AS and the technology of its operation – the structure of SEAs – allow us to obtain an analytical solution to the Enterprise Control Problem. These specific conditions are introduced in this chapter (section 3.4); and in Chapter 4 (section 4.3) it is demonstrated that they are sufficient conditions for the existence of an optimal solution to the Enterprise Control Problem. On the other hand, from a management point of view, these conditions integrate a large share of best practices implemented in leading firms. In Chapter 8, devoted to practical issues of Enterprise Control, a relevant comparative analysis is presented.

All this allows us to introduce the term *perfect Enterprise* and to use the same to designate an Enterprise that meets sufficient conditions for obtaining an analytical Optimal Solution to the Enterprise Control Problem. We refer to these conditions as *perfect Enterprise conditions* and systematically formulate them in Chapter 8, while developing the Enterprise Control Framework.

3.2.5 BRIEF

So, the Enterprise Control Problem is formulated as follows:

I. A controlled entity is a hierarchical set of complex actors of elements of the complex activity of an Enterprise – SEAs (see Figure 3.1), considered in discrete time. Complex actors, in turn, are active elements, and a controlled entity is a hierarchical dynamic active system.

II. Actions directly performed by actors constitute the behavior of a controlled entity.

During each time period, each complex actor of an SEA performs several actions ordered by a cause–effect structure – CA technology. All the technologies are known at the beginning of a period.

III. Events of measurable and true uncertainty influence the output of the behavior of a controlled entity – a hierarchy of actors of SEAs.

IV. Actors of SEAs have the property of active (possibly group) choice; therefore, control actions over them are implemented in the form of contracts, specifying the goals of SEAs, technology (ways, methods, and means to achieve the goals), and a response by the controlling actor for achieving the goal, in particular, payment of remuneration.

V. Control action by an external controlling actor is implemented in the form of one or more contracts offered to the actors of SEAs. Due to the hierarchical structure of an aggregate of SEAs, actors of superior SEAs also control subordinate SEAs through contracts that establish relations between the superior and subordinate actors of SEAs.

VI. The objective function of Enterprise control is defined as an economic output – the difference between value or utility obtained as a result of achievement of the CA goal and expenses incurred to achieve this goal over a certain period of time. The objective function stated in this way determines the criterion of efficiency of an Enterprise, since it characterizes the earned value and the incurred expenses.

VII. Control – the influence on the behavior of the actors of SEAs – is formed by solving the following Enterprise Control Subproblems (Thesis 10, Section 2.5): (a) Coordination of the interests of CA actors; (b) Complex activity and resource planning (coordination), including the detection of mismatches of LCs of CA; (c) Technology management. These tasks are formulated for the hierarchy of complex actors (clauses I–VI) considering their dynamics and uncertainty.

3.3 ENTERPRISE CONTROL PROBLEM AMONG RELATED KNOWLEDGE DOMAINS

This book is an attempt to bridge the gap between management theory and systems engineering, on the one hand (MCA is closer to this), and mathematical models of optimization, on the other. However, any attempt to both generalize and itemize has its own "cost." Therefore, let us make a small epistemological digression in order to consider, following Novikov and Novikov (2013), gains and losses from the use of the developed approaches.

3.3.1 "EPISTEMOLOGICALLY WEAK" AND "STRONG" SCIENCES AND THE ENTERPRISE CONTROL PROBLEM

The core idea used today in any *mathematical modeling* act is as follows. The application of *optimal solutions* leads to the fact that, as a rule, they cease to be optimal for small variations in model parameters. A possible way to overcome this drawback is to expand the set of "optimal" solutions by including so-called *approximate* or *suboptimal solutions* (that is, "slightly worse" than optimal). It turns out that weakening the "optimality" of the solution allows one (once an interconnection has been established between possible inaccuracy in the model description and the amount of loss in the solution efficiency) to guarantee a certain level of efficiency of the set of solutions in a given class of real/modeled systems. That is, the range of applicability of solutions may be expanded due to the use of less efficient ones from them. In other words, instead of considering a fixed model of a real system, a family of models is researched.

The qualitative considerations given above bear witness that there is a certain dualism between the effectiveness of a solution and the area of its applicability, the area of its stability, and/or the area of adequacy.

Methods like *scenario analysis*, *simulation* of expected situations, and "what-if" analysis (what happens if such-and-such conditions change?) are used for optimization in the practice of *systems design* (as well as in many other areas of professional activity not yet amenable to "mathematization").

The following regularity can be distinguished: the wider the area of the subject matter is, the more difficult it is to obtain general scientific results for it (Novikov and Novikov 2013). This effect manifests itself most vividly in *mathematics*: any formal statement (for example, a theorem) consists of two parts: assumptions ("Let ...") and a conclusion ("Then ..."). The stronger the assumptions (conditions) – in other words, the constraints – introduced, the easier the proof for one and the same result, or the deeper the results that can be obtained. Minimal (weak) assumptions (conditions, constraints) lead to the weakest conclusions and obtained results. And vice versa: the stronger the result needed, the more restrictive the assumptions, as a rule, that should be introduced. Thus, there is a certain "balance" between the assumptions introduced and the results obtained. A "breakthrough" in mathematics (and also in other sciences that essentially use a formal apparatus) is either to obtain more general (new) results under the existing assumptions or to weaken the assumptions under which the known conclusions remain reasonable.

From the point of view of the epistemological division of sciences into *sciences of the strong version* and *sciences of the weak version* (see Novikov and Novikov (2013)), this regularity can be formulated in the following way: "weaker" sciences introduce the most minimal restrictive assumptions (or do not even introduce them at all) and get the most "fuzzy" results; "strong" sciences, on the contrary, introduce many restrictive assumptions and use specific scientific languages, but also get clearer and stronger (and, often, more reasonable) results, the applicability area of which is very much narrowed (clearly limited by the assumptions introduced).

When introduced, assumptions (conditions) limit the applicability (adequacy) area of the results that follow from them. For example, in the field of management (control) of organizational and technical systems, mathematics (operations research, optimization theory, optimal control, etc.) gives optimal solutions, but their applicability (adequacy) area is rigorously limited by the introduced assumptions. On the other hand, social sciences and humanities, which also study management/control of STSs, barely introduce assumptions and offer "universal recipes" (that is, the applicability or adequacy area is wide), but the effectiveness of these "recipes" rarely differs from the results of using common sense or from such a generalization of the positive practical experience. Indeed, without proper comprehensive research, no guarantees can be given that a managerial decision that has proven effective in one situation will be equally effective in another, even very similar, situation.

Therefore, it is possible to conventionally place various sciences on the plane "Reasonableness of results" – "Their applicability (adequacy) area" – and formulate (again conventionally, by analogy with Heisenberg's uncertainty principle) the following *"uncertainty principle"* (Novikov and Novikov 2013): **the current level of development of science is characterized by a certain "volume of knowledge" acting as a joint constraint on the "reasonableness" of results and their generality** (see Figure 3.3).

In other words, let us conventionally say that the "multiplication" of an applicability area and a reasonableness area does not exceed a certain constant; an increase in one "multiplier" inevitably leads to a decrease in another. This constant, also conventionally, is interpreted as "the volume of knowledge accumulated to date."

A possible explanation for this phenomenon is that the "weakening" of sciences occurs as the subject matter of research becomes more complicated. From this position, strong sciences can also be referred to as "simple" ones, and weak sciences as "complicated" ones (judging by the complication of the entity of research). Conventionally, the boundary between them is living systems, explored by biology. Research on individual body systems (anatomy, physiology, etc.) still gravitates toward strong sciences (empiricism is confirmed by repeated tests and experiments and is justified by "simpler" sciences – biophysics, biochemistry, etc.); therefore, based on empiricism, formal constructions are possible, both in physics and in chemistry. Furthermore, in research on living systems, experiments in the classical sense (reproducibility, etc.) are becoming more and more cumbersome. And then, when shifted to people and social systems, experiments become almost completely impossible.

The foregoing does not mean at all that development is impossible – each specific study is an advance towards either an increase in "reasonableness" and generality and/or an expansion of the applicability (adequacy) area. Indeed, the entire history of the development of science, as a whole, is an illustration of a shift of the curve shown in Figure 3.3 up and to the right, i.e., an increase in the volume of accumulated knowledge – the constant appearing on the right side of the inequality! Below, at the end of Section 3.3.3, it is shown how the models and methods proposed to solve the Enterprise Control Problem "dominate" (in the terms of Figure 3.3) over related sciences and areas of knowledge.

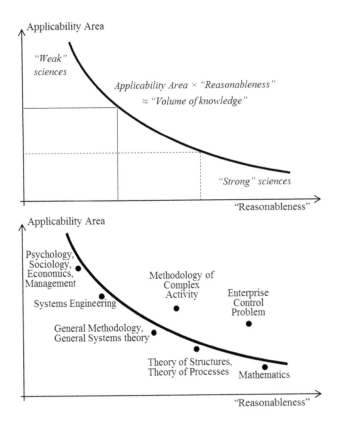

FIGURE 3.3   Illustration of the Principle of Uncertainty.

3.3.2 ENTERPRISE CONTROL PROBLEM AND THEORY OF CONTROL IN ORGANIZATIONS

Problems of *coordination of the interests* of actors possessing the properties of *active choice* are studied in *contract theory* (Bolton and Dewatripont 2005, Laffont and Martimort 2001, Salanie 2005), in the *theory of active systems* (Burkov 1977, Burkov and Kondratyev 1981), and in the *theory of control in organizations* (TCOr). The definition of a "general control problem" in TCOr (Novikov 2013) describes a control structure, comprising a principal, an agent, and an agent-controlled entity, by considering both one-time and multiple repeating modes of the functioning of an active system.

It is assumed in TCOr that the choice of an action of an actor (principal or agent) is a process of his or her decision-making that is described by a corresponding mathematical model, usually by a *game–theoretic* one or by a collective behavior model. Several types of control (based on the classification of the controlled subject) are considered (Novikov 2013).

Institutional control (control by imposed constraints – conditions, requirements, principles – and norms of activity) is the most rigid and consists of the fact that a principal deliberately constrains sets of feasible technologies, norms, principles, actions, and outputs of a controlled agent. Such a constraint can be established by explicit or implicit impacts – legal acts, decrees, orders, instructions, and so on or moral and ethical norms, corporate culture, etc.

Motivational (incentive) *control* (control by an impact on preferences, i.e., by choosing a criterion for the evaluation of an activity output) is "softer" than the institutional one, and consists of a purposeful change to the preferences of an agent. Such a change can be carried out by introducing a system of penalties and/or rewards for the choice of certain actions and/or the achievement of certain outputs of activity.

The "softest" (indirect) control, as opposed to institutional and motivational ones, is *informational control*, which consists of affecting an actor's awareness of the essential parameters.

Below, the focus is on problems and mathematical models of motivational control (see Chapters 4, 6, and 7); such is reasoned by the fact that

- first, as shown in the ninth chapter of the monograph (Novikov 2013), a wide class of such models makes it possible to consistently deconstruct norms of activity and to reduce the problems of institutional control to the corresponding problems of motivational control;
- second, as shown in Chapter 8, a perfect Enterprise implies the existence of a set of information models of activity shared by all participants; this fact "degenerates" the problem of informational control.

A controlled entity in the Enterprise Control Problem is a hierarchy of interconnected *agents* that constitute a multi-level *organizational system* (OS) as an essential part of the STS/Enterprise. Its subsystems are also OSs, each of which represents a complex *network structure*.

The fundamentals of TCOr (Burkov 2013) attribute two types of actions to a principal. The first one is the definition of the operational mechanism of the OS; the second is the actions within the framework of this mechanism: (a) implementation of predetermined information processing procedures; (b) "calculation" of the values of control variables. Agents – subordinate elements – act in two ways: they transmit information to the principal and choose their states or direct actions. The operational *mechanism* (procedure of decision-making) defines the objective functions of the system (principal) and its elements, operational constraints, planning procedures, causal–temporal order of the principal's and agent's actions, as well as procedures used by the principal to collect information about the agents (Burkov 2013).

In all this, the foundations of TCOr are generally close to the model of an SEA. However, TCOr postulates that the technology of activity of any elements (agents or principal) is invariable and a priori known to all participants (Novikov 2013); this aspect fundamentally differentiates TCOr from the Enterprise Control Problem, where the evolution of the technology is one of the key factors.

The consequence of this aspect is another significant difference between the Enterprise Control Problem and TCOr: if the technology is known and invariable, there is no need to consider a lifecycle of activity, because an analysis of the design phase of an LC and expenses does not make sense. Therefore, TCOr does not study the lifecycle of activity. Any control problem in TCOr is solved only while concretization is being performed (Sections 1.4.1, 2.4) and does not consider the problems of the creation of technology or resource management (except for their choice during concretization). Therefore, TCOr models and methods can and should be used, but they do not create, to the full extent, a solution to the problem of coordinated control of the lifecycles of SEAs.

In terms of TCOr, a hierarchy of actors, or implementing SEAs, corresponds to the expansion of the basic model by introducing dynamics, multiple agents, a hierarchy, and other factors. In fact, it is an expansion and complication of the incentive problem explored in contract theory, by taking into account the dynamics (the multi-period model), or hierarchy, of multiple agents (a hierarchical aggregate of SEAs) and uncertainty (expenses of actors).

In Novikov and Shokhina (2003) and Novikov (2013), the *principle of decomposition of the agents game* is presented; it states that in a deterministic, two-level, multi-agent, static AS, the governing entity – the *principal* – can always (without loss of effectiveness) formulate and use an incentive system for agents, implying that the dominant strategy of each agent consists of the choice of an action desired by the principal. In Chapter 4, this idea is generalized to the case of a dynamic and hierarchical multi-level AS with uncertainty.

General research principles of TCOr. Let us consider a hierarchy of *scientific laws** and *principles*[†] (Novikov 2016): philosophical laws are the most general; logical and other general scientific laws and principles are more "specific"; laws, rules, and principles of concrete sciences follow those.

Two classes of principles might be distinguished: those that describe the structure and operations of certain classes of systems (these *"entity-based" principles* are an outcome of scientific studies of these systems), and internal *principles* (conventionally speaking, *"epistemological,"* research ones), used within the framework of a relevant science (its fundamental provisions, paradigms, and research methodology: approaches, general methods of study, etc.).

As a science, control theory, on the one hand, has its own laws and principles; on the other hand, it uses the laws and principles of other sciences related to the corresponding controlled system.

As applied to *sociotechnical systems* (STSs), "entity-based" principles include general laws of control and principles of complex systems organization and operation, as well as principles of organizational control, which can be supplemented, with an appropriate adaptation, with principles of operations of living systems and social systems (Novikov 2013b, Novikov 2016).

---

* The *law* is a statement of an order or relation of a phenomenon that as far as is known is invariable under the given conditions (Merriam-Webster.com Dictionary).
[†] The *principle* is a comprehensive and fundamental law, doctrine, or assumption (Merriam-Webster. com Dictionary)

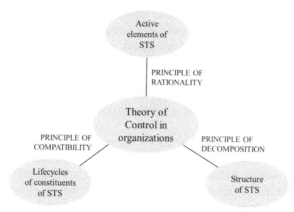

FIGURE 3.4 Research principles of theory of control in organizations.

Let us consider the general "epistemological" principles of the *theory of control in organizations* (TCOr), the subject matter of which is control of organizational systems and STSs (see Foreword). These principles (see Figure 3.4) – rationality, coordination, and decomposition – reflect the specifics of organizational system as controlled entities that have a complicated structure (logical, cause–effect, process, etc.), require coordination of the lifecycles (LCs) of their elements (see Section 2.5), and include actors implementing active behavior (independent goal-setting, active choice, and decision-making).

The principle of rationality consists of the need to take into account and constructively model *the active behavior* of controlled and controlling actors of an STS, carried out in interaction with the environment and other active elements of the STS. This research principle includes a number of hypotheses.

The basic *hypothesis of rational behavior* is that an actor, taking into account all the information available to them, chooses actions that lead to an output of activity that they prefer most (Novikov 2013). Decision theory, choice theory, and other related fields of science provide an apparatus to model and study such a choice. If an actor chooses solutions that are not optimal (the best among the feasible ones; the most effective one) but are rational (with an efficiency no less than a given one or differing from the maximum by no more than a given value), it is a case of *bounded rationality* (Simon 1978), which takes into account time spent on decision-making, as well as the cognitive capabilities of the actor. In the framework of this study, we introduce

Assumption A1	The validity of the hypothesis of rational behavior (possibly taking into account limited rationality) is assumed.

If the output of an actor's activity depends not only on his/her actions but also on other factors, maybe uncertain ones, then, when making decisions, he or she must *eliminate uncertainty* (we distinguish between so-called *natural uncertainty* – related to environmental factors – and *game uncertainty*, dealing with the behavior of other actors).

The determinism hypothesis is that an actor seeks to eliminate (with all the information available to them taken into account) the existing uncertainty and to make decisions being fully aware (in other words, the final criterion that guides a decision-maker should not contain uncertain parameters) (Novikov 2013).

In the case of game uncertainty studied by the apparatus of game theory, the *equilibrium principle* is used, according to which a combination of actions chosen by actors is effective and/or stable in one sense or another. In *hierarchical games*, the equilibrium actions by controlled actors depend on the actions of controlling actors (Germeier 1986). In *reflective games*, the equilibrium actions by actors also depend on their mutual awareness of natural uncertainty and on principles of behavior with regard to each other (Novikov and Chkhartishvili 2014).

The use of the principle of rationality allows one to create a model of controlled actors to describe the dependence of their behavior on control parameters. With this model, it is possible to solve the *control problem* – the search for such feasible control actions that would ensure such a behavior of actors, controlled by a controlling actor, which is desired from the point of view of the latter.

The principle of compatibility. Since both controlling and controlled actors are active, then, by virtue of the hypothesis of rational behavior, each of them strives to achieve the best output for themselves. But, since their interests do not generally coincide, the *principle of compatibility* requires a compromise (taking into account the asymmetry of the roles of actors), i.e., *coordination of interests* (Burkov 1977, Novikov 2013), and, in the general case, compatibility of the lifecycles of all constituents of STS (including conditions, resources, preferences, and interests).

The *principle of compensation* states that (in the case of a transferable utility, i.e., in an active system with side payments) an actor must be compensated by other actors for losses in productivity (gains, etc.) due to the fact that he or she chooses the actions according to the interests of other actors but not the best action for himself or herself (Novikov 2013).

In incentive problems, the *principle of compatible control* states that a controlling actor can predict that a controlled actor chooses only such actions that are profitable (with the control taken into account) for the latter (Burkov 1977). The principle of compatible control allows one to guarantee a required behavior (within a certain range) of controlled actors (the coincidence of actions or results by controlled actors with *plans* – desirable from the point of view of the controlling actor), reducing the complicated game-theoretic problem to a simple optimization problem – one of *incentive-compatible planning*, i.e., the choice by a controlling actor of such coordinated states of actors, controlled by him/her, that are the most favorable to him/her.

In planning problems (when a principal makes decisions based on information reported by controlled agents), the *open control principle* (synonyms: *fair play principle* or *revelation principle*) directs a controlling actor (to ensure the accuracy of the information they receive) to make decisions that are the most beneficial to controlled actors by believing that information communicated by the latter is true (Burkov 1977).

In *systems with distributed control* (multiple controlling principals), the *principle of compromise* states that a stable outcome of the interaction of controlling actors is either a *Pareto-effective* situation for them or a "monopolization" of the subordinate actor by one of them.

If the coordination principle allows solving control problems in an STS with a sufficiently simple, *basic* structure (one controlling actor and multiple weakly coupled controlled actors), then the next class of research principles makes it possible to reduce complex problems of control of STSs to a set of basic ones.

The **decomposition principle** assumes that a control impact on a separate actor should be based on his or her observable actions and/or outputs of activity. Such control should provide him or her with a beneficial choice of actions desired by the controlling actor, regardless of other factors, namely:

- actions and outputs of activity of other actors (*principle of decomposition of agents' game*);
- a prehistory (*principle of decomposition of periods of functioning*);
- the technology of interaction of STS participants (*principle of technology decomposition*);
- a multilevel structure of organizational subordination (*principle of hierarchical_decomposition*).

The possibility of such a decomposition is justified below and, on top of that, for all of the above factors simultaneously.

Thus, the principle of decomposition makes it possible to reduce the problem of control of a multi-element, multi-level, dynamic STS to a set of interconnected basic control problems.

Joint implementation of the above classes of research principles (rationality, compatibility, and decomposition) is a universal tool for the definition and solution of STS control problems, taking into account the dynamics, the multiplicity of interrelated actors, the multilevel hierarchy, distributed control, uncertainty, technological constraints of cooperative activity, information exchange, and other factors.

Indeed, all known STS models are based on general research principles (see Table 3.1). Moreover, when considering these models, certain assumptions with respect to the properties of a researched STS are introduced.

A **researcher** executes the following **general algorithm**:

1) Describe the composition and structure of the STS (an aggregate of controlling and controlled actors and relationships among them);
2) Describe an aggregate of feasible actions of the participants;
3) Describe the awareness of the participants, including that about uncertain parameters, as well as the causal–temporal order (a sequence of information exchange and decision-making operations);

TABLE 3.1

General Research Principles of TCOr for STS Control

Principle	Outcome of Use
Rationality Principle	
Rational behavior hypothesis	(3.1), (3.2), (3.3), (4.1), (4.2), (4.12), (4.39), Propositions 4.10, 4.11
Determinism hypothesis	(3.6), (3.8), (3.10), (4.6), (4.13), Proposition 4.7
Equilibrium principle	(4.45), Proposition 4.12
Compatibility Principle	
Principle of compensation	(4.3), (4.9), Lemma 4.1, (4.19), Proposition 4.1, Proposition 4.2, Proposition 4.4, (4.45)
Principle of coordinated control	(4.4), (4.29), (4.33), (6.1), (6.2)
Principle of open control	This book does not study mechanisms of information exchange from agents to the principal (Novikov 2013).
Principle of compromise	This book does not examine STS with distributed control (Novikov 2013).
Decomposition Principle	
Principle of decomposition of agents' game	(4.45), Proposition 4.12, (4.48)
Principle of decomposition of periods	(4.45), Proposition 4.12, (4.48), Proposition 4.13
Principle of technology decomposition	(3.2), (3.11)
Principle of hierarchy decomposition	(3.12), (3.13), (4.52), (4.53), Proposition 4.13

4) Within the framework of the principle of rationality, describe procedures of decision-making by participants by setting their preferences (Assumption A1 on the validity of the rational behavior hypothesis) and procedures for uncertainty elimination (the determinism hypothesis), taking into account the interaction with each other (the equilibrium principle);

5) For all the feasible *planned trajectories* of vectors of actions or those of outputs by controlled actors, find the most desired actions for the controlling actor. These control actions should encourage (the compensation principle) the controlled actors to choose such planned actions or achieve such planned outputs that are the equilibrium of their game (the principle of equilibrium), regardless of their interaction, dynamics, and organizational structure (the decomposition principle). The result of this step is a set of pairs – compatible plans and "expenses" of the controlling actor for the implementation of this plan;

6) Solve the problem of optimal compatible planning (the principle of compatible control) – choose compatible plans which are optimal from the point of view of the controlling actor (Chapter 7).

3.3.3 ENTERPRISE CONTROL PROBLEM AND MATHEMATICAL MODELS IN RELATED DISCIPLINES

The Enterprise Control Problem as a whole and each of the Enterprise Control Subproblems (Thesis 10, Section 2.5) fall under a wide group of scientific domains, which, one way or another, studies complex systems, including people, and the control of such systems. The relations between the Enterprise Control Problem and general systems theory, management, and other "weak" sciences are examined in Section 1.1.3 above. Let us now consider a connection between the management tasks (Section 2.5, Figure 2.6) and similar mathematical problems being solved in related fields.

3.3.3.1 Operations research

Problems of complex activity and resource planning (coordination), including the detection of mismatches of LCs of CA, are *Operations Research* (OR) (synonym: Quantitative Approaches to Decision Making); OR is a substantially broad field of mathematics (see classical textbooks Ackoff and Sasieni (1968), Wagner (1975), the methods and approaches of which are aimed primarily at solving optimization problems. OR models and methods can be classified on the following bases (Ackoff and Sasieni 1968):

1) resource management and distribution (appointment and allocation) – linear programming (including duality theory and sensitivity analysis), integer programming;
2) inventory control – continuous optimization (including optimal control), stochastic processes;
3) replacements and repairs – probability theory, reliability theory;
4) mass service – queueing theory, probability theory, stochastic processes;
5) ordering and coordination – discrete optimization (scheduling theory), dynamic programming;
6) routing – graph theory, network planning, scheduling;
7) competition – game theory;
8) search – mathematical statistics, design of experiments.

There is another possible basis for the classification (OR in business and manufacturing): marketing and advertising, assortment planning, production planning, logistics, resource planning, optimization (labor, machines, and finance), etc.

"Branches" like the military, business, urban planning, energy, and healthcare might be used as one more basis to classify OR models.

Any OR problem can be "complicated" due to the presence of:

1) uncertain factors (probabilistic or fuzzy ones) – mathematical statistics or fuzzy-sets theory;
2) several effectiveness criteria – multi-criteria decision-making;
3) nonlinearity of effectiveness criteria or/and constraints – nonlinear optimization.

It is of interest to note that, despite the fact that OR dates back three quarters of a century in its history, classical and modern textbooks barely differ in content. Modern mass textbooks (Anderson et al. 2018, Hillier and Lieberman 2010, Taha 2016, Rardin 2017) or encyclopedias and reference books on OR (Gass and Fu 2013) have approximately the same content, differing in their accent on mathematical methods or on meaningful interpretations. Not many monographs on OR are devoted to the use of one of the classes of mathematical methods in OR, for example (Sethi 2019), to optimal control, to use "at the intersection" with one of the directions/schools/trends of management, for example (Ramón and Mateo 2015), to project management (Daellenbach and McNickle 2005), to Soft Systems Thinking (Mind Maps, etc.), etc.

The *detection of mismatches* of LCs of CA consists of detecting a change in the properties of an uncertain process by indirect observations and belongs to the field of *statistical sequential analysis* (starting with the pioneering paper (Wald 1947)) and the class of *sequential disorder problems* (see, for example, (Nikiforov 2016)). Traditionally, sequential decision rules based on the likelihood ratio are used to solve such problems. The peculiarity of these problems within the framework of the Enterprise Control Problem is the need to take into account the active properties of actors of CA, which requires an adaptation of well-known models and methods to these conditions. These problems and models and the methods to solve them are discussed in more detail in Section 7.3.

Problems of technology management, at a descriptive level, are studied by methods and means of *systems engineering* (for example, Pyster and Olwell 2013, Haskins 2015, ISO/IEC/IEEE 15288 2015, MITRE 2014). However, technology management problems in the framework of Enterprise Control are new and require an adequate formalization and the development of special quantitative models and methods based on the approaches of *probability theory*, the *theory of stochastic processes*, *sequential statistical analysis*, and various sections of *operations research*. Technology management problems are considered in detail in Chapter 5.

Moreover, in the framework of the TRL concept (technology readiness levels), problems of maximization of a system's readiness levels have been increasingly considered recently under restrictions on TRL and the integration readiness level (Sauser 2010, Sauser 2011).

3.3.3.2 Models of structures and processes

The hierarchical and/or network structure of a controlled entity is the essential distinguishing feature of the Enterprise Control Problem.

Sequences of actions and structures are traditionally modeled by formalisms of *graph theory*; notably, this approach has been successfully used for a long time to describe transport, production, social, economic, and other networks (see reviews in the papers (Jackson 2010, Oxford 2016)) and project and program management (Burkov 1997, Daellenbach and McNickle 2005), including resource management and allocation, scheduling, and project risk management. Indeed, network models successfully express "cause–effect" relationships among elements, implementing the descriptive and forecast function (from causes to effects), the explanatory function (from effects to causes), and the normative function (from causes to optimal effects or optimal causes leading to the desired effects). The technological structure of CA can be described by various classes of models that reflect the substantial properties of CA, among them:

- semantic, logical, and Bayesian networks: probabilistic logic networks (Goertzel 2008), Markov logic networks (Richardson 2006), and binary neural networks (Kohut 2014), as well as their applications in the fields of transport, electricity networks, logistics and manufacturing, and many others (Kelly 2014);
- knowledge models: those such as production, network (semantic networks, ontologies), frame-based, etc. (see reviews in Brachman 2004, Handbook 2007);
- models of science development in terms of bibliometric and citation networks (Lucio-Arias 2012);
- models of diffusion, innovation, epidemics to describe the development of scientific ideas (Vitanov 2012);
- estimation and assessment models (information aggregation and complex assessment (Burkov 2013, Novikov 2013), etc.) for the integration of a set of values of particular indicators into one or more general indicators.

Thus, a large number of models and methods have been developed to solve various control problems in the considered and related areas of science (TCOr, OR, modeling of structures and processes). However, each of the Enterprise Control Subproblems (Thesis 10, Section 2.5) are distinguished by a combination of specific factors that present obstacles to the use of known solutions. To successfully solve the Enterprise Control Problem, the following factors must be considered:

1. the entire lifecycles of key controlled constituents (Enterprises, SEAs, and their procedural components);
2. the creation and modernization of the technology of CA;
3. the active properties of actors of SEAs;
4. the hierarchical structure of a controlled entity – a fractal hierarchy of SEAs;
5. measurable and true uncertainty.

In Chapters 4–7 that follow, an analysis of specific formulations of the Enterprise Control Problem is carried out, and original models and methods to solve each of them are presented.

Based on the "uncertainty principle" for the sciences of the "strong and weak versions" and the graphical metaphor of Figure 3.3 (Section 3.3.1), we can say that the methodology of complex activity possesses a greater practical applicability than the general methodology and general systems theory. At the same time, it possesses a greater reasonableness and rigor relatively to psychology, sociology, and management.

Models and methods of the Enterprise Control Problem, in turn, differ in the significantly greater reasonableness than the methodology of complex activity, as well as having a much larger area of practical applicability relative to classical mathematical methods.

That is to say conventionally that the developed models and methods to solve the Enterprise Control Problem shift the curve of Figure 3.3 to the upper-right; they increase the "volume of accumulated knowledge" in the scientific domain at hand.

3.4 ENTERPRISE CONTROL PROBLEM AS AN OPTIMIZATION PROBLEM

Let us now turn to the quantitative formalization of the Enterprise Control Problem; the definition of four necessary components of an optimization problem, discussed in Section 3.1:

1. variables of states of a system and an environment;
2. constraints;
3. laws and rules reflecting connections among the variables;
4. an objective function and constraints.

The following theses are used as a basis:

- An Enterprise is a complex system and therefore is the subject matter of research in various fields of scientific knowledge. In each of them, a number of models have been developed that allow studying individual aspects of an Enterprise with varying degrees of rigor. The existence of heterogeneous models requires a reasonable choice of approaches to the development of a quantitative model of an Enterprise.
- At the same time, being a system, an Enterprise requires, for its research, a systematic approach and adherence to the principle of holism. Therefore, an optimization problem should be set as a single holistic problem, covering all aspects of an Enterprise and all kinds of its CA. The multidisciplinary nature of the CA of an Enterprise impedes the development of a unified formalization. Modeling and optimization of individual types of CA of an Enterprise are the traditional practical approaches; they are characteristic, for example, of operations research and allied disciplines (for example, Ackoff and Sasieni 1968, Sethi 2019). However, the optimality of the parts does not entail the optimality of the whole. Therefore, the formalization of a holistic optimization problem is fundamentally important without canceling the correctness of its subsequent "top-down" decomposition in order that it be solved using various mathematical methods.
- Humans constitute the basic elements of an Enterprise; taking into account their activity, an Enterprise is presented in the form of a multi-level dynamic active system (in terms of contract theory and TCOr), corresponding to a hierarchy of SEAs. In addition, the presence of people in an Enterprise and their key role in the implementation of CA are universal properties that are characteristic of all Enterprises, without exception. Therefore, a quantitative model of an Enterprise in terms of contract theory and TCOr should

be built by supplementing the same by necessary mechanisms to describe factors not directly related to the manifestation of the active properties of people.

In Sections 3.4.1–3.4.3, we consider a "simple" Enterprise in the form of one SEA – a dynamic active system consisting of one principal and several agents. This AS plays the role of a complex actor of an SEA implementing the SEA; agents, in turn, execute exactly valuable activity, delivering value to stakeholders, while the principal manages the agents, motivating and incentivizing them and providing them with technology. Valuable activity executed by actors is quite complex, so Section 3.4.1 is devoted to formalization of CA actors. Management activity executed by the principal consists of designing an incentive scheme – a set of contracts – and offering them to agents. Participants in the AS play a hierarchical repeated game: the principal, making the first move, offers the agents contracts, after which the agents make the second move – to choose (and execute) their actions, and then the principal remunerates the agents according to the contracts. An incentive scheme and a game of agents caused by it are considered in Section 3.4.2. In Section 3.4.3, we formulate the problem of optimal control of a "simple" Enterprise (one SEA as a dynamic active system).

In Section 3.4.4, we enrich the model of an active system with a hierarchy of active subsystems, each of which is a dynamic AS, and formulate the Enterprise Control Problem in the general case.

A generalized scheme of the optimal solution of the Enterprise Control Problem is developed and presented in Section 3.4.5.

3.4.1 FORMAL DESCRIPTION OF A STRUCTURAL ELEMENT OF ACTIVITY AS A DYNAMIC ACTIVE SYSTEM*

Let us consider a "simple" Enterprise, a dynamic active system consisting of one principal and a set of agents subordinated to him/her (to be denoted by $N = \{1, 2, ..., n\}$ – a finite aggregate of agents, $n \geq 2$).

The *technology* of joint activity of agents is described by *network* $G = (N, E)$ with correct numbering,[†] and we assume that the agents are labeled exactly with these numbers. The nodes of the network correspond to actions of the agents, and the set of arcs $E \subseteq N \times N$ reflects "technological" connections among them. The set of *predecessors* of the i-th agent in network G ($i \in N$) is denoted as $N(i) = \{j \in N \mid (j; i) \in E\}$. We assume that the network has $M_0 \subseteq N$ – the set of *inputs* and the only *output* – the n-th node, characterized by the fact that generated utility (for example, a market one) belongs only to the outcome of activity of the network's output – the output of the

---

* For readers who are not very familiar with game theory and contract theory, it is recommended to study the basic models and approaches (Sections 4.1 and 4.2 of this book and/or Novikov (2013)) first and then continue reading this section.

† The numbering of the graph nodes is deemed correct (Burkov 1974) if each node has input arches only from nodes with lower numbers. The absence of cycles in a graph is a sufficient condition for the existence of correct numbering.

active system as a whole that brings income to the principal. Through M_k, we denote a set of nodes that has input arcs only from nodes belonging to sets $\{M_j\}, j \in \{1; \dots; k-1\}$; number k is the *rank* of a node belonging to the set M_k.

The functioning of this AS is considered during discrete time periods $t \in \{1; 2; \dots; T\}$, where T is a *time horizon*.

During period t, the *i-th* agent chooses and implements their *action*, which is characterized by an aggregate of parameters $y_i(t) \in Y_i$, where Y_i is a set of possible values of the parameters of their actions, including refusal to participate in the AS as one of admissible actions. An action of the *i-th* agent (combined with the results of their predecessors) determines the *output* of their activity, which in turn is described by an aggregate of parameters $z_i(t) \in Z_i$, where Z_i is a set of possible values of the parameters of their output; we assume that Y_i and Z_i are subsets of Euclidean space or of some finite set. In technological networks, sets Y_i and Z_i may depend on the choice of actions by the predecessors of the *i-th* agent. That is, the sets of admissible values are functions of the outputs of their predecessors $Y_i(\{Z_k; k \in N(i)\})$ (where $N(i)$ is a set of predecessors of the *i-th* agent). However, as demonstrated below, the presence or absence of these dependences does not affect the outputs obtained; therefore, we do not mention these dependences explicitly, where this does not lead to discrepancies.

We denote through $y_D(t)$ a vector of action of agents with numbers from subset $D \subseteq N$; through $z_D(t)$, a vector of the outputs of actions; through $y_{-i} = (y_1, \dots, y_{i-1}, y_{i+1}, \dots, y_n)$, a vector of actions of all agents except the *i*-th.

We denote through $\tilde{W}_i^t$ a set of possible actions by the *i*-th agent and his or her predecessors during periods $\overline{1; t}$ by noting that $\tilde{W}_i^t \subseteq (Y_i)^t \times \prod_{k \in N(i)} (Z_k)^t$. The depen-

dence of the output of activity of an agent on his/her action and on the outputs of other agents to be used by him/her in the process of this activity is determined by the *technological function* $Q_i^t : \tilde{W}_i^t \to Z_i$, i.e. $z_i(t) = Q_i^t(y_i[1^*t]; z_{N(i)}[1^*t])$ (hereinafter, using notation $\xi[1^*t]$, we denote sets of all values of $\xi(\tau)$, possibly being multidimensional, for all time periods $\tau = \overline{1, t}$). For all $i \in M_0$, $N(i) = \emptyset$ is true; therefore, we assume $z_i(t) = Q_i^t(y_i[1^*t]; z_0[1^*t])$, where z_0 is the known L-dimensional vector of *inputs* of the network.

In this case, a network determines the technological dependence among the actions by agents, a multi-step implementation of activity is being considered.

We consider and solve the control problem in two versions: when either Assumption A2 or A3 "about the technological transparency of an Enterprise's activity" is valid.

Assumption A2   The principal, during each period, observes only the network output $z_n(t)$.

Technological functions $Q_i^t(\cdot)$ are biunique with respect to the actions of the *i*-th agent and to the outputs of all his or her predecessors during the current period.

This assumption means that, given outputs of activity of the agent's predecessors during the current period $z_{N(i)}(t)$ (and known $y_i[1*(t-1)]$ and $z_{N(i)}[1*(t-1)]$ during previous periods), the current agent action $y_i(t)$ uniquely determines the output $z_i(t)$. And, conversely, by knowing previous actions $y_i[1*(t-1)]$, output $z_i(t)$, and outputs of predecessors $z_{N(i)}(t)$, one can unambiguously restore action $y_i(t)$ in the current period.

Assumption A3   The principal, during the current period, observes the actual actions of all agents during this period.

Let us discuss conditions under which Assumptions A2 and A3 are valid.

First of all, note that Assumption A3 (as well as A3' presented below in Section 3.4) is rather rarely fulfilled in practical complex activity, because the observation of all actions requires from the principal such time and cognitive expenditures that are comparable to the implementation of the actions by the principal. As a rule, the working time of a principal is significantly more valuable than that of controlled agents; therefore, control in one form or another is usually based on the observation of the aggregated outputs. Direct observation of actions is possible and justified in the case of sufficiently simple and standardized activity that allows binary testing, whether or not the technological requirements are met.

Assumption A2 (similar to A2' in Section 3.4.2) characterizes the technological function of joint activity of agents for the case where the action of each of them affects the output in such a way that it cannot be replaced by any other. That is, the technology of each of the agents is unique within the AS. The uniqueness of technology can be manifested, for example, in the fact that the action by each agent can be executed only in the case of certain combinations of the outputs of his or her predecessors (although, in the general case, the relations between agents are not a necessary condition for the uniqueness of the technology of each of them). Both individuals, i.e., employees of enterprises, and entire organizations can play the role of agents. As an example, we can consider an assembly line (or a section of one) of an aerospace enterprise or shipyard, the construction site of a petrochemical plant, or a machinery shop.

The technology of just a complex activity is characterized by the following important particular feature: each agent uses the outputs of predecessors in his or her activity; therefore, the output of his or her activity is more complicated than the outputs of his or her predecessors' activities (and the output of subordinate subsystems) and as such requires a "richer" description. This explains an increase in the dimensionalities of sets of possible values of the outputs of agents, as compared to the outputs of predecessors. The principle of output complication contraposes this problem against the traditional approach of considering multilevel active systems (Novikov and Tsvetkov 2001), assuming an "aggregation" of outputs of predecessors and subordinate subsystems, which does not increase the complexity (consequently – the dimensionality of a vector of characteristics) of an output. When the actions of agents do not complicate the output, one may use various incentive mechanisms proposed in Novikov and Tsvetkov (2001), for example, the "ideal aggregation theorem."

In practically all the cases mentioned, the sets of possible actions of agents and their outputs might be considered to be finite: agents perform "typical operations," so the values of (possibly multidimensional) characteristics of their actions and outputs belong to a finite number of sets, inside each of which the values of the characteristics are indistinguishable from the principal's point of view.

In such a way, let us consider an i-th agent over time interval $t = \{1; 2; \dots T\}$ and denote by $N(i)$ the set of his or her predecessors. According to the definition of the technological function given above, output $z_i(t)$ of actions of the i-th agent (and his or her predecessors) depends on a tuple of $t \times (|N(i)| + 1)$ values $\{y_i(\tau); z_k(\tau) : \tau \in \{1; 2; \dots t\}; k \in N(i)\}$; in this regard, their dependence on $|N(i)| + 1$ is biunique. When agents perform "typical operations," then sets Y_i of their possible actions are finite (from the point of view of the principal). In addition, the sets Z_i of possible outputs are also finite. In this case, technological function $Q_i^t(\cdot) : \tilde{W}_i^t \to Z_i$ is some rule of numbering of feasible (performed by agents) combinations $\{y_i(\cdot); z_k(\cdot)\}$.

We believe that the choice of action $y_i(t)$ requires expenditures from the i-th agent, which generally depend on the actions of all agents in the AS; let $c_i^t(y_N[1^*t])$ be nonnegative *cost functions* $c_i^t(\cdot) : \prod_{k \in N} (Y_k)^t \to \mathfrak{R}_+^1$.

The proposed type of dependence of expenses on the prehistory of agents' actions is also characteristic of practical CA, examples of which are discussed above. In particular, the time consumption of a group of mechanical fitters/assemblers (and each of them individually) on the final assembly line of the aerospace enterprise depend on the prehistory of their actions and the actions of their colleagues.*

Thus, the *technology of CA* of the i-th agent is described by tuple $<N(i), c_i^t(\cdot), Q_i^t(\cdot), t \in \{1; 2; \dots; T\}>$.

Network G and technological functions $\{Q_i^t(\cdot)\}$ for each trajectory of actions $y_N[1^*t]$ define the single trajectory of the network output; we denote this trajectory through $z_n^t(y_N[1^*t])$.

3.4.2   GAME OF AGENTS IN A DYNAMIC ACTIVE SYSTEM

In order to describe the repeated game of agents, it is necessary to complete the AS definition by a sequence of moves and an awareness of who, when, and what regarding decisions (from which sets) made: what who knows at the time of decision-making.

We assume that the principal, knowing the network, the technological functions, and the cost functions of the agents, first offers them an *incentive scheme* – a set of functions $\{\sigma_i^\tau\}$ $\tau = \overline{1, T}$ for all subsequent time periods (the principal thereby carries out "*programmed control*"), without changing the incentive function. Based on the study of cost functions, incentive functions, and other factors in each time period, agents, in turn, choose an action and implement it.

---

* In most traditional settings of similar problems, agent expenses do not depend on the actions of all the agents, but only on those of their predecessors. However, the dependence on "everyone" is more general and does not narrow the outputs obtained.

If Assumption A2 is valid, the principal can form nonnegative *incentive functions* $\sigma_i^t(\cdot)$ for the *i*-th agent during period *t*, the arguments of which are network output, so $\sigma_i^t(z_n[1*t]) : (Z_n)^t \to \mathfrak{R}_+^1$. If Assumption A3 is valid, the principal can use incentive functions, whose arguments are the observed actions: $\tilde{\sigma}_i^t(y_N[1*t]) : \prod_{k \in N}(Y_k)^t \to \mathfrak{R}_+^1$.

The network, sets of admissible actions, technological functions, and cost functions of all the agents during each period are common knowledge to all participants. Knowing the current game history (the actions chosen in previous periods and the outputs of activity of all the agents) and the incentive functions, the agents choose their actions in this period once and implement them, without forming coalitions, in a sequence, corresponding to the numbers in network *G*, thus adhering to the technology of joint activity.

Let the agents be far-sighted and rational (Assumption A1). When choosing current action $y_i(t)$ and predicting future actions $y_i(\tau)$, $\tau \in \{t+1; ...; T\}$, the *i*-th agent seeks to maximize the following objective function:

$$F_i(\{\sigma_i^\tau\}\tau = \overline{t,T}; y_N[1*T]) = \sum_{\tau=t}^{T} \delta_i(t;\tau)\, f_i^t(\sigma_i^t; y_N[1*\tau]). \qquad (3.1)$$

where $\delta_i(\cdot) \geq 0$ is the distribution of the agent's *farsightedness*,* and $f_i^t(\cdot)$ is the objective function of the agent during period *t*, being equal to the difference between remuneration $\sigma_i^\tau(\cdot)$ and expenses $c_i^t(\cdot)$ (a *reserve utility* in the case of refusal to participate in the AS should be taken into account in incentive functions $\{\sigma_i^\tau\}$):

The described game-theoretic model, which includes a set of agents *N* (with their interests and preferences), network *G*, and set $Q = \{Q_i(\cdot)\}$ of technological functions, is referred to as a *dynamic networked active system* (DNAS). A DNAS is a dynamic generalization of the model of a networked active system.

$$f_i^t(\sigma_i^t; y_N[1*t]) = -c_i^t(y_N[1*t]) + \begin{cases} \sigma_i^t(z_N(z_N[1*t])) & \text{if A1}; \\ \tilde{\sigma}_i^t(y_N[1*t]), & \text{if A2}, \end{cases} i \in N, t = \overline{1,T}. \quad (3.2)$$

The assumption that the principal knows the agent's cost functions and reserve utility has been made above. In practice, a manager does not know the amount of remuneration that compensates an agent's expenses for performing certain work, since this amount is determined by the agent's subjective estimation of the utility of the remuneration, in comparison with his or her expenses. However, in the case of a developed and mature labor market, a manager can use "average market estimates" and therefore well-known cost functions, instead of the individual cost function of each employee, which actually happens in reality. At the same time, it is feasible to consider the deviation of each employee's individual preferences from the "average market" ones as a measurable uncertainty of the active choice (by the employee),

---

* *Farsightedness* is the capability of an actor to predict and consider the circumstances in some future periods of time when making a decision now.

which results in the uncertainty of an employee's traffic between the company and the labor market (the traffic model is discussed in detail in Section 6.2.1). Therefore, we use here and below practically important Assumption A4, which is valid in a developed labor market:

Assumption A4   The awareness of the principal about the "average market" cost function and reserve utility of all agents is assumed.

In the repeated *game* of agents, the *dominant strategy* (DS) of the i-th agent (given incentive system $\{\sigma_N^\tau\}$ $\tau = \overline{1,T}$) is defined as the trajectory of actions $y_i^d[1*T]$, such that

$$\forall y_{-i}[1*T] \in \prod_{k \in N; k \neq i} (Y_k)^T; \forall t_1 \in \overline{1;T}; \forall t_2 \in \overline{t_1;T};$$

$$\forall s[t_1 * t_2] \in (y_i)^{t_2 - t_1 + 1}; s[t_1 * t_2] \neq y_i^d[t_1 * t_2]:$$

$$F_i(\{\sigma_N^\tau\}; \{y_i^d[1*T], y_{-i}[1*T]\})$$

$$\geq F_i(\{\sigma_N^\tau\}; \{y_i^d[1*(t_1 - 1)], s[t_1 * t_2], y_i^d[(t_2 + 1)*T], y_{-i}[1*T]\}).$$

DS $y_i^d[1*T]$ provides the maximum of the objective function of the i-th agent, regardless of the choice of other agents $y_{-i}[1*T]$.

Dominant Strategies Equilibrium (DSE) is a set of dominant strategies of all agents:

$$y_N^d[1*T] = \left\{ y_1^d[1*T]; \ldots; y_i^d[1*T]; \ldots; y^d[1*T] \right\}.$$

3.4.3   OPTIMAL CONTROL OF THE STRUCTURAL ELEMENT OF ACTIVITY: A DYNAMIC ACTIVE SYSTEM

Let us formulate the *incentive problem in a DNAS*. We denote through σ_D^τ an incentive vector-function for agents from set $D \subseteq N$ during time period $t = \overline{1,T}$. Consider a repeated game of agents during periods from 1 to T. Denote by $E(\{\sigma_D^\tau\}; \tau = \overline{1,T})$ trajectories $y_N[1*T]$ of a set of actions, i.e., a set of solutions from the agents game (being equilibria in any sense, for example, subgame perfect equilibria) being implemented by incentive scheme $\{\sigma_D^\tau\}$. Let us assume the principal is fully *farsighted* (Novikov et al. 2002) with the horizon of farsightedness T.

Then, the *objective function of the DNAS* – a criterion of control efficiency of the DNAS – is the difference between the income of the principal and his or her total expenses for incentives:

$$\Phi(\{\sigma_N^\tau\};\Psi) = \max_{y_N[1*T]\in E(\{\sigma^\tau_N\};t=\overline{1,t})} \left\{ \sum_{t=1}^{T} \delta(1;t)\phi(z_n^t(y_N[1*t]);\Psi \right\} \qquad (3.3)$$

$$\phi(z_n^t(y_N[1*T]);\Psi) = h^t(z_n^t(y_N[1*t]);\Psi) - \left\{ \begin{array}{l} \sum_{i=1}^{n}\sigma_i^t(z_n^t(y_N[1*t])), \text{ if A2 is valid;} \\ \\ \sum_{i=1}^{n}\tilde\sigma_i^t(y_N[1*t]), \quad \text{ if A3 is valid.} \end{array} \right\},$$

$$(3.4)$$

where $h^t(z_n^t(\cdot));\Psi) \geq 0$ is the principal's *income function* during period t, $\delta(\cdot)\geq 0$ is the *distribution of farsightedness* of the principal, and Ψ is a vector of some parameters of the Enterprise and the external environment, on which the implementation of the CA of the Enterprise depends, but which do not directly relate to the active choice of participants in the DNAS. In fact, Ψ characterizes the technology of the CA, the actor, and the external environment in which the CA is implemented. Such a characteristic is specific to various Enterprises; it depends on the industry and types of activity. Here and below, we assume that a vector Ψ is a composition of three vectors $\Psi=(\Psi_c; \Psi_k; \Psi_u)$, and a controlling actor

- can define the value of Ψ_c, *controlled parameters*;
- knows the value of Ψ_k, *known parameters*, but cannot influence them;
- knows laws and regularities describing Ψ_u, *uncertain parameters*, cannot influence them, but can eliminate uncertainty (assuming that this uncertainty is a true one).

The calculation in (3.3) of the maximum over the set of equilibria $E(\cdot)$ corresponds to the *hypothesis of benevolence* (Novikov 2013): from the set of equilibria $E(\cdot)$, the agents choose the most favorable one for the principal. If the hypothesis of benevolence is not valid, one should use the *principle of guaranteed result* (3.5) and take the minimum among the trajectories belonging to the set of equilibria $E(\cdot)$:

$$\Phi(\{\sigma_N^\tau\};\Psi) = \min_{y_N[1*T]\in E(\{\sigma^t_N\};t=\overline{1,T}} \left\{ \sum_{t=1}^{T} \delta(1;t)\phi(z_n^t(y_N[1*t]);\Psi \right\}. \qquad (3.5)$$

The *control problem* consists of constructing incentive scheme $\{\sigma_N^t\}$ and choosing such values of controlled parameters Ψ_c that provide *optimal control*, i.e., the maximum of the objective function of the principal $\Phi(\cdot)$, given known values of parameters Ψ_k, as well as of the elimination of the uncertainty of parameters Ψ_u (using notation $\underset{\Psi}{\text{def}}\{\cdot\}$, we denote an operator for eliminating the uncertainty of parameters Ψ):

$$\underset{\Psi_u}{\text{def}}\{\Phi(\{\sigma_N^t\};\psi)\} \to \underset{\sigma_N^t;\psi_c}{\max}. \qquad (3.6)$$

The value of functional $\Phi(\cdot)$, obtained as a result of the solution to problem (3.6), is referred to as the *efficiency of the DNAS*: the value of $\Phi(\cdot)$ numerically characterizes the income and expenses to achieve the goal of complex activity, implemented by the DNAS. In such a way, a solution to problems (3.1–3.6) allows one to design the optimal control of a "simple" enterprise, in the form of one SEA, consisting of one controlling principal and many controlled agents subordinated to him/her.

Let us now consider an extension of this problem to the case where the expenses of agents are uncertain. This may be a consequence of the occurrence of uncertainty events, causing uncertainty about the actor's expenses* required to achieve the goal. This extension corresponds to Assumption 5, that the technology of CA is mature (a qualitative definition of a "mature technology" is given in Section 2.3).

Assumption A5   The maturity of CA technology is assumed, whence it follows that an
                           uncertain variation in the duration of actions does not exceed one discrete
                           time period.

We consider the expenses $\tilde{c}_i(t)$, required from each i-th agent for the implementation of action during any period t, to be uncertain at the time when the participants in the AS are making decisions. Let us assume that a posteriori expenses become known to the agents but remain unknown to the principals (if a posteriori expenses are known to the principals, the problem reduces to a deterministic case). We study an interval and probabilistic models of uncertain expenses.

Interval uncertainty model. Let the conditions below for expenses be

$$\forall t, i : c_i^t \left(y_N[1*t] \right) \geq \tilde{c}_i(t), \tag{3.7}$$

i.e., let us assume that functions $c_i^t(\cdot) : \prod_{k\in N} (y_k)^t \to \mathfrak{R}_+^1$ define the maximum values of the possible expenses of the i-th agent for choosing and implementing the action in any period t.

If functions $c_i^t(\cdot)$ and inequalities (3.7) are *common knowledge*[†] to all participants in the AS at the time when they choose actions in each period, then the cost uncertainty can be eliminated based on the method of guaranteed result. Control problem (3.8) in this case will consist of the formation of an incentive scheme $\{\sigma_N^t\}$ and the choice of such values Ψ_c that provide the maximum of the objective function of the principal $\Phi(\cdot)$ for the worst values of expenses of all agents $\tilde{c}_i(t)$ during all periods t:

---

* In this case, we consider uncertainty to reflect the specificity of implementation of the actions by a particular agent, while in Assumption A4 above we consider uncertainty to reflect a mismatch between the individual preferences of a particular agent and the "average market" ones.

† Models of ASs with asymmetric awareness of participants, considered by contracts theory (for example, (Bolton and Dewatripont 2005, Salanie 2005)) and the theory of control in organizational systems (Novikov 2013) are certainly of great interest, but are not considered in this book, being an avenue of further research.

$$\underset{\psi_u \ \{c_i{}^t(y_N[1*t])\geq \tilde{c}_i(t)\}}{\text{def}\ \min}\ \{\Phi(\{\sigma_N{}'\};\psi)\} \to \underset{\{\sigma_N^t\};\psi_c}{\max}\ . \qquad (3.8)$$

Probabilistic uncertainty model. Let cost $\tilde{c}_i(t)$ for all t and i allow a probabilistic description, i.e., its representation as random variables with some distribution functions $F_c(\cdot;\ y_N[1*t])$, depending on $y_N[1*t]$ as on parameters, being such that*

$$E[\tilde{c}_i(t)] = \int_z z dF_c(z;\ y_N[1*t]) = c_i{}^t(y_N[1*t]). \qquad (3.9)$$

So, functions $c_i{}'(\cdot): \prod_{k \in N}(y_k)^t \to \Re_+^1$ determine the mathematical expectations of expenses of the i-th agent with regard to the choice and implementation of an action during any period t.

The uncertainty regarding expenses can be eliminated based on the principle of expected utility if functions $c_i{}'(\cdot)$ (knowledge of distribution functions $F_c(\cdot;\ y_N[1*t])$ as such is not necessary) and conditions (3.9) are common knowledge to all participants in the AS at the time they choose actions in each period.

We assume that the agent chooses their action proceeding, speaking metaphorically, from the fact that some expected value of expenses is realized, without knowing it a priori. Moreover, in some cases (depending on the realized value of an uncertain parameter), the incentive may not compensate for the expenses incurred for the action chosen by the agent, but in other cases it may exceed the expenses. The agent believes that, during a sufficiently long time interval, these discrepancies are compensated, and, on average, the mathematical expectation of the cost function for the uncertain parameter is implemented. In this case, any uncertainty of expenses can be eliminated using a method of expected utility. Control problem (3.10) is set as searching for an incentive scheme $\{\sigma_N\}$ and such Ψ_c values that provide the maximum of the mathematical expectation of the objective function of the principal:

$$\underset{\psi_u}{\text{def}}\{E[\{\Phi(\{\sigma_N{}'\};\psi)]\} \to \underset{\{\sigma_N^t\};\psi_c}{\max} \qquad (3.10)$$

3.4.4 OPTIMAL CONTROL OF AN ENTERPRISE: A HIERARCHICAL DYNAMIC ACTIVE SYSTEM

Based on formalization (3.1–3.10), Sections 3.4.1–3.4.3, let us make the model of an active system more intricate by introducing a hierarchy of active subsystems, each of which is a DNAS and, being a complex actor, implements a corresponding structural element of activity. Such a complex AS implements a hierarchy of SEAs and in so doing allows us to formulate the problem of Enterprise control in general. In short,

---

* Hereinafter, in this study, unless otherwise specified, we use symbols $E[\cdot]$ to denote the operator of the calculation of mathematical expectation. A subscript, if used, defines the stochastic variable by which the expectation is calculated.

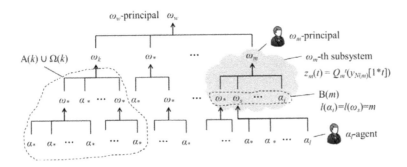

FIGURE 3.5   Hierarchy of active elements: agents and intermediate principals.

we refer to the hierarchy of an AS as a *multilevel DNAS*, an m-DNAS (implying that each of the subsystems is a DNAS).* The hierarchical structure of such a multi-level AS (see Figure 3.5) is defined by the hierarchy of active elements.

Let us denote a set of agents as $A = \{\alpha_1, \ldots, \alpha_a\}$ by using the notation α_i-agent applied to the particular AE. Active elements, which act as principals of subsystems[†] (ω_m-subsystems, their set being denoted by $\Omega = \{\omega_1, \ldots, \omega_w\}$), are referred to, following (Novikov and Tsvetkov 2001), as *intermediate principals*, i-principals, or ω_m-principals.

The hierarchy of AEs is modelled by a connected acyclic graph $\Gamma = <A \cup \Omega, D>$ (where $A \cup \Omega$ is a set of nodes and $D \subseteq (A \cup \Omega) \times \Omega$ is a set of arcs $d_{im} \in E$), being such that (a) for any node $\alpha_i \in A$, there are no inputting arcs ε_{li}, (b) there is a single node, *the root node* (we assume that this is ω_w), into which there are paths from all nodes $\alpha_i \in A$ and $\omega_m \in \Omega$ ($\omega_m \neq \omega_w$), (c) exactly one arc outputs from each node (except for the root ω_w).

For each node $\omega_m \in \Omega$, let us define $A(m) \subseteq A$ as a subset of agents/nodes, from which there is a path into ω_m; similarly, $\Omega(m) \subseteq \Omega$ as a subset of intermediate principals/nodes, from which there is a path into ω_m. Then, $A(m) \cup \Omega(m)$ forms a set of subsystems and agents, subordinated to the ω_m-subsystem. Each of the nodes of graph Γ corresponds to one and only one AE: the α_i nodes to agents, the ω_m nodes to i-principals, and the root node ω_w to the principal of the upper level (also the goal and output of an Enterprise as a whole).

Let us introduce Assumption A6 "about the tree-like structure of SEAs."

Assumption A6	The structure of SEAs (and goal structure of an Enterprise) has the form of a single tree (with a single root node).

---

* The hierarchy of networks with correct numbering can be reduced to a single network with correct numbering, and, from the point of view of the technology, an m-DNAS can be reduced to a DNAS, just as the hierarchy of SEAs is reduced to a single SEA (Chapter 1). However, a hierarchy of "incentivizing" (controlling) intermediate principals is built over such a technological network, which distinguishes this problem from the one considered above in Section 3.4.1.

† It is important to note that subsystems of ASs are ASs, which reflects the fractal nature of this model.

Let us discuss the correctness of Assumption A6. One of the main results of MCA is that the structure of the SEAs corresponds to the structure of the goals of CA, following top-down from the goal of the upper level to more detailed ones (see Chapters 1 and 2). Thus, no subordinate goal can be a result of the decomposition of two superior goals, i.e., no SEA can be subordinated to two or more different SEAs.

In most cases, a separate AE is created for the implementation of each SEA. Such an AE plays the *role* of the actor of an SEA and, in this case, any controlled AE has a single controlling AE. In some cases, it might be feasible to create a single AE (an individual or an Enterprise) to fulfill the role of the actor of several SEAs.

Let a decision be made to create a single AE to play the roles of actors of SEAs ω_d and ω_f(Figure 3.6).

The decision to create a single AE (ω') to fulfill the roles of the actors of several SEAs can be made by the actor, who is superior to all such SEAs. In this example, this is ω_k or any superior to him/her, since none of the actors subordinated to ω_k (such as ω_m and ω_l) has enough information about both SEAs ω_d and ω_f to make such a decision. Having made such a decision, actor ω_k faces the problem of coordinating the interests of AE ω' with their own interests, because the interests of AE ω', which is created to achieve the combination of goals ω_d and ω_f, "go beyond" the interests of the actors of each SEA ω_m and ω_l. All the above means that actor ω_k will transform the structure of the SEAs (and the cause-and-effect structures of SEAs ω_k, ω_m, and ω_l, respectively) to a form of Figure 3.7 and will perform control functions with respect to AE ω'.

Thus, we can affirm that the structure of SEAs should be tree-like with a single root node.

Let us define a unified numbering of elements in the whole set $A \cup \Omega$ of all AEs and refer to it as technological or t-numbering. Below, we use t-numbers as indices ω_i or α_i in such a way that ω_i or α_i uniquely identifies an i-principal and/or an agent. At hierarchy Γ, due to its properties, a *correct numbering* (see definition in Section 3.4.1) of all AEs can be set, and in each subsystem ω_m a correct numbering of all AEs

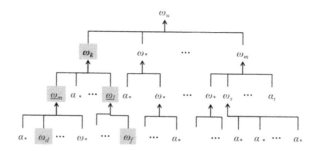

FIGURE 3.6   Initial structure of goals and SEAs.

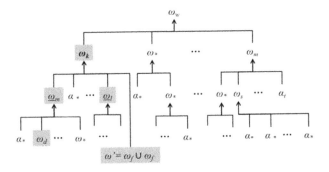

FIGURE 3.7 Transformed structure of goals and SEAs.

can also be set following technological network G_m. We build t-numbering using the following algorithm:

1. According to hierarchy Γ, let us set an intermediate correct numbering in the set of all AEs (agents and i-principals) and refer to its numbers as Γ-numbers, thus distinguishing them from technological numbering. We introduce auxiliary integer variable η and assign $\eta = 0$. We assume that initially no t-number is assigned to any AE.

2. Among all i-principals that have not yet been assigned a t-number, we choose the one for which the Γ-number is minimal; let it be ω_μ-principal. For all AEs (agents and i-principals) belonging to the ω_μ-subsystem, we perform a correct numbering, according to network G_μ; we refer to the corresponding numbers as Γ-numbers.

3. We increase η by one ($\eta = \eta + 1$). Among all agents belonging to the ω_μ-subsystem that have not yet been assigned a t-number, we choose the one for which the Γ-number is minimal, and we assign a t-number equal to η to it.

4. We check if there are still agents belonging to the ω_μ-subsystem that are not assigned a t-number. If there are such agents, we return to Step 3; otherwise, we go to Step 5.

5. We increase η by one ($\eta = \eta + 1$). We assign to ω_μ-principal a t-number equal to η.

6. We check if there are still i-principals that have not been assigned a t-number. If there are such i-principals, we return to Step 2; otherwise, the algorithm is complete.

The t-numbering constructed in such a way has an important property: the output of the actions by any AE depends on the actions of the AE itself and the outputs of AEs with lower t-numbers and does not depend on the actions of AEs with higher t-numbers.

Below, unless otherwise specified, we assume that a reference to the number of AE means the technological number, with prefix t not to be mentioned. In a certain sense, due to the "renumbering" of the elements of the AS, we succeed in reducing the "hierarchy of networks" to one equivalent network with a correct numbering.

Let us denote through $B(m)$ a set of AEs in the ω_m-th subsystem ($B(m) \subseteq A(m) \cup \Omega(m)$), as illustrated in Figure 3.5): α_i-agents are such that, for $\forall \; \alpha_i \in B(m) \; \exists \; d_{im} \in D$, and ω_k-principals are such that, for $\forall \; \omega_k \in B(m) \; \exists \; d_{km} \in D$. In the set $A \cup \Omega$ of all AEs, we introduce function $l(\cdot)$ as the number of the i-principal, being superior to an AE, α_i-agent, and/or a ω_k-principal, such that $\alpha_i \in B(l(i))$ and $\omega_i \in B(l(i))$. For the "root" ω_w-principal, the function $l(\cdot)$ is not defined.

According to the general concept of complex activity (Chapter 1, Section 3.1), agents directly implement valuable activity, and i-principals organize agents and control them. The activity of agents and i-principals during each and any period consists of making a decision to participate in an AS, to choose an action $y_i(t) \in Y_i$ (refusal to participate is a special case of action), and to execute the chosen action. The action of each ω_m-principal consists of assigning to all subordinate AEs constituting the m-th subsystem ($\alpha_i \in B(m)$ and $\omega_k \in B(m)$) incentive functions and remuneration according to the incentive functions. Following a common notation, the actions of the i-principal are denoted as $y_i(t) \in Y_i$, which means $y_i(\cdot)$ is an aggregate of the parameters of the developed incentive scheme.

Analogously to the formalization of the DNAS, we believe that the expenses of each α_i- agent depend on the actions of all agents in the $\omega_{l(i)}$-th subsystem, to which the agent belongs ($\alpha_i \in B(l(i)) \cap A$), $c_i^t(y_{B(i)\cap A}[1*t])$:

$$\prod_{\alpha_k \in B(l(i)) \cap A} (Z_k)^t \to \mathfrak{R}_+^1 \text{ and}$$

the expenses $c_i^t(\cdot)$ principal depend on the actions of agents in the $\omega_{l(m)}$-th and all subordinate subsystems $\alpha_k \in A(l(m))$ $c_m^t(y_{A(l(m))}[1*t])$:

$$\prod_{\alpha_k \in A(l(m))} (Z_k)^t \to \mathfrak{R}_+^1 \text{ (for}$$

illustration, see Figure 3.5). Since $\forall m \; A(m) \subseteq A$ and $\{A \cap B(m)\} \subseteq A$, without loss of generality, it can be assumed that all cost functions depend on the actions of all the agents, so $c_i^t(y_A[1*t])$:

$$\prod_{\alpha_k \in A} (Z_k)^t \to \mathfrak{R}_+^1.$$

Let us suppose that each subsystem and the entire m-DNAS during each period $t \in \{1, 2, ..., T\}$ functions as follows (Figure 3.8):

a. At the beginning of period t, each ω_m-principal (except for the ω_w-th one) successively, in *descending* order of the technological numbers, receives information on incentive function σ_m^t from a superior $\omega_{l(m)}$-principal, after which he or she makes a decision whether to participate in the AS or not (considering $\sigma_m^t(\cdot)$ and his or her cost function $c_m^t(\cdot)$. The ω_w-principal, being superior in the m-DNAS, is the first to make the decision on the basis

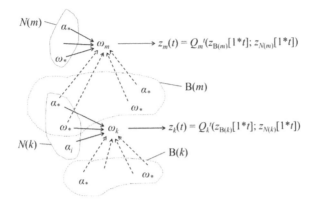

FIGURE 3.8 Technological relations in subsystems of an m-DNAS.

of his or her income function $h^i(\cdot)$, given in set Z_w of possible values $z_w(t)$ of the output of the m-DNAS as a whole, $h^i(z_w[1*t]):(z_w)^t \rightarrow \mathfrak{R}_+^1$, and of his or her expenses.

b. Having decided to participate in the AS, the ω_m-principal implements his/her action $y_m(t) \in Y_m$, that is, assigns incentive functions $\sigma_i^i(\cdot)$ to all participants in the ω_m-th subsystem. Agents $\alpha_i \in B(m)$ and i-principals $\omega_k \in B(m)$ make decisions to participate in the AS or not. Agents participating in the AS choose their actions, $y_i(t)$, and ω_k-principals choose theirs, $y_k(t)$: they build and assign incentive systems in the ω_k-th subsystems. If the ω_m-principal refuses to participate in the AS, no subordinates $\alpha_i \in A(m)$ and $\omega_k \in \Omega(m)$ participate in the AS either.

c. Sequentially, in *ascending* order of the technological numbers, agents $\alpha_i \in B(m)$ choose and implement actions $y_i(t)$; their outputs $z_i(t)$ and the output $z_m(t)$ of each ω_m-subsystem during period t are formed. The output $z_i(t)$ of each α_i-agent (similar to the DNAS, Section 3.3) is determined by: (a) the action $y_i(\cdot)$; (b) the outputs of his or her predecessors $\alpha_j \in N(i)$ and $\omega_j \in N(i)$ in network G_m; and (c) the technological function $Q^i (\cdot)$ in such a way that $z_i(t)=Q^i{}_i (y_i[1*t]; z_{N(i)}[1*t])$. The output $z_m(t)$ of the ω_m-subsystem (Z_m is a set of its values, $z_m(t) \in Z_m$) is determined by: (a) the outputs of all elements of the ω_m- subsystem, i.e., the α_r-th agents $\alpha_r \in B(m)$ and the ω_s-th subsystems $\omega_s \in B(m)$; (b) the outputs of the "predecessors" in the superior subsystem $N(l(\omega_m))$; and (c) the aggregation function

$$z_m(t) = (Q_m)^t (z_{B(m)}[1*t]; \; z_{N(l(m))}[1*t]),$$

$$Q_m{}^t(\cdot): \prod_{\alpha_i \in B(m) \cup N(l(m))} (Z_i)^t + \prod_{\omega_k \in B(m) \cup N(l(m))} (Z_k)^t \rightarrow Z_m.$$

   d. At the end of the period, sequentially, in *descending* order of the technological numbers, each ω_m-principal receives compensation for expenses from
the superior, $\omega_{l(\omega_m)}$-th, principal $\sigma_m{}'(\cdot)$ (or reserve utility u_m) and compensates
expenses to all subordinate participants of the ω_m-th subsystem, following
the incentive functions $\sigma_i{}'(\cdot)$.

   e. A transfer to the next time period $t \rightarrow t+1$ occurs.

The technological functions and the aggregation functions $Q_m{}'(\cdot)$, as well as technological networks G_m and hierarchy Γ, uniquely determine the dependence of the
outputs of the activity of agents $z_J(y_A[1*t])$ for any sets J of agents and i-principals:
$J \subseteq A \cup \Omega$.

   An assumption "about the technological transparency of the activity of an
Enterprise" in this case has a more complex structure. First, we believe that each
ω_m-principal observes the actual actions by all such ω_k-principals, being parts of
the ω_m-subsystem, $\omega_k \in B(m)$, that are directly subordinated to him/her during the
current period. Thus, each i-principal knows the incentive schemes assigned by each
subordinate i-principal within the subordinate subsystems.

   Second, with regard to agents, we assume two possible cases, i.e., the validity of
one of the Assumptions A2' and A3', similar to Assumptions A2 and A3.

Assumption A2'   Each ω_m-principal observes only the output of subsystem $z_m(t)$, but aggregation
functions $Q_m{}'$ $(\cdot)$ are biunique with respect to the outputs of α_r-agents $\alpha_r \in B(m)$
and the ω_s-th subsystems $\omega_s \in B(m)$ (subordinate active elements), as well as those
of the α_r-agents $\alpha_r \in N(l(m))$ and ω_s-subsystems $\omega_s \in N(l(m))$ (its predecessors in
the superior subsystem) during the current period.

Discussion of the validity of Assumption A2 presented in Section 3.3 is also characteristic of Assumption A2'.

Assumption A3"   Each ω_m-principal observes the actual actions of α_r-agents $\alpha_r \in B(m)$ and the ω_s-th
subsystems $\omega_s \in B(m)$ (subordinate active elements), as well as those of α_r-agents
$\alpha_r \in N(l(m))$ and the ω_s-th subsystems $\omega_s \in N(l(m))$ (his/her predecessors in the
superior subsystem) during the current period.

Let us assume the following awareness of the participants in an AS at the time of
their decision-making during each period t (in any case, of the validity of A2' or
A3'):

- all participants in each ω_m-th subsystem (the ω_m-principal, the α_l-agents $\alpha_l \in$
B(m), and the ω_k-principals $\omega_k \in B(m)$) know sets of the values of actions Y_l
and outputs Z_k, objective functions $Fi(\cdot)$, including cost functions and incentive systems, awareness and farsightedness of each other, the prehistory of
actions $y_l[1*t-1]$, and outputs $z_k[1*t-1]$.

- the ω_m-principal also knows aggregation functions $Q_m{}'(\cdot)$, set Σ of possible incentive functions, and the incentive function assigned to him or her by superior principal $\sigma_m{}'(\cdot)$.
- the ω_w-principal also knows the income function $h'(\cdot)$.

If Assumption A2' is valid, the ω_m-principal forms the incentive functions for every i-th subordinate agent based on the output z_m $[1*t]$ of the ω_m-th subsystem $\sigma_i{}'(z_m [1*t])$: $(Z_m)' \to \mathfrak{R}_+^1$, and if Assumption A3' is valid, the incentive function is designed based directly on the observable action of the i-th agent $\sigma_i{}'(y_i [1*t])$: $(Y_i)' \to \mathfrak{R}_+^1$. Since the actions of ω_m-principals are observable from the perspective of the superior i-principals, their incentive functions are always formed on the basis of their actions $\sigma_m{}'(y_m[1*t])$: $(Y_m)' \to \mathfrak{R}_+^1$. Then, the objective functions of agents and principals will take the following form (3.11–3.16):

the objective function of α_i-agent $\alpha_i \in A$ during the t-th period:

$$f_i{}^t(\sigma_i{}^t; y_A[1*t])) = -c_i{}^t(y_{A(l(i))}[1*t])) + \begin{cases} \sigma_i^t(z_{l(i)}(y_A[1*t])), & \text{if A2' is valid;} \\ \sigma_i^t(y_i[1*t]), & \text{if A3' is valid.} \end{cases} \tag{3.11}$$

the objective function of the α_i- agent $\alpha_i \in A$, during periods $t \in \{1; 2; ...; T\}$:

$$F_i(\{\sigma_i{}^\tau\}\tau = \overline{t,T}; y_A[1*T] = \sum_{\tau=t} \delta_i(t;\tau) f_i{}^\tau(\sigma_i{}^\tau; y_A[1*\tau]); \tag{3.12}$$

the objective function of the ω_m-principal $\omega_m \in \Omega$ ($\omega_m \neq \omega_u$) during the t-th period:

$$f_m{}^\tau(\sigma_m{}^\tau; y_A[1*T] = \sigma_m{}^\tau(y_m[1*t])) - c_m{}^\tau(y_{A(l(m))}[1*t]) - \sum_{\alpha_i; \omega_i \in B(m)} \sigma_i^\tau(\cdot); \tag{3.13}$$

the objective function of the ω_m-principal $\omega_m \in \Omega$ ($\omega_m \neq \omega_u$) during periods $t \in \{1; 2; ...; T\}$:

$$F_m(\{\sigma_m^\tau\}\tau = \overline{t,T}; y_A[1*T] = \sum_{\tau=t}^T \delta_m(t;\tau) f_m{}^\tau(\sigma_m{}^\tau; y_A[1*\tau]); \tag{3.14}$$

the objective function of the root ω_w-principal and of an Enterprise, as a whole, during the t-th period:

$$\phi^t(\{\sigma^\tau{}_{A\cup\Omega}\}; z_w(y_A[1*t])); \Psi) = h^t(z_w(y_A[1*t])); \Psi) - c_w{}^t(y_w[1*t]) - \sum_{\alpha_i; \omega_m \in B(w)} \sigma_i^\tau(\cdot); \tag{3.15}$$

and the objective function of the root ω_w-principal and of an Enterprise, as a whole, with the distribution of farsightedness $\delta_w(\cdot)$ taken into account, during periods $t \in \{1; 2; ...; T\}$:

$$\Phi((\{\sigma^t{}_{A\cup\Omega}\};\psi) = \sum_{t=1}^{T}\delta_w(1;t)\phi^\tau(\{\sigma^t{}_{A\cup\Omega}\};z_w(y_A[1*t]);\Psi) \qquad (3.16)$$

The control problem (3.17) is to construct an incentive scheme $\{\sigma^t{}_{A\cup\Omega}\}$ for all i-principals ($\omega_m \in \Omega$) and all agents ($a_l \in A$), constituting the m-DNAS, and choose such values of controlled parameters Ψ_c that optimize the objective function $\Phi(\cdot)$ of the root ω_w-th subsystem for known values of parameters Ψ_k and the elimination of uncertainty Ψ_u:

$$\det\{\Phi(\{\sigma^t{}_{A\cup\Omega}\};\psi)\} \to \max_{\sigma^t{}_{A\cup\Omega} \in \Sigma;\Psi_c} . \qquad (3.17)$$
$$\scriptstyle \Psi_u$$

The value of functional $\Phi(\cdot)$, obtained as a result of solving problem (3.17), is referred to as the *efficiency of the m-DNAS* or the *efficiency of an Enterprise as a whole.*

The solution to problem (3.11–3.17) allows one to obtain the optimal control of an Enterprise in the general case.

In the case of uncertain expenses of an agent, similarly to Section 3.4.1, problem (3.17) is transformed to (3.18) and (3.19) as follows:

In the case of the interval uncertainty model, control problem (3.18) consists of the design of incentive scheme $\{\sigma^t{}_{A\cup\Omega}\}$ and choice of such values of Ψ_c that provide the maximum of the objective function of the principal $\Phi(\cdot)$ for the worst values of expenses $\tilde{c}_i(\cdot)$ of all agents and i-principals during all periods:

$$\det_{\Psi_u}\ \min_{\{c_i^t(y_N[1*t])\ge\tilde{c}_i(t)\}}\{\Phi(\{\sigma^t{}_{A\cup\Omega}\};\psi)\} \to \max_{\sigma^t{}_{A\cup\Omega}\in\Sigma;\Psi_c} . \qquad (3.18)$$

In the case of the probabilistic uncertainty model, control problem (3.19) is set as the design of incentive scheme $\{\sigma^t{}_A\cup\Omega\}$ and the choice of such values Ψ_c that provide the maximum of the mathematical expectation of the objective function of the principal:

$$\det_{\Psi_u}\{E[\Phi(\{\sigma^t{}_{A\cup\Omega}\};\psi)]\} \to \max_{\{\sigma^t{}_{A\cup\Omega}\}\in\Sigma;\Psi_c} . \qquad (3.17)$$

Expression (3.17) represents the Enterprise Control Problem in the most general form, and expressions (3.18–3.19) are its special cases. In Section 3.4.3, a generalized scheme of the solution to this optimization problem is presented. All subsequent Chapters (4–7) of Part II are devoted to the mathematical models and methods that constitute the solution to the problem: game-theoretic contract models (Chapter 4); models of technologies (Chapter 5); human capital models (Chapter 6); and planning models (Chapter 7).

3.4.5 ENTERPRISE CONTROL OPTIMIZATION SCHEME

Let us set forth a generalized setup for the search for the optimal solution to the Enterprise Control Problem as formulated in the previous sections in the form of (3.17)–(3.19).

Let us consider an Enterprise to be an m-DNAS, a multi-element, multi-level, dynamic, active system, with constraints on the joint activity of elements in the form of technological networks, the objective functions of agents and principals being represented by expressions (3.11–3.16). The problem of the search for optimal control is reduced to the construction of an incentive scheme $\{\sigma'_{A\cup\Omega}\}$ for all principals and agents and the choice of such values of the controlled parameters Ψ_c (which characterize agents and principals, technology, and the external environment) that optimize the objective function $\Phi(\cdot)$ of the Enterprise as a whole (3.17). Participants in the m-DNAS play a hierarchical game: the principal, making the first move, offers the agents contracts (the incentive scheme $\{\sigma'_{A\cup\Omega}\}$), after which the agents make the second move: to choose (and execute) their actions, and then the principal remunerates agents according to the contracts. In the *hierarchical games theory* (Germeier 1986), such a game is called a game Γ_2 with *side payments*; it is also necessary to note that the contract theory models are particular cases of the games Γ_2 with side payments. A general scheme to solve control problems in active systems with side payments consists of two steps (Novikov 2013a):

a. For each feasible vector of players' actions or a vector of outputs of their activity (denote any of these vectors by $x[1*t]$), using the principles of decomposition and compensation of players' expenses (see above), a problem of coordination is solved: a compensatory incentive scheme $\{\sigma'_{A\cup\Omega}\}$ (and $x[1*t]$ are the parameters of $\{\sigma'_{A\cup\Omega}\}$) that implements these actions/outputs* with minimal expenses of the principal is constructed.

b. Then, the optimal planning problem is solved: vector $x[1*t]$ of actions or outputs, the implementation of which is the most beneficial for the principal, should be found.

Such a two-step scheme greatly simplifies the solution to problem (3.17): a direct solution is the search for functions $\{\sigma'_{A\cup\Omega}\}$, which optimize the functional $\Phi(\cdot)$, defined in the set depending on the desired functions $\{\sigma'_{A\cup\Omega}\}$. And the reduced solution is (a) finding a relatively simple incentive scheme and (b) then, "parametric" optimization, optimal planning.

The main output of Chapter 4 is Theorem 4.2, which proves the existence of the compensatory incentive scheme in the m-DNAS and determines its form (4.52)–(4.53) under 12 different versions of conditions and for any values of the parameters Ψ. If we use this incentive scheme, the objective function of an Enterprise during each period (3.15) takes the form

$$\phi'(\{\sigma^\tau{}_{A\cup\Omega}\}; x[1*t]; \Psi) = h'(x[1*t]; \Psi) - \sum_{\alpha_i \in A; \omega_i \in \Omega} (c_i^\tau(y_{A\cup\Omega}(x[1*t]); \psi) + u_i).$$

In general, we assume that the cost functions $c(\cdot)$ also depend on the vector of parameters Ψ.

---

* According to the definitions accepted in TCOr, it is said that an incentive system *implements* specific actions of an agent if the incentive system is such that the choice of these specific actions is the most advantageous for the agent.

Let us introduce a notation:

$$\tilde{\phi}'(x[1*t];\psi_c;\psi_k) = \operatorname*{def}_{\psi_u}\{\phi'(\{\sigma^t{}_{A\cup\Omega}\};\phi'(x[1*t];\psi))\}$$

$$= \operatorname*{def}_{\psi_u}\{h'(x[1*t];\psi)\} - \sum_{\substack{\alpha_i \in A;\\ \omega_i \in \Omega}}\left(\operatorname*{def}_{\psi_u}(c_i^t\{y_{A\cup\Omega}(x[1*t];\psi)\}+u_i\right);$$

$$\Phi^+(x[1*T];\psi_c;\psi_k) = \operatorname*{def}_{\psi_u}\{\Phi(\{\sigma^t{}_{A\cup\Omega}\};\psi_c;\psi_k;\psi_u)\}$$

$$= \operatorname*{def}_{\psi_u}\left\{\sum_{t=1}^{T}\delta_w(1;t)\phi'(\{\sigma^t_{A\cup\Omega}\};x[1*t];\psi)\right\}$$

$$= \sum_{t=1}^{T}\delta_w(1;t)\tilde{\phi}'(x[1*t];\psi_c;\psi_k) = \sum_{t=1}^{T}\delta_w(1;t)\operatorname*{def}_{\psi_u}\left\{h'(x[1*t];\psi) - \sum_{\substack{\alpha_i \in A;\\ \omega_i \in \Omega}}(c_i^t(y_{A\cup\Omega}(x[1*t]);\psi)+u_i)\right\}.$$

As a result of the application of the optimal compensatory incentive scheme (see Theorem 4.2), optimization problem (3.17) is formulated as follows:

To find optimal values of controlled parameters Ψ_c (parameters of an actor, technology, and the environment) and vector $x[1*T]$ of the output of the CA of an Enterprise, which provides maximum possible value of the objective function $\Phi(\cdot)$ of the Enterprise after eliminating the uncertainty of unknown parameters Ψ_u at given known values Ψ_k of uncontrollable parameters.*

Optimization problem (3.17) takes the following form:

$$\Phi^+(x[1*T];\psi_c;\psi_k) = \sum_{t=1}^{T}\delta_w(1;t)\tilde{\phi}'(x[1*t];\psi_c;\psi_k) \to \max_{x[1*T];\psi_c} \qquad (3.20)$$

Without loss of generality, problem (3.20) can be transformed into a sequential composition of optimization subproblems:

1. *The optimal planning of the output of complex activity (or the actions) using the given technology*: After eliminating the uncertainty of unknown parameters Ψ_u for the given values of uncontrollable Ψ_k and for all possible values of controlled parameters Ψ_c (by considering Ψ_k and Ψ_c to be known), to find such optimal values $x[1*T]$ of characteristics of the output of CA,

---

* We believe that the characteristics of a model of uncertainty of parameters Ψ_u are known and are parts of Ψ_k.

i.e., the output of an Enterprise, which provide the maximum possible value of the objective function of the Enterprise $\Phi^+(\cdot)$:

$$\Phi^+(x[1*T];\psi_c;\psi_k) \to \max_{x[1*T]}.$$

2. *The choice of the optimal values of parameters of the technology of CA:*
   After eliminating the uncertainty of unknown parameters Ψ_u and completing the optimal planning of the output $x^*[1*T]$ for the given values of uncontrollable Ψ_k, to choose those values of controlled parameters Ψ_c of an actor, technology, and the environment that provide the maximum possible value of the objective function of an Enterprise, as a whole, $\Phi^{++}(\cdot)$:

$$\Phi^{++}(\psi_c;\psi_k) = \max_{x[1*T]}\{\Phi^+(x[1*T];\psi_c;\psi_k)\} \to \max_{\psi_c}.$$

These subproblems, together with the choice of the incentive scheme $\{\sigma^t_{A \cup \Omega}\}$ according to Theorem 4.2 (let's call it subproblem 0), illustrate the step-by-step nature of the solution to the optimization problem (3.17) during the implementation of the lifecycle of the CA of an Enterprise, Figure 3.9.

It is easy to see that this *backward induction* – the logical decomposition of problem (3.17) into subproblems 0–1–2 – corresponds to the logic of the implementation of the lifecycles of the CA of an Enterprise and to the application of the backward induction* (or backward search) method to find the optimal solution. By comparison, any other decomposition is contrary to the practice of Enterprise operations. Although, within the framework of implementation of LCs of CA, it is the second subproblem that corresponds to the synthesis of technology (choice of the optimal values of parameters Ψ_c of the technology), and, therefore, it is solved in time before any others (see the process model, Section 1.4.2), as shown in Figure 3.9. After that, planning is carried out (subproblem 1), the results of which are used to establish specific contracts with agents – the incentive scheme $\{\sigma^t_{A \cup \Omega}\}$ (subproblem 0).

The functions $\operatorname*{def}_{\psi_u}\{h^i(\cdot)\}$, $\operatorname*{def}_{\psi_u}\{c^i_i(\cdot)\}$, and $\delta_w(\cdot)$ constituting problem (3.20) are

known deterministic functions, but their specific form is determined by the

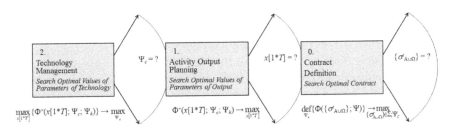

FIGURE 3.9   Backward induction: three-step solution to optimization problem.

---

* This method is widely used in game theory and optimization theory in general, starting with the classical papers by Zermelo (1912) and von Neumann and Morgenstern (1944).

industrial specifics of an Enterprise. It does not seem possible to propose unified common approaches to an analytical solution to problem (3.20) under such circumstances. Therefore, in Section 7.1, an algorithmic model is proposed that supports a compatible planning process in a hierarchical dynamic system and allows obtaining a reasoned plan that is, perhaps, not the optimal one, but is feasible in practice.

At the same time, the practices of engineering and controlling an Enterprise demonstrate an important system-wide feature, which allows us to highlight three typical cases of planning tasks that permit an analytical solution (these cases and solutions are presented in Chapter 7).

1. *Planning of cyclical execution of CA.*

In most cases, an Enterprise evolves in such a way that, once developed, the technology is cyclically used in repeated valuable CA, and, once incurred, expenses for the Enterprise and technology development are paid off owing to the multiply obtained goal-oriented effect.

The cyclical use of the same technology is beneficial only if the adequacy of the technology to the external conditions and to the CA goals is maintained; otherwise, the CA goals cannot be achieved, and the activity becomes meaningless. In other words, in most cases, valuable activity is implemented in stationary conditions. This means that both control variables – the optimal plan $x^*[1*T] = \underset{x[1*T]}{\mathrm{argmax}}\{\Phi^+(x[1*T]; \Psi_c; \Psi_k)\}$ and the values of the controlled parameters

$\Psi^*_c = \underset{\Psi_c}{\mathrm{arg\,max}}\left\{\underset{x[1*T]}{\max}\{\Phi^+(x[1*T]; \Psi_c; \Psi_k)\}\right\}$ – form stationary sequences, and some

of their parameters remain constant.

In practice, some elements of the information model of a CA technology (conditions, criteria, forms and methods of attaining the CA goal) and characteristics of CA actors are constants: their optimal values are chosen once during the phase of technology creation (Figure 1.12). Meanwhile, the parameters of CA resources (means of attaining the CA goal) must be chosen repeatedly, before each cycle of valuable CA, following changes in the external environment, which are described by the known laws of measurable uncertainty. This is a case of repeated implementation of a productive stage of CA using a well-known, well-developed, and fixed technology (its information model). Obviously, in such a case, the constant parameters of controls ($x^*[1*T]$ and Ψ^*_c) are calculated once during the stage of technology synthesis, and the optimization problem (3.20) itself is reduced to regularly repeating resource planning under conditions of stationary measurable uncertainty. Problems of resource planning are typical of any enterprises and any type of CA; human resource planning models (of dynamic programming) are discussed in Section 7.4.

2. *Planning of the transition from technology development to its productive use.*

An implementation of the lifecycle of any CA consists of design (technology development), execution (productive use), and reflection stages; therefore, planning for the transition from one stage to another is characteristic of any Enterprise, and optimal transition planning is critically important for an Enterprise's efficiency. Models and methods of transition planning from technology development (design stage) to productive use of technology for valuable activity execution (execution stage) are proposed in Section 7.2.

3. *Planning under conditions of a possible change in the characteristics of the external environment.*

External environment variability is one of key specifics of any Enterprise and CA. Thus, sooner or later, the evolution of the external environment leads to the fact that the CA technology becomes inadequate for the external conditions. Models and methods of CA implementation planning under conditions of a possible change in the characteristics of the external environment and/or the CA technology are developed in Section 7.3.

Note that the considered setting of problem (3.20) and the Enterprise Control Optimization Scheme describe, as special cases, almost all well-known models of operations research and allied fields of knowledge in application to an Enterprise.

CONCLUSION

In conclusion, let us note that this chapter is, to a certain extent, central: here, rather than everywhere, a single integral optimization problem, the Enterprise Control Problem, is formulated, and a generalized schema for its solution, which implements its correct decomposition into subproblems, is proposed. The formation of a single holistic setting of the optimization problem for such a complicated and heterogeneous controlled entity was made possible thanks to the development of the unified model of an Enterprise and its CA of various types, in the form of the hierarchy of LCs of SEAs. Using approaches of the theory of control in organizations, the optimization problem is laid out as a search for optimal control actions in a multi-element, multi-level, dynamic, active system with constraints imposed on the joint activity of elements in the form of technological networks, i.e., expressions (3.1)–(3.19).

In the following chapters, to solve the posed problems, mathematical models and methods are considered which, due to the complexity and variety of properties of a controlled entity, fall under different areas of applied mathematics. The chosen sequence of presentation of mathematical models and methods differs from the traditional sequence of problem-solving in *managerial cycles* (for instance, the PDCA cycle (Tague 2005) and the Fayol cycle (Fayol 1917)) and is determined by the following considerations.

Models of contract theory (as a subsection of game theory), on the one hand, describe the key properties of people as the main elements of an Enterprise, and on the other hand, they allow us to prove theorems (Section 4.3) on the decomposition of agents' games in an active system, which determine sufficient conditions for the existence of a simple structure for optimal control of an Enterprise; therefore, these models are set forth in Chapter 4 as a first priority.

Models of technologies (Chapter 5) are, in a sense, original, i.e., such mathematical models that generalize and systematically describe the processes of creating, testing, and using CA technologies, as a whole, are proposed for the first time.

Models of human capital (Chapter 6) describe people as the most important element of an Enterprise.

Planning models (Chapter 7) integrate all other models, make the model system complete, and therefore are set forth last in the logical chain.

REFERENCES

Ackoff, R. and Sasieni, M. 1968. *Fundamentals of Operations Research*. New York: John Wiley & Sons.

Anderson, D., Sweeney, D., Williams, T., Camm, J., Cochran, J.2018. *An Introduction to Management Science: Quantitative Approaches to Decision Making*. 15th edition. Mason, OH: Cengage Learning.

Bolton, P. and Dewatripont, M. 2005. *Contract Theory*. Cambridge: MIT Press.

Brachman, R. 2004. *Knowledge Representation and Reasoning*. New York: Morgan Kaufmann.

Bramoullé, Yann, Galeotti, Andrea, and Rogers, Brian W. 2016. *The Oxford Handbook of the Economics of Networks*. Oxford: Oxford University Press.

Burkov, V. 1977. *Foundations of Mathematical Theory of Active Systems*. Moscow: Nauka (in Russian).

Burkov, V., Gorgidze, I., and Lovetsky, S. 1974. *Applied Problems of the Graph Theory*. Tbilisy: VC GAN (in Russian).

Burkov, V. and Novikov, D. 1997. *How to Manage Projects*. Moscow: Sinteg (in Russian).

Burkov, V., Burkova, I., Chkhartishvily, A., Chtepkin, A., Dinova, N., Enaleev, A., Goubko, M., Kondratyev, V., Korgin, N., Novikov, D., Tsvetkov, A. 2013. *Mechanism Design and Management: Mathematical Methods for Smart Organizations*. New York: Nova Scientific Publishing.

Daellenbach, H. and McNickle, D. 2005. *Management Science: Decision Making Through Systems Thinking*. New York: Palgrave Macmillan.

Encyclopedia of Operations Research and Management Science. 2013. Third edition / S. Gass and M. Fu. (eds.). New York: Springer.

Fayol, H. 1917. *Administration industrielle et générale*. Paris: Dunod et Pinat.

Germeier, Yu. 1986. *Non-Antagonistic Games*. Dordrecht: D. Reidel Publishing Company.

Goertzel, B. 2008. *Probabilistic Logic Networks*. Heidelberg: Springer.

Harmelen, Frank van, Lifschitz, Vladimir, Porter, Bruce (eds.), *Handbook of Knowledge Representation*. 2007. Amsterdam: Elsevier.

Haskins, C. (ed.). 2015. *INCOSE Systems Engineering Handbook Version 3.2.2 – A Guide for Life Cycle Processes and Activities*. INCOSE. Fourth edition. San Diego, CA: John Willey & Sons.

Hillier, F. and Lieberman, G. 2010. *Introduction to Operations Research*. Ninth edition. Boston, MA: McGraw Hills.

ISO/IEC/IEEE 15288:2015. 2015. *Systems and Software Engineering. System Life Cycle Processes*. Internatonal Standard Organisation.

Jackson, M. 2010. *Social and Economic Networks*. Princeton, NJ: Princeton University Press.

Kelly, F. and Yudovina, E. 2014. *Stochastic Networks*. Cambridge: Cambridge University Press.

Kohut, R. 2014. Decomposition of Boolean Function Sets for Boolean Neural Networks. https://www.researchgate.net/publication/228865096_decomposition_of_boolean_function_sets_for_boolean_neural_networks.

Laffont, G. and Martimort, D. 2001. *The Theory of Incentives: The Principal-Agent Model.* Princeton, NJ: Princeton University Press.

Lucio-Arias, D. and Scharnhorst, A. 2012. Mathematical Approaches to Modeling Science from an Algorithmic-Historiography Perspective. In Lucio-Arias, D., Scharnhorst, A., Börner, K., Van Den Besselaar, P. (eds.), *Models of Science Dynamics. Understanding Complex Systems.* Heidelberg: Springer, 23–66.

MITRE. 2014. *Systems Engineering Guide.* Bedford: MITRE Corporation.

Nikiforov, I. 2016. Sequential Detection/Isolation of Abrupt Changes. *Sequential Analysis* 35(3), 268–301.

Novikov, D. 2013a. *Theory of Control in Organizations.* New York: Nova Science Publishers.

Novikov, D. 2013b. *Control Methodology.* New York: Nova Science Publishers.

Novikov, D. 2016. *Cybernetics: From Past to Future.* Heidelberg: Springer.

Novikov, D. and Chkhartishvili, A. 2014. *Reflexion and Control: Mathematical Models.* London: CRC Press.

Novikov, A. and Novikov, D. 2013. *Research Methodology: From Philosophy of Science to Research Design.* Boca Raton, FL: CRC Press.

Novikov, D. and Shokhina, T. 2003. Incentive Mechanisms in Dynamic Active Systems. *Automation and Remote Control* 64(12), 1912–1921.

Novikov, D. and Tsvetkov, A. 2001. Decomposition of the Game of Agents in Problems of Incentive. *Automation and Remote Control* 62(2), 317–322.

Pyster, A. and Olwell, A. (eds.). 2013. *The Guide to the Systems Engineering Body of Knowledge (SEBoK)*, v. 1.2. Hoboken, NJ: The Trustees of the Stevens Institute of Technology. http://www.sebokwiki.org [Accessed 16 December 2019].

Ramón, J. and Mateo, S. 2015. *Management Science, Operations Research and Project Management.* Burlington: Gower.

Rardin, R. 2017. *Optimization in Operations Research.* Second edition. Hoboken, NJ: Pearson.

Richardson, M. and Domingos, P. 2006. Markov Logic Networks. *Machine Learning* 62, 107–136.

Salanie, B. 2005. *The Economics of Contracts.* Cambridge: MIT Press.

Sauser, B., Magnaye, R., Tan, W., Ramirez-Marquez, J. 2010. Optimization of System Maturity and Equivalent System Mass for Space Systems Engineering Management. In *Proceedings of the Conference on Systems Engineering Research*, Hoboken, NJ.

Sauser, B., et al. 2011. *Development of Systems Engineering Maturity Models and Management Tools.* Stevens Institute of Technology. Report No. Serc-2011-Tr–014.

Sethi, S. 2019. *Optimal Control Theory: Applications to Management Science and Economics.* Third edition. Heidelberg: Springer.

Simon, H. 1978. Rationality as Process and as Product of Thought. *American Economic Review* 68(2), 1–16.

Tague, N. 2005. *Plan–Do–Study–Act Cycle. The Quality Toolbox.* Second edition. Milwaukee, WI: ASQ Quality Press.

Taha, H. 2016. *Operations Research: An Introduction.* Tenth edition. New York: Prentice Hall.

Vitanov, N. and Ausloos, M. 2012. Knowledge Epidemics and Population Dynamics Models for Describing Idea Diffusion. In Scharnhorst, A., Börner, K., and Van Den Besselaar, P. (eds.), *Models of Science Dynamics. Understanding Complex Systems.* Heidelberg: Springer, 69–125.

von Neumann, J. and Morgenstern, O. 1944. *Theory of Games and Economic Behavior.* Princeton: Princeton University Press.

Wagner, H. 1975. *Principles of Operations Research.* Second edition. Upper Saddle River, NJ: Prentice Hall.

Wald, A. 1947. *Sequential Analysis*. New York: John Wiley & Sons.

Zermelo, E. 1912. Über eine Anwendung der Mengenlehre auf die Theorie des Schachpiels. In E.W. Hobson and E.H. Love (eds.), *ProceedingsFifth International Congress of Mathematicians in Cambridge*. Cambridge: Cambridge University Press, volume II, pp. 501–504.

4 Contracts

People are the main element of any Enterprise. In this regard, the key feature that distinguishes people from other entities in the surrounding world is the property of *active choice* – behavior according to one's own motives and preferences. As a consequence, in order to model this human feature, the category of *active element* is introduced above in Section 3.2.2. It is also determined that the direct tool of control in an Enterprise is the *contract*, a means to coordinate the preferences of a controlled AE with the preferences of a controlling AE, i.e., to motivate and incentivize the controlled AE to behave so as to yield an output that meets the goals of the one doing the controlling. The contract also plays a key role in the Enterprise Control Optimization Scheme (Section 3.4.5, Figure 3.9).

Problems with coordinating the interests of actors with the interests of the superior actor performing control are the subject matter of the *theory of control in organizations, TCOr,* (Novikov 2013) and *contract theory* (Bolton and Dewatripont 2005, Laffont and Martimort 2001, Salanie 2005). Basic approaches of TCOr, as well as some original advanced models applicable to the Enterprise Control Problem, are described in Sections 4.1 and 4.2 of this chapter.

The activity of an Enterprise is always extended in time; as a result, the interaction of AEs within an Enterprise is repeated over time more than once, so a need arises to consider dynamic contracts, as described in the theory of repeated games in discrete (Ljungqvist and Sargent 2004, Renner and Schmedders 2016) or continuous (Cvitanic and Zhang 2012, Sannikov 2008) time (see also the review in Horne (2016)).

Technology is the most important component of the CA of STS; therefore, there is a need to develop and study a set of models that simultaneously describe both the technology and the active properties of its actors. For this purpose, in Section 3.4 above, an original model of a dynamic network multi-element AS was introduced. Section 4.3 is devoted to the study of various aspects of coordination of the preferences of CA actors, taking into account their lifecycles and technologies. As a result, theorems on the decomposition of the agents' game are presented. These theorems are keys to solving the Enterprise Control Problem.

4.1 STATIC PRINCIPAL-AGENT MODELS

4.1.1 DETERMINISTIC CASE

Let us consider an active system consisting of one controlling entity – a *principal* – and one entity, controlled by that entity – an *agent*. The agent chooses a non-negative *action* $y \geq 0$, which, together with implementation of some uncertain parameter, i.e., *a state of nature* $\theta \in [0; \Delta]$, uniquely determines the output $z = z(y, \theta)$ of his/her activity (for example, the so-called *additive model* of uncertainty $z = y - \theta$, in which uncertainty "additively worsens" the action of an agent). Let us suppose that the

119

expenses of an agent $c(y, r)$ depend on his/her *action* y and the agent's *type* $r>0$ (parameter, reflecting the effectiveness of his activity). We assume that *cost function* $c(\cdot, r)$ is the strictly monotonically increasing, continuously differentiable, convex function of the first argument, which equals to zero, if the agent chooses zero action, and the monotonically decreasing function of the second argument. Modeling of an agent's expenses using a function of two variables is traditional for theory of control in organizations (see, for example, Novikov (2013)). However, in most cases considered below, type of agent r is fixed and/or insignificant, from a substantive point of view. Therefore, we omit type of agent in the formulas, using the notation $c(y)$ for the cost function where this does not lead to ambiguity.

A principal offers an agent to accept a *contract* $\sigma(z)\geq 0$, which determines the amount of nonnegative remuneration (and the conditions for its receipt), depending on the output z achieved. The agent's objective function is the difference between the remuneration and the expenses:

$$f(\sigma(\cdot), y, z) = \sigma(z) - c(y, r).$$

The principal receives *income H(z)* caused by the agent's activity (where $H(\cdot)$ is a continuous non-decreasing function) and incurs incentive expenses, i.e. principal's objective function is equal to the difference between the income and the incentive expenses:

$$\Phi(\sigma(z), z) = H(z) - \sigma(z) \tag{4.1}$$

Let us assume such an *order of functioning*, that is traditional for incentive problems in the contract theory (Bolton and Dewatripont 2005, Laffont and Martimort 2001, Salanie 2005, Stole 1997), theory of hierarchical games (Germeyer 1976) and the theory of control in organizations (Novikov 2013):

1. the principal designs and offers the agent a contract $\sigma(z)$,
2. the agent chooses and implements an action y, resulting an output z (the refusal is a special case of the chosen action);
3. the principal remunerates the agent (in amount of $\sigma(z)$) based on actual value of output z.

Let the participants of the AS, making decisions, seek to maximize their objective functions. Since the output of the agent's activity depends on both the action and a state of nature, so, in order to eliminate *uncertainty of the state of nature* θ, both the principal and the agent must use all the information they have. Depending on the *awareness* of the participants, the following types of uncertainty are defined (let us note that all these cases correspond to measurable uncertainty):

- *a deterministic* case – the absence of uncertainty $\theta \equiv 0$, and this is common knowledge for the principal and the agent);
- a case *of complete awareness* – a decision-maker knows the true value of the state of nature;

- *interval uncertainty* – a decision-maker knows only a set of possible values of the uncertain parameter, the state of nature $\theta \in [0; \Delta]$;
- *probabilistic* uncertainty – a decision-maker knows probability distribution at a set of possible values of the uncertain parameter, the state of nature or the output of the agent's activity;
- *fuzzy uncertainty* – a decision-maker knows the membership function of the uncertain parameter defined, at a set of its possible values.

Let us denote by $f(\sigma(\cdot), y)$ and $\Phi(\sigma(\cdot), y)$ "deterministic" objective functions of the agent and principal, resulting from the eliminating θ uncertainty of nature. The *principle of the maximum guaranteed result* (in case of interval uncertainty) and the principle of expected utility (in case of probabilistic uncertainty) are usually used to eliminate uncertainty; an overview of methods for eliminating uncertainty might be found in Novikov (2013).

Let us denote by $P(\sigma(\cdot)) = \operatorname{Arg} \max_{y \geq 0} \{f(\sigma(\cdot), y)\}$ a set of the actions (optimal for the agent) of the agent, within the framework of the contract $\sigma(\cdot)$ and through $M - a\ set$ *of admissible contracts.* Following terminology TCOr (Novikov 2013) we say that the *contract $\sigma(\cdot)$ implements the agent's action y^* (or the action y^* is implemented by the contract $\sigma(\cdot)$)* if the action y^* is the most beneficial for the agent considering the contract $\sigma(\cdot)$, i.e. $y^* \in P(\sigma(\cdot))$.

Let us accept the *hypothesis of benevolence* (Novikov 2013), according to which the agent chooses from the set of implementable actions the action that is the most preferable for the principal. Then the *incentive problem* for principal consists in designing the *optimal contract $\sigma^*(\cdot)$*, i.e. such admissible contract that maximizes the principal's objective function:

$$\sigma^*(\cdot) \in \operatorname{Arg} \max_{\sigma \in M} \{ \max_{y \in P(\sigma)} \{\Phi(\sigma(\cdot), y)\}\} \tag{4.2}$$

If the *hypothesis of benevolence* is not satisfied, then an incentive system (contract) is sought that has the maximum *guaranteed effectiveness*:

$$\sigma_g^*(\cdot) \in \operatorname{Arg} \max_{\sigma \in M} \{ \min_{y \in P(\sigma)} \{\Phi(\sigma(\cdot), y)\}\}.$$

Let us note that if only one uncertain parameter is present, the number of possible combinations of the awareness of the principal and the agent is quite large (more precisely, it is $17 = 1 + 4^2$; cases of nontrivial mutual awareness (Novikov and Chkhartishvily 2014) are outside the subject-matter of this book). Let us analyze some of them for the additive model of uncertainty $z = y - \theta$.

4.1.1.1 Deterministic case

Within this framework $\theta \equiv 0$ and $z \equiv y$, and *the jump-like* (lump sum) *incentive scheme* (by solving problem (4.2)), that employs the principle of *agent's expenses compensation* (Novikov 2013), is optimal:

$$\sigma_C(x_0, y) = \begin{cases} c(x_0), & y \geq x_0, \\ 0 & y < x_0, \end{cases} \tag{4.3}$$

where x_0 is the optimal *plan for actions* (desired for the principal agent's actions) is defined by

$$x_0 = \arg \max_{z \geq 0}\{H(z) - c(z)\} \qquad (4.4)$$

Inserting (4.3) and (4.4) into (4.1), we easily find the principal's optimal gain $K_0 = \max_{z \geq 0}\{H(z) - c(z)\}$. In this case, the value of the agent's objective function is equal to zero.

If the hypothesis of benevolence is not satisfied, then the following incentive scheme is ε- optimal (where $\varepsilon > 0$ is an arbitrarily small constant):

$$\sigma_{Cg}(x_0, y) = \begin{cases} c(x_0) + \varepsilon, & y \geq x_0, \\ 0 & y < x_0, \end{cases}$$

4.1.1.2 Full awareness of the principal and agent

Let the agent and the principal at the time of making decisions know the value of the state of nature θ. Then the principal can use the so-called *flexible planning mechanism* (Novikov 1997), in which both the optimal plan $x^*(\theta) = \arg \max_{y \geq 0}\{H(y - \theta) - c(y)\}$ and the incentive scheme

$$\sigma_C(x^*(\theta), z) = \begin{cases} c(x^*(\theta)), & z \geq x^*(\theta) - \theta, \\ 0, & z < x^*(\theta) - \theta, \end{cases}$$

depend explicitly on the state of nature θ. In this case, the final value of the agent's objective function is equal to zero, and the principal's optimal gain (4.5) is equal to

$$K(\theta) = \max_{y \geq 0}\{H(y - \theta) - c(y)\} \qquad (4.5)$$

Due to the nondecrease of the agent's cost function, $\forall \theta \geq 0$ $K(\theta) \leq K_0$, i.e. the effect of uncertainty on the principal's gain is negative.

4.1.2 INTERVAL MODEL OF UNCERTAINTY

In situations of incomplete awareness, it is reasonable to separate the cases of *symmetric* (equal) and *asymmetric* awareness of the principal and the agent. It is usually assumed that the agent is informed of uncertain parameters no worse than the principal (Novikov 2013). So within the framework of *asymmetric awareness*, it is assumed below that the agent, at the time of decision-making, knows the actual value θ of the state of nature, while the principal makes decisions unknowing θ the uncertain state of the nature. Let us note that we do not consider the possibility that the agent briefs information to the principal (Novikov 2013).

Asymmetric awareness. In this case, the principal, knowing only the range $[0; \Delta]$ of possible values of the state of nature, have to guarantee compensation of agent's expenses:

$$x_{PGR} = \arg \max_{y \geq 0} \min_{\theta \in [0;\Delta]} \{H(y-\theta) - c(y)\} = \arg \max_{y \geq 0} \{H(y-\Delta) - c(y)\}$$

i.e. to use the following incentive scheme

$$\sigma_C(x_{PGR}, z) = \begin{cases} c(x_{PGR}), & z \geq x_{PGR} - \Delta, \\ 0, & z < x_{PGR} - \Delta. \end{cases} \tag{4.6}$$

In this case, the agent, knowing the implemented value of the state of nature θ, chooses the action $y^*(\theta) = x_{PGR} - \Delta + \theta$ leading to the output of activity, "expected" by the principal, $x_{PGR} - \Delta$ (it is easy to verify that it is profitable for the agent to fulfill the plan by comparing the amount of gains when fulfilling and not fulfilling the plan).

The principal's optimal gain is

$$K_\Delta = \max_{y \geq 0} \{H(y-\Delta) - c(y)\} \tag{4.7}$$

In the case of asymmetric awareness, given any value of the state of nature, the gain is not higher than one in the case of full awareness (compare 4.5 and 4.7). While the value of the agent's objective function is nonnegative

$$f(\sigma_C(x_{PGR}, x_{PGR}), y^*(\theta), x_{PGR}) = c(x_{PGR}) - c(x_{PGR} + \Delta + \theta) \geq 0. \tag{4.8}$$

Value (4.8) is referred to as the *information rent*, i.e. the gain that an actor receives (in this case, the agent) due to his better awareness in comparison with other actors (the principal).

Symmetric awareness. In this case, neither the principal nor the agent at the time of decision-making knows θ the state of nature, but they know the range $\theta \in [0; \Delta]$. Therefore, the principal uses incentive scheme (4.6) and receives gain (4.7), and the agent is forced to choose such action $y_{PGR} = x_{PGR}$ that guarantees non-zero renumeration, which yields zero gain. At that, "overproduction," equaling to $\Delta - \theta \geq 0$, is produced by the system.

4.1.3 ADDITIVE PROBABILISTIC MODEL OF UNCERTAINTY

Let symmetrical awareness take place and the state of nature θ be a random variable with the *distribution function* $\hat{F}_\theta(\cdot)$: $[0; \Delta] \to [0; 1]$, for which there exists a probability density function (p.d.f.) $p_\theta(\cdot)$. Hereinafter the following distribution function $F_\theta(\cdot)$: $(-\infty; +\infty) \to [0; 1]$ is used:

$$F_\theta(\zeta) = \begin{cases} 0, & \zeta \leq 0, \\ \hat{F}_\theta(\zeta), & \zeta \in [0;\Delta], \\ 1, & \zeta \geq \Delta. \end{cases}$$

Consequently the output of activity $z = y - \theta$ is a random variable with the distribution function $F_z(\cdot, y)$: $[y - \Delta; y] \rightarrow [0; 1]$: $F_z(\xi, y) = 1 - F_\theta(y - \xi)$, in which the action y plays the role of parameter.

Suppose the principal is limited by a parametric class (4.9) of jump-like incentive systems with the parameters: $\pi \geq 0$, $\lambda \geq 0$. In this case, jump-like incentive systems may be not optimal (Goubko 2000, Novikov 2013), see also below, but, nevertheless, they are simple and widespread in practice:

$$\sigma_C(\pi, z) = \begin{cases} \lambda, & z \geq \pi, \\ 0, & z < \pi, \end{cases} \tag{4.9}$$

where π is the plan for output (the output of the agent's activity desirable for the principal).

When the agent is choosing the action $y \geq \pi$, the mathematical expectation of the amount of remuneration (4.9) is

$$E_z[\sigma_C(\pi, z)] = \lambda F_\theta (y - \pi) \tag{4.10}$$

Assume that the agent chooses the action that maximizes its expected utility (Bolton and Dewatripont 2005, Novikov 2013), therefore, from the first-order conditions of optimality, we can write down that the agent's action $y^*(\pi, \lambda) \geq \pi$ must satisfy the equation

$$\lambda \, p_\theta (y^*(\pi, \lambda) - \pi) = c'(y^*(\pi, \lambda)) \tag{4.11}$$

The principal's problem consists in choosing the parameters $\pi \geq 0$, $\lambda \geq 0$ of the incentive system (contract), maximizing its expected utility:

$$\int_0^\Delta H(y^*(\pi, \lambda) - \zeta) p_\theta(\zeta) d\zeta - \lambda F_\theta(y^*(\pi, \lambda) - \pi) \rightarrow \max_{\pi \geq 0, \lambda \geq 0} \tag{4.12}$$

Example 4.1 Let the principal have a linear income function $H(z) = \gamma^* z$, where $\gamma > 0$ is a known constant; the agent has a quadratic cost function $c(y, r) = y^2/2r$, where $r > 0$ is the type of agent (Novikov 2013), reflecting the effectiveness of its activities; and the probability distribution θ is uniform: $F_\theta(v) = v/\Delta$, $v \in [0; \Delta]$.

From expression (4.10), it follows that the mathematical expectation of the amount of the agent's remuneration is equal to $\lambda^*(y - \pi)/\Delta$. Therefore, when the agent chooses the action $y \geq \pi$, the mathematical expectation of the value of objective function is equal to

$$E_z[f(\sigma_C(\pi, z, y, z) = \lambda (y - \pi) / \Delta - y^2 / 2r \tag{4.13}$$

By maximizing his expected gain (4.13), the agent will choose the following action (see also expression (4.11))

$$y^*(\pi,\lambda) = \begin{cases} \dfrac{\lambda r}{\Delta}, & \text{if } \pi \le \dfrac{\lambda r}{2\Delta}, \\[2mm] 0, & \text{if } \pi > \dfrac{\lambda r}{2\Delta}. \end{cases} \qquad (4.14)$$

The mathematical expectation of the value of the principal's objective function is equal to:

$$E_z[\Phi(\sigma_C(\pi,z),z)] = \gamma(y-\Delta/2) - \lambda(y-\pi)/\Delta \qquad (4.15)$$

By inserting (4.14) into (4.15), we obtain the problem (see (4.12)) of the principal's choice for the parameters of incentive system (4.9)

$$\gamma(\lambda\ r/\Delta - \Delta/2) - \lambda(\lambda\ r/\Delta - \pi)/\Delta \to \max_{\lambda \ge 0, \pi \le \lambda r/(2\Delta)} \qquad (4.16)$$

The solution to problem (4.16) has the form $\lambda^* = \gamma\ \Delta$, $\pi^* = \gamma^* r/2$. At the same time, the expected gain of the principal is equal to $\gamma\ (\gamma^* r - \Delta)/2$, and the expected gain of the agent is zero. •*

Let us solve the problem of synthesis of optimal incentive for the additive proba-bilistic model, being under consideration. The general scheme for solving probabi-listic incentive problems is as follows (Novikov 2013): first, for each action of the agent x, the minimum (from the point of view of the principal's expected expenses for incentive) incentive scheme $\sigma_{\min}(x, \cdot)$, *implementing* x, is sought, i.e. impelling the agent to choose the action $x \in P(\sigma_{\min}(x, \cdot))$. Then, such an action x^* is sought, implementation of which is the most beneficial for the principal (which maximizes its expected gain – see also expression (4.2))

$$x^* = \arg\max_{x \ge 0} E[\Phi(\sigma_{\min}(x,\cdot),x)].$$

It is easy to show that the following lemma is true, illustrating the well-known *principle of cost compensation* (Novikov 2013) as applied to the problem under consideration.

Lemma 4.1: in the probabilistic incentive problem, for any action of agent $x \ge 0$, there exists no incentive scheme implementing this action x on condition that the principal's expected expenses for incentive are strictly less than the agent's expenses, hence $\sigma_{\min}(x, \cdot) \ge c(x)$.

Proof of Lemma 4.1. Let such an agent action is $\hat{x} \ge 0$ and an incentive scheme $\hat{\sigma}(z)$ exist, that the following is satisfied

$$E_z[\hat{\sigma}(z) \mid \hat{x}] = \int_0^{+\infty} \hat{\sigma}(z) p_z(v,\hat{x}) dv < c(\hat{x}), \qquad (4.17)$$

and the incentive scheme $\sigma\ (z)$ implements the action $x \ge 0$, i.e. $\forall\ y \ge 0$ is satisfied

---

* Hereinafter the symbol «•» denotes the end of an example or a proof.

$$E_z[\hat{\sigma}(z) \mid \hat{x}] - c(\hat{x}) \geq E_z[\hat{\sigma}(z) \mid y] - c(y) \tag{4.18}$$

For $y=0$, formula (4.18), with the condition $c(0)=0$ taken into account, takes the form

$$E_z[\hat{\sigma}(z) \mid \hat{x}] \geq c(\hat{x}) + E_z[\hat{\sigma}(z) \mid 0]$$

which, due to the non-negativity of the incentives (and, therefore, such of its mathematical expectation), contradicts (4.17), and thus Lemma 4.1 is proved. ●

Let's find sufficient conditions for the optimality of an incentive scheme of type (4.9), namely, the same of a contract

$$\sigma_C(\pi, z) = \begin{cases} \lambda, & z \geq \pi, \\ 0, & z < \pi, \end{cases} \tag{4.19}$$

Denote $x^{**} = \arg\max\limits_{x \geq \Delta} \left\{ \int_0^{\Delta} H(x - \zeta) p_\theta(\zeta) d\zeta - c(x) \right\}$ and $c'(\cdot)$ – derivative of function $c(\cdot)$.

Proposition 4.1. (a sufficient condition for the optimality of a jump-like incentive scheme in an additive probabilistic model of uncertainty). If, in an additive probabilistic model of uncertainty, the p.d.f. $p_\theta(\cdot)$ of the state of nature satisfies the condition

$$p_\theta(x^{**} - x) \geq c'(x) / c(x^{**}) \forall x \in [x^{**} - \Delta; x^{**}], \tag{4.20}$$

then jump-like incentive scheme (4.19) implements the action of agent x^{**} with the principal's minimum expected incentive expenses, being equal to $c(x^{**})$, and is optimal.

Proof of Proposition 4.1. Let us calculate the mathematical expectation of remuneration when the agent chooses the action y given the plan x:
$E_z[\sigma_C(x,z) \mid y] = \int_0^{\Delta} \sigma_C(x - \Delta, y - \zeta) p_\theta(\zeta) d\zeta$., It follows from expression (4.10) that

$E_z[\sigma_C(x,z) \mid y] = c(x) F_\theta(y - x + \Delta)$. The agent's expected utility is

$$E_z[\sigma_C(x,z) \mid y] - c(y) = \begin{cases} -c(y), & y \leq x - \Delta \\ c(x) F_\theta(y - x + \Delta) - c(y), & y \in [x - \Delta, x], \\ c(x) - c(y), & y \leq x. \end{cases}$$

Given the plan $x = x^{**}$, by virtue of condition (4.20), the maximum of the given expected utility is achieved, if the agent chooses either zero action or an action that coincides with the plan x^{**} (condition (4.20) guarantees non-decrease in the agent's expected utility with respect to his action along the interval $[x^{**} - \Delta; x^{**}]$). By virtue of the hypothesis of benevolence, the agent chooses the action x^{**}, which will lead to the principal's expected incentive expenses being exactly equal to the agent's expenses. Therefore, by virtue of Lemma 4.1, incentive system (4.19) is optimal. Proposition 4.1 is proved. ●

Obviously, if the hypothesis of benevolence is not satisfied, then the following incentive scheme is ε-optimal incentive scheme under condition (4.20):

$$\sigma_{C_\varepsilon}(x,z) = \begin{cases} c(x)+\varepsilon, & z \geq x-\Delta, \\ 0, & z < x-\Delta. \end{cases}$$

Example 4.2. Under the conditions of example 4.1, the condition (4.20) takes the form of: $\gamma r \geq 2 \Delta$. ●

Now let us examine sufficient optimality conditions for the compensatory incentive scheme. To do this, we find the incentive scheme $\hat{\sigma}(z)$, which nullifies the agent's expected utility for any of his actions, i.e. such for which the following is satisfied

$$\int_{y-\Delta}^{y} \hat{\sigma}(z)p_\theta(y-z)dz = c(y) \qquad (4.21)$$

Proposition 4.2. If, in an additive probabilistic model of uncertainty, there exists a contract $\hat{\sigma}(z) \geq 0$, that satisfies expression (4.21), then contract $\hat{\sigma}(z)$ is optimal.

The validity of the proposition follows from property (4.21) of the incentive scheme $\hat{\sigma}(z)$ and Lemma 4.1. So, the compensatory incentive scheme $\hat{\sigma}(z)$ is optimal, if there exists a positive-valued solution to integral equation (4.21).

Let us formulate

Proposition 4.3. If the derivatives of the functions $p'_\theta(\cdot)$ and $c'_y(\cdot)$ are continuous over the domains of definition, then integral equation (4.21) has the unique solution that can be found by the method of successive approximations:

$$\begin{cases} \hat{\sigma}_0(z) = \dfrac{c'(z)}{p_\theta(0)} \\[3mm] \hat{\sigma}_{i+1}(z) = \dfrac{c'(z)}{p_\theta(0)} - \displaystyle\int_0^z \hat{\sigma}_i(u)\dfrac{p'_\theta(z-u)}{p_\theta(0)}du, \quad i=1,2,\dots \end{cases} \qquad (4.22)$$

A necessary condition for the positiveness of the integral equation solution (4.21) is:

$$c'(y) \geq \int_0^y \hat{\sigma}_i(u)p'_\theta(z-u)du, \quad i=1,2,\dots \qquad (4.23)$$

Proof of Proposition 4.3. Let us differentiate expression (4.21):

$$\hat{\sigma}(z)p_\theta(0) - \hat{\sigma}(z-\Delta)p_\theta(\Delta) + \int_{z-\Delta}^{z} \hat{\sigma}(u)p'_\theta(z-u)du = c'(z) \qquad (4.24)$$

Let's solve (4.24) given $z \leq \Delta$: $\hat{\sigma}(z)p_\theta(0) + \int_0^z \hat{\sigma}_i(u)p_\theta'(z-u)du = c'(z)$.

Let us rewrite this expression in the form:

$$\hat{\sigma}(z) = \frac{c'(z)}{p_\theta(0)} - \int_0^z \hat{\sigma}(u)\frac{p_\theta'(z-u)}{p_\theta(0)}du \qquad (4.25)$$

Equation (4.25) is a Volterra integral equation of the second kind. It is known (see, for example, Tricomi (1957)) that, within the conditions of the proposition being proved, such has a unique solution (4.22), which can be found by the method of successive approximations. For the value of the solution to be positive, the satisfaction of (4.23) is necessary. Thus, a solution for $z \leq \Delta$ is obtained.

Based on (4.25) a similar solution can be obtained for $z \in [j\Delta; (j+1)\Delta]; j=1, 2, \ldots$:

$$\hat{\sigma}(z) = \frac{\{c'(z) + p_\theta(\Delta)\hat{\sigma}(z-\Delta)\}}{p_\theta(0)} - \int_0^z \hat{\sigma}(u)\frac{p_\theta'(z-u)}{p_\theta(0)}du$$

at that, it is sufficient to perform a proof of the positiveness of the solution only for the solution along the first interval, and further $c'(z) + p_\theta(\Delta)\sigma(z-\Delta) \geq c'(z)$. Proposition 4.3 is proved. ●

Example 4.3. Let the p.d.f. $p_\theta(\cdot)$ be uniform, i.e.

$$p_\theta(v) = \begin{cases} \dfrac{1}{\Delta} & \text{if } v \in [a_0; a_1] \\ 0 & \text{if } v \notin [a_0; a_1] \end{cases}, \text{ where } 0 < a_0; a_1 = a_0 + \Delta.$$

Then (4.21) takes the form $\int_{z-a_1}^{z-a_0} \hat{\sigma}(u)dz = \Delta c(z)$. Differentiating both sides we obtain the functional equation $\sigma(z-a_0) - \sigma(z-a_1) \geq \Delta c'(z)$.

Considering that $c(y)=0$ $c'(y)=0$ given $y \leq 0$, the solution of the final equation is obtained in the form of a functional series: $\sigma(z-a_0) = \Delta \sum_{i=0}^{\infty} c'(z-\Delta i)$.

Since $c(\cdot)$ is continuously differentiable and convex, the sum of the functional series is positive and increases, which corresponds to the basic requirement to the incentive function $\sigma(\cdot)$. In particular, under the conditions of example 4.1, $c(y, r) = y^2/2r$, and $c'(y, r) = y/r$ given

$y > 0$, then $\sigma(z-a_0) = \dfrac{\Delta}{r} \sum_{i=0}^{\infty} (z-\Delta i)\theta(z-\Delta i)$, where $\theta(\cdot)$ is a Heaviside function

$(\theta(u)=1$ at $u \geq 0$ and $\theta(u)=0$ given $u<0)$.

4.1.4 "Simple" Agent (Probabilistic Model of Uncertainty)

An alternative to the additive uncertainty model, considered above, is a so-called
simple agent model (Goubko 2000), in which the p.d.f. of the agent's activity outputs
has the form

$$F_z(\zeta, y) = \begin{cases} G(\zeta), & \zeta \le y, \\ 1 & \zeta > y, \end{cases} \tag{4.26}$$

where $G(\cdot)$: $[0; +\infty) \to [0; 1]$ is the known distribution function ($g(\cdot)$ is p.d.f., corresponding to the same), $G(0)=0$, i.e., as in the additive model, the action of agent y
determines the maximum possible output, and the distribution $G(\cdot)$ does not explicitly depend on the action y. Let us denote p.d.f., corresponding to distribution function (4.26), by $p_z(q, y)$.

If the principal uses jump-like incentive scheme (4.9) and the agent chooses the
action $y \ge \pi$, then the mathematical expectation of the amount of the remuneration is
$\lambda(G(y) - G(\pi))$. An analog of first-order condition (4.11) for the simple agent model is
$\lambda g(y^*(\pi, \lambda))=c'(y^*(\pi, \lambda))$.

It is proved (Novikov 2013) that in the model of a risk-neutral simple agent, compensatory incentive schemes are optimal, and it is proved (Goubko 2000) that in this
class of models, the following incentive schemes are optimal:

- for a risk-averse agent, *compensatory incentive schemes*:

$$\sigma_K(z) = \int_0^z \frac{c'(v)}{1-G(v)} dv; \tag{4.27}$$

- for a risk-seeking agent, incentive schemes:

$$\sigma_C(x,z) = \begin{cases} \dfrac{c(x)}{1-G(x)}, & z = x, \\ 0, & z \ne x. \end{cases} \tag{4.28}$$

It is easy to see that incentive function (4.27) is non-negative, increasing, and convex.
By analogy with Lemma 1 from (Goubko 2000), one can prove the following properties of incentive schemes (4.27) and (4.28):

Proposition 4.4. In the simple agent model, $\forall y \ge 0$ is satisfied:

$$1)\ \int_0^{+\infty} \sigma_K(q)p_z(q,y)dq = c(y); \quad 2)\ \int_0^{+\infty} \sigma_C(y,q)p_z(q,y)dq = c(y).$$

The result of the first clause of Proposition 4.4 means that, for any action of agent,
the mathematical expectation of remuneration (4.27) is exactly equal to the agent's
expenses for the choice of this action. Therefore, if the principal offers a *contract*
(4.27), then the agent's expected utility for any actions (!) turns to zero. This makes the

agent indifferent to the choice of actions; so, within the framework of the hypothesis of benevolence, the agent chooses the action that is the most preferable for the principal.

When the principal uses incentive scheme (4.28), the agent is indifferent between zero action (refusal of the contract) and plan fulfillment. So it is necessary to increase the amount of remuneration for the plan realization by an arbitrarily small positive value ε, in order to maximize the agent's expected utility of an action, matching the plan. However, such an incentive scheme would no longer be optimal, but would be ε-optimal. It is easy to verify that the following proposition is true.

Proposition 4.5. In the simple agent model $\forall x \geq 0$, the incentive scheme

$$\sigma_C^\varepsilon(x,z) = \begin{cases} \dfrac{c(x,r)+\varepsilon}{1-G(x)}, & z \geq x, \\ 0, & z < x. \end{cases}$$

is ε-optimal, i.e. implements the action of agent x with the minimal principal's expected incentive expenses.

No matter which, compensatory or jump-like, incentive scheme is used by the principal, but the optimal plan (from principal point of view) is the following action:

$$x^* = \arg\max_{y \geq 0} \left\{ \int_0^y H(z)g(z)dz + (1-G(Y))H(y) - c(y,r) \right\} \qquad (4.29)$$

The first-order condition for expression (4.29) is

$$(1-G(x^*))H'(x^*) = c'(x^*,r) \qquad (4.30)$$

Example 4.4. Let, in the conditions of example 4.1, $G(z)=z/(1+z)$. From expression (4.27), it follows that $\sigma_K(z)=z^2/2r+z^3/3r$, and we can find $x^* = (\sqrt{1+4\gamma r}-1)/2$ from (4.30). •

Thus in the model of a simple agent with risk-neutral agent the jump-like incentive scheme (4.28) is preferable to the compensatory one (4.27) since such is, firstly, simpler, and secondly, its ε-optimal analogue forces the agent to choose the action that matches the plan (Proposition 4.4).

The main results of this section, devoted to the basic static problems of contract theory, are analytic dependencies of type (4.21), (4.27), which allow us to set and solve more complicated problems, in particular, dynamic ones. However, let us firstly consider a direct generalization of the model with one agent and additive uncertainty to a multi-agent case (Section 4.2) especially a practically important case of an "extended" Enterprise.

4.2 STATIC MULTI-AGENT MODELS

4.2.1 MULTIPLE AGENTS AND ADDITIVE PROBABILISTIC MODEL OF UNCERTAINTY

Let a principal control n subordinated agents (let us denote through $N=\{1, ..., n\}$ a set of these agents) which chose actions simultaneously and independently, and the cost function of the i-th agent be $c_i(y_i, r_i) = c(y_i, r_i)$, where $y_i \geq 0$ is the action, $r_i > 0$ is the type (hereinafter we denote an agent's number by inferior index). The output of the action of each of the agents is equal to $y_i - \theta_i$, where θ_i reflects the impact of probabilistic uncertainty, and all θ_i are independent and equally distributed according to $F_\theta(\cdot)$.

Let us denote through $y = \sum_{i \in N} y_i$ a sum of the actions of all agents, and the total

output is $\sum_{i \in N} y_i - \sum_{i \in N} \theta_i$. Let us suppose that the goal of the principal is to ensure the

total output be more than given $X \geq 0$ with a probability not less than a given value α $\in [0; 1]$. The value α is called *contract reliability* (Burkov and Novikov 1997).

For the additive model of uncertainty accounting, this condition will take the appearance of the following constraint on the actions of agents:

$$Y \geq X + {}_n F_\theta^{-1}(\alpha) \tag{4.31}$$

where ${}_n F_\theta^{-1}(\cdot)$ means the inverse distribution function of the sum $\sum_{i \in N} \theta_i$, i.e. the con-

volution n of the distribution functions $F_\theta(\cdot)$. The value of ${}_n F_\theta^{-1}(\alpha)$ can be considered as "*uncertainty costs*" related to nature.

Let us consider the problem: which should be the optimal plans for actions?

The expected incentive expenses of the principal for each agent are exactly equal to the expenses of the agent who chose the corresponding action (see Proposition 4.1): if the principal uses an incentive scheme that meets (4.21), the agent's expected gain is constant regardless of the chosen action; by virtue of the hypothesis of benevolence the agent chooses the action that matches the plan. Since the expenses of agents are non-decreasing, so condition (4.31), in the optimal solution, is satisfied as equality. Therefore, search for optimal plans is reduced to the following problem of conditional optimization:

$$\begin{cases} \sum_{i \in N} c(x_i, r_i) \to \min_{\{x_i \geq 0\}}, \\ \sum_{i \in N} x_i = X + {}_n F_\theta^{-1}(\alpha). \end{cases} \tag{4.32}$$

Using the method of Lagrange multipliers, we obtain that the following is true

Proposition 4.6. In an additive probabilistic model of uncertainty the optimal plans $\{x_i^*\}$, in a contract to ensure the cumulative output $X \geq 0$ with the reliability α, have the appearance (hereinafter $c'^{-1}(\cdot)$ is an inverse function to the derivative of the function $c(\cdot)$)

$$x_i^* = c'^{-1}(\mu, r_i), i \in N, \tag{4.33}$$

where $\mu > 0$ is a solution of the following equation:

$$\sum_{i \in N} c'^{-1}(\mu, r_i) = X + {}_n F_\theta^{-1}(\alpha). \tag{4.34}$$

Due to the monotony of p.d.f., we obtain from analysis (4.32) that the following is true *Proposition 4.7.* In an additive probabilistic model of uncertainty, with contract reliability increasing, the principal's minimum expenses to ensure the given cumulative output of agents' activity is not decreasing.

Example 4.5. Let agents have cost functions of Cobb–Douglas type, i.e. $c(y, r) = \delta^{-1} y^\mu r^{1-\mu}$, $\mu > 1$. Let us denote $\rho = \sum_{j \in N} r_j$. From expressions (4.33) and (4.34), we obtain

$$x^*_i = r_i \rho^{-1}(X + {}_n F_\theta^{-1}(\alpha)), i \in N \tag{4.35}$$

Knowing optimal plans (4.35), we calculate the optimal value of efficiency criterion:

$$\sum_{i \in N} c(x^*_i, r_i) = \mu^{-1} \rho^{\mu-1}(X + {}_n F_\theta^{-1}(\alpha))^\mu. \tag{4.36}$$

The right side of expression (4.36) does not decrease with respect to α (see Proposition 4.6). The amount of the "uncertainty costs" (the difference between (4.36) and the value of efficiency criterion in a corresponding deterministic problem) are $\mu^{-1} \rho^{\mu-1}[(X + {}_n F_\theta^{-1}(\alpha))^\mu - X^\mu]$ and are not decreasing with contract reliability increasing. ●

4.2.2 INCENTIVE PROBLEM IN AN "EXTENDED ENTERPRISE"

Over the past decades, integration in the modern world has become global and the foundations of relationships in STS and Enterprises have dramatically transformed: technological ties between the constituents began to prevail over traditional legal and shareholder links. Such organizational form as *extended enterprises*, i.e. aggregates of enterprises and firms, united by common technological processes and connections but legally and financially independent, has become widespread (see for instance Jagdev and Browne (1998)).

An AS can be considered as the model of an extended enterprise where the integrator (principal) organizes joint activity of constituent firms (agents), offers them appropriate contracts (incentive scheme) and forms the entire "production cooperation" (technological network) based on joint technology.

A linear incentive scheme (the remuneration is proportional to the agent's action or output, and the proportionality coefficient is called rate or price) can be considered as a model, where purchase of production factors is carried out on the market or inside an extended Enterprise and the "final assembly" is carried out following given technology.

Let us consider a model, in which an agent, in addition to ensuring his required output for the AS, can deliver output to an external market as well using the same production capacities. Agent executes the same actions (possessing certain "additivity") in a volume $v_i \geq 0$, at a price $\rho_i \geq 0$, which are known to the agent and the principal. We assume that the cost functions $c_i(y)$ are monotonically non-decreasing, convex, and differentiable for all values of $y \geq 0$. The model of AS with independent time periods is considered; therefore the dynamic problem is reduced to a single-step one. The objective function of the agent has the appearance:

$$g_i(x, v_i) = c_i(y_i(x)) + u_i + \rho_i v_i - c_i(y_i(x) + v_i), i = \overline{1, n} \qquad (4.37)$$

where x is the output, $y_i(x)$ is action corresponding to output x and u_i is reserve utility

Since, given fixed x and a compensatory incentive scheme, the first two summands in expression (4.37) are constants, so, due to the convexity and differentiability of $c_i(\cdot)$, the optimal level of actions y_i corresponding to the output delivered to the market, is defined as

$$v_i(x) = c_i'^{-1}(\rho_i) - y_i(x), i = \overline{1, n} \qquad (4.38)$$

The first summand in expression (4.38) is monotonical with respect to the market price ρ_i, therefore, the minimum market price, at which it is still profitable for the i-th agent to offer "additional" (over $y_i(x)$) actions to the market, is $c_i'(y_i(x))$.

Let us consider two alternatives for an agent. The first one is to participate in the AS and, perhaps, deliver a surplus to an external market; the second one being to refuse to participate in the system and totally deliver the output to an external market in optimal volume $c_i'^{-1}(\rho_i)$. Comparison of the agent's gain in these two cases (taking into account the principle of cost compensation) justifies

Proposition 4.10. Participation in an AS is beneficial for the agent if

$$\sigma_i(y_i(x)) \geq \max\{\rho_i y_i(x); c_i(y_i(x)) + u_i\}, i = \overline{1, n}. \bullet \qquad (4.39)$$

Based on Proposition 4.10, a set of feasible values of joint activity of the agents takes the appearance $Z_0 = \{x \geq 0 \mid \sigma_i(y_i(x)) \geq \max\{\rho_i y_i(x); c_i(y_i(x)) + u_i\}, i = \overline{1, n}\}$.

It was shown above that $\rho_i \geq c_i'(y_i(x)), i = \overline{1, n}$.

Proposition 4.11. In case of linear incentive schemes, an agent having a possibility to deliver the output to the external market, agrees to participate in the AS if

$$\sigma_i'(y_i(x)) \geq \rho_i, i = \overline{1, n}. \bullet \qquad (4.40)$$

The validity of Proposition 4.11 follows from the fact that the combination of two conditions, (4.38) and (4.39), is consistent, if and only if condition (4.40) is satisfied.

Meaningfully, Proposition 4.11 is trivial: if the principal designs a linear incentive scheme and offers the agent a rate lower than the market price, then the latter will not agree to participate in the AS. Let us note that in this case we do not take into account the organizational and informational expenses of the principal and agents;

these expenses deserve a separate study, and their introduction into the model can change the conclusions corresponding to the Propositions 4.10 and 4.11.

Example 4.8. Let the price λ be constant, the cost function be quadratic: $c_i(y_i) = (y_i)^2/(2\ r_i)$, where the constants $r_i > 0$, and the technological function (see Section 3.4) is linear:

$$Q_i(y_i, z_{i-1}) = B_i y_i + z_{i-1}, \quad \text{where } B_i > 0.$$

Under these conditions, expression (4.38) takes the appearance: $v_i = (\rho_i - \lambda\ B_i)\ r_i$, $i = \overline{1, n}$, and system of inequalities (4.39) takes the appearance $\lambda\ B_i\ r_i\ (\rho_i - \lambda\ B_i/2) \le u_i$, $i = \overline{1, n}$. •

The above considered "external market" model corresponds to a case of:

- the agent's shortage of the resources, when the agent is forced to optimize resource distribution to obtain the maximum gain;
- "conflict" relations between the principal and the agent, when they "fight for the gain" from the cooperative activity.

These a priori assumptions lead to the fundamental conclusion that such a compensatory incentive scheme is optimal that is based on the principle of "compensate as much as the agent needs to carry out the action desired by the principal." This is partly due to the fact that the principal is the first to make a move, offering the agent "rules of the game" (see the discussion of set of the compromise in Novikov (2013)). In other words, it is the shortage of the resources that forces the principal and agent to "fight for" a limited gain.

However, the current progress of technology and the economy as a whole substantially alleviates the shortage of financial, material, labor, and other types of resources. This makes the prerequisites for creating other cooperative relations between the principal and the agent, when they not only "fight for" the limited gain, but increase it together. Therefore, it makes sense to expand the problem statement considered above.

Let us supplement the two above discussed alternatives for the agent (to participate in the AS or totally deliver the output to external market) by a third option, that is, the expansion of the agent's activity.

Let us suppose that the i-th agent (independently or in cooperation with the principal) can attract additional resources and transform its technology of activity: substitute, in the network G, a single manufacturing element, having the technological function $z_i = Q_i(y_i, z_{i-1})$, $i = \overline{1, n}$ and the cost function $c_i(y_i(x))$, by a set of M_i identical elements, having the same technological function and cost function. The "additivity" of the agent's actions implies the possibility for the agent to share the "plan" $y_i(x) + v_i$ between M_i manufacturing elements. If $c_i(0) = 0$, then the monotonicity and convexity of the cost function clearly suggest the feasibility of assigning, to each of the manufacturing elements, a plan of as small a volume as possible, and choosing the number of elements M_i in accordance with the required plan $y_i(x) + v_i$.

At the same time, obviously, there exists a lower constraint on the feasible scope of a plan being assigned, i.e. the technological function $Q_i(y_i, z_{i-1})$ cannot be implemented for actions y_i, smaller than the a priori known level α_i, depending on the technology. Then, for each plan $y_i(x)+v_i$, an optimal organization of the agent can be found, consisting of $M_i=[(y_i(x)+v_i)/\alpha_i]$ manufacturing elements (where $[\cdot]$ denotes the integer part of a number). The "optimally organized agent" has the initial technological function $z_i=Q_i(y_i, z_{i-1})$, while the cost function transforms into

$$c^*_i(y_i) = \left[y_i / \alpha_i\right]c_i(\alpha_i) + c_i(y_i - [y_i / \alpha_i]\alpha_i) + b_i, \tag{4.41}$$

where b_i is a known constant, reflecting expenses for the agent's organization. As an aside, let us note that, in order to get rid of the requirement $c_i(0)=0$, one can assume that b_i is expenses for organization of one manufacturing element and assume the second summand in the expression for the cost function to be equal to $[y_i/\alpha_i]b_i$. Let us note that, for the "transformed" cost function (4.41), the following interrelation is valid:

$$c^*_i(y_i) \le \frac{c_i(\alpha_i)}{\alpha_i} y_i + b_i \tag{4.42}$$

at that, equality being achieved at points $y_i=\alpha_i P$, where P takes natural values.

Such a transformation is beneficial primarily to the principal. The transformation reduces the amount of an agent's expenses compensated by the principal for any scopes of the plan $y_i(x) \ge y_i^{bnd}$, where the boundary value y_i^{bnd} is a solution to the equation

$$c_i(y) = \left[y / \alpha_i\right]c_i(\alpha_i) + c_i(y - [y / \alpha_i]\alpha_i) + b_i.$$

Let's analyze an agent's benefit from the transformation, by using the expression for objective function (4.37), by taking into account transformed cost function (4.41) and condition (4.42):

$$g^*_i(x,v_i) = c^*_i(y_i(x)) + u_i + \rho v_i \quad [(y_i(x)+v_i)/\alpha_i]c_i(\alpha_i) -$$
$$-c_i(y_i(x)+v_i - \alpha_i[(y_i(x)+v_i)/\alpha_i]) - b_i, \quad i = \overline{1,n}. \tag{4.43}$$

Let us study the objective function when v_i increases from zero. First, define the minimum price level ρ_i, at which the agent is interested to deliver the output to the external market; for this purpose we differentiate the objective function (4.43) with respect to v_i ($i = \overline{1,n}$):

$$\frac{dg^*_i(x,v_i)}{dv_i} = \rho_i - c'_i(y_i(x)+v_i = [y_i(x+v_i)/\alpha_i]\alpha_i). \tag{4.44}$$

From expression (4.44), one can see that an agent is interested in delivering the output to the external market only at the prices $\rho_i \ge c'_i(y_i(x) - [y_i(x)/\alpha_i]\alpha_i)$. Let us note that this *threshold price* is strictly less than the threshold value $c_i'(y_i(x))$ in the case of the cost function without transformation (see expression (4.40)).

In expression (4.43), the first two summands $(c_i^*(y_i(x)) + u_i)$ and the last one (b_i) are independent of v_i. Therefore, for further analysis, let us rewrite the objective function, by omitting these summands:

$$g_i^{**}(x,v_i) = \rho_i v_i [(y_i(x)+v_i)/\alpha_i]c_i(\alpha_i) - c_i(y_i(x)+v_i - [(y_i(x)+v_i)/\alpha_i]\alpha_i), i = \overline{1,n}.$$

It is easy to show, by taking into account (4.42), that for $\rho_i > c_i(\alpha_i)/\alpha_i$, starting with some argument value v_i, the function $g_i^{**}(x, v_i)$ is strictly positive and unlimitedly increasing with the growth of v_i. So, the optimal level of agent supply equals the entire volume of the market.

Thus, the benefit of the transformation for an agent consists, first of all, in lowering the threshold price, at which it is profitable to deliver the output to the market, second in the appearance of conditions, under which the optimal level of the actions $v_i(x)$, being implemented on the market, coincides with the volume of the market, i.e. it is profitable for the agent to "capture the entire market."

The principal and the agent can cooperate to increase and share joint benefits depending on their mutual awareness. Consider two options:

- The principal knows the agent's cost function and manages the transformation initiative. The principal captures the whole gain, knowing and using the transformed cost function (4.41) instead of the initial one; in turn, the agent benefits from the delivery of the output to the external market and lower costs.
- The principal is not informed about the possibility of transformation initiative. The principal doesn't benefit anything; in turn, the agent captures the whole gain from lower costs and from the delivery of the output to the external market.

Let's note that the transformation of an agent's CA should usually be coordinated with the changes in the technology of the entire STS; and this coordination can be done only by the principal. Therefore, an agent, as a rule, cannot fail to inform the principal about changes in the technology. In turn, the principal may need for additional expenses to transform the entire STS technology, which can be compensated from the joint gain (in particular, from the delivery of output to the external market) depending on the agreements. Thus, the need for cooperative strategies for the described transformation is manifested.

The mentioned model illustrates well the benefits of *cooperative behavior* of the agent and the principal, but does not take into account such factors as: the need for resources for the transformation, uncertainty of demand, i.e. available market share, competitors, market dynamics, evolution of the agent and principal over time. All these factors complicate the model and are the subject-matter of further research.

4.3 DYNAMIC MULTI-AGENT MODELS

Studies of *repeated games* follow one common idea (see reviews of the so-called "Folk Theorems"): for normal-form repeated games (Demeze-Jouatsa 2018, Fudenberg and Maskin 1986, Fudenberg and Tirole 1995, Myerson 1997), for hierarchical repeated games (Gorelov and Kononenko 2015, Maschler et al. 2013, Rohlin and Ugolnitsky 2018) the idea of "sufficiently strong" punishment of any agent for any (even one-time) deviation from the choice required (by a principal and/or by other agents) from him. Germeier theorem for Γ_2 games (Germejer 1976) underlies all *incentive problems* and is also based on the same idea. This idea also forms the basis for the *principle of the decomposition* of a game of agents (Novikov 2013) in a deterministic two-level multi-element static AS: a principal can always (without loss of effectiveness) use such an incentive scheme of agents, whereby the choice of an action required for the principal is the dominant strategy of an agent.

In this section, this idea, by following Novikov and Shokhina (2003), is generalized to the case of dynamic and multi-level AS, with a constraint on agents' actions in the form of a technology of joint activity and given agents' uncertain expenses. Definitions of such DNAS and m-DNAS are introduced in Section 3.4.

4.3.1 CONTRACTS IN DYNAMIC SYSTEM WITH ONE PRINCIPAL AND MULTIPLE AGENTS

Let's design a compensatory incentive scheme in a *dynamic networked active system* (DNAS), defined in Section 3.4.1, which is optimal from the point of view of a principal (minimizing total by periods and agents costs to incentivize agents – see the deductible in (3.4)) in two settings, when assumption A2 or assumption A3 is true.

Let's firstly consider an incentive problem with deterministic agents' cost functions $c_i^t(y_N\,[1^*t])$. Let's fix some network output trajectory $x[1^*t]$, being desirable for the principal – a trajectory of *plans for output*, and a trajectory of *plans for actions* $y_N(x[1^*t])$ – an ordered set of vectors of agents' actions, leading to the trajectory-output $x[1^*t]$.

If assumption A2 is true, it is easy to show that for any feasible output-trajectory $x[1^*t]$, sequentially with respect to $t = 1, 2, \ldots T$, one can construct the single (!) trajectory of plans of all agents' actions $y_N(x[1^*t])$, causing the given network output $z_n[1^*t] = x[1^*t])$.

We denote as follows:

$y_N^p[1^*t]$ – a trajectory of plans for all agents' actions (we omit the record $x[1^*t]$ where this does not lead to ambiguity);

$y_i^p[1^*t]$ – a trajectory of plans for the i-th agent's action;

$y_i^p(t)$ – the t-th element of the trajectory of plans for the i-th agent's action $y_i^p[1^*t]$;

$Z_i^t(y) \subseteq Z_n$ – a subset of the set Z_n of possible network outputs, each element of which corresponds to an output $z_n(t)$, provided that the i-th agent chose the action y in the t-th period, and other agents chose any actions admissible for them, given any trajectories of all agents' actions $y_N[1*(t-1)]$ during previous periods, that is

$$Z_i^t(y) = \left\{ z_n(\{y, y_{-i}(t), y_N[1*(t-1)]\}) : \right.$$

$$\left. \forall y_{-i}(t) \in \prod_{k \in N; k \neq i} Y_k; \forall y_N[1*(t-1)] \in \prod_{k \in N} (Y_k)^{t-1} \right\};$$

$u_i > 0$ – *the reserve utility* of the i-th agent (the agent's gain in case of refusal to participate in the DNAS) in one period.

Let's form an incentive function for each agent $i \in N$ and $t \in \overline{1;T}$, assuming that the *hypothesis of benevolence* is valid:

$$\hat{\sigma}_i^t(z_n[1*t]) = \begin{cases} c_i^t(y_N(z_n[1*t])) + u_i, & z_n(t) \in z_i^t(y_i^P(t)); \\ 0, & z_n(t) \notin z_i^t(y_i^P(t)). \end{cases} \tag{4.45}$$

Incentive scheme (4.45) is such that in each period each agent is guaranteed to receive the compensation for actual costs ($c_i^t(\cdot)$) and the reserve utility (u_i), if agent chooses required (or planned) action $y_i^P(t)$, in any game environment $y_{-i}(t) = (y_1(t), \ldots, y_{i-1}(t), y_{i+1}(t), \ldots, y_n(t))$, occurred in the current period (for any actions of other agents), and given any history of the game (any trajectory of all agents' actions in the previous periods). Otherwise, remuneration is zero.

Proposition 4.12. If assumption A2 is satisfied, then incentive scheme (4.45) implements the trajectory of plans for actions $y_N(x[1*t])$ as the DSE (*dominant strategies equilibrium*) with the principal's minimal expenses for incentive. All agents' gains during each period in this equilibrium are identically equal to their reserve utilities. The principal's expenses for incentive are equal to

$$C(x[1*T]) = \sum_{t=1}^{T} \delta(1;t) \sum_{i=1}^{n} (c_i^t(y_N(x[1*t])) + u_i). \tag{4.46}$$

Proof. Let's consider an arbitrary period of time $t \in \overline{1;T}$ and an arbitrary agent number $i \in N$. Let $y_N[1*(t-1)]$ be some *game history*, and $y_{-i}(t)$ be some game environment for this agent. Let us consider all possible alternatives of the i-th agent's behavior.

a) Let the agent i chooses the planned action $y_i^P(t)$ during the period t. Then $y_N[1*t] = \{y_i^P(t); y_{-i}(t); y_N[1*(t-1)]\}$ and $z_n(y_N[1*t]) \in Z_i^t(y_i^P(t))$. According to (4.45), the value of the agent's objective function is:

$$f_i(\hat{\sigma}_N^t; y_N[1*t]; t) = \hat{\sigma}_N^t(z_n(y_N[1*t])) - c_i^t(y_N[1*t]) = c_i^t(y_N[1*t]) + u_i - c_i^t(y_N[1*t]) = u_i > 0.$$

b) Let the agent i refuses to participate in the DNAS during the period t, then the value of objective function is: $f_i(\hat{\sigma}_N^t; y_N[1*t]) = u_i > 0$. Let us note the significance of the fact that the last inequality is strict. Because if both inequalities $u_i \geq 0$ and $c_i^t(\cdot) \geq 0$ are non-strict, then from (4.47) it follows that the set of DSEs contains not only "the strategies of any agent, consisting of an arbitrary combination of planned actions and refusal to participate in the DNAS during each period," but also possibly some other ones else. Therefore, it is necessary to require one of the inequalities to be strict: either $u_i > 0$ or $c_i^t(\cdot) > 0$ (the latter assumption is too strong, since it is usually assumed that an agent incurs zero costs when refusing to participate in the DNAS).

c) Let the agent i choose during the period t an action $s \in Y_i$, different from a planned one: $s \neq y_i^P(t)$. Then the game history is: $y_N[1*t] = \{s; y_{-i}(t); y_N[1*(t-1)]\}$ and $z_n(y_N[1*t]) \notin Z_i^t(y_i^P(t))$ (by virtue of assumption A2). According to (4.45), the value of the objective function is

$$f_i^t\left(\hat{\sigma}_N^t; y_N[1*t]\right) = \hat{\sigma}_N^t\left(z_n(y_N[1*t])\right) - c_i^t\left(y_N[1*t]\right) = 0 - c_i^t\left(y_N[1*t]\right) \leq 0.$$

Let's note that options a) – c) for each agent and for each time period t are obtained independently from previous and subsequent actions of all the agents.

As a result, the objective function of the agent takes the value

$$F_i\left(\{\hat{\sigma}_N^t\}; y_N[1*T]\right) = u_i \Delta_i - \sum_{\tau \in \Theta_i} \delta_i\left(1;\tau\right)[u_i + c_i^t\left(y_N[1*\tau]\right)]. \qquad (4.47)$$

where Θ_i is a set of periods, during which the agent participated in the DNAS, but deviated from the planned trajectory $y_i^P[1*T]$, and $\Delta_i = \sum_{\tau=1}^{T} \delta_i(1;\tau)$.

In (4.47), the minuend $u_i \Delta_i$ does not depend on the choice of the agent, and, since $c_i^t(\cdot) \geq 0$, $u_i > 0$, $\delta_i(\cdot) \geq 0$, then objective function (4.47) reaches its maximum, if the set $\Theta_i = \emptyset$.

Whence it follows that such a strategy of any agent (that consists in an arbitrary combination of planned actions and refusal to participate in the DNAS during each period) is dominant. In particular, a trajectory of implementation of plans for actions is a dominant strategy: $\Theta_i = \emptyset$, then $F_i(\{\hat{\sigma}_N^t\}; \{y_i^P[1*T]; y_{-i}[1*T]\}) = u_i \Delta_i$.

Check this statement. Let's consider a trajectory of the i-th agent's actions, when

- over the periods from the first to the t_1-th (not including the latter), the agent implements planned actions $y_i^P[1*(t_1 - 1)]$;
- over the periods from the t_1-th to the t_2-th the agent participates in the DNAS, but implements some actions $s[t_1*t_2]$, different from the plan: $s[t_1*t_2] \neq y_i^P[t_1*t_2]$;

- over the periods from the $t_2 + 1$-th to the T-th the agent follows the plan for actions $y_i^P[(t_2 + 1)*T]$.

The value of the agent's objective function in case of such trajectory correlates with the maximum value in case of the planned trajectory as follows

$$F_i\left(\left\{\hat{\sigma}_N^t\right\};\left\{y_i^P\left[1*(t_1-1),s\left[t_1*t_2\right],y_i^P\left[(t_2+1)*T\right],y_{-i}\left[1*T\right]\right]\right\}\right)$$

$$= u_i\Delta_i - \sum_{\tau=t_1}^{t_2}\delta_i(1;\tau)\left[u_i + c_i^{\tau}(\{y_i^P[1*(t_1-1)],s[t_1*\tau],y_{-i}[1*\tau]\})\right] < u_i\Delta_i$$

$$= F_i\left(\left\{\hat{\sigma}_N^t\right\};\left\{y_i^P[1*T],y_{-i}[1*T]\right\}\right).$$

Similarly, the i-th agent's refusal to participate in the DNAS over any interval from the t_1-th to t_2-th periods does not increase the value of the objective function.

According to (4.47), the maximum values of the i-th agent's objective function (u_i Δ_i) do not depend on the actions of other agents; therefore the trajectory $y_N(x[1*T])$, when all agents follow the plans for actions during each period, is (one of) the DSE(s). Then, assuming the hypothesis of benevolence to be satisfied, all agents choose $y_N(x[1*T])$. Consequently, incentive scheme (4.45) implements the planned trajectory, i.e. the vector of all agents' actions $y_N(x[1*T])$, as the DSE, while the principal's total costs are determined by (4.46).

Let us demonstrate that the incentive scheme (4.45) ensures that the principal's costs stand at the lowest possible level (4.46) among all the incentive schemes that implement the network output $x[1*T]$.

Let there exist another incentive scheme $\{\sigma_N^{\prime t}\}$, implementing the network output $x[1*T]$ and, therefore, the same vector of agents' actions $y_N(x[1*T])$, and being characterized by the principal's total incentive costs being strictly lower. Then there is at least one agent $j \in N$, for which at least during one period $t \in \overline{1;T}$ the expression $\sigma_j^{\prime t}$ $(y_N(x[1*t])) < c_j^t (y_N(x[1*t])) + u_j$ is satisfied. That is to say that the value of the objective function is strictly less than the reserve utility. But then it is feasible for this agent, during such a period, to refuse participation in the DNAS and to receive the reserve utility. We have the contradiction; so the Proposition 4.12 is proved. •

Proposition 4.12 means that, over any possible farsightedness of the agents, compensatory incentive scheme (4.45)

- implements those trajectory of agents actions (as the DSE of their game) that lead to the required trajectory of network outputs,
- decomposes the control (incentive) problem with respect to agents and periods,
- guarantees the principal's minimum costs for the implementation of the trajectory of network outputs.

At that, incentive system (4.45) is such that the agent receives compensation for costs and reserve utility if he strictly follows the plan independently from all other agents and does not receive anything in case of deviation from the plan. Using this incentive scheme, the principal:

- firstly, makes it unprofitable for the agent to deviate from the planned trajectory even once, regardless of the agent's farsightedness (how many future periods of time he takes into account when making the current decision);
- secondly, "takes upon himself" the full weight (efforts for information storage, calculations, etc.) of solution of a planning problem (Chapter 7), including consideration of the mutual influence of decisions, made during different periods, etc.

Let now assumption A3 be satisfied (the principal observes agents' current actions during each period). In this case, the principal can form an incentive scheme based on the trajectory of the planned actions. Let us fix such a trajectory of *plans for actions*, that is desired for the principal, $y_N^P[1*t]$. An incentive function for each $i \in N$ and $t \in \overline{1;T}$, assuming the hypothesis of benevolence to be satisfied can be designed as:

$$\hat{\sigma}_i^t(y_N^P[1*t]) = \begin{cases} c_i^t(y_N[1*t]) + u_i & y_i(t) = y_i^P(t); \\ 0, & y_i(t) \neq y_i^P(t). \end{cases} \tag{4.48}$$

The proof of Proposition 4.12 above can be repeated to this case (4.48) considering correspondent substitution of the designations.

If the hypothesis of benevolence is not satisfied, incentive functions (4.45) and (4.48) should be supplemented by *incentive premiums* $\varepsilon_i > 0$, which accordingly increases the principal's costs: (4.50) if A2 is satisfied, and (4.51) if A3 is true.

$$\hat{\sigma}_i^t(z_n[1*t]) = \begin{cases} c_i^t(y_N(z_n[1*t])) + u_i + \varepsilon_i, & z_n(t) \in Z_i^t(y_i^P(t)); \\ 0, & z_n(t) \notin Z_i^t(y_i^P(t)). \end{cases}$$
$$\tag{4.50}$$

$$C(x[1*T]) = \sum_{t=1}^T \delta(1;t) \sum_{i=1}^n \left(c_i^t \left(y_N^*(x[1*t]) \right) + u_i + \varepsilon_i \right).$$

$$\hat{\sigma}_i^t(y_N^P[1*t]) = \begin{cases} c_i^t(y_N[1*t])) + u_i + \varepsilon_i, & y_i(t) = y_i^P(t); \\ 0, & y_i(t) \neq y_i^P(t); \end{cases}$$
$$\tag{4.51}$$

$$C(y_N^P[1*T]) = \sum_{t=1}^T \delta(1;t) \sum_{i=1}^n \left(c_i^t \left(y_N^P[1*t] \right) + u_i + \varepsilon_i \right).$$

The proof of Proposition 4.12 can be repeated in this case as well, considering correspondent substitution of the designations; at that, such DSE, in which all agents during each period choose the actions, required from them, $y_i^P(t)$, will be the single one.

Similar propositions can be formulated and proofs can be repeated, considering correspondent substitution of the designations, for each of combinations of conditions when:

- the assumption A2 vs A3 is true,
- the hypothesis of the agents' benevolence satisfied vs not satisfied,
- the agents' costs are determinate vs described by models of interval uncertainty (the functions $c_i^t(y_N[1*t])$ mean the maximum costs), vs those of probabilistic uncertainty (the functions $c_i^t(y_N[1*t])$ mean the mathematical expectations of costs) (see Section 3.4.1).

Thus there are twelve combinations of such conditions; let us formulate them in the appearance of the **Theorem 4.1** on the existence of the optimal incentive system in a DNAS (see Table 4.1 below).

In a DNAS, under various combinations of conditions for any implementable trajectory of DNAS outputs $z_n[1*T]$, over any possible farsightedness of the agents, there exists such compensatory incentive scheme, defined by (4.45), or (4.48), or (4.50), or (4.51) that: (a) decomposes the problem with respect to agents and periods; (b) implements those trajectories of agents actions (as the DSE of their game) that lead to the required trajectory of DNAS output $z_n[1*T]$; (c) guarantees the principal's minimum costs for the implementation of the given trajectory of DNAS output $z_n[1*T]$.

It is important to note that the decomposition of the problem with respect to agents and periods does not annul the interactions of agents. Subject to assumptions A2 or A3 and other conditions of the problem, the principal manages to construct an optimal incentive scheme (4.45) or (4.48), or (4.50), or (4.51).

Such scheme guarantees equilibrium in the dominant strategies of the game of agents regardless of their interconnections defined by DNAS technology: the structure of the network G and a combination of technological functions.

4.3.2 CONTRACTS IN DYNAMIC HIERARCHICAL MULTI-AGENT ACTIVE SYSTEM

Let us design for an m-DNAS (analogously to as it was done for DNAS in section 4.3.1) such compensatory incentive scheme that is optimal with respect to the ω_w-principal's expenses and implements given actions of agents and the i-principals (see definition in Section 3.4.4).

Let assumption A2' be true. Let us fix some admissible trajectory of the output of the system as a whole (of the ω_w-th subsystem) $x[1*t]$ – the trajectory *of plans for output* of the m-DNAS as a whole. Let us denote by $y_A(x[1*t])$ a trajectory of *plans for actions*, i.e. sets of such vectors of the agents' actions that lead to the trajectory of output $x[1*t]$.

Let us denote by $Z_i^t(y) \subseteq Z_{l(i)}$ a subset of the set $Z_{l(i)}$ of feasible outputs of the $\omega_{l(i)}$-th subsystem, superior to the α_i-th agent, $\alpha_i \in B(l(i))$, each element of which corresponds to the output $z_{l(i)}(t)$, on the condition that the i-th agent during the t-th period chooses the action y, and the other agents and i-principals chose any actions

TABLE 4.1
Summary formulation of Theorem 4.1 on decomposition of a game of agents

	If the Hypothesis of Benevolence Is Satisfied	If the Benevolence Hypothesis Is Not Satisfied
	incentive scheme (4.45):	incentive scheme (4.48):
	• when assumption A2 is true, it implements the trajectory of plans for actions $y_N(x[1*t])$ as the DSE of the game of agents, with the principal's minimal incentive costs, equal to: $$C(x[1*T]) = \sum_{t=1}^{T} \delta(1;t) \sum_{i=1}^{n} (c_i^t(y_N(x[1*t])) + u_t\ .$$ • when assumption A3 is true, it implements the trajectory of plans for actions $y_N^p[1*t]$ as the DSE of the game of agents with the principal's minimal incentive costs equal to: $$C(y_N^p[1*t]) = \sum_{t=1}^{T} \delta(1;t) \sum_{i=1}^{n} (c_i^t(y_N^p[1*t]) + u_i)$$	$$C(x[1*T]) = \sum_{t=1}^{T} \delta(1;t) \sum_{i=1}^{n} (c_i^t(y_N^*(x[1*t])) + u_t + \varepsilon_i)$$ $$C(y_N^p[1*t]) = \sum_{t=1}^{T} \delta(1;t) \sum_{i=1}^{n} (c_i^t(y_N^p[1*t]) + u_t + \varepsilon_i)$$
	In this equilibrium, during each period, each of the agents has a gain	
Det	identically equal to the reserve utility	identically equaling to the reserve utility, increased by the incentive premium ε_i
Int	not less than the reserve utility.	not less than the reserve utility, increased by the incentive premium ε_i
Pro	the mathematical expectation of which is identically equal to the agent's reserve utility	the mathematical expectation of which is identically equal to the agent's reserve utility, increased by the incentive premium ε_i

admissible for them, given any trajectories of actions $y_{B(l(i))}[1*(t-1)]$ of all participants of $\omega_{l(i)}$-subsystem during previous periods, that is

$$z_i^t(y) = \{z_k(\{y, y_{-i}(t), y_{B(l(i))}[1*(t-1)]\}) : \forall y_{-i}(t)$$

$$\in \prod_{s \in B(l(i)); s \neq i} Y_s; \forall\, y_{B(l(i))}[1*(t-1)] \in \prod_{s \in B(l(i))} (Y_s)t - 1.$$

For each of the feasible trajectories of outputs $x[1*t]$ and trajectories $y_A(x[1*t])$ of vectors of actions of all α_i-th agents $\alpha_i \in A$ let's construct an incentive function:

$$\hat{\sigma}_i^t(z_{l(i)}[1*t]) = \begin{cases} c_i^t(y_{B(l(i))}(z_{l(i)}[1*t])) + u_i, & z_{l(i)}(t) \in Z_i^t y_i^n(t); \\ 0, & z_{l(i)}(t) \notin Z_i^t y_i^n(t). \end{cases} \quad (4.52)$$

For each of the ω_m-th subsystems $\omega_m \in \Omega$, let's define function $C_m(\cdot)$ of costs for implementation of the trajectory of such output of the subsystem $z_m[1*t]$ that corresponds to $x[1*t]$:

$$C_m^{\,t}(y_{A \cup \Omega}(x[1*t])) = C_m^{\,t}(y_A(x[1*t])) + u_m$$

$$+ \sum_{\alpha_l \in B(r)} \left(c_l^t(y_A(x[1*t])) + u_1 \right) + \sum_{\omega_\kappa \in B(r)} c_k^t(y_A(x[1*t])),$$

and, based on function $C_m(\cdot)$, let's construct the incentive functions of the ω_m-principals:

$$\hat{\sigma}_m^t(\{\chi, y_m[1*(t-1)]\}) = \begin{cases} c_m(y_A(x[1*t])), & \chi = y_m^p(t); \\ 0, & \chi \neq y_m^p(t). \end{cases} \quad (4.53)$$

where χ is the ω_m-principal's action during the period t (the incentive scheme assigned by the ω_m- principal to all participants of the ω_m-th subsystem).

Let's show that functions (4.52)–(4.53) form such an incentive scheme, in which the trajectory of the vectors of the agents and i-principals' actions, regardless of their farsightedness, assuming their rationality (Assumption A1), make up the hierarchy of equilibria in each of the subsystems.

Let's consider feasible decisions of some ω_i-principal during the t-th period; let $y_{A \cup \Omega}[1*(t-1)]$ be some game history, and $y_{-i}(t) = (y_1(t), \ldots, y_{i-1}(t), y_{i+1}(t), \ldots, y_{|A \cup \Omega|}(t))$ be the game environment for the ω_i-principal.

At the beginning of each period, the ω_i-principal faces one of the situations (Figure 4.1 illustrates these options):

1. ω_i-principal doesn't receive an offer, if at least one of the superior i-principals refused to participate in the m-DNAS. There is no choice in such

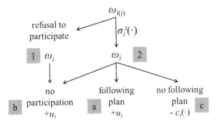

FIGURE 4.1 Decisions tree of the ω_i-principal during the period t.

case: ω_i-principal does not participate in the m-DNAS and get the reserve utility u_i.

2. ω_i-principal receives (if all superior i-principals decided to participate in the m-DNAS) from a superior $l(\omega_i)$-principal an offer to participate in the m-DNAS: to execute the activity and to get remuneration in accordance with the incentive function $\hat{6}_i{}^t$ (·) (4.53). In this case ω_i-principal has the following options:

a) to offer contracts – incentive scheme (4.52) –(4.53) – to all subordinate participants in the ω-th subsystem, which corresponds to the action $y_i^p(t)$ desired by superior i-principal. Then according to (4.53), the objective function of ω_i-principal takes the value

$$f_i^t\left(\hat{\sigma}_N^t; y_{A\cup\Omega}\left[1*t\right];t\right)=\hat{\sigma}_i^t(y_i[1*t])-c_i^t(y_{A\cup\Omega}[1*t])$$

$$= c_i^t(y_{A\cup\Omega}[1*t])+u_i-c_i^t(y_{A\cup\Omega}[1*t])=u_i>0.$$

b) to refuse to participate in the m-DNAS, then the objective function of ω_i-principal takes the value $f_i^t\left(\hat{\sigma}_N^t; y_{A\cup\Omega}[1*t];t\right)=u_i>0$

c) choose an action $s \in Y_i$, different from the planned one $s \neq y_i^*(t; x[1*t])$. Then, according to (4.52) the objective function of ω_i-principal takes the value

$$f_i^t(\sigma_N^t; y_{A\cup\Omega}[1*t])=\sigma_i^t(y_{A\cup\Omega}[1*t]) \quad c_i^t(y_{A\cup\Omega}[1*t])=0 \quad c_i^t(y_{A\cup\Omega}[1*t])\le 0.$$

Consequently, the objective function of the ω_i-principal on the interval $\overline{1;T}$ takes the value (similar to (4.47)):

$$F_i\left(\{\hat{\sigma}_N^t\}; y_{A\cup\Omega}\left[1*t\right]\right)=u_i\Delta_i-\sum_{\tau\in\Theta_i}\delta_i\left(1;\tau\right)[u_i+c_i^\tau\left(y_{A\cup\Omega}[1*\tau]\right)]. \qquad (4.54)$$

where Θ_i is a set of periods, during which the ω_i-principal participated in the m-DNAS, but deviated from the planned trajectory $y_i^p[1*T]$, and $\Delta_i-\sum_{\tau=1}^{T}\delta_i(1;\tau)$.

For each of the α_i-th agents, by repeating the calculations of Section 4.3.1, it is easy to show that the objective function takes the value (similar to (4.47) and (4.54)):

$$F_i\left(\left\{\hat{\sigma}_N^t\right\};y_A\left[1*T\right]\right)() = u_i\Delta_i - \sum_{\tau\in\Theta_i}\delta_i\left(1;\tau\right)[u_i + c_i^{\tau}(y_A[1*\tau])].$$

where Θ_i is a set of periods, during which the α_i-th agent participated in the m-DNAS, but deviated from the planned trajectory $y_i^p[1*T]$.

Thus, subject to the hypothesis of benevolence, the optimal strategy of each active element of an AS (a ω_i-principal and/or an α_i-agent) consists in choosing planned action, during each period, in which a contract is offered by the superior i-principal, regardless of any other actions of the other participants. If the superior i-principal doesn't offer a contract, active element has no chance to participate in the game and realizes the reserve utility.

Analogously to the proof of Proposition 4.12, it is easy to show that no expenses less than $C_w'(y_{A\cup\Omega}(x[1*t]))$ ensure implementation of the trajectory $y_A(x[1*t])$, therefore, it is true as follows

Proposition 4.13: If assumption A2' is satisfied, then incentive scheme (4.52)–(4.53) implements the trajectory of plans for actions $y_N(x[1*t])$ as the DSE of the game of agents with the principal's minimal incentive costs. The gains of all agents during each period in this equilibrium are identically equal to their reserve utilities. The principal's incentive costs are equal to

$$C(x[1*T]) = \sum_{\tau\in\Theta_i}\delta_i(1;\tau)[u_i + c_i^{\tau}(y_{A\cup\Omega}[1*\tau])]. \tag{4.55}$$

If assumption A3' is true, incentive functions (4.52)–(4.53) can be modernized and the proof of Proposition 4.13 can be repeated considering correspondent substitution of the designations. Just as in Section 4.3.1, analogous propositions can be formulated and the proofs can be repeated for each of twelve combinations of conditions. Let us summarize all of them in Table 4.2 and formulate them in the form of **Theorem 4.2** on the existence of the optimal incentive system in an m-DNAS.

So, in a multi-level multi-element dynamic active system, under various combinations of conditions for any implementable trajectory of m-DNAS outputs, over any possible farsightedness of the agents, there exists such compensatory incentive scheme, defined by (4.45), or (4.48), or (4.50), or (4.51) that: (a) decomposes the problem with respect to agents, i-principals and periods; (b) implements those trajectories of agents' and i-principals' actions (as the DSE of their game) that lead to the required trajectory of m-DNAS output; (c) guarantees the principal's minimum costs for the implementation of the given trajectory of m-DNAS output.

Just like for DNAS, let us note that, subject to assumptions A2' or A3' and other components of the control problem, the principal manages to construct such optimal incentive scheme that guarantees existence of an equilibrium in the dominant strategies of the game of agents regardless of their interconnections, i.e. regardless of the

TABLE 4.2
Summary Formulation of Theorem 4.2 on Decomposition of a Game of Agents

If the Hypothesis of Benevolence Is Satisfied	If the Hypothesis of Benevolence Is Not Satisfied
incentive scheme (4.52)–(4.53):	modernized incentive scheme (4.52)–(4.53):

- when assumption A2' is true, it implements the trajectory of plans for actions $y_N(x[1*t])$ as the DSE of the game of agents, with the principal's minimal incentive costs, equal to:

$$C(x[1*t]) = \sum_{t=1}^{T} \delta(1;t) \sum_{a_i \in A; \omega \in \Omega} (c_i^t(y_{A;\Omega}(x[1*t])) + u_i)$$	$$C(x[1*t]) = \sum_{t=1}^{T} \delta(1;t) \sum_{a_i \in A; \omega \in \Omega} (c_i^t(y_{A;\Omega}(x[1*t])) + u_i + \varepsilon_i)$$

- when assumption A3' is true, it implements the trajectory of plans for actions $y_N(x[1*t])$ as the DSE of the game of agents, with the principal's minimal incentive costs, equal to:

$$C(y_N^p[1*t]) = \sum_{t=1}^{T} \delta(1;t) \sum_{a_i \in A; \omega \in \Omega} (c_i^t(y_{A;\Omega}^p[1*t]) + u_i)$$	$$C(y_N^p[1*t]) = \sum_{t=1}^{T} \delta(1;t) \sum_{a_i \in A; \omega \in \Omega} (c_i^t(y_{A;\Omega}[1*t]) + u_i + \varepsilon_i)$$

In this equilibrium, during each period, each of the agents has a gain

	If the Hypothesis of Benevolence Is Satisfied	If the Hypothesis of Benevolence Is Not Satisfied
Det	identically equal to his reserve utility.	identically equal to his reserve utility, increased by the incentive premium ε_i.
Int	not less than the reserve utility.	not less than the reserve utility, increased by the incentive premium ε_i
Pro	the mathematical expectation of which is identically equal to the agent's reserve utility	the mathematical expectation of which is identically equal to the agent's reserve utility, increased by the incentive premium ε_i

technology of m-DSAS – the technological functions and aggregation functions, the technological networks G_m and the hierarchy Γ.

CONCLUSION

Incentive systems, i.e., contracts, are explored in Chapter 4 as the basic means of control in an Enterprise.

Static principal–agent and multi-agent models (Sections 4.1 and 4.2) are studied and a number of original propositions are given. In particular, incentive systems in extended enterprises are researched and the following results are obtained: the necessary conditions (Propositions 4.10 and 4.11) for the participation of an agent in a system and the model of expansion of an agent's technological capabilities, which illustrates the benefits of the cooperative behavior of the agent and the principal.

Dynamic multi-agent models playing key roles in the optimal solution to the Enterprise Control Problem are proposed and researched in Section 4.3.

For various combinations (there are 12 variants) of conditions, Theorems 4.1 and 4.2 are proved, stating that, for any feasible trajectory of outputs of DNAS or m-DNAS covering any possible farsightedness of the agents, such a compatible compensatory incentive system can be designed that:

- decomposes the control problem with respect to active elements (agents and i-principals) and periods;
- implements those trajectories of agents' and i-principals' actions (as the DSE of their game) that lead to the desired trajectory of the system output;
- guarantees the principal's minimum costs for the implementation of the given trajectory of m-DNAS output;
- makes the entire hierarchy of active elements "transparent" and accessible for end-to-end planning.

We should note that in such incentive systems the remuneration costs depend only on the corresponding values of cost functions, which, in turn, are indirectly determined by the technological functions, the network structure, and the structure of the AS as a whole, i.e., the actual organizational and technological structure of the Enterprise.

Let us discuss Theorems 4.1 and 4.2 and their theoretical and practical roles.

First, compensatory incentive systems, decomposing problems by active elements and periods, are designed for rather complicated models of organizations – hierarchical, multi-element, dynamic, active systems under uncertainty.

There are two particular reasons that allow problem decomposition:

- it can be done in active systems with *side payments*; such ASs generalize the contract theory models (see brief discussion in Section 3.4.5 and also Germeier (1986) and Novikov (2013) for more details);
- such ASs must satisfy assumptions A2/A2' or A3/A3' on the "technological transparency" of joint activity of all active elements.

This allows not only sequentially (by periods) reconstructing the desired trajectories of the agents' actions based on the trajectory of the plan for the "output of the entire Enterprise," but also controlling the agents' actions by observing only the actual values of the "output of the entire Enterprise." Therefore, under conditions of such rigid technological dependences, to speak conventionally, an incentive for an output is equivalent to an incentive for an action. Let us also note that all of the above results can be extended to the case where the known sets of admissible agents' actions and their outputs both change in time and depend on the previous actions of all active elements.

Second, rigid technological dependences make it possible to decompose the problem not only by agents, but also by periods. The possibility of such a decomposition is usually characteristic of the exact opposite case, i.e., the complete absence of connections: independent agents and unrelated periods. Here, conversely, the possibility of decomposition is ensured precisely due to the mutual uniqueness of the generalized technology of the agents' activity.

Third, such implementation of incentive-compatible control over a hierarchical set of technologically interconnected active systems naturally models a control problem in modern large businesses/Enterprises, which are based on the cooperation and control of tens of thousands of relatively autonomous business units, some of which, in turn, are Enterprises. It is important to note that results are obtained in the framework of both deterministic and uncertain models of active systems (with uncertain costs of the participants, allowing interval or probabilistic representation).

Fourth, the theorems divide mathematical models and methods of control of complex organizations into two domains: game-theoretic approaches – based on the study of the active choice of the AS participants – and planning models (including resource planning and allocation) employing optimization methods. As well, the independence of incentive systems from both technological graphs and technological functions allows one to research the technology management problem separately from other control subproblems (see Chapter 5). So, formulated holistically, the Enterprise Control Problem should be correctly solved as three subproblems (coordination of the interests of CA actors, CA and resource planning, and technology management; see Sections 2.5 and 3.4.5) based on separate mathematical models and methods. The three-step Enterprise Control Optimization Scheme proposed in Section 3.4.5 integrates all three groups of mathematical models and methods and the solutions to subproblems.

REFERENCES

Bolton, P. and Dewatripont, M. 2005. *Contract Theory*. Cambridge: MIT Press.

Cvitanic, J. and Zhang, J. 2012. *Contract Theory in Continuous-Time Models*. Heidelberg: Springer.

Demeze-Jouatsa, G. 2018. *A Complete Folk Theorem for Finitely Repeated Games*. Bielefeld: Center for Mathematical Economics.

Fudenberg, D. and Maskin, E. 1986. The Folk Theorem in Repeated Games with Discounting or with Incomplete Information. *Econometrica* 54(3), 533–554.

Fudenberg, D. and Tirole, J. 1995. *Game Theory*. Cambridge: MIT Press.

Germeier, Yu. 1976. *Nonatogonistic Games*. Moscow: Nauka (in Russian)

Germeier, Yu. 1986. *Non-Antagonistic Games*. Dordrecht: D. Reidel Publishing Company.

Goubko. 2000. "Simple agent" model in contract theory. Large-Scale Systems Control, vol. 2, pp. 22–27 (in Russian).

Gorelov, M. and Kononenko, A. 2015. Dynamic Models of Conflicts. III. Hierarchical Games. *Automation and Remote Control* 76(2), 264–277.

Horne, M. 2016. *Essays on Dynamic Contract Theory*. Ann Arbor, MI: The University of North Carolina.

Jagdev, H. and Browne, J. 1998. The Extended Enterprise – A Context for Manufacturing. *International Journal of Production Planning and Control* 9(3), 216–229.

Laffont, G. and Martimort, D. 2001. *The Theory of Incentives: The Principal–Agent Model*. Princeton, NJ: Princeton University Press.

Ljungqvist, L. and Sargent, T. 2004. *Recursive Macroeconomic Theory*. Cambridge: MIT Press.

Maschler, M., Solan, E. and Zamir, S. 2013. *Game Theory*. Cambridge: Cambridge University Press.

Myerson, R. 1997. *Game Theory: Analysis of Conflict*. London: Harvard University Press.

Novikov, D. 1997. Mechanisms of Flexible Scheduling in Active Uncertain Systems. *Automation and Remote Control* 58(5), 810–816.

Novikov, D. 2013. *Theory of Control in Organizations*. New York: Nova Science Publishers.

Novikov, D. and Chkhartishvili, A. 2014. *Reflexion and Control: Mathematical Models*. Boca Raton, FL: CRC Press.

Novikov, D. and Shokhina, T. 2003. Incentive Mechanisms in Dynamic Active Systems. *Automation and Remote Control* 64(12), 1912–1921.

Renner, P. 2016. *Dynamic Principal-Agent Models*. Swiss Finance Institute Research Paper No. 16–26. Zurich: University of Zurich.

Rohlin, D. and Ugolnitsky, G. 2018. Stackelberg Equilibria in Dynamic Deterministic Incentive Problem. *Automation and Remote Control* 79(4), 701–712.

Salanie, B. 2005. *The Economics of Contracts*. Cambridge: MIT Press.

Sannikov, Y. 2008. A Continuous-Time Version of the Principal–Agent Problem. *Review of Economic Studies* 75(3), 957–984.

Stole, L. 1997. *Lectures on the Theory of Contracts and Organizations*. Chicago, IL: University of Chicago.

Tricomi, F. 1957. *Integral Equations*. New York: Interscience Publishers, Inc.

5 Technology

The methodological analysis of the Enterprise paired with CA carried out in Chapters 1 and 2 made it possible to formulate the corresponding Enterprise Control Subproblems, one of the most important of which is the *technology management* (section 2.4).

Section 5.1 is devoted to formalizing the technology management problem. A review of models and methods of related fields of knowledge is presented in Section 5.2. Mathematical models reflecting the system-wide properties of the technology management process are presented in Sections 5.3–5.5.

5.1 TECHNOLOGY MANAGEMENT PROBLEM

The *technology of CA* has been defined (Chapter 1) as a system of conditions, criteria, forms, methods, and means for sequentially achieving a desired goal. In Section 2.4, *technology management* was defined as an activity for creating technology components in the form of corresponding information models and their integration, testing, use, and maintenance in an adequate state depending on the environment during the entire lifecycle of the CA.

An Enterprise is a complex system and, according to the concepts of *systems engineering* (Pyster and Olwell 2013, ISO/IEC/IEEE 15288:2015), a set of various models is needed to study the Enterprise, describing it from various viewpoints. Chapter 4 presents models of active systems that reflect the properties of the organized groups of people who are the foundation of an Enterprise. In Chapter 7, models and methods for planning the activities of an Enterprise as a whole will be given. In this chapter, we develop models that describe the system-wide features of the technology management process: the synthesis, integration, testing, and use of the technology of CA.

On the one hand, each technology component is determined by the characteristics of the Enterprise industry, the subject area in which the activity is performed. Therefore, any technology has specific, unique properties. However, all technologies have common, basic properties; we single them out and study them with mathematical methods.

1. Any technology, one way or another, evolves during the lifecycle of a CA (which, in fact, implements this technology). It is advisable to reflect the evolution of technology by the level of maturity of the technology, reflecting the possibility of productive use of technology under various conditions. Technology evolution models are developed in Section 5.3.
2. The technology of any complex activity necessarily has a complex internal structure that reflects the structure of activity goals. Models for integrating technology components are proposed in Section 5.4.

3. The existence of an external environment in which complex activity is implemented (as is, in fact, the technology) also requires its reflection in the models developed. Technology evolution models, taking into account the system-wide properties of the external environment, are presented in Section 5.5.

An integrated model of the technology management process, Figure 5.1, has been introduced and analyzed in Belov and Novikov (2020).

This model describes an Enterprise and its CA from the viewpoint of the creation and implementation of CA technology.

The integrated model illustrates the basic specificity of the evolution of the technology during the implementation of the lifecycle of CA itself: multiple cyclicality (see Figure 2.5).

First, during the creation or modernization of technology after direct synthesis (see item 1 in Figure 5.1), repeated testing of the (information models of the) technology components (item 2) is performed. If the testing is unsuccessful, a return to synthesis occurs (from d to a). Upon successful completion of the tests, the technology is repeatedly used in the cycle b → 3 → c → b → 3 .... If external conditions (for example, demand) change, the technology may become inadequate for them, which necessitates its modernization – a return from "c" to "a." And all these cycles together form the lifecycle of the corresponding element of CA.

Obviously, since each of the elements "1–2–3" of the model represents an element of CA, all of them, if necessary, can be decomposed in more detail according to the approaches introduced in Chapter 1.

The technology management process, specified by the integrated model, will be represented as a discrete-time process in which each time is associated with the implementation of precisely one CA element (one of the blocks 1–2–3 of the model in Figure 5.1) under precisely one state of the environment from a finite *set of possible states of the environment.*

If at some time the environment evolves into a new state never observed before, then an event of *uncertainty* occurs. This event leads to additional costs for the synthesis (or testing or adaptation, depending on what operation is being considered) of the technology component under the new conditions. When the state of the environment retakes this value at a later period, it is assumed that the technology is already mature enough to be productively used in this state of the environment, and no additional cost is required to manage it.

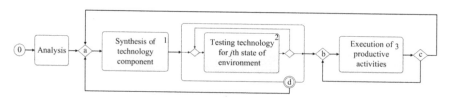

FIGURE 5.1   Integrated model of technology management.

The concept of environment uncertainty implies that the actor is unable to affect the choice of a current state of the environment; the uncertainty will be described using probabilistic methods.

Let the set of possible *states of the environment* be composed of K different values. Assume at each time that the environment takes on precisely one of them, regardless of the past states. Denote by p_k the probability that the environment takes on the k-th value (obviously, $\sum_{k=1}^{K} p_k = 1$).

At time t, the current state of the technology management process is described by a K-dimensional row vector $x_t = (x_{1t}, x_{2t}, \ldots, x_{kt}, \ldots, x_{Kt})$. Each of x_{kt} characterizes the local *technology maturity level* in relation to the k-th state of the external environment and takes the value:

  0 – if the external environment has not yet taken on the k-th state, and the technology has not yet been synthesized/tested/adapted in relation to it;
  1 – if the external environment has taken on the k-th state at least once, and therefore the technology for it has already been synthesized/tested/adapted.

Accordingly, the k-th element of the vector x_t may move from state 0 to 1 but not vice versa.

Therefore, the technology management process is characterized by the dynamics of the states of the environment: which values from the set of states the environment has already taken on (and how many times) and which it has not.

The technology maturity level (its readiness for productive use) at time t will be measured by the index $L_t = \sum_{k=1}^{K} x_{kt} p_k$, $0 \leq L_t \leq 1$ (note that $(1 - L_t)$ can also be used).

The value L_t gives the share of the states of the environment for which the technology has been synthesized/tested/adapted during the past t times, or the probability that at the next time $(t + 1)$ the environment will take one of its previous states. The value L_t is called the maturity level of the technology or, following the conventional approach of *learning models* (Jaber 2017), the *learning level* (accordingly, the sequence of its values is called the *learning curve*). Interestingly, the term "learning curve" is widespread with a similar meaning in modern science, starting with the Ebbinghaus "forgetting curves" (Ebbinghaus 1885), proceeding to the psychology of the 20th century (e.g., see the classical papers (Thurstone 1919, Thurstone 1930, Tolman 1934) and monographs (Atkinson et al 1967, Bush 1955, Hull 1943)) and the models suggested by Wright (Wright 1936) and his followers (Crawford 1944, Henderson 1984) (who consider the effect of learning on production costs in the aircraft industry), and up to the learning models of artificial neural networks.

In this setup, the technology management process can be considered from another viewpoint – as the sequential observation of different *series* of the well-known states of the environment that are interrupted by newly occurring ones. The length of such a series (from a newly observed state to the next one) has a Bernoulli (binomial) distribution parameterized by the learning level. This parameter is constant during each series and has a jump at the end point of the series when a new state is observed. Then, at each time t, the expected value of the current series length (till a nearest new state of the environment is observed, excluding this moment) can be calculated as $L_t (1 - L_t)^{-1}$. The series length corresponds to the number of repetitions required to increase the maturity (learning) level. In turn, this characterizes, e.g., the time cost of the next learning level increment (in fact, the cost of acquiring new knowledge). Therefore, in some cases the *expected series length* might be employed together with the learning level to describe the technology management process. It will be denoted by $N_t = L_t (1 - L_t)^{-1}$, where $L_t < 1$.

A natural formulation of the technology management problem is to reach a required technology maturity level as fast as possible or using as few resources as possible. Thus, the optimized and/or restricting parameters may be the consumption of resources or time.

Generally, the technology management process can be optimized by:

- partitioning all states of the environment into non-intersecting subsets so that the states from each subset are considered to be equivalent;
- choosing a sequence of the excessive number of all states of the environment to create tests and adoption of technology;
- redistributing these operations between the design level of a technology component and the component integration level;
- allocating limited resources among separate technology management operations;
- determining an admissible amount of attracted resources (in terms of risk) to manage all technology components.

Two technology management problems might be defined depending on the actor's knowledge about the environment.

The *first problem* (further referred to as basic) rests on the assumption that the list and probabilities of all possible states of the environment are constant and known to the actor (in other words, K and all $\{p_k\}$ are given, independent, and time-invariant). This problem surely arises and is basic in the following sense: the actor performs an initial synthesis of the CA technology and testing process using a definite set of all states of the environment. The basic problem is to derive a relation between the technology's maturity level and time and to optimize this relation in terms of the available resources.

The *second problem* is characterized by the *unknown properties of the environment*, i.e., the set and probabilities of all states of the environment (the set K) or at least some of the probabilities $\{p_k\}$ are either unknown to the actor or may vary. This problem arises during continuous repeated use of the technology when (due to the natural variability of the environment) the previously designed technology becomes inadequate in new conditions, which is identified as the result of productive activities. The second problem with the unknown properties of the environment is solved using the laws established for the first problem. Thus, our attention below will be focused on the first (basic) issue.

Complex technology is developed by integrating various components within the logical and cause–effect structures of CA. At the general system level, the logical models of any structural elements (with a nontrivial internal structure) of CA are equivalent and have a "fan" structure; see Chapter 1 for details. To put together cause–effect structures, the following list of integration tasks is sufficient: (a) sequential integration; (b) parallel conjunctive integration; (c) parallel disjunctive integration. In addition, a complex integration process that deserves analysis is (d) integration with "learning to learn," in which a technology component is created simultaneously with its technology. This complex case arises in "pioneering" innovations. For each integration process, the learning level of a complex technology component has to be optimized in terms of time and resources.

Thus, the study of the technology management process generates two CA technology management issues (the basic issue and the one with unknown properties of the environment) as well as the four integration tasks for the CA technology components (see cases (a)–(d) above), all being covered by the integrated model (Figure 5.1). All these tasks are studied in subsequent sections of this chapter.

5.2 KNOWN MODELS AND METHODS IN RELATED SCIENTIFIC DOMAINS

Formally speaking, the technology management process is the sequential repetition of cycles within the integrated model (Figure 5.1); see details in the previous subsections of this chapter. Such questions arise in many fields of knowledge (e.g., complex systems testing, software analysis, and testing), in which a large number of corresponding solutions are found. Let us consider a series of well-known models and methods for solving them:

- testing and verification of characteristics of complex systems (Ali and Yue 2015, Henriques 2012, Mikami and Kakazu 1993);
- large-scale manufacturing and improvement in its efficiency during adoption (Crawford 1944, Grant 2013, Gray et al 2016, Hax 1982, Henderson 1984, Ingram 2016, Jaber 2017)
- software testing (Aichernig and Schumi 2017, Alagoz and German 2017, Ali and Yue 2015, Bourque, P. and Fairley 2014, Legay et al 2010, Yizhen et al 2017);
- knowledge management and elicitation/acquisition (Orseau et al 2013, Stocia and Stack 2017, Wong, A. and Wang 2003) and machine learning (Sutton and Barto 2016);
- iterative learning in pedagogics, psychology, and human and zoophysiology (Chui and Wong 1986, Leibowitz 2010, Thurstone 1919, Thurstone 1930);
- knowledge testing for trainees in pedagogics (van der Linden and Hambleton 1996).

Like technology management, all these issues contain uncertainty and are often described using probabilistic models and/or the framework of random processes.

The testing procedure of complex systems (in particular, aircraft facilities) is represented as a hierarchical structure in which nodes describe the tests of elements, units, and systems. The efficiency of a product's components is assumed to have an exponential (or logistic) dependence on the duration of the tests; as a rule, the rate of growth of this efficiency is assumed to be proportional to the unreliability detected at a given time. The expected test times required to reach a given efficiency level and the corresponding costs are calculated at each level of the hierarchy. The total expected test time of a system (product) is the sum of the expected test times at each level of the hierarchy. Actually, the assumption that the efficiency of the system's components depends on the duration of the tests is not completely justified, while the integration of component tests by simply summing the average times seems to be a significant simplification (although this general framework can be used as a basis for further development and correction).

The optimization problem of the testing procedure is written using the well-known approximations of random functions in terms of their means and variances. The testing problems of various products and mathematical models are often posed as problems of hypothesis verification and experiment planning.

The potential improvement in manufacturing efficiency as the result of technology adoption has been discussed by economists since the early development of machines in the 19th century, but the per-unit cost reduction effect for large production outputs was first described by Wright only in 1936; see (Wright 1936). Wright's approach postulated an exponential model of the learning curve. Wright's model was generalized by Henderson (Boston Consulting Group) in the paper by Henderson (1984). During the research performed by Boston Consulting Group in the 1970s, the specific cost reduction effects were identified for various industrial sectors; they varied from 10 to 25% under a doubling of production output.

This topic remains relevant at the present time. For example, in management practice, the leading aerospace company, Boeing, takes into account and even plans to significantly reduce unit costs (primarily labor and time) in the development of new aircraft models (Gray 2016, Ingram 2016), which sometimes even leads to discussions about the legitimacy of reflecting such planned effects in official financial statements.

Model checking and a variant – statistical model checking – are popular methods to test complex systems and complex software (Aichernig and Schumi 2017, Henriques et al 2012). These methods are used for complex systems with a finite set of states and quantitative properties specified by logical expressions. Such an approach allows measuring the correspondence between system properties and their required values. A stochastic system is tested by verifying the hypothesis that its properties satisfy given requirements. Logical descriptions of the system can be used to integrate elementary tests into complex ones. General testing approaches were presented in many classical studies; for example, see the "Guide to the Software Engineering Body of Knowledge", version 3.0, in Bourque and Fairley (2014).

Another popular software testing method is regression testing and its numerous variations (Alagoz and German 2017). Regression testing is intended to verify the software in use and to prove its quality after changes and modernizations. Collections of tests are gradually growing in number following the rapid development of software, which makes the execution of all tests for each change very costly. Regression testing includes such techniques as the minimization, selection, and prioritization of tests, which are implemented as formal procedures. A software engineer eliminates all redundant test examples by minimizing the collection of tests, employs those tests directly connected with previous changes by selecting test examples, and adjusts the sequence of tests by prioritizing test examples, so that errors can be detected as fast as possible.

Among other common methods, we note model-based testing, various sequential testing procedures, and sequential analysis procedures (Shiryaev 1973), simulation modeling (Mikami and Kakazu 1993), and special testing methods for cyber-physical systems (Ali and Yue 2015).

In the paper by Mikami and Kakazu (1993), the coordinated planning problem for a group of autonomous agents (mobile robots) on a pendulum plane was considered. The goal of the group was to stabilize the plane. This problem was solved using an original collective learning procedure with the cyclic generation of learning signals and the statistical reinforcement of "skills."

Today, many descriptive models exist for the process of knowledge elicitation/acquisition; all of them implement sequential processes to analyze the subject matter and improve the models. Let us consider several examples as follows. In Wong and Wang (2003), a general decision support algorithm based on the analysis of large mixed data was suggested. As was claimed in Orseau et al (2013) and Stocia and Stack (2017), stochastic knowledge and deterministic knowledge supplement and improve each other; a stochastic model of acquired knowledge based on the diffusion approximation was also introduced. The paper by Orseau et al (2013) was dedicated to the optimal Bayesian agent – an algorithm that describes the process of knowledge elicitation in the course of sequential observations of a stochastic environment with a denumerable set of states. The algorithm rested on Solomonoff's theory of inductive inference.

In D. Chui and Wong (1986), methods to generalize knowledge acquired from empirical observations were considered. Knowledge was synthesized by a clustering algorithm using the identification of statistically significant events. The algorithm, with a probabilistic information measure, performed the grouping of ordered and unordered discrete data in two phases as follows. During cluster initiation, the distribution of the distances between nearest neighbors was analyzed to choose a proper clustering criterion for the samples. During cluster refinement, the clusters were regrouped using the event-covering method, which identified the subsets of statistically significant events.

Recall that learning is the process and result of acquiring *individual experience*. In pedagogics, psychology, and human and zoophysiology, *iterative learning* models (Novikov 1998) describe the process of learning in which a learned system (whether living, technical, or cybernetic) repeats some actions, trials, attempts, etc. over and over again to achieve a fixed goal under constant external conditions. In Novikov (1998), tens of well-known and widespread iterative learning models were surveyed and a general model combining the properties of separate models was formulated. Both the separate and general learning models have restrictions as follows. First, they postulate certain learning laws. Second, there are no proper integration processes of partial learning elements into a complex learning system.

In pedagogical measurements, the methods of item response theory (van der Linden and Hambleton 1996) have recently become very popular. This theory is intended for evaluating the latent (unobservable) parameters of respondents and test items using statistical measurement models. In item response theory, the relation between the values of the latent variables and the observable test results is defined as the conditional probability of respondents correctly answering test items. The conditional probability is given by a logistic curve or a Gaussian probability distribution. The most widespread models of this class are the Rush and Birnbaum models, which use the specific values of the coefficients of the logistic curve.

Summarizing this short overview of well-known results, we emphasize that the models mentioned are actually some elements of a cycle of the integrated model (Section 5.1) in a relatively simple form: (1) without the iterativeness and fractality of such cycles; (2) with the postulated character of basic laws (e.g., the exponential or logistic relation between the efficiency of the product's components and the duration of tests; the exponential or logistic relation between the learning level and time). Generally speaking, the basic laws are a consequence of more sophisticated processes that have to be analyzed and modeled. At the same time, the results of the methodological approach (Chapter 1) have been adopted to study the peculiarities of this cycle and reflect them using the general system integrated model (Figure 5.1). Consequently, this model further generalizes, specifies, and refines the well-known models.

5.3   TECHNOLOGY EVOLUTION AND MANAGEMENT

5.3.1   CORE PROPERTIES OF THE BASIC MODEL OF THE TECHNOLOGY EVOLUTION PROCESS

We now study the properties of the *technology evolution process* (as a constituent of technology management) and the properties of the learning level L_t, where K and all values $\{p_k\}$ are known to the CA actor.

This process (row vector x_t) represents a Markov chain with a finite number of states whose numbers y_t are formed from the elements of x_t by the rule $y_t = \sum_{k=1}^{K} x_{kt} 2^{k-1}$.

Then, the process y_t is also a Markov chain taking any integer values from 0 to

$$I = \sum_{k=1}^{K} 2^{k-1} = 2^K - 1, \text{ inclusive.}$$

We will construct the transition probability matrix $\Pi = \{\pi_{ij}; i=0, 1, \ldots, I; j=0, 1, \ldots, I\}$ of the process y_t. At the initial time $t=0$, the process y_t is in the 0th state $y_0 = 0$ ($x_{k0} = 0$ for all k) with probability 1. The process may move from state "0" only to those states with numbers 2^{k-1} with probabilities p_k as follows: to state "1" with probability p_1; to state "2" with probability p_2; to state "4" with probability p_3, and so on. The process may not stay in state "0."

From state "1," the process may not return to state "0"; it may stay in this state with probability p_1 and may move to the state $2^{k-1}+1$ with probability p_k for each $1 < k \leq K$.

Let us calculate the elements of the i-th row of the matrix Π, where $1 < i \leq I$. We consider the binary representation of the number i under the assumption that the first digit is least significant. We denote by $b(i,k)$ the value of the k-th digit in this representation; thus, $i = \sum_{k=1}^{K} b(i,k)2^{k-1}$.

The probability that the process will stay in the i-th state at the next time is

$$\pi_{ii} = \sum_{k=1}^{K} b(i,k)p_k.$$

The transition to any other state with a number $j < i$ is impossible ($\pi_{ij}=0$). For each k such that $x_k=0$, the probability of transition to the state $i+2^{k-1}$ is p_k. Finally, transitions to other states with numbers exceeding i are also impossible.

Thus, the elements of the transition probability matrix are given by

$$\pi_{ij} = \begin{cases} 0 & \text{if} \quad j \neq i+2^n, n=1,2,...,K, \\ \sum_{k=1}^{K} b(i,k)p_k & \text{if} \quad j=i, \\ p_n & \text{if} \quad j=i+2^n, \ n=1,2,...,K \text{ and } j \leq I, \end{cases} \quad \text{where } i=0,1,...,I \text{ and } j=0,1,...,I.$$

Then, the transition probability matrix Π of the Markov chain y_t is upper-triangular, and the state with the maximum number $I=2^K-1$ is absorbing: $\pi_{II}=1$ and $\pi_{Ij}=0$ for $j \neq I$.

We write the distribution of the state probabilities $q_{it}=\Pr(y_t=i)$ of this chain in the vector notation $q_t=(q_{0t}, q_{1t}, ..., q_{it}, ..., q_{It})$. At the initial time $t=0$, the distribution is $q_0=(1, 0, ..., 0)$. Hence, $q_t=q_{t-1}\Pi$ for any $t>0$ and $q_t=e_0\Pi^t = (1, 0, 0, ..., 0)\Pi^t$. Hereinafter, we denote by e_i a row vector of the appropriate dimension in which all elements are 0 except for the i-th one, which equals 1.

Let us divide all states of the *Markov chain* into groups by the number of units in their binary representations, i.e., $\sum_{k=1}^{K} b(i,k)$. These groups have two properties, one following from the other:

1) Any state from the l-th group can be reached from the 0th state in l steps.
2) Any state from the l-th group can be reached only from the states of the $(l-1)$-th group. There are $K+1$ groups, since l varies from 0 to K.

Proposition 5.1. The probability q_{it} of each state with number $0 < i < I$ from the l-th group satisfies the condition $q_{it} < l!t^{l-1}v^{t-l+1}$, where $0 < v < 1$ are some constants.

Proof of Proposition 5.1. Consider states from the first group; for each of them, $q_{it}=p_k^t$, where k is the number of the corresponding state of the environment, the following inequality then holds: $q_{it} < 1!t^0v_1^t$, where $v_1=\max\{p_k\} < 1$.

Let $q_{it} < l! t^{l-1} v_l^{t-l+1}$ for all states of the l-th group. The distribution of the state

probabilities of the Markov chain evolves in accordance with the law $q_{it} = \sum_{j=0}^{i-1} \pi_{ji} q_{jt-1}$

$+ \pi_{ii} q_{it-1}$. For any state from the $(l+1)$-th group, $q_{it} \equiv 0$ if $t < l$, and

$$q_{it} = \sum_{\theta=0}^{t-l} \pi_{ii}^{\theta} \sum_{j=0}^{i-1} \pi_{ji} q_{jt-1-\theta} = \sum_{j=0}^{i-1} \pi_{ji} \sum_{\theta=0}^{t-l} \pi_{ii}^{\theta} q_{jt-1-\theta} \quad \text{if } t \geq l. \text{ This gives the following}$$

bound   on q_{it}: $q_{it} = \sum_{j=0}^{i-1} \pi_{ji} \sum_{\theta=0}^{t-l} \pi_{ii}^{\theta} q_{jt-1-\theta} < \sum_{j=0}^{i-1} \pi_{ji} \sum_{\theta=0}^{t-l} \pi_{ii}^{\theta} l!(t-1-\theta)^{l-1} v_l^{t-l-\theta}$

$$< l!(t-1)^{l-1} \sum_{j=0}^{i-1} \pi_{ji} \sum_{\theta=0}^{t-l} \pi_{ii}^{\theta} v_l^{t-l-\theta} < t^{l-1}(l+1)!(t-l)(\max\{\pi_{ii}; v_l\})^{t-1} < (l+1)! t^l v_{l+1}^{t-l},$$

where $v_{l+1} = \max\{v_l; \max_i \{\pi_{ii}\}\}$ and the maximum is calculated over all states i belong-

ing to the $(l+1)$-th group.

Therefore, the inequality $q_{it} < (l+1)! t^l v_{l+1}^{t-l}$ holds for all states of the $(l+1)$-th
group.

If we denote $v = \max_i \{\pi_{ii}\}$, then $v_l \leq v$ for all l; therefore, $q_{it} < (l+1)! t^l v^{t-l}$. And
the desired result follows by mathematical induction for all i-th states except the I-th
one. The proof of Proposition 5.1 is complete. ●

Proposition 5.1 means that the probabilities of all states except the I-th one
decrease with a minimum time of $t^{l-1} v^{t-l+1}$; conversely, a stationary distribution of
the Markov chain y_t exists and is unique, $s = (0, 0, \ldots, 0, 1) = e_I$, which is the unique

solution of the matrix equation $s = s\Pi$ (or the system $s_i = \sum_{i=0}^{I} \pi_{ji} s_j$).

Hence, the evolution of the technology model described in this section has a
unique stable equilibrium – the state in which all possible states of the environment
are tested. In other words, any learning level (arbitrarily close to 1) can be reached
on a sufficiently large horizon.

Let us now study the *learning/maturity curve* – the behavior of the expected value

of the process $L_t = \sum_{k=1}^{K} x_{kt} p_k$. We denote by $E[\cdot]$ the expectation operator.

First of all, in accordance with Proposition 5.1, the learning level converges in
probability to 1: $\forall \varepsilon > 0$, $\lim_{t \to \infty} \{ \Pr(|L_t - 1| > \varepsilon) \} = 0$.

First, by the definition of the process* L_t, its increments are always nonnegative:
$\Delta L_t = L_t - L_{t-1} \geq 0$. In addition, the values of L_t and also the increments ΔL_t are
nonnegative and do not exceed 1. Second, the process L_t is also a Markov chain, i.e.,
L_t and ΔL_t are independent random variables for any t. Then,

---

* Recall that the learning curve L_t describes the probability that the environment will take a new value
at step $(t + 1)$. This probability is estimated using observations over t steps, inclusive.

$$E[L_t] = \sum_{k=1}^{K} p_k E[x_{kt}] = \sum_{k=1}^{K} p_k \left(1 - (1-p_k)^t\right) = 1 - \sum_{k=1}^{K} p_k (1-p_k)^t \qquad (5.1)$$

On the other hand, expression (5.1) of $E[L_t]$ can be obtained using the distribution of the state probabilities q_t: $E[L_t] = \sum_{i=1}^{I} \left(\sum_{k=1}^{K} b(i,k) p_k \right) q_{it} = e_0 \Pi^t \beta$, where β denotes a column vector composed of the elements $\sum_{k=1}^{K} b(i,k) p_k$. They, in turn, are the diagonal elements of the matrix Π.

From (5.1), the series length can be calculated as

$$N_t = E[L_t](1 - E[L_t])^{-1} = \left(1 - \sum_{k=1}^{K} p_k (1-p_k)^t\right)\left(\sum_{k=1}^{K} p_k (1-p_k)^t\right)^{-1}$$

Since $\Delta L_t = L_t - L_{t-1} \geq 0$, the first finite differences of the sequence $E[L_t]$ are strictly positive for all t. The formulas of the m-th differences, $m \geq 2$, are derived using the $(m-1)$-th differences in the following way:

$$\Delta E[L_t] = 1 - \sum_{k=1}^{K} p_k (1-p_k)^t - \left(1 - \sum_{k=1}^{K} p_k (1-p_k)^{t-1}\right) = \sum_{k=1}^{K} p_k^2 (1-p_k)^{t-1} > 0,$$

Generally, $\Delta^m[L_t] = (-1)^{m+1} \sum_{k=1}^{K} p_k^{m+1} (1-p_k)^{t-m}$.

Note that, for any time t, the finite differences of the learning curve form an alternating sequence whose values decrease by the absolute value ($|\Delta^m E[L_t]| > |\Delta^{m+1} E[L_t]|$). In addition, the first differences satisfy the inequality $1 - E[L_t] > \Delta E[L_t]$.

Thus, the following important result has been established.

Proposition 5.2. The learning curve $E[L_t]$ has several properties, as follows.

- At the initial time $t=0$, its value is $E[L_0]=0$.
- It increases monotonically: $\Delta E[L_t] > 0$.
- Its first finite differences are bounded by the inequality $1 - E[L_t] > \Delta E[L_t]$.
- Its growth rate decreases monotonically: $\Delta^2 E[L_t] < 0$ and $\Delta^3 E[L_t] > 0$.
- It has an asymptotic convergence to unity.

5.3.2 APPROXIMATIONS OF MATURITY/LEARNING CURVE

We will consider some approximations of the maturity/learning curve $E[L_t]$ (see formula (5.1)) depending on the probability distribution $P = \left\{ p_k; k = \overline{1, K}; \sum_{k=1}^{K} p_k = 1 \right\}$ of all possible states of the environment.

A) **Uniform distribution** P. For the sake of simplicity, we denote $\delta = 1/K$. Then,

$$E[L_t] = 1 - \sum_{k=1}^{K} \delta(1-\delta)^t = 1 - (1-\delta)^t = 1 - \exp(-\gamma t), \quad (5.2)$$

where $\gamma = \ln(1 + 1/(K-1))$ is the rate of variation of the learning level – the *rate of learning*.

The *exponential learning curve* (5.2) is classical for the theory of learning (see the survey in (Anzanello 2011) and also the pioneering book (Hull 1943)), and its analog in the finite-difference form is defined by $E[L_t] = E[L_{t-1}] + \gamma (1 - E[L_{t-1}]) = \gamma + (1 - \gamma) E[L_{t-1}]$.

At the same time, for the model under consideration, this curve is a special case that corresponds to the uniform distribution of all possible states of the environment.

In the uniform distribution case, the expected series length has an exponential growth, $N_t = \exp(\gamma t) - 1$. This is intuitively clear: with a further increase in the learning level (and hence the share of the "known" states of the environment), the acquisition of new knowledge requires more effort to "find" the new states.

The difference equation of N_t has the simple form $N_{t+1} = \exp(\gamma)N_t + \exp(\gamma) - 1$; hence, the expected series length grows multiplicatively.

For $K \gg 1$, the rate of learning becomes $\gamma = \ln(1 + 1/(K-1)) \approx 1/(K-1) \approx 1/K$, and

$$E[L_t] \approx 1 - \exp(-t / K). \quad (5.3)$$

As will be demonstrated in Section 5.5, the uniform distribution of all possible states of the environment actually maximizes the expected learning level.

B) **Distribution** (n, δ) (n highly probable states and $(K - n)$ lowly probable states with $\delta \ll 1/K$).

This distribution is given by

$$P = \{p_k = (1 - \delta(K-n))/n \text{ for } k = \overline{1, n}; p_k = \delta \text{ for } k = \overline{n+1, K}\}. \quad (5.4)$$

It makes sense to consider the case in which the probabilities $(1 - \delta(K - n))/n$ of the states from the first group are considerably greater than the probabilities δ of the states from the second group. The case in which these probabilities differ insignificantly can be well approximated by a uniform distribution (see above). In other words, let $(1 - \delta(K - n))/n \gg \delta$, which implies $\delta K \ll 1$. We find the learning curve for this distribution:

$$E[L_t] = 1 - \sum_{k=1}^{n} \frac{1-\delta(K-n)}{n}\left(1 - \frac{1-\delta(K-n)}{n}\right)^t - \sum_{k=n+1}^{K} \delta(1-\delta)^t$$

Since $\delta \ll 1/K$ and $n < N$, $(1 - 1/n) < (1 - \delta)$. Hence, for large t, distribution (5.4) tends to the uniform one: $E[L_t] \approx 1 - (K - n)\delta(1 - \delta)^t$.

For small t, the approximation is $E[L_t] \approx 1 - (1 - \delta(K - n))(1 - 1/n + \delta(K/n - 1))^t$.

C) **"Disturbed uniform" distribution**. Let the uniform distribution be defined on a "large" set of domains of all possible states of the environment in the following way:

$$P = \left\{ p_k; k = \overline{1, K}; \sum_{k=1}^{K} p_k = 1; p_k \ll 1; K \gg 1 \right\}. \tag{5.5}$$

For small t, the learning curve is approximated by

$$E[L_t] = 1 - \sum_{k=1}^{K} p_k(1 - p_k)^t \approx 1 - \sum_{k=1}^{K} p_k(1 - tp_k) = t \sum_{k=1}^{K} p_k^2. \tag{5.6}$$

i.e., it has a linear growth in t with the rate $\sum_{k=1}^{K} p_k^2$.

For large t, there are two possible behavior patterns of the learning curve as follows. If all domains of all possible states of the environment are nearly equivalent and their probabilities differ insignificantly ($p_k \approx 1/K$; $k = \overline{1, K}$), then the uniform distribution estimate (5.2) also holds. If a certain number n of the domains substantially differ from the others, then an adequate description is the approximation $E[L_t] \approx 1 - (1 - n/K)(1 - 1/K)^t$ (distribution B).

Interestingly, the analytical expressions (5.2), (5.3), and (5.6), as well as the properties of the learning curve $E[L_t]$ established within the current model, well match many conventional models of learning. However, the well-known models postulate the form of the learning curve or its equations, whereas the model suggested in this section describes the technology evolution/management process and learning – the design process – as a particular case. And the equations and properties of the learning curve are derived during model analysis.

5.3.3 Expected Maturity/Learning Time

In this section, the expected time to reach a required learning (maturity) level $L_{req} \in (0; 1)$ (the technology's maturity level) will be calculated. This is the expected time t at which

$$L_t = \sum_{k=1}^{K} x_{kt} p_k \geq L_{req}.$$

For this purpose, we study the behavior of the Markov chain y_t, in particular, the evolution of the probability distribution $q_{it} = \Pr(y_t = i)$ of its states. As established earlier, the initial distribution for $t=0$ is $q_0=(1, 0, ..., 0)$ and also $q_t=q_{t-1}\Pi$ for any $t>0$, $q_t=e_0\Pi^t=(1, 0, 0, ..., 0)\Pi^t$.

The matrix Π is upper-triangular, which indicates several properties of the matrix Π^t as follows.

- The determinant of the matrix Π (denoted by $\Delta\Pi$) is the product of all its diagonal elements: $\Delta\Pi = \prod\limits_{i=1}^{I} \pi_{ii}$.

- The matrix Π^t is also upper-triangular. (This fact follows from the multiplication rules of matrices.)
- The diagonal elements of the matrix Π^t are the powers of the diagonal elements of the matrix Π: $\pi^t_{ii}=(\pi_{ii})^t$.
- The determinant of the matrix Π^t is the product of the determinant Π:

$$\Delta\Pi^t = (\Delta\Pi)^t = \left(\prod_{i=1}^{I}\pi_{ii}\right)^t.$$

We will construct a "mask" – a column vector r of the same dimension as the row vector q_t – using the rule:

$$r_i = \begin{cases} 1, & \text{if } \sum\limits_{k=1}^{K} b(i,k)p_k < L_{req} \\ 0, & \text{if } \sum\limits_{k=1}^{K} b(i,k)p_k \geq L_{req} \end{cases} \qquad i = \sum\limits_{k=1}^{K} 2^k b(i,k) = 0,1,...,I$$

This mask vector "extracts" the states of the process y_t for which the learning levels are below the required one. Then, for each time, the probability that the learning level has reached or exceeded the required level is $\Pr(L_t \geq L_{req})=1 - q_t r$ or $\Pr(L_t < L_{req})=q_t r$. The probability that the time t_{reach} it takes to reach the required learning level exceeds the current time is $\Pr(t_{reach}>t)=q_t r$; the probability that the required learning level has been reached by the current time is $\Pr(t_{reach} \leq t)=1 - q_t r$. Obviously, $r_1=0$. In accordance with Proposition 5.1, the probabilities $\Pr(L_t<L_{req})=\Pr(t_{reach}>t)$ can be majorized by the function $l!t^l v^{t-l}$ as $t \to \infty$.

Consequently, $\Pr(t_{reach} > t) = \sum\limits_{i=0}^{I} r_i q_t < \sum\limits_{i=0}^{I} r_i l! t^l v^{t-l}$.

Using the relation $q_t = e_0 \Pi^t$, let us write $\Pr(t_{reach}>t)=q_t r=e_0 \Pi^t r$. Since $\Pr(t_{reach}>t-1)=\Pr(t_{reach}=t)+\Pr(t_{reach}>t)$, it follows that $\Pr(t_{reach}=t)=\Pr(t_{reach}>t-1)-\Pr(t_{reach}>t)$. The expected time can then be calculated as

$$\bar{t}_{reach} = \sum\limits_{t=0}^{\infty} t \Pr(t_{reach} = t) = \sum\limits_{t=0}^{\infty} t \left(\Pr(t_{reach} > t-1) - \Pr(t_{reach} > t) \right)$$

Because all probabilities $\Pr(t_{\text{reach}} > t)$ are majorized by $\sum_{i=0}^{I} r_i l! t^l v^{t-l}$, the series $t\Pr(t_{\text{reach}} > t)$

– when $t \to \infty$ – converges and has a finite sum: $\sum_{t=0}^{\infty} t\Pr(t_{\text{reach}} > t)$. As a result,

$$\bar{t}_{\text{reach}} = \sum_{t=0}^{\infty} t\Pr(t_{\text{reach}} = t) = \sum_{t=0}^{\infty} t\left(\Pr(t_{\text{reach}} > t-1) - \Pr(t_{\text{reach}} > t)\right) =$$

$$= \sum_{t=0}^{\infty} (t+1)\Pr(t_{\text{reach}} > t) - \sum_{t=0}^{\infty} t\Pr(t_{\text{reach}} > t) = \sum_{t=0}^{\infty} \Pr(t_{\text{reach}} > t).$$

Thus,

$$\bar{t}_{\text{reach}} = \sum_{t=0}^{\infty} \Pr(t_{\text{reach}} > t) = \sum_{t=0}^{\infty} e_0 \Pi^t r = e_0 \left(\sum_{t=0}^{\infty} \Pi^t \right) r = e_0 (E - \Pi)^{-1} r, \qquad (5.7)$$

where E is an identity matrix of the same dimension as the matrix Π.

The existence of the inverse $(E - \Pi)^{-1}$ follows from the upper-triangular property of the matrix $(E - \Pi)$. All its diagonal elements can be found from the above expression for π_{ij}, and their product is positive.

This theoretical development naturally leads to the following result:

Proposition 5.3. For any Markov chain, the expected time to first reach a state from the given set is $\bar{t}_{\text{reach}} = \sum_{t=0}^{\infty} \Pr(t_{\text{reach}} > t)$. If this series converges, then

$\bar{t}_{\text{reach}} = e_0 (E - \Pi)^{-1} r$.

Generally speaking, formula (5.7) can be used to calculate $\bar{t}_{\text{reach}}$ depending on the probability distribution $\{p_k; k = 1, 2, \ldots, K\}$ of all possible states of the environment (as the values p_k are taken into account through the matrix Π) and also on the required learning level (as the value L_{req} is taken into account through the vector m). Unfortunately, formula (5.7) is not constructive, because neither the probabilities p_k nor the level L_{req} enter it in explicit form. Furthermore, the considerable dimensions of the matrix Π ($2^K \times 2^K$) make the use of (5.7) difficult in practice.

In some cases, simpler and more constructive expressions can be obtained. Let us consider one of them – the uniform distribution $\{p_k = 1/K = \delta; k = 1, 2, \ldots, K\}$ of all possible states of the environment. In this case, instead of the Markov chain y_t with the values $i = 0, 1, \ldots I$, consider a chain $\tilde{y}_t$ whose values correspond to the number of states of the environment for which the technology has been tested. In other words, the chain $\tilde{y}_t$ takes values from 0 to K, inclusive. Then, $L_t = \delta \tilde{y}_t$, and the transition probabilities have the form

$$\pi_{ij} = \begin{cases} 0 & \text{if} \quad j < i \text{ or } j > i+1, \\ 1-\delta i & \text{if} \quad j = i+1, \\ \delta i & \text{if} \quad j = i, \end{cases} \qquad \text{where } i = 0,1,...,K.$$

The matrix $(E - \Pi)$ is then upper-triangular, band matrix, and has the elements

$$\varepsilon_{ij} = \begin{cases} 0 & \text{if} \quad j < i \text{ or } j > i+1, \\ 1-\delta i & \text{if} \quad j = i, \\ \delta i - 1 & \text{if} \quad j = i+1, \end{cases} \qquad \text{where } i = 0,1,...,K.$$

The inverse $(E - \Pi)^{-1}$ is also an upper-triangular matrix with the elements

$$\varepsilon_{ij}^{-} = \begin{cases} 0 & \text{if} \quad j < i, \\ (1-\delta i)^{-1} & \text{if} \quad i \le j < K, \quad \text{for } i = 0,1,...,K. \\ 1 & \text{if} \quad j = K, \end{cases}$$

The operation $(1, 0, 0, ..., 0)(E - \Pi)^{-1} r$ "cuts" the first row from the matrix $(E - \Pi)^{-1}$ and sums those elements of this row for which $\sum_{k=1}^{K} x_k p_k < L_{\text{req}}$. In the case of uniform distribution, the sum consists of the first $L_{\text{req}}/\delta = KL_{\text{req}}$ elements, and the expected time to reach the required learning level L_{req} is

$$\bar{t}_{\text{reach}} = \sum_{i=0}^{KL_{\text{req}}} (1-\delta i)^{-1} = \sum_{i=0}^{KL_{\text{req}}} K(K-i)^{-1} = K \sum_{j=K(1-L_{\text{req}})}^{K} j^{-1}$$

For $K \gg 1$, the value $\bar{t}_{\text{reach}}$ has the compact approximation

$$\bar{t}_{\text{reach}} = \sum_{i=0}^{KL_{\text{req}}} \frac{K}{K-i} = K \sum_{i=0}^{KL_{\text{req}}} \frac{1}{1-K^{-1}i} K^{-1} \approx K \int_0^{KL_{\text{req}}} \frac{1}{1-K^{-1}x} K^{-1}dx = -K \ln(1-K^{-1}x)\Big|_0^{KL_{\text{req}}},$$

and

$$\bar{t}_{\text{reach}} \approx -K \ln(1-L_{\text{req}}). \tag{5.8}$$

Note that expression (5.8) coincides with the approximate solution $\hat{t}$ of the equation $E[L_t] = 1 - (1-\delta)^t = L_{\text{req}}$ (see (5.2)), for which $\hat{t} = \ln(1 - L_{\text{req}})/\ln(1 - \delta) \approx -\ln(1 - L_{\text{req}})/\delta = K\ln(1 - L_{\text{req}})$.

The special case of the expected time to reach the "absolute" learning level $L_t = 1$ is studied in Appendix 5.1, and the expression for the expected time in this case is formulated:

$$T_{L=1} = \sum_{k=1}^{I} (-1)^{k+1} \sum_{i_1;i_2;...;i_k} \left(\sum_{j=1}^{k} p_{i_j} \right)^{-1}. \tag{5.9}$$

Thus, the properties of the technology evolution/management process and expected learning time in the basic model are studied in this section.

5.3.4 EXTENSION OF THE BASIC MODEL OF THE TECHNOLOGY EVOLUTION PROCESS

We will expand the basic model with the effects of environmental variability and more complex dynamics of local levels of technology maturity – elements of the process x_t (see Section 5.1).

As in the basic model (Section 5.3.1), we assume that the external environment in each period can take one of K possible states, regardless of previous values, all the probabilities of the onset of states $\{p_k\}$ are known, and $\sum_{k=1}^{K} p_k \equiv 1$.

We now assume a more complicated process of technology evolution.

At the first occurrence of the k-th state, synthesis/testing/adaptation of technology with respect to state k ($x_{kt}=1$) occurs with a known probability $0 \leq p_{\tilde{k}} \leq 1$, and with a probability of $1 - p_{\tilde{k}}$, this change does not happen ($x_{kt}=0$), that is, $\Pr(x_{kt+1}=1|x_{kt}=0)=p_k p_{\tilde{k}}$.

After the synthesis/testing/adaptation of the technology at the k-th state has occurred ($x_{kt}=1$), the local maturity level x_{kt} changes as follows at each subsequent period of time $t+1$:

- If the external environment has adopted a state other than k, the local maturity level does not change: $x_{kt+1}=x_{kt}$.
- If the external environment has taken the state k, then, with a probability of $0 \leq p_k^* \leq 1$, the local maturity level reached is "forgotten" (obviously, the "forgetting" effect in this model is equivalent to the effect of the evolution of the external environment), $x_{kt+1}=0$, and, with a probability of $1 - p_k^*$, doesn't change: $x_{kt+1}=x_{kt}$, that is, $\Pr(x_{kt+1}=0|x_{kt}=1)=p_k p_k^*$.

The expectation of the local maturity level at the k-th state $E[x_{kt}]$ is equal to $\Pr(x_{kt}=1)$, the probability that $x_{kt}=1$, then

$$E[x_{kt+1}] = \Pr(x_{kt+1}=1) = \Pr\left(x_{kt+1}=1|x_{kt}=1\right)\Pr\left(x_{kt}=1\right) + \Pr\left(x_{kt+1}=1|x_{kt}=0\right)\Pr\left(x_{kt}=0\right) =$$

$$= \left(1 - p_k p_k^*\right)E[x_{kt}] + p_k p_{\tilde{k}}\left(1 - E[x_{kt}]\right) = p_k p_{\tilde{k}} + \left(1 - p_k p_{\tilde{k}} - p_k p_k^*\right)E[x_{kt}].$$

Given $E[x_{k0}] \equiv 0$, we obtain $E[x_{kt}] = \dfrac{p_{\tilde{k}}}{p_{\tilde{k}} + p_k^*}\left(1 - (1 - p_k(p_{\tilde{k}} + p_k^*))^t\right)$.

We then find the learning curve in the form

$$E[L_t] = \sum_{k=1}^{K} p_k \frac{p_{\tilde{k}}}{p_{\tilde{k}} + p_k^*}\left(1 - (1 - p_k(p_{\tilde{k}} + p_k^*))^t\right). \tag{5.10}$$

It is easy to see that when maturation occurs with a probability of 1 at the first occurrence of a new state ($p_{\tilde{k}}=1$), and forgetting does not occur ($p_k^*=0$), the expression for the maturity/learning curve in the extended model is reduced to the base one.

Let us analyze the finite differences of the maturity/learning curve $E[L_t]$.

Similarly to the way in which it was done for the maturity/learning curve of the base model, it is easy to get an expression for the m-th differences:

$$\Delta^m E[L_t] = (-1)^{m+1} \sum_{k=1}^{K} p_k^{m+1} p_{\tilde{k}} (p_{\tilde{k}} + p_k^*)^{m-1} \left(1 - p_k(p_{\tilde{k}} + p_k^*)\right)^{t-m}.$$

When $\forall\, k\ p_k(p_{\tilde{k}}+p_k^*)<1$ for the maturity/learning curve in the extended model, the properties of the curve of the base model are valid (Proposition 3.2):

- at the initial moment $t=0$, its value is zero: $E[L_0]=0$;
- it monotonically increases: $\Delta E[L_t]>0$;
- its growth rate decreases monotonically: $\Delta^2 E[L_t]<0$ and $\Delta^3 E[L_t]>0$;
- its finite differences for any time t form an alternating sequence whose values decrease modulo: $\left|\Delta^m E[L_t]\right| > \left|\Delta^{m+1} E[L_t]\right|$;

- $\lim\limits_{t\to\infty} E[L_t] = \sum\limits_{k=1}^{K} p_k \dfrac{p_{\tilde{k}}}{p_{\tilde{k}} + p_k^*}.$

In the case of a uniform distribution and the same probabilities of maturation and forgetting for all states ($p_{\tilde{k}}=p^{\tilde{}}$ and $p_k^*=p^*\ \forall k$), the maturity/learning curve is also exponential:

$$E[L_t] = \frac{p^{\tilde{}}}{p^{\tilde{}} + p^*} \sum_{k=1}^{K} \frac{1}{K}\left(1-\left(1-\frac{1}{K}(p^{\tilde{}}+p^*)\right)^t\right) = \frac{p^{\tilde{}}}{p^{\tilde{}} + p^*}\left(1-\left(1-\frac{p^{\tilde{}}+p^*}{K}\right)^t\right)$$

We now consider the case where the condition $p_k(p_{\tilde{k}}+p_k^*)<1$ is not satisfied.

Suppose that there is a certain state of the external environment (we assume that its number is $k=1$) for which $p_1(p_{\tilde{1}}+p_1^*)>1$. Since $p_{\tilde{1}}\leq1$ and $p_1^*\leq1$, there must be $p_1>1/2$, which implies that the condition $p_k(p_{\tilde{k}}+p_k^*)<1$ can be violated for no more than one state of the external environment.

It also follows that the probability of the occurrence of this state is greater than the probability of the occurrence of all other states combined. In this case, all finite differences form time-alternating sequences, and the maturity/learning curve represents some "damped oscillatory process" (since $|\Delta^m E[L_t]|>|\Delta^{m+1}E[L_t]|$ remains valid).

Let us turn to a description of models for integrating technology components.

5.4   INTEGRATION OF TECHNOLOGY COMPONENTS

We will consider the *integration* of partial *technology components*, each described by the basic model, as the following processes: (A) sequential; (B) parallel conjunctive; (C) parallel disjunctive; (D) parallel evolution/learning with complete information exchange; (E) integration with "learning to learn."

To examine their properties, consider the management process of several technology components with an appropriate integration of their results. The states of partial processes are Markov chains with the properties studied in Section 5.3. Then, an integrated process will also evolve as a Markov chain on the state set defined by the direct product of the state sets of the partial processes.

Following the same approach as before, we introduce a $\tilde{K}$-dimensional process

$$\tilde{x}_t = (x_{1t}, x_{2t}, \ldots x_{kt}, \ldots x_{\tilde{K}t}, \quad \tilde{K} = \sum_{m=1}^{M} K^m, \text{ each element of which, } x_{kt}, \text{ reflects a local}$$

maturity level in the corresponding state of the environment (in a new state set) and takes the value 0 or 1. We also introduce a process $\tilde{y}_t$ that reflects the number of the current state of the process $\tilde{x}_t$. Both processes $\tilde{x}_t$ and $\tilde{y}_t$ are Markov chains. The transition probability matrix of the process $\tilde{y}_t$ is upper-triangular, and this process satisfies Proposition 5.1 (on the asymptotic behavior of the probability distribution of states) and Proposition 5.3 (on the expected time to reach a given maturity/learning level).

5.4.1 PARALLEL AND SEQUENTIAL MATURING/LEARNING

A. Let the integration process be intended to "mature" all partial technology components (the conjunction of all M partial components). Then, the level $L_t^{1\ldots M}$ (the maturity level of complex integrated technology) equals the probability that in the next period of time all the states of the environment in all particular processes will occur, for each of which an appropriate technology component is mature ($x_{kt} = 1$). This probability, in turn, is the product of the maturity/learning levels

L_t^m of all partial technology components: $L_t^{1\ldots M} = \prod_{m=1}^{M} L_t^m$. Consequently,

$$E\left[L_t^{1\ldots M}\right] = \prod_{m=1}^{M} E\left[L_t^m\right] = \prod_{m=1}^{M}\left[1 - \sum_{k=1}^{K} p_k^m (1 - p_k^m)^t\right]. \tag{5.11}$$

Formula (5.7), which determines the expected time it takes to reach a required learning level of a single technology component, can easily be extended to the case of M elements as follows:

$$\bar{t}_{A \text{ reach}} = \sum_{t=0}^{\infty} \Pr(t_{A \text{ reach}} > t) = \sum_{t=0}^{\infty} \Pr\left(\max_m\{t_{m \text{ reach}}\} > t\right) = \sum_{t=0}^{\infty}\left(1 - \prod_{m=1}^{M}(1 - e_0 \Pi_m{}^t r_m)\right). \tag{5.12}$$

If the management process of all technology components has the same characteristics, then

$$\bar{t}_{A \text{ reach}} = \sum_{t=0}^{\infty}\left(1-(1-e_0\Pi'r)^M\right) = \sum_{t=0}^{\infty}\left(\sum_{m=1}^{M} C_M^m(-1)^{m-1}(e_0\Pi'r)^m\right)$$

$$= M\sum_{t=0}^{\infty} e_0\Pi'r + \sum_{t=0}^{\infty}\left(\sum_{m=2}^{M-1} C_M^m(-1)^{m-1}(e_0\Pi'r)^m\right) + (-1)^{M-1}\sum_{t=0}^{\infty}(e_0\Pi'r)^M.$$

Using the sequence of the expected times $\bar{t}_{A \text{ reach}}$ for different increasing values M, we

can calculate the first and second differences $\Delta\bar{t}_M = \sum_{t=0}^{\infty} e_0\Pi'r(1-e_0\Pi'r)^{M-1}$ and

$\Delta^2\bar{t}_M = -\sum_{t=0}^{\infty}(e_0\Pi'r)^2(1-e_0\Pi'r)^{M-2}$. Clearly, $\bar{t}_{A \text{ reach}}$ grows with M, but the rate of

growth decreases with M. In addition, the first differences are bounded above and below:

$$\bar{t}_{\text{reach}} - \sum_{t=0}^{\infty}(e_0\Pi'r)^2 = \sum_{t=0}^{\infty} e_0\Pi'r(1-e_0\Pi'r) \le \Delta\bar{t}_M < \sum_{t=0}^{\infty} e_0\Pi'r = \bar{t}_{\text{reach}}.$$

B. Let all partial processes be independently implemented in parallel and also let the integration process be intended to create at least one of the partial components (the disjunction of M partial components). Then, the "non-maturity" level of the complex technology is the share of the "non-matured" states of the complex environment,

$1-L_t^{1-M} = \prod_{m=1}^{M}\left(1-L_t^m\right)$, and hence

$$E\left[L_t^{1-M}\right] = 1 - \prod_{m=1}^{M}\left[\sum_{k=1}^{K} p_k^m\left(1-p_k^m\right)^t\right]. \tag{5.13}$$

In this case, the expected time needed to reach a required learning level of M elements is calculated as

$$\bar{t}_{B \text{ reach}} = \sum_{t=0}^{\infty} \Pr(t_{B \text{ reach}} > t) = \sum_{t=0}^{\infty} \Pr\left(\min_m\{t_{m \text{ reach}}\} > t\right) = \sum_{t=0}^{\infty}\left(\prod_{m=1}^{M}(e_0\Pi_m{'}r_m)\right). \tag{5.14}$$

If the partial processes have the same characteristics, then

$$\bar{t}_{B \text{ reach}} = \sum_{t=0}^{\infty}\left(\prod_{m=1}^{M}(e_0\Pi_m{'}r_m)\right) = \sum_{t=0}^{\infty}(e_0\Pi'r)^M.$$

For the parallel implementation of several partial processes with the same characteristics (cases A and B), the expected time is

$$\bar{t}_{A\text{ reach}} = M\bar{t}_{\text{reach}} + \sum_{t=0}^{\infty}\left(\sum_{m=2}^{M-1}C_M^m(-1)^{m-1}(e_0\Pi^t r)^m\right)+(-1)^{M-1}\bar{t}_{B\text{ reach}},$$

where $\bar{t}_{\text{reach}}$, $\bar{t}_{A\text{ reach}}$, and $\bar{t}_{B\text{ reach}}$ denote the expected times of maturation of a partial process, all M partial processes, and at least one M partial process, respectively. In addition, the following bounds hold:

$$M\bar{t}_{\text{reach}} - (M-1)\bar{t}_{B\text{ reach}} \leq \bar{t}_{A\text{ reach}} < M\bar{t}_{\text{reach}}.$$

For the parallel implementation of two partial processes with the same characteristics (cases A and B), the expected time formula gives $\bar{t}_{A\text{ reach}} = 2\bar{t}_{\text{reach}} - \bar{t}_{B\text{ reach}}$. Hence, the expected times are related by $\bar{t}_{\text{reach}} = (\bar{t}_{A\text{ reach}} + \bar{t}_{B\text{ reach}})/2$.

C. Let two technology components be managed sequentially, so that the second component is initiated directly after the completion of the first one. This case is described by two independent Markov chains: the second chain starts evolving from a known state as soon as the state of the first chain reaches a given maturity/learning level. Such a complex technology consists of two components, and the second component can be designed only after the completion of the first one. The probability distribution of the completion time of this complex technology – the time to reach a given maturity/learning level for the second chain – is the convolution of the probability distributions of the times for both chains. This law can be used to calculate the integrated maturity/learning curve and the expected maturity/learning time as the sum of the expected times of the partial technologies.

D. Let a technology component be independently synthesized/tested/adapted in parallel within several (M) processes with complete information exchange. Then, M independent actions are executed during one time period and, hence,

$$E\left[L_t^{1\|M}\right] = 1 - \sum_{k=1}^{K} p_k (1-p_k)^{Mt}. \tag{5.15}$$

The expected time to reach a required maturity/learning level can be calculated as

$$\bar{t}_{\text{reach}} = \sum_{t=0}^{\infty} \Pr(t_{\text{reach}} > t) = \sum_{t=0}^{\infty} e_0\Pi^{Mt}r = e_0\left(E-\Pi^M\right)^{-1}r. \tag{5.16}$$

As is easily demonstrated, the maturity/learning curves (5.11), (5.13), and (5.15) satisfy all statements of Proposition 5.2.

5.4.2   COMPLEX INTEGRATION: "LEARNING TO LEARN"

Let us consider two processes that are implemented simultaneously:

- process "A" – "core" technology evolution;

- process "B" – evolution of the technology of process "A" (synthesis/testing/adaptation of the technology of process "A").

Consider that the intensity of process "A" varies according to the maturity level of process "B". Let a level $L_t = \sum_{k=1}^{K} x_{kt} p_k$ describe the "core" technology evolution (process "A"), and level $\tilde{L}_t = \sum_{j=1}^{J} \tilde{x}_{jt} q_j$ describe process "B" – the evolution of the technology of the synthesis/testing/adaptation of process technology "A."

Processes L_t and $\tilde{L}_t$ will be assumed to be statistically independent.

At each period t, the "core" technology is managed with the probability $\tilde{L}_t$ or "skipped" with the probability $1 - \tilde{L}_t$: the state of the environment is not considered and the processes x_{kt} don't change.* Consequently,

$$E[x_{kt+1}|x_{kt}] = \begin{cases} x_{kt} & \text{with probability } 1 - \sum_{j=1}^{J} \tilde{x}_{jt} q_j, \\ x_{kt} + (1 - x_{kt}) p_k & \text{with probability } \sum_{j=1}^{J} \tilde{x}_{jt} q_j, \end{cases}$$

where $E[\cdot|x_{kt}]$ denotes the conditional expectation operator given x_{kt}.

Then, $E[x_{kt+1}|x_{kt}] = x_{kt} + \Gamma_t p_k (1 - x_{kt})$, where $\Gamma_t = E\left[\sum_{j=1}^{J} q_j \tilde{x}_{jt}\right] = 1 - \sum_{j=1}^{J} q_j (1 - q_j)^t$.

Switching from conditional to unconditional expectations yields the finite-difference equation, which allows us to sequentially calculate $E[x_{kt}]$ for any $t \geq 0$:

$$E[x_{kt+1}] = E[x_{kt}] + \Gamma_t p_k (1 - E[x_{kt}]). \tag{5.17}$$

We introduce the notation $\Psi_t = 1 - E[x_{kt}]$ (or $E[x_{kt}] = 1 - \Psi_t$). Then, $E[x_{kt+1}] = 1 - \Psi_{t+1} = \Psi_t \Gamma_t p_k + 1 - \Psi_t$, and $\Psi_{t+1} = \Psi_t (1 - \Gamma_t p_k)$.

Since $\Psi_0 = 1$, it follows that $\Psi_t = \prod_{\tau=0}^{t-1} (1 - \Gamma_\tau p_k)$ and, consequently

$$E[x_{kt}] = 1 - \prod_{\tau=0}^{t-1} (1 - \Gamma_\tau p_k) = 1 - \prod_{\tau=0}^{t-1} \left(1 - p_k + p_k \sum_{j=1}^{J} q_j (1 - q_j)^\tau\right).$$

---

* This model may have an alternative interpretation as follows. Checks are performed at each step, while a technology for a new state is designed with some probability determined by a metaprocess. In the logistic model, this probability is equal to the learning level in the process itself; in the hyperbolic model, it is equal to the probability of "error" raised to some power with the proportionality factor μ.

And then,

$$E[L_t] = \sum_{k=1}^{K} p_k E[x_{kt}] = \sum_{k=1}^{K} p_k \left(1 - \prod_{\tau=0}^{t-1} (1 - \Gamma_\tau p_k) \right)$$

$$= 1 - \sum_{k=1}^{K} p_k \prod_{\tau=0}^{t-1} \left(1 - p_k + p_k \sum_{j=1}^{J} q_j (1 - q_j)^\tau \right). \tag{5.18}$$

Let us study in detail the sequence $E[x_{kt}]$ defined by expression (5.17). We calculate the first differences of the sequence: $\Delta E[x_{kt}] = \Psi_t \Gamma_t p_k$. Note that $\Delta E[x_{kt}]|_{t=0} = 0$ for any p_k because $\Gamma_0 = 0$ and $\Delta E[x_{kt}] > 0$ for any $t > 0$. In other words, $E[x_{kt}]$ grows for $t > 1$, which seems intuitively clear. Let us calculate the second differences:

$$\Delta^2 E[x_{kt}] = \Gamma_{t+1} p_k \left(\Psi_t - \Psi_t \Gamma_t p_k \right) - \Gamma_t p_k \Psi_t = p_k \Psi_t \left(\Gamma_{t+1} (1 - \Gamma_t p_k) - \Gamma_t \right) \tag{5.19}$$

Above all, $\Delta^2 E[x_{kt}]|_{t=0} = p_k \Gamma_1 > 0$. However, Γ_t monotonically increases from 0 and asymptotically converges to 1 as $t \to \infty$. Then, $\Delta^2 E[x_{kt}]|_{t\to\infty} = -p_k^2 \Psi_t < 0$ and $\Delta^2 E[x_{kt}]|_{t\to\infty} \to 0-$.

The maturity/learning curve $E[L_t] = \sum_{k=1}^{K} p_k E[x_{kt}]$ is a linear combination of the processes $\Delta E[x_{kt}]$ with strictly positive coefficients. Hence, the first and second differences of the curve satisfy all statements formulated for $E[x_{kt}]$. More specifically,

- $E[L_t]|_{t=0} = 0$;
- $\Delta E[L_t]|_{t=0} = 0$ and $\Delta E[L_t] > 0$ for all $t > 0$ (the learning curve increases in t from 0 and asymptotically converges to 1);
- $\Delta^2 E[L_t]|_{t=0} > 0$, $\Delta^2 E[L_t]|_{t\to\infty} < 0$ and $\Delta^2 E[L_t]|_{t\to\infty} \to 0-$ (the learning curve has an *inflection point*, being strictly convex on the left and strictly concave on the right of it).

Let us consider an example of "learning to learn." Let all possible states of the environment be uniformly distributed, $P = \{p_k = 1/K; k = \overline{1,K}\}$, and also $Q = \{q_j = 1/J; j = \overline{1,J}\}$. Using the notation $\eta = 1/J$, we write

$$G_t = E\left[\sum_{j=1}^{J} q_j \tilde{x}_{jt} \right] = 1 - \sum_{j=1}^{J} J^{-1} (1 - J^{-1})^t = 1 - (1 - J^{-1})^t = 1 - (1 - \eta)^t.$$

The corresponding maturity/learning curve has the form

$$E[L_t] = 1 - \prod_{\tau=0}^{t-1} \left(1 - \delta \left(1 - (1-\eta)^\tau \right) \right) \tag{5.20}$$

The second difference formula (5.19) can be employed to estimate the inflection point t of the learning curve (5.20) in the case of complex technologies ($K \gg 1, J \gg 1$, and $K < J$). The resulting estimate is $\hat{t} \approx \sqrt{KJ + 0.25K^2} - 0.5K$.

We will write (5.20) in the equivalent form $E[L_t] = 1 - \exp[\sum_{\tau=0}^{k-1} \ln(1 - \delta \exp(-\varphi\tau))]$, where $\varphi = \ln(1 + 1/(J-1))$. Then,

$$E[L_t] = E[L_{t-1}] + \delta\left(1 - (1-\eta)^{t-1}\right)\prod_{\tau=0}^{k-2}\left(1 - \delta\left(1 - (1-\eta)^\tau\right)\right) =$$

$$= E[L_{t-1}] + (1 - E[L_{t-1}])\delta(1 - (1-\eta)^{t-1}) = \beta_t + (1 - \beta_t)E[L_{t-1}],$$

where $\beta_t = \delta(1 - (1-\eta)^{t-1}) = \delta(1 - \exp(-\varphi(t-1)))$.

Thus, learning curve (5.20) is a "generalization" of learning curve (5.2) in which the coefficients $\{\beta_t\}$ of the difference equation depend on the time variable.

Let us consider several special cases of "learning to learn" in which the intensity of the technology evolution/management process depends on the technology maturity level achieved. Moreover, this dependence can be either increasing (see the model of the logistic learning curve below) or decreasing (see the model of the hyperbolic learning curve below).

This class of management processes will be formally called *auto-learning*.

Logistic learning curve. Consider an important special case of "learning to learn" as follows. For a sufficiently large number of practical situations, the intensity of the synthesis/testing/adaptation process is proportional to the maturity/learning level: $\Gamma_t = \mu E[L_t]$.

In fact, when testing new (e.g., aerospace or transport) equipment or commissioning new production facilities, at the first stages the product or facility is often tested for a limited set of operating modes (bench and ground tests, idling, etc.). As experience is gained, the range of modes is expanded to the complete set of all possible modes and conditions of the environment, and a transition to standard use takes place, which well matches the formal assumption that the "rate of maturation/learning" is proportional to the level reached.

This situation corresponds to a special case of the self-learning model in which the design process $\tilde{L}_t$ of the technology coincides with its adoption process L_t.

We will rewrite the difference equation (5.17) in a slightly modified form as follows and analyze it:

$$\Delta E[x_{kt+1}] = \Gamma_t p_k \left(1 - E[x_{kt}]\right) \tag{5.21}$$

If all states of the environment are equally probable ($p_k = \delta = 1/K$), then the difference equation $\delta\Delta E[x_{kt+1}] = \Gamma_t \delta^2(1 - E[x_{kt}]) = \Gamma_t \delta^2 - \Gamma_t \delta(\delta E[x_{kt}])$ follows from (5.21). Summation of these expressions over k yields

$$\Delta E[L_{t+1}] = \Gamma_t K \delta^2 - \Gamma_t \delta E[L_t] = \Gamma_t \delta(1 - E[L_t]) \tag{5.22}$$

For $\Gamma_t = \mu E[L_t]$, the difference equation of the learning level takes the form (a similar result for the continuous-time model was established in (Leibowitz et al 2010))

$$\Delta E[L_{t+1}] = \mu \delta E[L_t](1 - E[L_t]) \tag{5.23}$$

Equation (5.23) represents a difference analog of the differential equation $dx/dt = \beta x (1 - x)$, where $\beta = \mu\delta$, whose solution is the *logistic learning curve*, a classical concept in the theory of learning; for example, see the survey in (Novikov 1998). The discrete form of the logistic curve is described by

$$E[L_t] = \cfrac{1}{1 + \left(\cfrac{1}{\lambda} - 1\right)\exp(-\beta t)} \tag{5.24}$$

This function monotonically increases from $\lambda > 0$ (at $t=0$) to 1 (as $t \to +\infty$).

As a rule, the solutions of similar difference and differential equations are not functions of the same form; generally speaking, the logistic curve in the discrete form (5.24) is not a solution of (5.23). Therefore, we will establish conditions under which function (5.24) approximates the solution of equation (5.23) well.

For the sake of local simplifications, we introduce the compact notation $x_t = (1 + ba^t)^{-1}$ for function (5.24).

First, we will prove that the difference equation describing (5.24) will turn into the differential equation $dx/dt = \beta x (1 - x)$ as $\Delta t \to 0$. (Here, Δt denotes the time increment.)

In view of the compact notation, we write $x_{t+\Delta t} = (1 + ba^{t+\Delta t})^{-1}$ and further transform this expression. The following chain of transformations is correct as $\Delta t \to 0$ (in fact, under the condition $\ln(a)\Delta t \ll 1$):

$$x_{t+\Delta t} = \frac{1}{1 + ba^{t+\Delta t}} \approx \frac{1}{1 + ba^t(1 + \ln(a)\Delta t)} = \frac{1}{1 + ba^t}\frac{1}{1 + ba^t(1 + ba^t)^{-1}\ln(a)\Delta t} \approx$$

$$\approx \frac{1}{1 + ba^t}\left(1 - \frac{ba^t}{1 + ba^t}\ln(a)\Delta t\right) = \frac{1}{1 + ba^t} - \frac{ba^t}{(1 + ba^t)^2}\ln(a)\Delta t = x_t + x_t(1 - x_t)\ln(a)\Delta t.$$

Therefore, $x_{t+\Delta t} = x_t + x_t(1 - x_t)\ln(a)\Delta t$ if $\ln(a)\Delta t \ll 1$.

As a result, $(x_{t+\Delta t} - x_t)/\Delta t = \ln(a) x_t(1 - x_t)$, which completes the proof.

Obviously, for $\ln(a) \ll 1$ and $\Delta t = 1$, all these transformations remain in force, and the difference equation describing the logistic curve in the discrete form (5.24) is approximated well by (5.23).

In accordance with the intermediate notations, $\ln(a) = \beta = \mu \delta = \mu/K$ and, hence, the condition $\ln(a) \ll 1$ can be written as $\mu/K \ll 1$. Thus, for a large dimension K of the set of all states of the environment, the logistic curve (5.24) is well approximated by the difference equation (5.23).

The logistic learning curve (5.24) is classical in the theory of learning (Novikov 1998). At the same time, this curve is a special case of the "learning-to-learn" model that corresponds to the uniform distribution of a "large" set of all states of the environment and the proportional relation between the intensity of testing different states of the environment and the learning level reached.

If the learning curve is logistic (see (5.24)), then the expected series length has the form $N_{t+1} = \lambda(1 - \lambda)^{-1} \exp(\beta t)$ generated by the compact difference equation $N_{t+1} = \exp(\beta)N_t$.

Hyperbolic learning curve. In another special case of auto-learning, the intensity of technology evolution decreases in the maturity level: $\Gamma_t = \mu (1 - E[L_t])^a$, where $a > 0$. In practice, this relation describes well the limited cognitive and/or computational capabilities of an actor (in particular, the finite capacity of short-term memory).

We will derive a difference equation of the learning level in this case by analogy with the logistic learning curve for the equally probable states of the environment; see above. In this special case, expression (5.22) remains in force too. Substituting $\Gamma_t = \mu (1 - E[L_t])^a$ into it gives

$$\Delta E[L_{t+1}] = \Gamma_t \delta \left(1 - E[L_t]\right) = \mu\delta \left(1 - E[L_t]\right)^{1+a} \qquad (5.25)$$

Equation (5.25) represents a difference analog of the differential equation $dx/dt = \beta (1 - x)^{1+a}$, where $\beta = \mu\delta$, the solution of which is the *hyperbolic learning curve*, a classical concept in the theory of learning; for example, see the survey in (Novikov 1998) and the pioneering papers (Thurstone 1919, Thurstone 1930).

The discrete form of the hyperbolic learning curve is described by

$$E[L_t] = 1 - \frac{1}{(1 + a\beta t)^{1/a}} \qquad (5.26)$$

This function monotonically increases from 0 (at $t=0$) to 1 (as $t \to +\infty$).

As for the logistic curve, we introduce the compact notation $x_t = 1 - \dfrac{1}{(1 + a\beta t)^{1/a}}$

and use the same considerations under the conditions $\beta \ll 1$ and $a\beta \ll 1$ to obtain $x_{t+1} = x_t + (1 - x_t)^{a+1}$

The condition $\beta \ll 1$ is equivalent to $\mu \delta = \mu/K \ll 1$. Consequently, the hyperbolic curve satisfies the difference equation (5.25) for a "large" dimension K of the set of all states of the environment.

In this case, the expected series length has the form $N_t = (1 + a\beta t)^{1/a} - 1$.

The difference equation of the expected series length is $N_{t+1} = [(N_t + 1)^a + a\beta]^{1/a}$. In particular, for $a = 1$, the equation turns into $N_{t+1} = N_t + \beta$.

Thus, the hyperbolic learning curve (5.26) (its difference analog $E[L_t] = E[L_{t-1}] + \beta (1 - E[L_{t-1}])^{1+a}$) is a special case of the learning-to-learn model that corresponds to the uniform distribution of a large set of all states of the environment and a decreasing relation between the intensity of testing different states of the environment and the learning level reached.

Auto-learning. We consider a continuous auto-learning model as follows. Let the dynamics of the learning level $z(t) \in [0; 1]$, $t \geq 0$ be described by the differential equation

$$\dot{z}(t) = \gamma(1-z)\tilde{p}(z) \tag{5.27}$$

with the initial condition $z(0) = \lambda \in [0, 1)$, where $\gamma > 0$; $\tilde{p}$ $(\cdot)$: $[0, 1] \to (0, A]$ is a continuous function; $0 < A < +\infty$. (If $\tilde{p}$ means probability, then $A = 1$.)

Due to the above assumptions, we have the following.

a) The solution of equation (5.27) exists and is unique.
b) The relation $z(t)$ is a strictly monotonically increasing function, i.e., $\forall t \geq 0$ $\dot{z}$ $(t) \leq \gamma$.
c) If $z(0) = 0$, then $\forall t \geq 0$ $z(t) \leq 1 - \exp(-\gamma A t)$.
d) The relation $z(t)$ is slowly asymptotic, i.e., $\lim_{t \to +\infty} z(t) = 1$, $\lim_{t \to +\infty} \dot{z}(t) = 0$.

Different auto-learning curves can be obtained by varying $\tilde{p}(z)$. Special cases include many of the learning curves considered:

1) the *exponential learning curve* ("degenerate case") – auto-learning is replaced by standard learning
   $$\tilde{p}(z) \equiv 1, \lambda = 0; \dot{z} \ (t) = \gamma(1 - z); z(t) = 1 - \exp(-\gamma t).$$
2) the *logistic learning curve*
   $$\tilde{p} \ (z) = z, \lambda > 0; \dot{z}(t) = \gamma z(1 - z); z(t) = (1 + (\lambda^{-1} - 1)\exp(-\gamma t))^{-1}.$$
3) the *hyperbolic learning curve*
   $$\tilde{p} \ (z) = (1 - z)^a, a > 0, \lambda = 0; \dot{z}(t) = \gamma (1 - z)^{1 + a}; z(t) = 1 - (1 + a\gamma t)^{-1/a}.$$

The auto-learning model (5.27) allows several extensions, namely, transitions to learning-by-doing and collective learning.

Consider the *learning-by-doing model* in which a learned actor (agent) can choose the intensity $w(t) \geq 0$ of his/her activity (the amount of work executed per unit time; the number of current states of the environment analyzed per unit time; etc.).

The amount of executed work $W(t) = \int_0^t w(\tau)d\tau$ can be treated as the experience accumulated by the agent, his/her "productive internal time" (Novikov 2012).

Replacing the function $\dot{p}$ (z) with the intensity $w(t)$ in equation (5.27) yields the differential equation

$$\dot{z}(t) = \gamma(1 - z)w(t), \tag{5.28}$$

its solution being the "exponential" learning curve

$$z_w(t) = 1 - \exp(-W(t)) \tag{5.29}$$

Following Novikov (2012), we assume function (5.29) specifies the probability of achieving the result at a time t – the share of all successful actions of the agent. Then, the cumulative expected result can be calculated as

$$W_+(t) = \int_0^t z_w(\omega)w(\omega)d\omega \equiv \int_0^t 1 - \exp(-\int_0^t w(\tau)d\tau)w(\omega)d\omega$$

Let $T \geq 0$ be a given interval and also let W_0 be the maximum amount of work in accordance with the agent's capabilities. In view of (5.28–5.30), the expected result maximization is the dynamic programming problem $W_+(T) \to \max\limits_{w(\cdot), W(T) \leq W_0}$.

Similar optimization problems (in particular, subject to the agent's cost constraints, etc.) interpreted in terms of the agent's optimal learning strategy were considered in Novikov (2012) (see also Chapter 7).

In concluding this section, we will describe the process of *collective learning* (Novikov 2012) in terms of auto-learning.

Up to this point, the agent's learning process has been considered under the assumption that the agent uses his/her "own" experience only. However, members of real groups exchange their experience: an agent can gain experience by observing the activity of the others (their achievements or challenges). Such models were described in Novikov (2012). For a proper reflection of this effect, let the experience $\tilde{p}$ accumulated by an agent be dependent on the learning levels of the other agents.

We will consider n agents and introduce the following notations: i is the agent's number; z_i is his/her learning level; and $\mathbf{z} = (z_1, z_2, ..., z_n)$ is the learning levels vector. For each agent, we write an analog of equation (5.27):

$$\dot{z}_i(t) = \gamma_i(1 - z_i)\tilde{p}_i(\mathbf{z}), i = \overline{1,n} \tag{5.31}$$

In model (5.31), agents may have different influences on each other as follows:

- if $\dfrac{\partial \tilde{p}_i(\mathbf{z})}{\partial z_j} > 0$, then agent i adopts the experience from agent j.

- if $\dfrac{\partial \tilde{p}_i(\mathbf{z})}{\partial z_j} < 0$, then the experience of agent j "confuses" agent i.

- if $\dfrac{\partial \tilde{p}_i(\mathbf{z})}{\partial z_j} \equiv 0$, then the experience gained by agent j does not affect agent i.

Within the framework of model (5.31), the optimal collective learning problem for a group of agents can be formulated and solved in the same way as in Novikov (2012).

5.5 TECHNOLOGY IN AN EXTERNAL ENVIRONMENT

5.5.1 "STANDARD SOLUTIONS" AND OPTIMAL TECHNOLOGY MANAGEMENT

Consider an actor (*agent*) that makes certain *decisions* during his/her activity (they are technology focused). Let the *efficiency* $x \in [0; 1]$ of the agent's decisions be described by a function $f(x, \theta)$ that depends on the realized *state of the environment* $\theta \in [0; 1]$. For the sake of simplicity, assume $\arg\max_{x \in [0,1]} f(x, \theta) = \theta$. An example of

such a function is $f(x, \theta) = 1 - (x - \theta)^2$. Assume the agent distinguishes among K values of the state of the environment that are realized with probabilities $\{p_k\}$, $k = \overline{1, K}$. We partition the unit interval* into K sequential subintervals Δ_k of lengths $\{p_k\}$ with

the boundaries $\left[\sum_{i=0}^{k-1} p_i; \sum_{i=0}^{k} p_i \right]$, where $p_0 = 0$.

Consider a discrete *technology evolution process* of the following form. At each time, a certain state of the environment $\theta \in \Delta_k$ is realized; if some state of the environment is realized again, then the agent chooses the corresponding optimal decision $x^*(\theta)$, where $x^*(\theta) = \arg\max_{x \in \Delta_j} f(x, \theta)$; if some state of the environment (e.g., the j-th one) is newly realized (never observed before), then the agent chooses an arbitrary decision from the corresponding subinterval Δ_j. On the one hand, this decision principle formally matches Aumann's model (Aumann 2008), in which decision-making based on act–rationality and rule–rationality was considered. On the other hand, the model suggested in this section well reflects the ideology of *standard solutions*, which is widespread in situational and adaptive management.

Let the function $f(\cdot, \theta)$ be uniformly l-Lipschitzian, where $l > 0$, for any states of the environment. (If $l \leq 0$, the efficiency turns out to be independent of the decisions.) Then, the maximum expected error of the agent's decision at time t (the difference between the efficiencies of the chosen and optimal solutions) can be estimated as

$\sum_{k=1}^{K} p_k (1 - p_k)^t l p_k$ (see formula (5.2)).

Fixing an arbitrary integer $K \geq 1$ and a minimum *threshold* ρ: $0 < \rho \leq 1/K$ in order to distinguish the states of the environment, we may formulate the optimal partition problem of all possible states of the environment (the unit interval) into K subsets as follows:

$$Q(\{p_k\}, t) = \sum_{k=1}^{K} (p_k)^2 (1 - p_k)^t l \rightarrow \min_{\{p_k \geq \rho\} : \sum_{k=1}^{K} p_k = 1} \tag{5.32}$$

Note that the nonzero threshold ρ allows us to avoid the trivial solution $p_1 = 1$, $p_j = 0$, $j = \overline{2, K}$. For a *uniform distribution* $(p_k = 1/K)$, the objective function of problem (5.32) takes the form

$$Q_0(K, t) = l / K(1 - 1/K)^t. \tag{5.33}$$

---

* All the results presented below in Sections 5.5.1 and 5.5.2 can be transferred – with an exactness up to the terms – to a model of partitions of the space of elementary events in an arbitrary probability space. Such a model is much "richer" than those with a unit segment.

Problem (5.32) can be interpreted as seeking an optimal set of standard solutions that minimize the expected error of the current decisions at a given time.

Proposition 5.4. $\forall \rho \in (0; 1/K] \ \exists \ t(\rho)$, such that the uniform partitioning $\forall \ \tau > t(\rho)$ is the unique solution of the problem

$$Q(\{p_k\}, \tau) \to \min_{\{p_k \geq \rho\}: \sum_{k=1}^{K} p_k = 1} . \tag{5.34}$$

The proof of Proposition 5.4 is given in Appendix A5.2.

Interestingly, the solution of problem (5.34) does not depend on the Lipschitz constant l.

Proposition 5.4 might be generalized to the following case. Let us denote by $C_k(x)$ the agent's "losses" incurred by the first realization of the k-th state of the environment (in a practical interpretation, the *cost* of obtaining the optimal solution in this situation).

The optimal partition problem of the set of all possible states of the environment (the unit interval) into K subsets in terms of the minimum expected losses at the current time t takes the form

$$Q_C(\{p_k\}, t) = \sum_{k=1}^{K} C_k(p_k) p_k (1 - p_k)^t \to \min_{\{p_k \geq \rho\}: \sum_{k=1}^{K} p_k = 1} . \tag{5.35}$$

Example 5.1. A graph of $Q(p, t)$ at $K=2$ is shown in Figure 5.2.

Corollary 1. Let the functions $C_k(\cdot)$, $k = \overline{1, K}$ be strictly positive and have bounded first- and second-order derivatives. Then, $\forall \rho \in (0; 1/K] \ \exists \ t(\rho)$, such that $\forall \ \tau > t(\rho)$ the uniform partition is the unique solution of problem (5.35).

The proof of the corollary is given in Appendix A5.2.

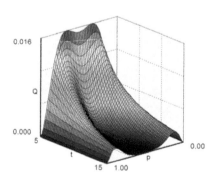

FIGURE 5.2 Graph of the function $Q(p, t)$ in Example 5.1.

Next, let us assume the agent will gain some payoff $H_k(p_k)$ if the k-th state of the environment is realized one or more times again. In this case, the optimal partition problem of the set of all possible states of the environment (the unit interval) into K subsets in terms of the maximum expected utility (the difference between the payoff and cost) at time t can be written as

$$Q_H(\{p_k\},t) \to \max_{\{p_k \geq \rho\}:\sum_{k=1}^{K} p_k = 1} . \qquad (5.36)$$

where $Q_H(\{p_k\},t) = \sum_{k=1}^{K} p_k \left\{ [1-(1-p_k)^t]H_k(p_k) - C_k(p_k)(1-p_k)^t \right\}$.

Proposition 5.5 (about optimal standard solutions). Let the functions $H_k(\cdot)$, $k = \overline{1,K}$ be such that the functions $x \, H_k(x)$ are strictly concave for $x \in [0; 1]$, and also let the functions $C_k(\cdot)$, $k = \overline{1,K}$ satisfy the hypotheses of Corollary 5.1. Then, $\forall \rho \in (0; 1/K] \, \exists \, t(\rho)$, such that the unique solution of problem (5.36) $\forall \tau > t(\rho)$ is the uniform partition.

Proof of Proposition 5.5: by the hypotheses of Proposition 5.4 and Corollary 5.1, each of the terms in the objective function (5.36) is a strictly concave function as the difference of strictly concave and strictly convex functions. Hence, the function $(\{p_k\}, t)$ is concave in $\{p_k\}$. Using the same considerations as in the proof of Proposition 5.4, we can easily show that the optimal values of $\{p_k\}$ are the same. The proof of Proposition 5.5 is complete. •

In Proposition 5.4, for any threshold, there is a time after which the uniform probability distribution will minimize the expected error of the agent's decisions. A natural question, which actually characterizes the converse property, is as follows. For sufficiently large times, does a threshold under which the uniform distribution is optimal exist? The answer is affirmative.

Proposition 5.6. $\forall \, t \geq [2K-3/2 + \sqrt{2(K^2 - K - 1)}] \, \exists \, \rho(t) \leq 1/K$, such that one of the solutions of the problem $Q(\{p_k\},t) \to \min_{\{p_k \geq \rho\}:\sum_{k=1}^{K} p_k = 1}$ is the uniform partition.

The proof of this result seems trivial: under the hypotheses of the proposition and for $\rho(t) = 1/K$, the convexity condition

$$2(1-K)^2 - 4t(1-1/K)/K + t(t-1)/K^2 \geq 0.$$

Up to this point, the number K of pairwise distinguishable states of the environment has been assumed to be fixed. Now, let's study how this number affects the expected error, i.e., find the optimal value of K. In view of Propositions 5.4 and 5.5, it suffices to study the class of uniform distributions only.

Example 5.2. The graph of (5.33) with $t = 50$ is shown in Figure 5.3; here, $K_* = 51$.

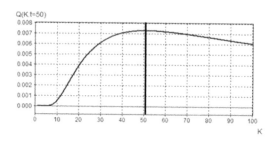

FIGURE 5.3   Graph of the function $Q(K, t=50)$ in Example 5.2.

A direct analysis of formula (5.33) gives the following result:

Proposition 5.7. For any $t \geq 0$, there is a unique "worst" value $K_*(t)=t+1$ that maximizes the error.

Error (5.33) reaches its minimum under small or quite large values of K. Hence, additional criteria should be introduced, e.g., the boundedness of the agent's cognitive capabilities or the relation between the learning level and the number of states of the environment.

Indeed, up to this point, the expected error (the objective function in the optimization problem (5.32)) has been adopted as the criterion.

Now, for this role, let us choose the learning level – the probability that a known state of the environment is realized; see (5.1).

Consider the expected maturity/learning level maximization problem

$$L(\{p_k\},\tau)=1-\sum_{k=1}^{K} p_k(1-p_k)^{\tau} \to \max_{\{p_k \geq \rho\}:\sum_{k=1}^{K} p_k=1} \qquad (5.37)$$

For this problem, an analog of Proposition 5.4 can be established using the convexity conditions of the objective function's terms as follows.

Proposition 5.8. $\forall \rho \in (0;\ 1/K]\ \exists\ t(\rho)=2/\rho -1$, such that the unique solution of problem (5.37) $\forall\ \tau > t(\rho)$ is the uniform partition.

Example 5.3. For a uniform partition, the dependence of the expected learning level on K has the following form.* A graph of (5.38) is presented in Figure 5.3.

$$L(K,t)=1-(1-1/K)^t. \qquad (5.38)$$

For any fixed time, the maturity/learning level decreases as the value of K increases; see expression (5.38) and also Figure 5.4. Moreover, in view of Proposition 5.7, the relation between the error and this number has a maximum point.

Why can we not choose $K=1$, assuming that the set of all possible states of the environment is a singleton? This question seems natural, but such an assumption will make the system's behavior independent of the states of the environment.

---

* Hereinafter in Section 5.5, to denote the learning curve and learning level, instead of the notation $E\ [L\ (\cdot)]$ used in Sections 5.3 and 5.4 earlier, we omit the mathematical expectation symbol and use $L\ (\cdot)$ to simplify the notation.

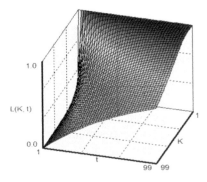

FIGURE 5.4   Graph of $L(K, t)$ in Example 5.3.

Hence, a reasonable approach is to hypothesize the existence of K_0 fundamentally different states of the environment that require meaningfully different responses from the agent. (The number K_0 has to be known a priori.) On the one hand, this number can be determined from some objective laws or retrospective data (in the case of measurable uncertainty in the states of the environment) or determined using some heuristics/expertise (in the case of true uncertainty in the states of the environment). On the other hand, this number imposes an explicit lower bound on the number of different states of the environment (inequality $K \geq K_0$) and must agree with the threshold ρ (inequality $\rho \leq 1/K_0$).

Let us now analyze which factors may restrict an infinite increase in parameter K. The natural restrictions on the number K are as follows.

- The inequality $p_k \geq \rho$ implies $K \leq 1/\rho$.
- Proposition 5.8 gives $t(\rho) \geq 2K - 1$.
- If δ is the agent's "differential threshold" for the values of the objective function, then $K \leq l/\delta$.

Thus, a rational choice is to partition the set of all possible states of the environment into K equally probable "situations" so that $K \geq K_0$, K guarantees a reasonable compromise between the expected error and the learning level at the current time, and K satisfies the above-mentioned upper bounds. For each situation, the agent will find optimal or typical solutions during technology synthesis/testing/adaptation.

Consider an example of the optimal management problem as follows. Given some K_0, l, and ρ, the problem is to reach a required learning level L_{req} by time τ so that the expected error will not exceed ε. Within Proposition 5.4, this system of requirements is consistent if a positive integer K exists such that (see also (5.33) and (5.38))

$$\begin{cases} K_0 \leq K \leq 1/\rho, \\ 1 - (1 - 1/K)^{\tau} \geq L_{req}, \\ 1/K(1 - 1/K)^{\tau} \leq \varepsilon \end{cases} \qquad (5.39)$$

In accordance with Proposition 5.7, for $K_0 \le K_*(\tau)$, it suffices to check all inequalities (5.39) for the number $K = K_0$ (higher values of K are pointless, because they will simultaneously reduce the maturity/learning level and increase the expected error); for $K_0 > K_*(\tau)$, the admissible values of the parameter K have to be found.

5.5.2 ENTROPY

We will describe the technology evolution/management process "in aggregate"; we assume that at each moment in time two events can take place – realizations of the known or unknown (new) states of the environment. The former event has the probability $L(\{p_k\}, t)$ defined by (5.37). In the case of two possible events, the *entropy* is

$$S\big(t,\ \{p_k\}\big) = -L\big(\{p_k\},t\big) \ln \big(L(\{p_k\},t)\big) - \big(1 - L(\{p_k\},t)\big) \ln \big(1 - L(\{p_k\},t)\big).$$

(5.40)

Let us study the dependence of entropy (5.40) on $\{p_k\}$, K, and t. More specifically, let us consider the entropy minimization problem at time t.

Proposition 5.9 (about entropy). $\forall \rho \in (0;\ 1/K]\ \exists\ t(\rho) = 2/\rho - 1$ such that the unique solution of the problem of minimizing the entropy $S(t, \{p_k\})$ is the uniform partition.

$$S(t, \{p_k\}) \to \min_{\{p_k \ge \rho\}:\sum\limits_{k=1}^{K} p_k = 1} .$$

(5.41)

Proposition 5.9 directly follows from the fact that entropy (5.40) is a minimum if one of the probabilities $L(\{p_k\}, t)$ or $(1 - L(\{p_k\}, t))$ reaches its maximum. In Proposition 5.8, precisely the uniform distribution maximizes (5.37).

The result of Proposition 5.9 is not trivial: the maximum variety of the initial states (the uniform probability distribution of all possible states of the environment) not only minimizes the expected error and maximizes the learning level (Propositions 5.4 and 5.8, respectively) but also minimizes the entropy of the agent's learning states.

Proposition 5.10. The maximum value of entropy (3.40) does not depend on the distribution $\{p_k\}$, being equal to $\ln(2)$.

Indeed, Proposition 5.10 follows from the fact that expression (5.40) is maximized with respect to the time variable if $L(\{p_k\}, t) = 1 - L(\{p_k\}, t)$, i.e., if the known and new states of the environment are realized with the same probability.

For the uniform distribution, relation (5.40) among the entropy, time, and parameter K takes the form

$$S(t, K) = -\frac{K^t - (K-1)^t}{K^t} \ln\left(\frac{K^t - (K-1)^t}{K^t}\right) - \frac{(K-1)^t}{K^t} \ln\left(\frac{(K-1)^t}{K^t}\right).$$

Entropy $S(t, K)$ reaches its maximum at the time $t_S(K) = -\ln(2)/\ln(1 - 1/K)$. Note that $t_S(K) \le t(\rho)$, i.e., the uniform distribution is optimal for times considerably exceeding the characteristic time for achieving the maximum entropy.

This model satisfies the *principle of the determinism destruction* (Foerster 1995), because a maximum point of entropy exists. (At the initial time, the entropy is 0,

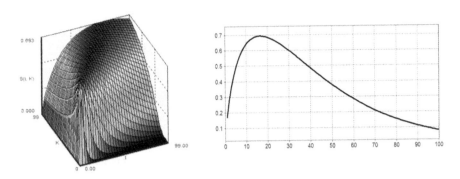

FIGURE 5.5 Graph of $S(t, K)$ under uniform distribution (left) and graph of $S(t, K)$ under uniform distribution with $K=25$, $t_S(K) \approx 17$ (right).

meaning that the system is completely deterministic; hence, any state of the environment realized at the initial time will be new for the agent; the entropy vanishes as → 0.)

Example 5.4. The figures below represent sketches of the general dependence $S(t, K)$ for uniform distribution and for $K=25$ (Figure 5.5).

Let us now study entropy $s(t, \{p_k\})$ of the technology evolution process in "detailed form." We consider a system with 2^K possible states. At time t, its dynamics are described by a K-dimensional binary vector, in which the k-th component is 1 if the state of the environment has taken the k-th value at least once up to and including this time, and 0 $s(t, \{p_k\})$ otherwise (Section 5.1). The entropy of this system has the form (5.42).

Proposition 5.11. $\forall \rho \in (0; 1/K] \exists t(\rho)$, such that $\forall \tau > t(\rho)$ the uniform partition is the unique solution of problem (5.42).

$$s(t,\{p_k\}) = -\sum_{k=1}^{K}(1-(1-p_k)^t)\ln(1-(1-p_k)^t) \to \min_{\{p_k \geq \rho\}:\sum_{k=1}^{K} p_k=1} . \quad (5.42)$$

This result is established by analogy with Propositions 5.4 and 5.5. (For sufficiently large t, we should demonstrate the strict convexity of the function $(1-(1-p)^t)\ln(1/(1-(1-p)^t))$ in the variable p.) The technical details are therefore omitted.

CONCLUSION

Chapter 5 is devoted to the study of the technology of the complex activities of an Enterprise and the formulation of and solution to the problem of technology management.

The main results in the chapter are as follows.

First, the formalization of the technology management problem and, above all, the identification of system-wide features of the problem, namely (a) the evolution of technology throughout the lifecycle of complex activities that actually put the technology into operation; (b) the complexity of the technology and the existence of its internal structure; and (c) the relationship between the technology and the external environment.

Second, the development of a set of mathematical models that describe the system-wide features of the technology:

- basic model of the technology evolution/management process and the extension of the model;
- models of the integration of technology components;
- models of "standard solutions" and entropy models, representing the relationship between the technology and the external environment.

Third, the system-wide foundations of these models and the universal methods of mathematics, which make them applicable for solving the problems of analysis and technology management of the complex activity of any Enterprise.

APPENDIXES

APPENDIX 5.1 EXPECTED TIME TO REACH THE "ABSOLUTE" MATURITY/LEARNING LEVEL

We calculate the expected time to reach the "absolute" maturity/learning level $L_t = 1$.

Assume several states of the environment have been tested by some time; let $I \le K$ states with the probabilities $\{p_i; i = \overline{1, I}\}$ still be unknown. Clearly, $\sum_{i=1}^{I} p_i \le 1$.

Let us denote by $T(\{p_i; i = \overline{1, I}\})$ the expected time to test the residual I states, i.e., the expected time to reach the learning level $L_t = 1$. Using mathematical induction, we prove the formula

$$T(\{p_i; i = \overline{1, I}\}) = \sum_{i=1}^{I} p_i^{-1} - \sum_{i;k} (p_i + p_k)^{-1} + \sum_{i;k;l} (p_i + p_k + p_l)^{-1}$$

$$- \sum_{i;k;l;m} (p_i + p_k + p_l + p_m)^{-1} + \dots$$

(A5.1)

We rewrite (A5.1) in another (equivalent) form:

$$T(\{p_i; i = \overline{1, I}\}) = \sum_{k=1}^{I} (-1)^{k+1} \sum_{i_1;i_2;\dots i_k} \left(\sum_{j=1}^{k} p_{i_j} \right)^{-1}.$$

(A5.2)

We will demonstrate that the expected time represents the sum of the alternating partial sums of all ks from $\{p_i; i = \overline{1, I}\}$, $k = \overline{1, I}$.

We introduce the compact notation $\Theta(k; I)$ for the sums of all ks from $\{p_i; i = \overline{1, I}\}$, $k = \overline{1, I}$ that appear in (A5.2):

$$\Theta(k;I) = \sum_{i_1;i_2;\ldots;i_k} 1/\sum_{j=1}^{k} p_{i_j} = \sum_{i_1;i_2;\ldots;i_k} 1/(p_{i_1} + p_{i_2} + \ldots + p_{i_k}). \qquad (A5.3)$$

In view of (A5.3), expression (A5.2) takes the form

$$T(\{p_i; i = \overline{1,I}\}) = \sum_{k=1}^{I} (-1)^{k+1} \sum_{i_1;i_2;\ldots i_k} \left(\sum_{j=1}^{k} p_{i_j} \right)^{-1} = \sum_{j=1}^{I} (-1)^{j+1} \Theta(j;I). \qquad (A5.4)$$

Let us assume a single state of the environment remains untested; then, $T(\{p_i; i = 1\}) = 1/p_1$.

Let relations (A5.1), (A5.2), and (A5.4) be valid for the $(I - 1)$ states, i.e.,

$$T(\{p_i; i = \overline{1,I-1}\}) = \sum_{k=1}^{I-1} (-1)^{k+1} \Theta(k;I-1).$$

We will show that, in this case, relations (A5.1), (A5.2), and (A5.4) are valid for the I states. The event that results in the sequential implementation of $I = \overline{1,I}$ states is equivalent to the union of I events, in each of which one of the I states has been real-ized first and the other $(I - 1)$ states sequentially after it. Then,

$$T(\{p_i; i = \overline{1,I}\}) = 1/\sum_{i=1}^{I} p_i + \sum_{j=1}^{I} p_j / \sum_{i=1}^{I} p_i T(\{p_i; i = \overline{1,I}; i \neq j\}), \qquad (A5.5)$$

where the first term is the expected time to the first of the realized states $i=1, 2, \ldots, I$. Each of the j-th terms in the summand gives the probability that the j-th state has been tested first; then, $T(\{p_i; i = \overline{1,I}; i \neq j\})$ gives the expected testing time of the residual $(I - 1)$ states.

Substituting (A5.4) into the right-hand side of (A5.5) yields

$$T(\{p_i; i = \overline{1,I}\}) = \left(\sum_{i=1}^{I} p_i \right)^{-1} \left(1 + \sum_{j=1}^{I} \left(p_j \sum_{k=1}^{I-1} (-1)^{k+1} \Theta(k;I-1) \right) \right). \qquad (A5.6)$$

Using (A5.3), we transform the second sum in the following way:

$$\sum_{j=1}^{I} \left(p_j \sum_{k=1}^{I-1} (-1)^{k+1} \Theta(k;I-1) \right) = \sum_{j=1}^{I} \sum_{k=1}^{I-1} (-1)^{k+1} \sum_{i_1;i_2;\ldots i_k} \frac{p_j}{p_{i_1} + p_{i_2} + \ldots + p_{i_k}}$$

None of the probabilities p_j in the numerators appears in the sum $p_{i_1} + p_{i_2} + \ldots + p_{i_k}$ in the denominators. Hence, the order of summation can be modified so that

$$\sum_{j=1}^{I}\left(p_j\sum_{k=1}^{I-1}(-1)^{k+1}\Theta(k;I-1)\right)=\sum_{j=1}^{I}\sum_{k=1}^{I-1}(-1)^{k+1}\sum_{i_1;i_2;...;i_k}\frac{p_j}{p_{i_1}+p_{i_2}+...+p_{i_k}}=$$

$$=\sum_{k=1}^{I-1}(-1)^{k+1}\sum_{i_1;i_2;...;i_k}(p_{i_1}+p_{i_2}+...+p_{i_k})^{-1}=\sum_{j=1;j\neq i_1;i_2;...;i_k}^{I}p_j.$$

Here, the summation procedure runs over all j from 1 to I not coinciding with any of $i_1, i_2, \ldots, i_k$. Consequently,

$$\sum_{j=1;j\neq i_1;i_2;...;i_k}^{I}p_j=\sum_{i=1}^{I}p_i-(p_{i_1}+p_{i_2}+...+p_{i_k}).$$

Using this relation in the second sum gives

$$\sum_{j=1}^{I}\left(p_j\sum_{k=1}^{I-1}(-1)^{k+1}\Theta(k;I-1)\right)=\sum_{k=1}^{I-1}(-1)^{k+1}\sum_{i_1;i_2;...;i_k}\frac{\sum_{i=1}^{I}p_i-(p_{i_1}+p_{i_2}+...+p_{i_k})}{p_{i_1}+p_{i_2}+...+p_{i_k}}=$$

$$=\left(\sum_{i=1}^{I}p_i\right)\sum_{k=1}^{I-1}(-1)^{k+1}\sum_{i_1;i_2;...;i_k}(p_{i_1}+p_{i_2}+...+p_{i_k})^{-1}-$$

$$-\sum_{k=1}^{I-1}(-1)^{k+1}\sum_{i_1;i_2;...;i_k}1=\left(\sum_{i=1}^{I}p_i\right)\sum_{k=1}^{I-1}(-1)^{k+1}\Theta(k;I)+\sum_{k=1}^{I-1}(-1)^k C_I^k,$$

where C_I^k is the number of k-combinations from the set of I elements. Substituting this formula into (A5.6) yields

$$T(\{p_i;i=\overline{1,I}\})=\left(\sum_{i=1}^{I}p_i\right)^{-1}+\left(\sum_{i=1}^{I}p_i\right)^{-1}\left(\left(\sum_{i=1}^{I}p_i\right)\sum_{k=1}^{I-1}(-1)^{k+1}\Theta(k;I)+\sum_{k=1}^{I-1}(-1)^k C_I^k\right)=$$

$$=\sum_{k=1}^{I-1}(-1)^{k+1}\Theta(k;I)+\left(\sum_{i=1}^{I}p_i\right)^{-1}\left(1+\sum_{k=1}^{I-1}(-1)^k C_I^k\right).$$

By definition, $\Theta(I;I)=\left(\sum_{i=1}^{I}p_i\right)^{-1}$, and also $1+\sum_{n=1}^{I-1}(-1)^n C_I^n+(-1)^I=(1-1)=0.$

Hence, $1+\sum_{n=1}^{I-1}(-1)^n C_I^n=(-1)^{I+1}.$ Finally, the desired expected time to reach the

"absolute" learning level $L_t=1$ (in form (A5.4)) is $T(\{p_i;i=\overline{1,I}\})=\sum_{k=1}^{I}(-1)^{k+1}\Theta(k;I)$

APPENDIX 5.2 PROOF OF PROPOSITION 5.4 AND COROLLARY 5.1

Proof of Proposition 5.4

Proposition 5.4. $\forall \rho \in (0; 1/K] \; \exists \; t(\rho)$, such that $\forall \; \tau > t(\rho)$ the uniform partitioning is the unique solution of the problem

$$Q(\{p_k\}, \tau) \to \min_{\{p_k \geq \rho\}: \sum_{k=1}^{K} p_k = 1} .$$

The proof of Proposition 5.4 will rest on an intermediate result as follows.

Lemma. $\forall \rho \in (0; 1/K] \; \exists \; t(\rho)$, such that the $\forall \; \tau > t(\rho)$ function $Q(\{p_k\}, \tau)$ is strictly convex in the variables $\{p_k\}$.

Proof of Lemma 1. Let us fix an arbitrary number $k = \overline{1, K}$. Omitting the subscript k below, we demonstrate that $\forall \rho \in (0; 1/K] \; \exists \; t(\rho)$, such that $\forall \; \tau > t(\rho)$ the function $G(p) = p^2 (1 - p)^t$ is convex in p. We calculate the second-order derivative of the function $G(\cdot)$:

$$\frac{d^2 G(p;t)}{dp^2} = (1 - p)^{t-2} \left[2(1 - p)^2 - 4p\, t(1 - p) + p^2 t(t - 1) \right]. \qquad (A5.7)$$

As $t(\rho)$ we choose the maximum in relation to $t \geq 2$, the root of the quadratic equation

$$\forall p \in [\rho; 1 - \rho], \; 2(1 - p)^2 - 4p\, t(1 - p) + p^2 t(t - 1) = 0.$$

This equation has a nonnegative solution, since its coefficient at the highest (quadratic) term is strictly positive. Clearly, any $\tau > t(\rho)$ satisfies the system of inequalities $\forall p \in [\rho; 1 - \rho] \dfrac{d^2 G(p;t)}{dp^2} > 0$. Hence, due to the continuity of the right-hand side of expression (A5.7) in t, it follows that $\forall p \in [\rho; 1 - \rho]$ and $\forall \; \tau > t(\rho) \dfrac{d^2 G(p;t)}{dp^2} > 0$.

Thus, each term of $\displaystyle\sum_{k=1}^{K} p_k (1 - p_k)^t l$ represents a convex function of p_k, because the Lipschitz constant is nonnegative by definition. Consequently, their sum is also a convex function, which concludes the proof of the lemma.

Now, we prove the main result – Proposition 5.4. Let us fix an arbitrary time $t > 0$. Assume $\{q_k\}$ is the solution of problem (5.34) for $t > t(\rho)$ and, in addition, a pair $i, j \in \overline{1, K}$ exists, such that $i \neq j$ and $q_i \neq q_j$. For the sake of definiteness, let $j > i$. Due to the strong convexity of the objective function, we have

$$Q(\{q_k\}, t) > Q\left(q_1, ..., q_{i-1}, \frac{q_i + q_j}{2}, q_{i+1}, ..., q_{j-1}, \frac{q_i + q_j}{2}, q_{j+1}, ..., q_K, t\right),$$

which contradicts the assumption. This means that in the optimal solution all values $\{q_k\}$ are the same. The uniqueness of this optimal solution follows from the strong convexity of the objective function. The proof of Proposition 5.4 is complete.

Proof of Corollary 5.1

Corollary 5.1. Let the functions $C_k(\cdot)$, $k = \overline{1, K}$ be strictly positive and have bounded first- and second-order derivatives. Then, $\forall \rho \in (0; 1/K] \,\exists\, t(\rho)$, such that $\forall\, \tau > t(\rho)$ the unique solution of problem (5.35) is the uniform partition.

The corollary is proved by analogy with Proposition 5.4, with the only exception being that the function $G(p)$ is replaced by the function $G_C(p) = C(p)\, p\, (1-p)^t$. We calculate the second-order derivative of $G_C(\cdot)$:

$$\frac{d^2 G(p;t)}{dp^2} = \left(1-p\right)^{t-2}\left[C''(p)p\left(1-p\right)^2 - 2C'(p)\left(1-p\right)(1-p-pt) + C(p)p\, t\left(t-1\right)\right].$$

In view of the hypotheses of the corollary, the coefficient at the highest (quadratic) term on the right-hand side of the expression is strictly positive, while the other coefficients are bounded. The proof of the corollary is complete.

REFERENCES

Aichernig, B. and Schumi, R. 2017. Statistical Model Checking Meets Property-Based Testing. In *2017 IEEE International Conference on Software Testing, Verification and Validation (ICST)*, Tokyo, 390–400.

Alagoz, H. and German, R. 2017. A Selection Method for Black Box Regression Testing with a Statistically Defined Quality Level. In *2017 IEEE International Conference on Software Testing, Verification and Validation (ICST)*, Tokyo, 114–125.

Ali, S. and Yue, T. 2015. U-Test: Evolving, Modelling and Testing Realistic Uncertain Behaviours of Cyber-Physical Systems. In *IEEE 8th International Conference on Software Testing, Verification and Validation (ICST)*, Graz, 1–2.

Anzanello, M. and Fogliatto, F. 2011. Learning Curve Models and Applications: Literature Review and Research Directions. *International Journal of Industrial Ergonomics* 41, 573–583.

Atkinson, R., Bower, G. and Crothers, J. 1967. *Introduction to Mathematical Learning Theory.* New York: John Wiley & Sons.

Aumann, R. 2008. *Rule-rationality versus Act-rationality.* Discussion paper No. 497. Jerusalem: Hebrew University.

Belov, M. and Novikov, D. 2020. *Models of Technologies.* Heidelberg: Springer.

Bourque, P. and Fairley, R. (eds.). 2014. *Guide to the Software Engineering Body of Knowledge.* Version 3.0, IEEE Computer Society. www.swebok.org.

Bush, R. and Mosteller, F. 1955. *Stochastic Models for Learning.* New York: Wiley.

Chen Y., Ying M., Liu D., Alim A., Chen F. Chen M., Chen H. 2017. Effective Online Software Anomaly Detection. In *Proceedings of the 26th ACM SIGSOFT International Symposium on Software Testing and Analysis (ISSTA)*, Santa Barbara, 136–146.

Chui, D. and Wong, A. 1986. Synthesizing Knowledge: A Cluster Analysis Approach Using Event Covering. *IEEE Transactions on Systems, Man, and Cybernetics* 16(2), 251–259.

Crawford, J. 1944. *Learning Curve, Ship Curve, Ratios, Related Data.* Lockheed Aircraft Corporation, 122–128.

Ebbinghaus, H. 1885. *Über das Gedächtnis*. Leipzig: Dunker.

Foerster, H. 1995. *The Cybernetics of Cybernetics*. Second edition. Minneapolis, MN: Future Systems.

Grant, R. 2013. *Contemporary Strategy Analysis*. New York: John Wiley & Sons.

Gray, C., Walker, K. and Terrell, E. 2016. A Case Study on the Effects of Program Accounting Boeing vs Airbus. https://www.cpajournal.com/2016/11/23/case-study-effects-pro gram- accounting/

Hax, A. and Majluf, N. 1982. Competitive Cost Dynamics: The Experience Curve. *Interfaces* 12(5), 50–61.

Henderson, B. 1984. The Application and Misapplication of the Learning Curve. *Journal of Business Strategy* 4, 3–9.

Henriques, D., Martins, J.G., Zuliani, P., Platzer, A. and Clarke, E. 2012. Statistical Model Checking for Markov Decision Processes. *International Conference on Quantitative Evaluation of Systems (QEST)*, London, 84–93.

Hull, C. 1943. *Principles of Behavior and Introduction to Behavior Theory*. New York: D. Appleton Century Company.

Ingram, D. and Aubin, D. 2016. Boeing Uses an Accounting Method that Others Have Left Behind. https://www.reuters.com/article/us-boeing-probe-accounting-idUSKCN0VL2 K0 [Accessed 16 December 2019].

ISO/IEC/IEEE 15288:2015. 2015. *Systems and Software Engineering. System Life Cycle Processes*. Internatonal Standard Organisation.

Jaber, M. 2017. *Learning Curves: Theory, Models and Applications*. Boca Raton, FL: CRC Press.

Leibowitz, N., Baum, B., Enden, G. and Karniel, A. 2010. The Exponential Learning Equation as a Function of Successful Trials Results in Sigmoid Performance. *Journal of Mathematical Psychology* 54, 338–340.

Legay, A., Delahaye, B. and Bensalem, S. 2010. Statistical Model Checking: An Overview, in Runtime Verification. *Lecture Notes in Computer Science* 6418, 122–135.

Mikami, S. and Kakazu, Y. 1993. Extended Stochastic Reinforcement Learning for the Acquisition of Cooperative Motion Plans for Dynamically Constrained Agents. *Proceedings of IEEE Systems Man and Cybernetics Conference (SMC)*, Le Touquet, 4, 257–262.

Novikov, D. 1998. *Regularities of Iterative Learning*. Moscow: Institute of Control Sciences.

Novikov, D. 2012. Collective Learning-by-Doing. *IFAC Proceedings Volumes* 45(11), 408–412.

Orseau, L., Lattimore, T. and Hutter, M. 2013. Universal Knowledge-Seeking Agents for Stochastic Environments. In: Jain S., Munos R., Stephan F., Zeugmann T. (eds) *Algorithmic Learning Theory. Lecture Notes in Computer Science* vol. 8139, Springer, Berlin, Heidelberg pp.158–172.

Pyster, A. and Olwell, A. (eds.). 2013. *The Guide to the Systems Engineering Body of Knowledge (SEBoK)*, v. 1.2. Hoboken, NJ: The Trustees of the Stevens Institute of Technology. http://www.sebokwiki.org [Accessed 16 December 2019].

Shiryaev, A. 1973. *Statistical Sequential Analysis: Optimal Stopping Rules*. New York: American Mathematical Society.

Stocia, G. and Stack, B. 2017. Acquired Knowledge as a Stochastic Process. *Surveys in Mathematics and Its Applications* 12, 65–70.

Sutton, R. and Barto, A. 2016. *Reinforcement Learning: An Introduction*. Cambridge, MA: MIT Press.

Thurstone, L. 1919. The Learning Curve Equation. *Psychological Monographs* 26(3), 1–51.

Thurstone, L. 1930. The Learning Function. *Journal of General Psychology* 3, 469–493.

Tolman, E. 1934. Theories of Learning. In Moss, F. (ed.), *Comparative Psychology*. New York: Prentice Hall, 232–254.

van der Linden, W. and Hambleton, R. 1996. *Handbook of Modern Item Response Theory*. New York: Springer.

Wong, A. and Wang, Y. 2003. Pattern Discovery: A Data Driven Approach to Decision Support. *IEEE Transactions on Systems, Man, and Cybernetics* 33(1), 114–124.

Wright, T. 1936. Factors Affecting the Cost of Airplanes. *Journal of Aeronautical Sciences* 3(4), 122–128.

6 Human Capital

People are the core constituents of any Enterprise and, in general, any sociotechnical system; more precisely, it is they who carry out the complex activity of the Enterprise and create value. Therefore, *human capital* (following modern trends, we use the term human capital or HC to denote people as the core constituents of an Enterprise) and *human resource* (HR) *management* have always been the focus of attention of both researchers and hands-on managers.

The activity of people in an Enterprise (as well as in any STS) is characterized by a combination of factors that, in a certain sense, contradict each other:

a. First of all, the key distinguishing characteristic of people – *active elements** – is their *active choice*, an action in accordance with their own interests and motives. This factor is considered in Chapter 4, and mathematical models are proposed that formally describe an active choice of AEs and the Enterprise as an active system. In this chapter, we also study the Enterprise as an active system (and, in some cases, we use the abbreviation AS).

b. People also have creative capabilities, which, as part of the complex activity of an Enterprise, are realized in the synthesis of new CA *technologies*. The system-wide aspects of technology synthesis processes are reflected in the technology models developed in Chapter 5.

c. At the same time, AEs are not only the decision-makers and actors involved in activity. The hierarchical structure of CA leads to the fact that, from the point of view of superiors, AEs are a specific kind (see a and b above) of *means* to reach a goal, i.e., *active resources*: AEs are those resources used from which superiors form subordinate actors.

d. The active choice of AEs shows up in their decisions to join and/or leave the Enterprise according to their internal motives. Therefore, the traffic of AEs (processes of AEs joining and leaving the Enterprise), first, reflects the uncertainty of AEs' active choice, and, second, significantly affects characteristics of the human capital and, as formally shown in Section 6.2.2, the efficiency of the Enterprise.

So, this chapter is devoted to modeling Enterprise human capital.

The problem of modeling human capital, the lifecycles of AEs, is studied in Section 6.1; the problem statement is based on the results of Sections 2.4 and 3.4.

In Section 6.2, the basic model of human capital is developed and the influence of AE lifecycle parameters on the efficiency of an Enterprise is investigated.

---

* Hereinafter, we use the term "active element" or "AE" as an equivalent to a person, an individual, an employee, or an active resource unit, and plural AEs as the equivalent to people, employees, or active resources.

Results and algorithms of statistical analyses of AE traffic are presented in Section 6.3.

HC models and the analytical output of this chapter are employed in Section 7.4 for optimal planning of human capital.

6.1   PROBLEM OF HUMAN CAPITAL MANAGEMENT

6.1.1   REQUIREMENTS TO THE MODEL OF HUMAN CAPITAL OF AN ENTERPRISE

Let's arrange the requirements to HC model.

First of all, the HC model should describe the main factors highlighted in the preceding chapters: lifecycles of AEs, the active choice and creativity of AEs, the AE associated costs and AEs' traffic.

The model should consider not only the quantitative economic aspects of the lifecycle of AEs, but, first of all, study human capital as a main constituent of the Enterprise/STS.

The model should consider all stages and phases of the lifecycle of AEs during the whole period of their interaction with the Enterprise (Figure 6.1) and the AEs' traffic between the Enterprise and the "labor market". The lifecycles of AEs must be modeled considering the interaction of AE with the Enterprise; and AE interacts with an actor of *human capital management* (HCM) from the Enterprise side.

Let's study employee, AE, lifecycle.

First of all, after determining the internal demand for a new kind of AEs or new AE, the HCM actor announces the need and performs standard procedures of searching for and selection of candidates (conducting interviews, testing, etc.), i.e. phase I in Figure 6.1. An AE (a potential participant of the Enterprise) decides to enter into a relationship with the Enterprise (with HCM actor) and participate in selection procedures. During this phase, the AE may at any time decide to terminate participation in the selection and leave the "queue" (Figure 6.1).

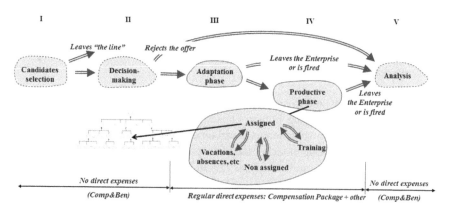

FIGURE 6.1   Employee lifecycle.

The selection procedures (phase I) end when the HCM actor makes a decision – selects a suitable candidate (candidates), forms and issues one or more offers to join the Enterprise (job offer as a particular case). Having received the offer, the candidate (phase II in Figure 6.1) decides whether to accept or reject it.

Having accepted the offer, the candidate joins the Enterprise. During an adaptation phase (phase III) standard procedures of on-boarding, adaptation, training, etc. are executed. The adaptation phase ends when the HCM actor makes a decision on the AE's readiness to fulfill his duties, i.e. implement a corresponding element of CA of the Enterprise.

During a productive phase (phase IV), the AE implements appropriate elements of complex activity, being alternately in the states (see Figure 6.1) of:

- Assigned to execute a concrete element of CA as an actor (or a constituent of a complex actor).
- Non assigned – the AE is waiting for a new assignment, training, or vacation.
- Training.
- Vacations, absences, etc.

The AE's productivity during the productive phase may be uneven, i.e. vary in different periods of the AE's activity, and such effects should be reflected in the model.

During both the adaptation phase and the productive phase, the AE can decide to leave the Enterprise, or the HCM actor can decide to fire the AE.

Cases of leaving, firing, and offers refusal are analyzed by the HCM actor (phase V, Figure 6.1).

In addition, all phases I – V, their duration, uncertainty, expenses, and created value must be considered in the model.

The model should take into account that AEs make the decision to join or leave an Enterprise or to reject an offer according to their internal interests and motives. Consequently, the traffic of AEs (processes of joining and leaving an Enterprise) is driven by the uncertainty of the active choice of AEs. In their turn, the parameters of the traffic of AEs determine most of the time parameters of the lifecycles of AEs.

It makes sense to note that the active choice of AE can be reduced to the two types of decisions, let's say positive and negative ones:

a) to join an Enterprise and execute CA according to prescribed technology;
b) to leave an Enterprise or reject the offer.

Indeed, any other choice can only affect the implementation of the CA element; and, in turn, the implementation of the CA element may lead to the achievement or non-achievement of the objectives of the CA (see Sections 2.3 and 3.4), which again is equivalent to solutions (a) and (b). Moreover, the decomposition Theorems 4.1 and 4.2 state that the optimal contract is "binary": AE is fully remunerated, if the required actions are chosen the required outputs are achieved, or AE is not remunerated at all in any other cases.

The model should reflect the secondary and subordinate role of human capital as a resource with respect to the internal demand formed by the CA actors, and, therefore, the uncertainty and unevenness of the internal demand for AEs over time. Stochastic modeling serves as a generally accepted approach, representing uncertain and heterogeneous processes, and such models can be employed in this case as well.

We consider Enterprise human capital as a set of organized aggregates of AEs, who possess certain knowledge, skills, qualifications and are motivated to solve the tasks posed to them. To formalize HC management we use the "functional houses" concept, introduced by McKinsey company (De Smet et al 2016). Groups of specialists with equivalent functional capabilities for solving business problems are defined as "*functional houses*," and an organized set of functional houses is considered as a prospective structure of an Enterprise.

Considering various forms of temporary resources acquiring (for example, outsourcing, out-staffing, and hiring freelancers), not only full-time employees but also temporary hired freelancers and out-staffers are usually counted as members of functional houses.

The concept of functional houses generalizes all known kinds of organizational structures (including matrix and project oriented), on the one hand, and demonstrates a standardization of any kind of business processes, and therefore work products (for example, product parameters and productivity rates), as well as unification of employees' skills and knowledge, on the other hand. Functional houses play the role of *pools of active resources* – identical AEs. In turn, AEs can be assigned (Figure 6.1) to carry out CA elements – regular tasks, projects, programs, etc.; and an assignment of AEs is a creation of CA actors. It is important to note that AEs execute valuable complex activity only being assigned (Figure 6.1) – being organized as CA actors (in working groups or alone).

In fact, HC management is the influence on the parameters of pools of active resources: their headcount and AEs' functional capabilities. Following the output of Chapter 2 we consider the management of a lifecycle of pools of active resources, as well as a lifecycle of AEs (Figure 6.1); and this approach corresponds to well-known and widely used concepts of enterprise asset management business processes and software supporting them (Rio 2018).

The idea of the pools of active resources is also reasoned by minimization of *transaction costs* (Coase 1937): organization and maintenance of the pool is beneficial, if transaction costs (all costs associated with phases I – III and V of an employee's lifecycle, Figure 6.1) exceed the costs (associated with phase IV) for maintaining resources during such periods of time, when resource units, awaiting the next assignment, are not used productively.

In a certain sense, active resources possess properties being analogous to other types of resources, for example, capital assets, i.e. equipment and buildings (Figure 6.2):

- The competencies, knowledge, skills of employees are analogous to the production characteristics of equipment, i.e. both of them drive a value/ utility being created.

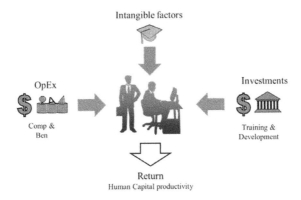

Intangible factors

OpEx

Comp &
Ben

Investments

Training &
Development

Return
Human Capital productivity

FIGURE 6.2   Human capital as an Enterprise asset.

- Wages and other compensation costs are analogous to maintenance and repairing costs. Both of them drive operational capabilities of employees and equipment.
- Costs for training employees are analogous to investments in the equipment modernization. Despite the fundamental differences in accounting for these types of costs, both affect the long-term qualitative and quantitative functional capabilities of assets – employees and equipment. Let us note that both kinds of assets are characterized by depreciation, amortization, aging, and obsolescence – wastage from an economic point of view.
- Transaction costs in both cases are associated with negotiation and execution of contracts (acquisition of capital assets and hiring of employees, respectively).
- Intangible factors such as, for example, implicit and/or undocumented knowledge of employees also affect their return.

To support the practical applicability of Enterprise Control Problem solution, the model should be based on the concepts and principles of management accounting, which implies a sufficiently high accuracy of modeling. However, business practice is complex, and when modeling any business object and its behavior, substantial assumptions and simplifications are usually made. The phenomena and parameters of HC that we model relate to the social and psychological spheres and are physically immeasurable or are not exactly known, and the parameterization of these dependencies is often arbitrary. The possibilities of using "statistical averaging" are also limited, since the practical interest presents not mass repetitive phenomena, but specific business implementations during this particular period of time and under these external conditions.

Therefore, it is very important to ensure stability and robustness of outputs and solutions to inaccurate parameters and regularities used in the model, for their applicability in practice. To meet this, we use interval estimates instead of point estimates where necessary, we control the sensitivity of solutions to initial parameter values, and we deliberately "do not increase" the detail and accuracy of the models.

Since HC management is an influence on the pools of active resources to meet the internal demand caused by the implementation of the enterprise CA, then the problem of human capital management can be formalized as the choice of the optimal parameters of the pools – the number of AEs and their functional capabilities – at every moment throughout the entire CA lifecycle.

The functional capabilities of AEs are highly dependent on the specific features of a CA technology, so the choice of capabilities might not be thought of as a general system problem and is considered a priori given. At the same time, the headcount of resource pools and numerical parameters of lifecycles of active resources are the main factors, determining costs for CA implementation (operation costs) and therefore directly and significantly affecting the economic output of the Enterprise. Such optimization problems are solved in the corresponding sections of Chapter 7.

6.1.2 KNOWN APPROACHES AND MODELS OF HUMAN CAPITAL

Today, at the era of "knowledge economy" all branches of traditional human resource management, organizational management, knowledge management, and related disciplines are usually considered as a united "human capital management" domain (Blackburn and Varvarigos 2008, Fan et al 2015, Gartner 2019, Palacios 2013, Smith 2013), playing critical role in any field of human activity.

The topic of HC management is not new, economists addressed it back in the 19th and 20th centuries, but the first use of the term in modern neoclassical economic literature is considered to be Mincer's paper (Mincer 1958).

By the time the paper appeared (Mincer 1958), knowledge-intensive firms, in which the main share of output is formed in the form of knowledge and through the use of employees' knowledge (Wu 2015), had widely developed. A value chain of such firms is mostly based on the knowledge and information creation and transformation. Those are, for example, professional services businesses (financial, legal, engineering, and other), banks, Internet companies, and other business entities whose core competence and business drivers are based on knowledge, employees' skills, high technologies, and low capital intensity.

To date, qualitative approaches, being specific to sociology, psychology, management sciences, and related disciplines, dominate in practically the entire field of HR and HC management. Employees' loyalty, involvement, satisfaction, commitment, and other similar concepts, as well as strategical aspects of people management, are widely considered and developed in a large number of researches (see for example Kahn (1990); Thie and Brown (1994)).

The theme of employee (active resources) modeling deals with both qualitative approaches, listed above, and quantitative methods, such as management accounting, operations research, stochastic modeling, and other related fields.

The concepts and practice of human resource accounting are well developed and presented in a considerable number of works, starting with the fundamental monograph of E. Flamholtz (Flamholtz 1999) and his other papers (Flamholtz 2002), which set out detailed models of accounting for actual labor cost, including not only compensations and benefits, but also expenses for employees' search, hiring, adaptation, training, etc.

The papers in the field of organizational economics analyze the organizational structure and HC of the firm in the relations with the strategy (Maister 1993, Menard 2000). These models well describe acts and operations that actually occurred, but they do not help much in HC strategic planning and management.

It is necessary to mention the recognized fundamental papers of G.S. Becker (Becker 1962, Becker 1975), who was awarded the Nobel Prize for the development of the theory of human capital. HC is defined as the stock of knowledge, skills, habits, and motivations that everyone has; education, job training, and other kinds of personnel development, healthcare, geographical mobility improvement can be considered as investments in HC. Investing in professional training and education, students and their parents behave rationally; analyzing the benefits and costs, they compare the expected marginal return from such investments with the return from alternatives (bank interests, dividends, etc.). Depending on what is economically feasible, a decision is made either to continue education or to terminate it and start working. Rates of return act, therefore, as a regulator of the distribution of investments between different types and levels of education, as well as between the educational system as a whole and the rest of the economy. High rates of return indicate underinvestment, while low ones overinvestment. In addition to theoretical reasoning, Becker was the first to carry out a practical, statistically correct calculation of the economic efficiency of education.

Uncertainty is an important factor of Enterprise human capital; stochastic approaches, queue models, and, in particular, Markov models are often used to model HC and to analyze, for example, waiting time, rejection probability, and other characteristics (Espinosa et al 2010, Gans et al 2003, Ibrahim et al 2016, Lee and Longton 1959).

The paper (Espinosa et al 2010) proposes an extension to the well-known BPMN-notation by the elements, called "Markov Decision Processes" and designated to represent the actions of employees executing task chains – decision-making. Such elements support full-scale simulation using a BPMN-model to obtain numerical estimates of the operating efficiency of the business as a whole. As a formal basis for the functioning of such elements, it is proposed to use various known formalisms, in particular, dynamic programming-based solutions.

The author of the paper (Badinelli 2010) considers the distribution of resources of a services enterprise. Stochastic models of the technological function (a function of converting inputs to outputs) are used to describe the uncertainty, being peculiar to services. A service enterprise as a whole is presented as a stochastic (generally speaking, Markov) network.

In the paper (Flamholtz et al 1984), the Markov chain is used to represent the behavior of employees of investment firms and to model future incomes that traders can generate. Such an assessment can be used to determine the HC volume (in financial terms) of the firm to support audit and due diligence of merge and acquisition.

The paper (Cao et al 2011) presents a set of tools developed for the personnel management at a service division of the IBM company (whose annual turnover at the time of writing the paper exceeded $4 billion). The purpose of development and introduction of the tools is to determine the level of investment in employee development to increase their productivity. The developers identified areas of investment as the most effective workforce management tools: hiring, training, career development, and retention (through incentives). The set of tools supports forecasting demand for human resources, planning based on risk analysis, assessment and optimization of employees' skills set, and related tasks.

It is important to note that in a considerable number of researches (Flamholtz et al (1984) and Cao et al (2011) are among them) employees are modeled as independently acting agents demonstrating Markov behavior.

Despite the large number of fundamental and applied works studying various factors of human capital, there is no model of active resource lifecycle that meets the set of requirements developed in the previous section, therefore, new quantitative methods and approaches should be developed for using as part of the Enterprise Control Problem solution.

6.2 POOLS OF ACTIVE RESOURCES AS A FORMAL REPRESENTATION OF HUMAN CAPITAL

6.2.1 BASIC MODEL OF POOL OF ACTIVE RESOURCES

Let's develop a HC model – a model of the evolution of the headcount of active resource pools, AEs' functional capabilities, operations costs, taking into account uncertainty and unevenness of the internal demand for active resources over time driven by external demand to the outputs of the Enterprise CA. The proposed model (Figure 6.3) describes the relationships of the above-listed factors with the objective function – economic output of the Enterprise (see Sections 3.4.2–3.4.4), and in Section 7.4 we demonstrate the use of the model to manage the HC. The discrete time model is used, as in the previous sections, and t means the number of the time period.

Active resource traffic (see also assumption A4). We model an Enterprise as a set of pools of active resources – AEs, having various functional capabilities; and AEs

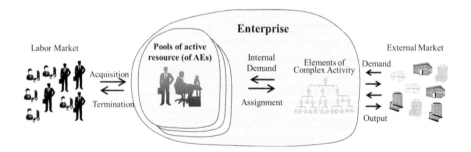

FIGURE 6.3   An Enterprise as a set of active resource pools.

are used to create the complex actors of CA. The AEs of each pool are thought to be statistically identical; let us denote by $n_i(\theta, t)$ the number of AEs of the i-th pool at the end of the t-th time period, who joined the Enterprise at $t - \theta$ ($\theta \geq 0$):

$$
\begin{cases}
n_i(0,t) = n_i^+(t) + n_i^{+\text{int}}(\theta,t); \\
n_i(\theta+1, t+1) = n_i(\theta,t) - n_i^{-\text{int}}(\theta,t) - n_i^{\text{lft}}(\theta,t) - n_i^{\text{fir}}(\theta,t).
\end{cases}
\tag{6.1}
$$

where $n_i^+(t)$ is the number of AEs of the i-th pool, newly hired during the t-th period, $n_i^{+\text{int}}(\theta,t)$ is the number of AEs transferred to the i-th pool from other pools as internal movements, $n_i^{-\text{int}}(\theta,t)$ is the number of AEs transferred from the i-th pool to other pools as internal movements, $n_i^{\text{fir}}(\theta,t)$ is the number of fired AEs, $n_i^{\text{lft}}(\theta,t)$ is the number of AEs that left the Enterprise.

Active resource traffic (6.1) is uncertain: the number of AEs leaving for their own motives $n_i^{\text{lft}}(\theta,t)$ (sometimes also $n_i^{+\text{int}}(\theta,t)$ and $n_i^{-\text{int}}(\theta,t)$) cannot be fully controlled by the actor of HCM.

Internal demand for the active resource caused by CA implementation is presented as a flow of actions of various types that need to be carried out to implement the CA of an Enterprise. Suppose that external deals requiring an implementation of the Enterprise CA appear as an uncertain result of some activity (for example, sales activity). We consider the actions of the same type to be statistically identical; let us denote by $d_j(\tau, t)$ the number of actions of the j-th type performed during τ periods ($\tau \geq 0$), counted at the end of the t-th time period:

$$
\begin{cases}
d_j(0,t) = d_j^+(t); \\
d_j(\tau+1, t+1) = d_j(\tau, t) - d_j^{\text{cml}}(\tau, t).
\end{cases}
\tag{6.2}
$$

where $d_j^+(t)$ is the number of actions of the j-th type initiated during the t-th period, $d_j^{\text{cml}}(\tau,t)$ is the number of actions of the j-th type completed during the t-th period.

Suppose, implementation of the k-th action of the j-th type requires AEs of the i-th pool in the number $m_i(k, j, \theta, t)$ to be assigned. The sum over all actions of all types $\sum_j \sum_{k=1}^{d_j(\tau,t)} m_i(k,j,\theta,t)$ determines the internal demand for active resources of the i-th pool. The flows $d_j^+(t)$ of the actions' initiations and $d_j^{\text{cml}}(\tau,t)$ terminations are uncertain ones (caused by uncertainty of the internal demand and the technology of CA) and create future uncertainty and unevenness in internal demand for active resources.

CA implementation. Let's consider implementation of activity. There are obvious constraints on the number of AEs assigned to implement actions:

$$
\sum_j \sum_{k=1}^{d_j(\tau,t)} m_i(k,j,\theta,t) \leq n_i(\theta, t); \quad \forall i, \tau, t;
\tag{6.3}
$$

To evaluate the economic output of an Enterprise, we follow the approaches of Flamholtz (1999) and take into account costs associated with the formation and use of active resources; let us denote different costs (for each l-th AE from i-th pool) as follows:

$c_{i,l}^{cmp}(\theta,t)$– compensation package (salary, bonuses and other financial benefits) and taxes,

$c_{i,l}^{trn}(\theta,t)$– professional training and education,

$c_{i,l}^{ad}(t)$– onboarding and adaptation,

$c_{i,l}^{off}(t)$ – search and offer preparation (including not hired),

$c_{i,l}^{imv}(\theta,t)$– internal movements and adaptation at a new position,

$c_{i,l}^{fir}(\theta,t)$– firing,

$c_{i,l}^{att}(\theta,t)$– attrition.

As well we take into account other costs $C^{oth}(t)$ not related to personnel; also we denote:

$u_i(t)$ – the number of job offers prepared and issued;

$v(i, \theta, j, \tau, t) > 0$ is the productivity – the output created by each AE of the i-th pool per period executing an action of the j-th type.

Following the definition given in Section 3.2.4, we consider the economic result of an Enterprise as the difference between the value or utility, obtained as an outcome of the Enterprise CA (the first sum over t in expression (6.4)), and the costs incurred for achieving this goal (the second, third, and fourth sums over t, deducted in expression (6.4)), expressed in unified numerical units. Then the Enterprise objective function, i.e. the output of HC as a whole, for the interval T, takes the form (as a special case of (3.16), Section 3.4.4):

$$\Phi\left(n[1*T]; d[1*T]; u[1*T]; v[1*T]; c^*[1*T]\right)$$

$$= \sum_{t=1}^{T} \delta(1;t) \sum_{\tau,\theta} \sum_{j,i} \sum_{k=1}^{d_j(\tau,t)} v(i,\theta,j,\tau,t) m_i(k,j,\tau,t)$$

$$- \sum_{t=1}^{T} \delta(1;t) \sum_{\theta=0}^{\infty} \sum_{i} \left[\sum_{l=1}^{n_i(\tau,t)} \left(c_{i,l}^{cmp}(\theta,t) + c_{i,l}^{trn}(\theta,t) \right) \right.$$

$$+ \sum_{l=1}^{n_i^{+int}(t)} c_{i,l}^{imv}(t) \sum_{l=1}^{n_i^{fir}(\theta,t)} c_{i,l}^{fir}(\theta,t) + \left. \sum_{l=1}^{n_i^{lft}(\theta,t)} c_{i,l}^{att}(\theta,t) \right]$$

$$- \sum_{t=1}^{T} \delta(1;t) \sum_{i} \left[\sum_{l=1}^{n_i^{+}(t)} c_{i,l}^{ad}(t) + \sum_{l=1}^{u_i(t)} c_{i,l}^{off}(t) \right] - \sum_{t=1}^{T} \delta(1;t) C^{oth}(t)$$

(6.4)

where $c^*(t)$ denotes* the vector of costs of all kinds.

In (6.4) the output of each AE activity is formed by multiplying AE's productive time (during which the AE is assigned to implement the required actions) by AE's productivity $v(i, \theta, j, \tau, t)$, and the output of the Enterprise is formed by summing the outputs of all AEs of all pools. The operation of summing is absolutely adequate to this problem, because the synergistic effects of the joint work of group of AEs (reflecting the complicated, systemic nature of an Enterprise CA) are taken into account through the needs functions $m_i(k, j, \theta, t)$ and the corresponding assignments. Expression (6.4) does not reflect the market value of the outputs of an Enterprise from the point of view of consumers. However, the problem (6.4) consists in resource management, which does not require consideration of market value, and the proposed expression just represents the contribution of active resources to the output creation.

Expressions (6.1) – (6.4), which correspond to the concepts and principles of management accounting, are accurate from a financial and economic point of view and being compiled without any simplifying assumptions are suitable for accounting of the actual outputs of an Enterprise CA. Solution of the problem (6.4) can be used for strategical and operational planning and management of any kind of Enterprises: the result $\Phi(\cdot)$ should be optimized based on the forecast of the future behavior of the Enterprise and all constituents depending on influencing factors.

As in expression (3.16), parts of the variables in the model (6.1–6.4) are known and manageable; these are costs of all types $c^*(t)$, the number of offers $u_i(t)$ and internal transfers $n_i^{+\mathrm{int}}(\theta,t)$, as well as $n_i^{\mathrm{fir}}(\theta,t)$ – the number of fired AEs by the actor of HCM. Another part of the variables is known, but is not controllable by the actor of the HCM – for example, the needs functions $m_i(k, j, \theta, t)$. The third part of the parameters is uncertain; those are the number of candidates who accepted/rejected offers $n_i^+(t)$ and such of transfer $n_i^{+\mathrm{int}}(\theta,t)$, the attrition $n_i^{\mathrm{att}}(\theta,t)$, as well as the internal demand for active resources $d_j^+(t)$. The optimization problem with respect to the result $\Phi(\cdot)$, taking into account conditions (6.1) – (6.3), can be formulated as a search for the values of the controlled variables $u_i(t)$, $n_i^{+\mathrm{int}}(\theta,t)$, $n_i^{-\mathrm{int}}(\theta,t)$, $n_i^{\mathrm{att}}(\theta,t)$, $c^*(t)$, by satisfying constraints (6.1–6.3) and ensuring a maximum to output (6.4), while taking into account the elimination of uncertainty, similarly to (3.17–3.19):

$$\operatorname*{def}_{n[1*T];d[1*T]} \left\{ \Phi\left(n[1*T]; d[1*T]; u[1*T]; v[1*T]; c^*[1*T] \right) \right\} \to \max_{u[1*T], \dots, c^*[1*T],} \quad (6.5)$$

However, the problem "in direct strict form" (6.5) is not so complicated due to the dimension (a large number of parameters that change values over time), as it has a very limited value due to the uncertainty of CA. True uncertainty leads to the fact that reasonable assumptions about the future CA execution cannot be rigorous and thoroughly consider "all the details" of CA (for example, the labor market state

---

* Without loss of generality, both the output and the costs can be interpreted as recognized upon completion of work, and as accrued parameters of work in progress, and as the accumulated amounts of payments, or other financial and economic indicators.

which affects personnel hiring, salary levels, and attrition intensity cannot be precisely forecasted for long periods).

Therefore, in order to solve the human capital management problem, in Chapter 7 we make assumptions that enable the practical use of the basic model (6.1–6.4) and transform the basic model to a form convenient for efficiency analysis and Enterprise optimization.

6.2.2 THE HUMAN CAPITAL EFFECT ON ENTERPRISE OUTPUT

Using the model of a pool of active resources (6.1–6.4), let's study the effect of the AEs' lifecycle on the CA effectiveness in a practical case; let's analyze how HC influences an output of an Enterprise. For simplicity, we consider one pool of resources (one category of AEs) in a stationary case.

We eliminate the uncertainty of the internal demand for active resources by averaging and assume that $D \underset{d[1*T]}{=} \operatorname{def} \sum_{j} \sum_{k=1}^{d_j(\tau,t)} m_i(k,j,\theta,t) = E\left[\sum_{j}\sum_{k=1}^{d_j(\tau,t)} m_i(k,j,\theta,t)\right]$, the

average value of the internal demand, expressed in the number of AEs needed to implement CA, is constant in time.

We also eliminate the uncertainty of AE traffic by averaging and characterizing the uncertainty of a candidate's decision (to accept or reject an offer) by an acceptance probability π to be constant in time. We also use a probabilistic approach to model the uncertainty of AE attrition. We assume AE's time-in-the-pool (from the entering to the leaving) to be a random integer positive variable with the distribution $\{\varphi_\theta\}$ also being constant in time.

Additionally, a possible unevenness of AE's productivity during various periods of the time-in-the-pool is introduced in the model: the AE's productivity is modelled by a function $S(\theta)$ of the average output (taking into account the operational costs) during the whole time-in-the-pool of θ periods (if AE leaves the pool exactly after θ periods).

All the abovementioned considerations allow for the expression of the output (6.4) to be reduced as follows:

$$\Phi(n_{off};\pi;c_{rpl};c_{off};T) = \Delta(T)\left\{ n_{off}\pi\left[\sum_{\theta=0}^{\infty}\varphi_\theta S(\theta) - c_{rpl}\right] - n_{off}c_{off}\right\} - \Phi^* \quad (6.6)$$

where

n_{off} is the average number of offers formed during one period of time,

c_{off} is the average costs of preparation of one offer, including search for candidates;

c_{rpl} is the average costs of replacement of left AE, including transaction costs for recruitment, adaptation, and other,*

---

* In the composition of these costs it also makes sense to include a cost to temporarily attract human resources for a period of searching for constant ones. For example, by organizing overtime work for regular employees.

$\Delta(T) = \sum_{t=1}^{T} \delta(1;t)$ is a cumulative farsightedness of a HCM actor,

Φ^* is a constituent of the output, not related to the resource pool.

To study (6.6) analytically we simplify productivity function $S(\theta)$: we suppose that the AE's productivity during the initial adaptation interval t_{ad} and terminal interval before leaving t_{trm} is lower than during the main interval of productive execution. The expression (6.6) is analytically researched and the effect of characteristics of LCs of active resources on the output of an Enterprise is studied in Appendix A6.1. The performed analysis can be easily extended to the case of several pools of active resources, as well as to the case of a nonstationary process (with a known trend) of the internal demand for AEs, required to implement complex activity.

The results of Appendix A6.1 can be formulated as a practical *Proposition 6.1.* "On a dependence of the Enterprise effectiveness on the characteristics of the life-cycle of active resources."

The output of an Enterprise, regardless of the probability distribution of AE's time-in-the-pool (from the entering to the leaving) increases monotonically if: (a) the acceptance probability π increases $\partial\Phi/\partial\pi > 0$; (b) the duration of adaptation interval t_{ad} decrease $\partial\Phi/\partial t_{ad.} < 0$ and the duration of the interval t_{trm} preceding leaving decrease $\partial\Phi/\partial t_{trm} < 0$; (c) the average time-in-the-pool t_{avg} increases $\partial\Phi/\partial t_{avg} > 0$ (due to a change in the probabilities of leaving later than the total duration of adaptation interval and prior to leaving interval). •

Proposition 6.1 states intuitively clear relationships, but does this on the basis of mathematically rigorous reasoning given in Appendix A6.1. The statement also illustrates the importance of on-line control of the characteristics of AEs' lifecycle, to ensure effective Enterprise operations.

6.3   STATISTICS OF THE ACTIVE RESOURCE TRAFFIC

As is noted above, the active choice of people comes down to two types of decisions: (a) acceptance/rejection of offers (when joining the Enterprise) and (b) leaving or staying at the Enterprise. These decisions affect the traffic and temporal characteristics of AEs' lifecycles, and, in turn, the characteristics considerably affect the Enterprise output (as Proposition 6.1 states). The foregoing emphasizes the actuality and importance of analyzing and controlling AEs' traffic to ensure the effectiveness of the Enterprise and to reach the optimal solution of Enterprise Control Problem.

6.3.1   NONPARAMETRIC STATISTICS OF THE ACTIVE RESOURCE TRAFFIC

Let's study the active resource traffic using the probabilistic model.

The AEs' pool is an organized set of functionally identical and statistically independent AEs, and the headcount must be maintained at a given level (in the general case, changing over time). That is, in case of an AE leaving, a new AE should be hired as soon as possible to fill a vacant position. We assume that a *pool* consists of identical functional roles, each of which is nearly always occupied by AEs whose behavior is statistically identical and independent of each other. Then events of AEs' leaving each of the roles form independent processes, consisting in the fact that, if the previous leaving (and replacement) occurred on the t_d-th period of time, then the next leaving will occur on the t-th period with a probability φ_{t-t_d}. If the *time-in-the-pool distribution* $\{\varphi_\theta\}$ is given and it is known that the previous leaving occurred at the moment t_d at some role, then the probability of the next leaving on the t-th period

equals to $\varphi_{t-t_d} / \sum\limits_{\theta=t-t_d}^{\infty} \varphi_\theta$ * (knowing that there was not any leaving of this role

between t_d and t).

The use of probabilities, calculated in such a way, for all roles of the pool is convenient for an analytical study of a pool headcount evolution. However, their use is hampered by the fact that the distribution of AEs' time-in-the-pool $\{\varphi_\theta\}$ is not a priori known and it is not based on objective fundamental laws, but is driven by the active choice of people. Thus, the statistical estimation technique is the only tool to get the distribution $\{\varphi_\theta\}$ (or its characteristics). It's reasonable to believe that nature in general and the external conditions of the attrition process in particular are characterized by certain variability. One can talk about the existence of successive periods of uniformity of conditions (*stationarity*), which fundamentally limits accessible observation intervals and the volume of data appropriate for statistical estimations.

Appendix A6.2 explores estimation techniques and the use of estimates $\{\varphi_\theta\}$ for analysis of the output of an Enterprise (see above and Appendix A6.1).

The study shows that even in case of a headcount of several tens of thousands AEs, the accuracy of the distribution estimate $\{\varphi_\theta\}$ is very poor. The width of confidential interval is more or less acceptable only for very small values of time-in-the-pool and increases sharply with increasing time-in-the-pool (see Appendix A6.2) that makes the estimated distribution practically inapplicable. The practical proposition follows from this research:

Proposition 6.2: A time-in-the-pool probability distribution (or an intensity function) can be used to analyze and make managerial decisions only for relatively very small values of time-in-the-pool. For all other cases, it is not correct to use the time-in-the-pool probability distribution (or the intensity function) for leaving the pool due to the impossibility of getting reliable estimates. •

It is stated above (Proposition 6.1) that the number of AEs leaving at low values of time-in-the-pool should be as small as possible; ideally this number should tend toward zero. Therefore, a reliable estimation and detailed analysis of the probability distribution for small values of time-in-the-pool can be used to analyze precisely this particular group of AEs, in order to make managerial decisions to reduce their share. In particular, it might be appropriate to use regression techniques for analyzing

---

* The probabilities calculated in this way correspond to the case of the impossibility of more than one leaving of each role per one time period, i.e. $\varphi_0=0$. If this is not so, the probabilities of one or more leaving is different, which, however, does not affect all other results of the work and conclusions.

factors affecting early flight. In other cases, it is feasible to use other approaches based on less "detailed" models based on aggregated characteristics of the AEs' traffic; for example, the average share of AEs who leave the pool over one period and the average share of offers accepted by candidates – such parameters are employed in the human capital planning models (Section 7.4).

6.3.2   SEQUENTIAL ANALYSIS OF THE ACTIVE RESOURCE TRAFFIC

The external environment of an Enterprise is characterized by considerable variability; periodic changes of key factors of external conditions significantly affect, in their turn, active resources and parameters of their lifecycles. A significant dependence of the Enterprise's productivity on the characteristics of the lifecycles of active resources actualizes a problem to detect, as expeditiously as possible and at the same time as reliably as possible, moments of a change ("disorder") in the characteristics of LCs of active resources.

Let's consider the problem of optimal detection of such changes using the probabilistic model.

We assume that, until the moment of disorder, the characteristics of the LC of active resources retain some constant values, and after a disorder they differ but are also constant. The characteristics of the LC of active resources are not a priori known either before or after disorder, and their values should be estimated based on observations of stochastic processes μ_t^1 of AEs' admission, and μ_t^2 AEs leaving. Let us preserve the assumption on the statistical equivalence (within one pool) and the independence of the AEs' behavior from each other and during different time periods. Suppose a priori there are observations during a preliminary time interval, about which it is known that it's a single interval of stationary external conditions. Based on the observations accumulated during this preliminary interval, the characteristics of LCs should be estimated. And after that it is necessary, based on current observations, to make sequential decisions on the presence or absence of disorder – to detect a change in the characteristics of lifecycles of the active resource.

By taking into account practical Proposition 6.2, about the impossibility of reliable identification of the probability distribution $\{\varphi_\theta\}$, the *attrition process* μ_t^2 will be considered not in detail for each AE, but aggregately, i.e. over the pool as a whole. The attrition flow intensity $\lambda(t)$ of the whole pool is used to model the attrition process – to estimate initial stationary value of $\lambda(t)$ and to detect its changes. Obviously, with such an approach, i.e. of deliberate "roughening" of the model, one loses some information that could theoretically be taken into account, if the probability distribution $\{\varphi_\theta\}$ was reliably known, but in practice this loss is inevitable.

The headcount N_t of the pool (we model the only pool) is observable over time:

$$N_{t+1} = N_t + \mu_t^1 - \mu_t^2 \tag{6.7}$$

where

μ_t^1 characterizes the *hiring process* – the sequence of independent random values, distributed binomially with parameters $n_{off}(t)$ and $\pi(t)$;

μ_t^2 characterizes the attrition process – the sequence of independent random variables distributed binomially with parameters N_t and $\lambda(t)$.

The average headcount evolves over time as $E[N_{t+1}] = (1 - \lambda(t))E[N_t] + \pi(t)n_{off}(t)$ or

$$E[N_{t+T}] = \prod_{\omega=1}^{T}(1 - \lambda(t+\omega))E[N_t] + \sum_{\tau=1}^{T}\prod_{\omega=\tau}^{T}(1 - \lambda(t+\omega))\pi(t+\tau)n_{off}(t+\tau).$$

In the stationary case ($\lambda(t) = \lambda = $ const, $n_{off}(t) = n_{off} = $ const and $\pi(t) = \pi = $ const), we get $E[N_{t+T}] = N_{st} + (1 - \lambda)^T(E[N_t] - N_{st})$, where $N_{st} = \lim_{T\to\infty} E[N_{t+T}] = \pi n_{off}\lambda^{-1}$.

Then, formally, the *disorder detection problem* can be posed as follows: the unobservable two-dimensional process $x(t) = (\pi(t); \lambda(t))^T$ takes a constant value until an a priori unknown moment of disorder, at which the process $x(t)$ changes its value to another constant. It is necessary to detect the disorder moment on the basis of sequential observations of the process $y(t) = (\mu_t^1; \mu_t^2; N_t; n_{off}(t))^T$, related to $x(t)$. The initial value of the process $x(t)$ is estimated on the basis of the observations $y(t)$ during the preliminary interval of a duration T_{prl} (conventionally at time points $-T_{prl}$; $-T_{prl} + 1$; $-T_{prl} + 2$; ...; 0), about which it is known that during the same, disorder did not occur.

We use *maximum likelihood estimates*. Let's denote: $N_{[u,v]} = \sum_{\tau=u}^{v} N_\tau$;

$\mu_{[u,v]}^1 = \sum_{\tau=u}^{v}\mu_\tau^1$; $\mu_{[u,v]}^2 = \sum_{\tau=u}^{v}\mu_\tau^2$; $n_{[u,v]} = \sum_{\tau=u}^{v} n_{off}(\tau)$. The estimate $(\hat{\pi}_0; \hat{\lambda}_0)^T$ of the initial value of the process $x(t)$ has the following form and characteristics:

$\hat{\pi}_0 = (n_{off[-T_{prl};0]})^{-1}\mu_{[-T_{prl};0]}^1$; $E[\hat{\pi}_0] = \pi_0$; $\text{cov}[\hat{\pi}_0; \hat{\lambda}_0] = 0$;

$var[\hat{\pi}_0] = \pi_0(1-\pi_0)(n_{off[-T_{prl};0]})^{-1}$; $\hat{\lambda}_0 = (N_{[-T_{prl};0]})^{-1}\mu_{[-T_{prl};0]}^2$; $E[\hat{\lambda}_0] = \lambda_0$;

$var[\hat{\lambda}_0] = \lambda_0(1-\lambda_0)(N_{[-T_{prl};0]})^{-1}$.

In business practice, the values $n_{off[-T_{prl};0]}; \mu_{[-T_{prl};0]}^1; N_{[-T_{prl};0]}$ and $\mu_{[-T_{prl};0]}^2$ are of the order of several hundred; therefore, the probability distribution for elements of the vector $y(t)$ is well approximated by a normal one, therefore, the estimate $(\hat{\pi}_0; \hat{\lambda}_0)^T$ is unbiased and consistent, and its deviation from the true value of $x(t)$ can be neglected.

The decision of disorder detection at each time point t actually consists in checking a family of hypotheses $\mathbf{H}_\tau$ if disorder occurred at the time point $t_p = t - \tau$ ($\tau \geq 1$) against a hypothesis $\mathbf{H}_0$ that there is no disorder.

Let's use a logarithmic relative likelihood function (l.r.l.f.) calculated at time t based on observations over the interval $[-T_{prl};t]$ for a couple of events: (a) that disorder occurred at the time point $t_p = t - \theta$; and (b) no disorder up to the current moment has occurred: $\Omega(t;\theta) = \ln(\Pr(y|_{-T_{prl}}^t; t;\theta)) = \sum_{\tau=t-\theta+1}^{t} \Delta l(\tau)$, where $\Delta l(t)$ are local l.r.l.f.s

for each time period $\Delta l(t) = \ln(\Pr(y(t)|t_p < t)) - \ln(\Pr(y(t)|t_p \geq t))$. A relative likelihood criterion has the form:

$$\begin{cases} H_0: \max_\theta \{\Omega(t;\theta)\} \le C; \\ H\text{-}: \max_\theta \{\Omega(t;\theta)\} > C; \end{cases} \quad \text{and} \quad \tau = \arg\max_\theta \{\Omega(t;\theta)\} \qquad (6.8)$$

In disorder problems in such a setting, a criterion equivalent to (6.8) is traditionally used (see, for example, Shiryayev (1977) and Nikiforov (2016)), based on statistics $L(t) = \max\{0; L(t-1) + \Delta l(t)\}$, of the form:

$$\begin{cases} H_0: L(t) \le C; \\ H\text{-}: L(t) > C; \end{cases} \quad \tau = \arg\min_\theta \{L(t-\theta) = 0\} \qquad (6.9)$$

Study of the characteristics of sequential criteria (errors of the first and second kind in a sequential interpretation) is always a difficult task, which has been explored by many researchers, starting with Wald's fundamental work (Wald 1947). To date, a significant number of results in the field of sequential analysis have been received and various methods of practical importance have been proposed, for example, in papers by Shiryayev (1977), Nikiforov (1983), Bartroff et al (2008), and Nikiforov (2016). In particular, in Nikiforov (1983), the problematics of obtaining analytical expressions of characteristics of those criteria that are similar to (6.9) are analyzed, and the impossibility of obtaining exact analytical expressions for the same is noted. At the same time, Nikiforov (1983, chapter 4) offers an exhaustive number of various approximations and boundary estimates for the average time between false disorder detection and the average time delay from the moment disorder occurs until such is detected. The mentioned boundary estimates are based on the values of the first and second moments of increments of the decision functions $\Delta l(t)$ before and after disorder, when $\Delta l(t)$ are independent normally distributed random values.

Normally, before the disorder, the average values of the process $\Delta l(t)$ are negative, and after a disorder they become positive. Under these conditions, analytical expressions can be obtained for the boundaries of each of the characteristics of the criterion, i.e. as the average time T_{fd} between false detections of disorder and T_{dl} as the average time from the moment of disorder to the moment of its revelation.

Let's introduce (using expressions (4.2.14–16) from Nikiforov (1983, p. 67)) a function $a(m, h)$, which depends on the normalized average value m of increments in the decision functions $\Delta l(t)$ and the threshold of the criterion h and has the form

$$a(m, h) = \frac{1}{2m^2}\left(e^{-2mh} - 1 + 2mh\right) + \frac{\varphi(m)}{m\Phi(m)} + 1,$$

$$\text{where } \varphi(x) = \frac{1}{\sqrt{2\pi}} e^{-\frac{x^2}{2}} \text{ and } \Phi(x) = \int_{-\infty}^{x} \varphi(\chi)\,d\chi.$$

The function $a(m, h)$ allows Nikiforov (1983) to obtain the boundary values of the characteristics of all criteria by inserting the process moments $\Delta l(t)$: $T_{fd} > a(m_0, h_0)$; $T_{dl} < a(m_\tau, h_\tau)$, where $m_\theta = E[\Delta l(t)|H_\theta]/(var[\Delta l(t)|H_\theta])^{1/2}$ and $h_\theta = C/(var[\Delta l(t)|H_\theta])^{1/2}$ for $\theta = 0; \tau$.

These expressions can be used to make a reasonable choice of the parameter's decision criterion: threshold C and the rate γ of the expected change of $x(t)$.

It should be noted that the solution of the problem occurs under conditions when the values of changes in the process $x(t)$ are a priori unknown. The detection of an attrition intensity increase $\hat{\lambda}_0 \to \hat{\lambda}_0 + \Delta\lambda$ and/or a decrease of the offer acceptance probability of $\hat{\pi}_0 \to \hat{\pi}_0 - \Delta\pi$ has practical significance. At the same time, usually there are no a priori reasons to consider simultaneous changes in both components π and λ; in the general case one should believe that these can change independently. Therefore, let's consider several scenarios of disorder: the independent or simultaneous increment $\hat{\lambda}_0 \to \hat{\lambda}_0 + \Delta\lambda$ and $\hat{\pi}_0 \to \hat{\pi}_0 - \Delta\pi$ in one or more pools

Scenario 1. Detection of the independent changes $\hat{\lambda}_0 \to \hat{\lambda}_0 + \Delta\lambda$ and $\hat{\pi}_0 \to \hat{\pi}_0 - \Delta\pi$ of one active resource pool (relatively significant changes, not less than, say, by $\gamma = 10\%$). In this case, the problem naturally splits into two parallel tasks, i.e. based on observations $y_{[-T_{prl};t]}$ to detect changes $\{\hat{\pi}_0 \to (1-\gamma)\hat{\pi}_0; \gamma \geq 0,1\}$ and $\{\hat{\lambda}_0 \to (1+\gamma)\hat{\lambda}_0; \gamma \geq 0,1\}$. Then, instead of criterion (6.9), two parallel and independent ones are used, having form (6.9), but differing in the values of the thresholds C_1 and C_2, as well as in the form of the functions of local l.r.l.f.s:

$$\Delta l^1(t) = \mu_t^1 ln(1-\gamma) + \left(n_{off,t} - \mu_t^1\right) ln\left(1 + \gamma\frac{\hat{\pi}_0}{1-\hat{\pi}_0}\right)$$

$$= n_{off,t} ln\left(1 + \gamma\frac{\hat{\pi}_0}{1-\hat{\pi}_0}\right) + \mu_t^1 ln\left(1 - \gamma\frac{1}{1-\hat{\pi}_0+\gamma\hat{\pi}_0}\right)$$

$$\Delta l^2(t) = \mu_t^2 ln(1+\gamma) + \left(N_t - \mu_t^2\right) ln\left(1 - \gamma\frac{\hat{\lambda}_0}{1-\hat{\lambda}_0}\right)$$

$$= N_t ln\left(1 - \gamma\frac{\hat{\lambda}_0}{1-\hat{\lambda}_0}\right) + \mu_t^2 ln\left(1 + \gamma\frac{1}{1-\hat{\lambda}_0+\gamma\hat{\lambda}_0}\right)$$

It is easy to see that $\Delta l^i(t) = a^i y(t)$, where a^i are constants (vectors-rows). Therefore, each of the processes $\Delta l^1(t)$, $\Delta l^2(t)$ forms a sequence of independent random variables, the probability distribution for which being adequately approximated by a normal one with the parameters:

$$E\left[\Delta l^1(t)\right] = n_{off,t}\, ln\left(1 + \gamma/(1-\hat{\pi}_0)\right) + E\left[\mu_t^1\right] ln\left(1 - \gamma/(1-\hat{\pi}_0+\gamma\hat{\pi}_0)\right);$$

$$var\left[\Delta l^1(t)\right] = \left(ln\left(1 - \gamma/(1-\hat{\pi}_0+\gamma\hat{\pi}_0)\right)\right)^2 var\left[\mu_t^1\right];$$

$$E\left[\Delta l^2(t)\right] = N_t\, ln\left(1 - \gamma/(1-\hat{\lambda}_0)\right) + E\left[\mu_t^2\right] ln\left(1 + \gamma/(1-\hat{\lambda}_0+\gamma\hat{\lambda}_0)\right);$$

$$var\left[\Delta l^2(t)\right] = \left(ln\left(1 + \gamma/(1-\hat{\lambda}_0+\gamma\hat{\lambda}_0)\right)\right)^2 var\left[\mu_t^2\right].$$

Scenario 2. Revelation of the simultaneous changes $\hat{\lambda}_0 \rightarrow \hat{\lambda}_0 + \Delta\lambda$ and $\hat{\pi}_0 \rightarrow \hat{\pi}_0 - \Delta\pi$ of one pool of active resources, also by $\gamma \geq 10\%$. If it is supposed that the changes $\Delta\pi$ and $\Delta\lambda$ occur simultaneously, then the decision is made on the basis of a single detection criterion of the changes $\{\hat{\pi}_0 \rightarrow (1-\gamma)\hat{\pi}_0; \hat{\lambda}_0 \rightarrow (1+\gamma)\hat{\lambda}_0; \gamma \geq 0,1\}$, in which the function of local l.r.l.f.s has the form:

$$\Delta l(t) = \Delta l^1(t) + \Delta^2 l(t) = \mu_t^1 \ln(1-\gamma) + \left(n_{off,t} - \mu_t^1\right) \ln\left(1 + \frac{\gamma\hat{\pi}_0}{1-\hat{\pi}_0}\right)$$

$$+ \mu_t^2 \ln(1+\gamma) + \left(N_t - \mu_t^2\right) \ln\left(1 - \frac{\gamma\hat{\lambda}_0}{1-\hat{\lambda}_0}\right)$$

where the first two summands detect $\hat{\pi}_0 \rightarrow \hat{\pi}_0 - \Delta\pi$, i.e. a decrease in probability, and the second two $\hat{\lambda}_0 \rightarrow \hat{\lambda}_0 + \Delta\lambda$, i.e. an increase in intensity.

The process $\Delta l(t)$ forms a sequence of independent random variables, the distribution of which is adequately approximated by a normal one with the parameters:

$$E[\Delta l(t)] = E[\Delta l^1(t)] + E[\Delta l^2(t)]; var[\Delta l(t)] = var[\Delta l^1(t)] + var[\Delta l^2(t)].$$

Scenario 3. A case where an Enterprise consists of a significant number of equivalent but independent (for example, geographically distributed) pools of active resources has practical significance; at that, there are grounds to assume that in the normal state the characteristics of all pools are identical. One treats as disorder the occurrence of anomaly behavior of the AEs of the different pools independently by $\hat{\lambda}_0 \rightarrow \hat{\lambda}_0 + \Delta\lambda$ and $\hat{\pi}_0 \rightarrow \hat{\pi}_0 - \Delta\pi$, while in the normal state, such behavior is stationary in time and identical for all pools. That is, for each i-th ($i = 1, 2, ..., I$) pool of active resources, it is necessary to check a family of hypotheses $\mathbf{H}_\tau$ that, starting from time $t - \tau$ ($\tau \geq 1$), the characteristics of this pool began to differ from the characteristics of all other pools against hypothesis $\mathbf{H}_0$ regarding the fact that the characteristics of this pool are equal to the characteristics of all other pools. In this case, it is feasible to form the local l.r.l.f.s $\Delta l_i^{1,2}(t)$ for all pools on each time period and apply the criterion of form (6.9). Let's consider the form of the local l.r.l.f.s $\Delta l_i^1(t)$ and $\Delta l_i^2(t)$ in this case, similarly to scenario 1.

$$\Delta l_i^1(t) = \mu_{i,t}^1 \ln(1-\gamma) + \left(n_{offi,t} - \mu_{i,t}^1\right) \ln\left(1 + \gamma\frac{\hat{\pi}_{0,i}}{1-\hat{\pi}_{0,i}}\right);$$

$$\Delta l_i^2(t) = \mu_{i,t}^2 \ln(1+\gamma) + \left(N_{i,t} - \mu_{i,t}^2\right) \ln\left(1 - \gamma\frac{\hat{\lambda}_{0,i}}{1-\hat{\lambda}_{0,i}}\right)$$

where $\hat{\pi}_{0,i} = \sum_{j\neq i} \mu_{j,[-T_{prl};0]}^1 / \sum_{j\neq i} n_{offj,[-T_{prl};0]};$ $E\left[\hat{\pi}_{0,i}\right] = \pi_0$;

$$var\left[\hat{\pi}_{0,i}\right] = \pi_0 (1-\pi_0) / n_{off,i,[-T_{prl};0]};$$

$$\hat{\lambda}_{0,i} = \sum_{j \neq i} \mu^2_{j,[-T_{prl};0]} / \sum_{j \neq i} N_{j,[-T_{prl};0]} \; ;$$

$$E\left[\hat{\lambda}_{0,i}\right] = \lambda_0; \quad var\left[\hat{\lambda}_{0,i}\right] = \lambda_0 / N_{i,[-T_{prl};0]}; \quad cov\left[\hat{\pi}_0;\hat{\lambda}_0\right] = 0.$$

Expressions for the moments $\Delta l_i^1(t)$ and $\Delta l_i^2(t)$ are similar to expressions for scenario 1.

Scenario 4. Many independent pools and a simultaneous change $\hat{\lambda}_0 \rightarrow \hat{\lambda}_0 + \Delta\lambda$ and $\hat{\pi}_0 \rightarrow \hat{\pi}_0$. For this case, local l.r.l.f.s are equal to $\Delta l_i(t) = \Delta l_i^1(t) + \Delta l_i^2(t)$, and their moments are similar to scenario 2.

Appendix A6.3 demonstrates the verification that for each of the scenarios the average values of the decision functions $\Delta l^i(t)$ before disorder are negative, and after the same those are positive; that is to say that all the considered decision functions have a property to detect disorder.

CONCLUSION

This chapter is devoted to modeling and studying the systemic aspects of the human capital of an Enterprise. Human capital is considered to be people organized within an Enterprise, with their knowledge, skills, habits, and personal and social attributes (including creativity) embodied in the ability to produce value in performing Enterprise CA.

Human capital is formalized as a set of pools of identical active elements – people – from whom superiors form subordinate CA actors.

Human capital management is considered to be the management of the capabilities of active resource pools, the functional capabilities of AEs, and their headcount, to meet the internal demand of the Enterprise's CA implementation at different moments of time. Methods and algorithms for optimal human capital planning are presented in Section 7.4.

A basic model of a pool of active resources, described in Section 6.2.1, as well as the results of its study, is the main result of the chapter. The model reflects, on the one hand, the uncertainty of the people's active choice (embodied in their traffic) and, on the other hand, all possible costs associated with the people within an Enterprise, adequately describing in such a way the lifecycles of active resources. It is important to note from a practical point of view that the proposed model and analysis results are formed based on management accounting approaches, without any simplifying assumptions, and allow all traditionally considered types of labor costs to be considered. At the same time, the models and methods of analysis take into account the main aspects of implementation of complex activity, primarily uncertainty in the internal demand for active resources and their traffic.

Proposition 6.1 is formulated based on an analytical study of the model (Section 6.2.2 and Appendix 6.1), fixing the dependence of an Enterprise's productivity on the parameters of lifecycles of active resources (a monotonic increase in productivity with an increase in the probability of accepting the offer, with a decrease in the duration of the adaptation phase and the duration of the phase preceding leaving, and with an increase in the average time-in-the-pool).

As a result of statistical research of the human capital model, Proposition 6.2 about the impossibility of obtaining reliable estimates of the detailed temporal characteristics of HC is formulated; consequently, it is reasonable to use aggregated and robust models of active resource traffic for practical purposes.

Based on the revealed (in Proposition 6.1) significant dependence of an Enterprise's productivity on the attributes of the active resource lifecycle (in particular, on their traffic), it is concluded that the problem of disorder parameters' control is relevant. Therefore, in Section 6.3.2, a sequential procedure is developed for disorder detection, scenarios of its practical implementation are analyzed, and its detecting characteristics are verified.

APPENDIXES

APPENDIX A6.1 THE EFFECT OF HUMAN CAPITAL ON ENTERPRISE OUTPUT

Consider concretized model (6.6) to analyze the effect of the attributes of AEs' lifecycles on the effectiveness of complex activity implemented by them in the practical case, i.e. let's analyze the effect of these characteristics on the productivity of an Enterprise.

An AE output $S(\cdot)$ during the entire time-in-the-pool is the sum of outputs over all the periods: $S(\cdot) = \sum_{\tau=1}^{\theta} s(\tau)$.

Let's consider the output $S(\cdot)$ in aggregated form: let us divide the AE's time-in-the-pool into three intervals: (a) adaptation, (b) productive work and (c) the one preceding leaving. Let us suppose that the output of an employee during intervals (a) and (c) is lower than during the interval of productive work:

$$s(\tau) = \begin{cases} s_{prd} - \Delta s_{ad} & \text{for } 0 \le \tau \le t_{ad} \\ s_{prd} & \text{for } t_{ad} < \tau \le \theta - t_{lv} \\ s_{prd} - \Delta s_{lv} & \text{for } \max\{t_{ad}; \theta - t_{lv}\} < \tau \le \theta \end{cases}$$

where
s_{prd} is the average output during the productive interval;
Δs_{ad} is the average output decrease during the adaptation interval;
t_{ad} is the average duration of the adaptation interval;
Δs_{lv} is the average output decrease of the interval preceding leaving;
t_{lv} is the average duration of the interval preceding leaving.

Thus the expression for $S(\cdot)$ is transformed into the form:

$$S(\theta) = \sum_{\tau=0}^{\theta} s(\tau) = s_{prd}\theta - \begin{cases} \Delta s_{ad}\theta & \text{for } 0 \le \theta \le t_{ad} \\ \Delta s_{ad}t_{ad} - \Delta s_{lv}(\theta - t_{ad}) & \text{for } t_{ad} < \theta \le t_{ad} + t_{lv} \\ \Delta s_{ad}t_{ad} - \Delta s_{lv}t_{lv} & \text{for } t_{ad} + t_{lv} < \theta \end{cases}$$

Wherefrom the average output S_{av} from an employee during the entire period of work in the pool (averaged by the duration of work in the pool) is:

$$S_{av} = \sum_{\theta=0}^{\infty} S(\theta)\varphi_\theta$$

$$= s_{prd} \sum_{\theta=0}^{\infty} \theta\varphi_\theta - \Delta s_{ad}\left[\sum_{\theta=0}^{t_{ad}} \theta\varphi_\theta + t_{ad} \sum_{\theta=t_{ad}+1}^{\infty} \varphi_\theta\right]$$

$$- \Delta s_{lv}\left[\sum_{\theta=t_{ad}+1}^{t_{ad}+t_{lv}} \theta\varphi_\theta + t_{lv} \sum_{\theta=t_{ad}+t_{lv}+1}^{\infty} \varphi_\theta\right]$$

Let's denote $v_{av} = \sum_{\theta=0}^{\infty} \theta\varphi_\theta$ as the average time-in-the-pool, as well as analogue val-

ues $t_{ad}^* = \sum_{\theta=0}^{t_{ad}} \theta\varphi_\theta + t_{ad} \sum_{\theta=t_{ad}+1}^{\infty} \varphi_\theta$ and $t_{lv}^* = \sum_{\theta=t_{ad}+1}^{t_{ad}+t_{lv}} \theta\varphi_\theta + t_{lv} \sum_{\theta=t_{ad}+t_{lv}+1}^{\infty} \varphi_\theta$. Let's note that,

$t_{ad}^* < t_{ad}$, $t_{ad}^* < t_{av}$; $t_{lv}^* < t_{lv}$, $t_{lv}^* < t_{av}$, then $S_{av} = \sum_{\theta=0}^{\infty} \varphi_\theta S(\theta) = s_{prd}t_{av} - \Delta s_{ad}t_{ad}^* - \Delta s_{lv}t_{lv}^*$.

Let us get an expression for the output of an Enterprise, by inserting the expression for S_{av} into (6.6):

$$\Phi\left(n_{off};\pi;c_{rpl};c_{off};T\right)$$

$$= \Delta(T)\left\{n_{off}\pi\left[s_{prd}t_{av} - \Delta s_{ad}t_{ad}^* - \Delta s_{lv}t_{lv}^* - c_{rpl}\right] - n_{off}c_{off}\right\} - \Phi^* \qquad \text{(A6.1)}$$

Obviously, πn_{off} is equal to the average number of new AEs joining an Enterprise during each period. And such, in its turn, is equal to the average number of those leaving, given the assumption about stationarity of processes.

The average headcount of a pool is driven by a demand (D) from the CA being implemented $\pi n_{off}t_{av} = D$. Let's insert $n_{off} = D/\pi t_{av}$ into (A6.1) and get:

$$\Phi\left(n_{off};\pi;c_{rpl};c_{off};T\right)$$

$$= \Delta(T)D\left\{s_{prd} - \left(\Delta s_{ad}t_{ad}^* + \Delta s_{lv}t_{lv}^* + c_{rpl} + c_{off}/\pi\right)/t_{av}\right\} - \Phi^* \qquad \text{(A6.2)}$$

Let's introduce $V(\cdot)$ as the effectiveness of one AE of the pool, normalized to one period:

$$V\left(\pi,\{\varphi_\theta\},t_{ad},t_{lv},c_{rpl},c_{off}\right)$$

$$= s_{prd} - \Delta s_{ad} t^*_{ad} / t_{av} - \Delta s_{lv} t^*_{lv} / t_{av} - c_{rpl} / t_{av} - c_{off} / (\pi t_{av}) \qquad (A6.3)$$

Then $\Phi(n_{off}; \pi; c_{rpl}; c_{off}; T) = \Delta(T)DV(\pi, \{\varphi_\theta\}, t_{ad}, t_{lv}, c_{rpl}, c_{off}) + \Phi^*$.

The parameters of AEs' lifecycles effect $\Phi(\cdot)$ in the same way as $V(\cdot)$, due to their linear connection; therefore, an analysis of the effect can be performed with respect to $V(\cdot)$ (A6.3); let's do this.

The first element of expression (A6.3) is the average output s_{prd} of AE during one period during the productive interval; obviously, an increase in s_{prd} monotonically increases $V(\cdot)$ and $\Phi(\cdot)$.

The values of the decrease in the output Δs_{ad} and Δs_{lv}, as well as the costs c_{rpl} and c_{off} are included in (A6.3) as additive members with negative coefficients $(-t^*_{ad}/t_{av}, -t^*_{lv}/t_{av}, -1/t_{av}, -1/(\pi t_{av}))$; therefore, it is obvious that the growth of each of the values monotonically decreases the output $\Phi(\cdot)$.

Let us analyze the dependence of $V(\cdot)$ on the characteristics of traffic $\pi, \{\varphi_\theta\}, t_{ad}, t_{lv}$.

First, the probability π has an effect on the value of the function $V(\cdot)$, only by being included in the element $c_{off}/(\pi t_{av})$. Therefore, it is obvious that the function $V(\cdot)$ monotonically increases by π given any values of all its parameters, that is $\partial V(\cdot)/\partial\pi > 0$ and $\partial\Phi(\cdot)/\partial\pi > 0$, at that, given π tends to zero, $V(\cdot)$ can decrease unlimitedly: $\lim\limits_{\pi\to 0}\{\Phi(n_{off}; \pi; c_{rpl}; c_{off}; T)\} = -\infty$.

Secondly, the duration of the adaptation period t_{ad} has an effect on the function $V(\cdot)$ only through the element $-\Delta s_{ad} t^*_{ad}/t_{av}$. At the same time, t_{av} does not depend on t_{ad}, and from $t^*_{ad} = \sum\limits_{\theta=0}^{t_{ad}}\theta\varphi_\theta + t_{ad}\sum\limits_{\theta=t_{ad}+1}^{\infty}\varphi_\theta$ it directly follows that t^*_{ad} increases monotonically with the growth of t_{ad}. Therefore, $\partial V(\cdot)/\partial t_{ad} < 0$ and $\partial\Phi(\cdot)/\partial t_{ad} < 0$. Similar considerations are also valid for the duration of the interval preceding leaving; therefore, $\partial V(\cdot)/\partial t_{lv} < 0$ and $\partial\Phi(\cdot)/\partial t_{lv} < 0$. From a business point of view, the monotonical decrease in the function $\Phi(\cdot)$ with an increase in the duration of adaptation and/or the interval of a decrease in productivity preceding leaving is intuitively obvious.

The type of probability distribution of time-in-the-pool $\{\varphi_\theta\}$ has an effect on the output $V(\cdot)$ in a more complicated way. Let's study this effect; for this purpose, let's use "small changes" of the function $\{\varphi_\theta\}$ of the following form:

$$\delta\varphi_\theta(x,i) = x\varepsilon_\theta(i); \quad \text{where } \varepsilon_\theta(i) = \begin{cases} 1 & \text{for } \theta = i \\ -1 & \text{for } \theta = i+1 \\ 0 & \text{for } \theta < i \text{ or } \theta > i+1 \end{cases}$$

It is easy to show that the difference between any probability distributions $\{\varphi_\theta\}$ and $\{\bar\varphi_\theta\}$ can be represented as the sum of a countable number of "small changes" $\delta\varphi_\theta(x,i)$.

Let's consider the effect of the "small changes" $\delta\varphi_\theta(x,i)$ $(x \to 0)$ for various i on the function $V(\cdot)$, i.e., let's estimate $\partial V(\pi, \{\varphi_\theta + \delta\varphi_\theta(x,i)\}, t_{ad}, t_{lv}, c_{rpl}, c_{off})/\partial x$. From the expression (A6.3) it follows (to simplify the notation, hereinafter we omit a part of the arguments of $V(\cdot)$):

$$\frac{\partial}{\partial x}V\big(\{\varphi_\theta + \delta\varphi_\theta(x,i)\},\cdot\big) = -\frac{\partial}{\partial x}\left(a\frac{t^*_{ad}}{t_{av}} + b\frac{t^*_{lv}}{t_{av}} + c\frac{1}{t_{av}}\right)$$

where the coefficients $a = \Delta s_{ad}$, $b = \Delta s_{lv}$ and $c = c_{rpl} + c_{off}/\pi$ are independent of x.

Also from the expressions for t_{av}, t^*_{ad} and t^*_{lv} it follows for all i.:

$$t_{av}\big(\{\varphi_\theta + \delta\varphi_\theta(x,i)\}\big) = \sum_{\theta=0}^{\infty}\theta\varphi_\theta + xi - x(i+1) = t_{av}(\{\varphi_\theta\}) - x$$

$$t^*_{ad}\big(\{\varphi_\theta + \delta\varphi_\theta(x,i)\}\big) = \begin{cases} t^*_{ad}(\{\varphi_\theta\}) - x & \text{for } 0 < i < t_{ad} \\ t^*_{ad}(\{\varphi_\theta\}) & \text{for } t_{ad} \le i \end{cases},$$

$$t^*_{lv}\big(\{\varphi_\theta + \delta\varphi_\theta(x,i)\}\big) = \begin{cases} t_{ad}x & \text{for } i = t_{ad}, \\ t^*_{lv}(\{\varphi_\theta\}) - x & \text{for } t_{ad} < i < t_{ad} + t_{lv}, \\ t^*_{lv}(\{\varphi_\theta\}) & \text{for } t_{ad} + t_{lv} \le i \text{ or } i < t_{ad}. \end{cases}$$

Wherefrom it is clear that for $i < t_{ad} + t_{lv}$ the sign of the derivative $\partial V(\{\varphi_\theta + \delta\varphi_\theta(x,i)\},)/\partial x$ can be different, depending on the interrelations a, b, and c; that is, the effect of the "small changes" $\delta\varphi_\theta(x, i)$ on the function $V(\cdot)$ over the part $0 \le i < t_{ad} + t_{lv}$ manifests itself ambiguously.

However, when $t_{ad} + t_{lv} \le i$ it is true that

$$\frac{\partial}{\partial x}V\big(\{\varphi_\theta + \delta\varphi_\theta(x,i)\},\cdot\big) = -\frac{\partial}{\partial x}\left(a\frac{t^*_{ad}}{t_{av}} + b\frac{t^*_{lv}}{t_{av}} + c\frac{1}{t_{av}}\right) = \frac{\big(at^*_{ad} + bt^*_{lv} + c\big)}{t_{av}^2}\frac{\partial t_{av}}{\partial x}.$$

Where from $\dfrac{\partial/\partial x\,V\big(\{\varphi_\theta + \delta\varphi_\theta(x,i)\},\cdot\big)}{\partial t_{av}/\partial x} = \dfrac{\partial V\big(\{\varphi_\theta\},\cdot\big)}{\partial t_{av}} = \dfrac{\big(at^*_{av} + bt^*_{lv} + c\big)}{t_{av}^2} > 0$, i.e.

$\partial V(\cdot)/\partial t_{av} > 0$ and $\partial\Phi(\cdot)/\partial t_{av} > 0$.

Let's interpret the obtained properties from the point of view of the practice of complex activity (business) management.

Firstly, $\partial\Phi(\cdot)/\partial\pi > 0$ and $\lim_{\pi\to 0}\{\Phi(n_{off};\ \pi;\ c_{rpl};\ c_{off};\ T)\} = -\infty$ meaning that a low efficiency of the procedures of search and recruitment (a low share of candidates accepting the offer compared to those being considered and invited), i.e., small π values, has a negative effect on the output of the Enterprise $\Phi(\cdot)$. Although, of course, an unlimited – uncontrolled – decrease in the output, including due to inefficient hiring, is rather an exception to the rule.

Secondly, from the economic point of view, a monotonical decrease in the output $\Phi(\cdot)$ with an increase in the duration of adaptation and/or the interval of a productivity decrease preceding leaving ($\partial\Phi(\cdot)/\partial t_{ad} < 0$ and $\partial\Phi(\cdot)/\partial t_{lv} < 0$) is intuitively obvious, since these are "desperate" intervals of an employee's lifecycle; a firm does not receive the main output from an employee during the same.

The type of probability distribution of an employee's time-in-the-pool $\{\varphi_\theta\}$ has effect on output in a more complicated way. To study this effect, "small changes" $\delta\varphi_\theta(x,i)$ were used. It is shown that effect of the "small changes" $\delta\varphi_\theta(x,i)$ on output manifests ambiguity. If the time-in-the-pool is less than $t_{ad} + t_{lv}$, the employee is not "in time" to reach the productive interval and, therefore, produce the required output. The presence of such employees witnesses inefficient processes of hiring, adaptation, and retention. That is, employees leaving earlier than the periods $t_{ad} + t_{lv}$ should be as few as possible, "ideally" not a single one. Therefore, a detailed economic analysis of the lifecycle of such employees does not make sense; it is enough to estimate their share and strive to reduce this share.

However, for "small changes" over the part of work time longer than $t_{ad} + t_{lv}$, $\partial\Phi(\cdot)/\partial t_{av} > 0$ is valid, regardless of the type of probability distribution of time-in-the-pool $\{\varphi_\theta\}$. This also corresponds to the logic of business: an increase in the average working time in this case increases the relative duration of the productive interval, in relation to the total lifecycle of an active resource.

Appendix A6.2 Nonparametric Statistics of the Active Resource Traffic

Let's consider a method for estimating the attributes of the process of leaving and using the estimates to analyze the output of an Enterprise. The probability distribution $\{\varphi_\theta\}$ most fully characterizes the process of leaving; so let's consider a possibility to directly estimate its values.

It is known that, in the general case, a sample distribution function of a random variable almost certainly converges to the theoretical distribution function (if its fourth moment is finite), and is also its asymptotically normal estimate, with the rate of decrease in the confidential interval value being inversely proportional to the square root of the sample size (Glivenko – Cantelli theorem and Kolmogorov theorem, see for example van der Vaart (1998)).

However, to estimate the probability distribution of such values as the time-in-the-pool one traditionally uses a procedure, proposed in the classical work (Kaplan and Meier 1958), for analysis of "survival time" based on censored data, widely used and known as the "Kaplan-Meier procedure." The procedure allows a consistent and unbiased estimate of the "survival function" ($\Phi(t) = \sum_{\theta=t+1}^{\infty} \varphi_\theta$) to be obtained. Based on well-known theorems (for example, Kaplan and Meier (1958), van der Vaart (1998)), it is not hard to show that the relative confidential intervals for estimates of both the "survival function" and the intensity of leavings ($\lambda(t) = \varphi_t / \sum_{\theta=t}^{\infty} \varphi_\theta = \varphi_t / \Phi(t-1)^{-1}$) are dependent on t and N of the form $(N\varphi_t)^{-1/2}$; that is, they distinctly increase by t, i.e., the duration of time-in-the-pool, even with the significant sample sizes N (in practice, φ_t decreases significantly with the growth of t). For example, for the geometric probability distribution of the time-in-the-pool $\varphi_t = \varphi(1 - \varphi)^{t-1}$, the dependence of the relative confidential intervals on t and N will have the character $O(N^{-1/2}(1 - \varphi)^{-t/2})$ for estimates of both the "survival function" and intensity.

Wherefrom it follows that it's impossible, in principle, to estimate the probability distribution $\{\varphi_t\}$ with an acceptable accuracy for large t time-in-the-pool. Because the above-noted variability of external conditions does not allow one "to accumulate" such large N (the number of AE in the pool), that would ensure the acceptably low values $(N\varphi_t)^{-1/2}$. This thesis is illustrated by graphs of estimates for attrition intensity in two Russian companies from different industries (a retail company – Figure A6.1 and an IT company – Figure A6.2).

In both graphs, the vertical axis corresponds to the attrition intensity for one period, periods being plotted along the horizontal axis. The dashed line shows estimates for intensity; the thinner solid lines are the upper and lower boundaries of the confidential intervals, admitted for illustrative purposes to be equal to plus–minus three standard root-mean-square deviations.

In the example Figure A6.1, the headcount of the pool of active resources under consideration is on the order of several tens of thousands of people (cashiers of the retail network).

The number of leavings during the initial periods is on the order of several thousand people during one period, drops to hundreds and then to tens of people. This allows a relatively accurate estimate for the first 20–30 periods to be obtained. Starting from the values of 90–100 periods, the number of leavings in the sample

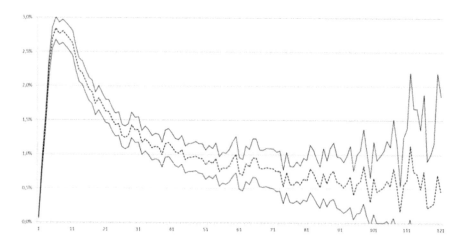

FIGURE A6.1   Estimate of the attrition intensity and its confidential interval for cashiers of the retail network.

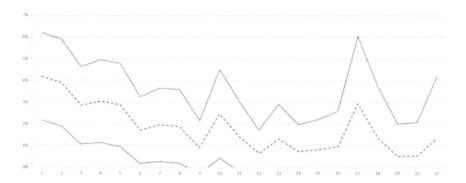

FIGURE A6.2   Estimate of the intensity of leavings and its confidential interval for the second example.

decreases to ten–twenty, which leads to the confidential interval becoming twice as large as the value of the estimate itself. Such an assessment can hardly be considered reliable.

In the second example (Figure A6.2), as a result of a significantly smaller head-count of the pool (several thousand people), the accuracy of the estimate, even for small values of seniority, is very small.

This means that even for companies with homogeneous employees of several tens of thousands of people, the possibilities to accurately assess the probability distribution of time in the company are limited: one can reliably estimate the intensity of leavings only for small durations, when the proportion of such employees is relatively large, and for large values of durations estimates become unreliable.

Appendix A6.3 Detection of Changes in the Active Resource Traffic

Verification of the fact that the average values of the decision functions before disorder are negative.

Let's verify that if the external conditions correspond to the hypothesis $\mathbf{H_0}$, then the average values $\Delta l^I(t)$, $\Delta l^2(t)$, $\Delta l(t)$ are negative for any γ, $\hat{\pi}_0$, and $\hat{\lambda}_0$.

Let's consider $E\left[\Delta l^I(u)\big| H_0\right] = \bar{n}_{off}\left(ln\left(1-\gamma\right)\hat{\pi}_0 + ln\left(1 + \dfrac{\gamma\hat{\pi}_0}{1-\hat{\pi}_0}\right)\left(1-\hat{\pi}_0\right)\right)$. The

factor $\bar{n}_{off}$ is positive, so we omit it. Let's denote $F\left(\hat{\pi}_0;\gamma\right) = ln\left(1-\gamma\right)\hat{\pi}_0 + ln\left(1 + \dfrac{\gamma\hat{\pi}_0}{1-\hat{\pi}_0}\right)\left(1-\hat{\pi}_0\right)$ and study the behavior of the function $F(\cdot)$

Firstly, $F(0; \gamma)=0$. Let's calculate the derivative with respect to the first argument.

$$\frac{\partial}{\partial \pi} F(\pi;\gamma) = ln(1-\gamma) - ln\left(1 + \frac{\pi\gamma}{1-\pi}\right) + (1-\pi)\frac{\partial}{\partial \pi} ln\left(1 + \frac{\pi\gamma}{1-\pi}\right)$$

$$= ln\frac{(1-\pi)(1-\gamma)}{1-\pi+\pi\gamma} + (1-\pi)\left[\frac{\partial}{\partial \pi} ln(1-\pi+\pi\gamma) - \frac{\partial}{\partial \pi} ln(1-\pi)\right]$$

$$= ln\frac{(1-\pi)(1-\gamma)}{1-\pi+\pi\gamma} + (1-\pi)\left[-\frac{1-\gamma}{1-\pi+\pi\gamma} + \frac{1}{1-\pi}\right]$$

$$= ln\frac{(1-\pi)(1-\gamma)}{1-\pi+\pi\gamma} + 1 - \frac{(1-\pi)(1-\gamma)}{1-\pi+\pi\gamma}.$$

Let's denote $x = \dfrac{(1-\pi)(1-\gamma)}{1-\pi+\pi\gamma}$, as $\forall x > 0$ $ln(x) + 1 - x < 0$, then $\partial F(\pi;\gamma)/\partial\pi < 0$

That is, $F(\pi; y)$ monotonically decreases by π for any γ. Let's find the limit of $F(\cdot)$ if $\pi \to 1$:

$$\lim_{\pi \to 1}\left\{ ln(1-\gamma)\pi + ln\left(1 + \frac{\gamma\pi}{1-\pi}\right)(1-\pi)\right\}$$

$$= ln(1-\gamma) + \lim_{\pi \to 1}\left\{(1-\pi)ln\frac{\gamma}{1-\pi}\right\}$$

$$= ln(1-\gamma) + \gamma \lim_{z \to \infty}\left\{\frac{ln(z)}{z}\right\} = ln(1-\gamma) < 0.$$

In such a way, $E[\Delta l^1(u)|H_0]$ is always negative; for $E[\Delta l^2(u)|H_0]$ the proof is similar. Since $E[\Delta l^1(u)|H_0] < 0$ and $E[\Delta l^2(u)|H_0] < 0$, then also $E[\Delta l(u)|H_0] < 0$.

Now then, if the external conditions actually correspond to the hypothesis $\mathbf{H_0}$, then the average values of the processes $\Delta l^1(t)$, $\Delta l^2(t)$ and $\Delta l(t)$ take negative values ($\Delta l_i^1(t)$, $\Delta l_i^2(t)$ and $\Delta l_i(t)$ analogously).

Verification of the fact that the average values of the decision functions after disorder are positive.

If the external conditions correspond to hypothesis $\mathbf{H}\tau$, then $x(u) = (\hat{\pi}_0; \hat{\lambda}_0)^T$ at $-T_{apr} \le u \le t - \tau$ and $x(u) = (\pi_d; \lambda_d)^T$ for $t - \tau \le u \le t$, at that $\pi_d \le (1-\gamma)\hat{\pi}_0$ and $\lambda_d \ge (1+\gamma)\hat{\lambda}_0$, then:

$$E\left[\Delta l^1(u) \mid H_\tau\right] = \bar{n}_{off}\hat{\pi}_0\left(1-\gamma\right)ln\left(1-\gamma\right) + \bar{n}_{off}\left(1-\hat{\pi}_0(1-\gamma)\right)ln\left(1 + \frac{\gamma\hat{\pi}_0}{1-\hat{\pi}_0}\right).$$

Let's consider $E[\Delta l^1(u)|H_\tau]$; let's denote

$$G\left(\hat{\pi}_0;\gamma\right) = \hat{\pi}_0(1-\gamma)\ln(1-\gamma) + \left(1-\hat{\pi}_0(1-\gamma)\right)\ln\left(1 + \frac{\gamma\hat{\pi}_0}{1-\hat{\pi}_0}\right).$$

and investigate the behavior of the function $G(x;y)$. Firstly, $G(0; y)=0$. Let's calculate the derivative with respect to the first argument.

$$\frac{\partial}{\partial x}G(x;y) = (1-y)ln(1-y) + \frac{\partial}{\partial x}\left(1-x(1-y)\right)ln\left(1+\frac{xy}{1-x}\right)$$

$$= (1-y)ln(1-y) - (1-y)ln\left(1+\frac{xy}{1-x}\right) + \left(1-x(1-y)\right)\frac{\partial}{\partial x}ln\left(\frac{1-x+xy}{1-x}\right)$$

$$= (1-y)\left[ln(1-y) - ln\left(\frac{1-x+xy}{1-x}\right)\right] + \left(1-x(1-y)\right)\left(-\frac{1-y}{1-x+xy} + \frac{1}{1-x}\right)$$

$$= (1-y)ln\left(\frac{(1-y)(1-x)}{1-x+xy}\right) + \left(1-x(1-y)\right)\frac{1-x+xy-(1-y)(1-x)}{\left(1-x(1-y)\right)(1-x)}$$

$$= (1-y)ln\left(\frac{(1-y)(1-x)}{1-x+xy}\right) + \frac{y}{(1-x)}.$$

Now then,

$$\frac{\partial}{\partial x}G(x;y) = (1-y)ln(1-x) + (1-y)ln(1-y) - (1-y)ln\left(1-x+xy\right) + \frac{y}{(1-x)}.$$

Let us show that the derivative is positive.

$$\frac{\partial}{\partial x}G(x;y)\bigg|_{x=0} = (1-y)ln(1-y) + y = -(1-y)\sum_{n=1}^{\infty}\frac{y^n}{n} + y$$

$$= y - \sum_{n=1}^{\infty}\frac{y^n}{n} + \sum_{n=2}^{\infty}\frac{y^n}{n-1} = y - y - \sum_{n=2}^{\infty}\frac{y^n}{n} + \sum_{n=2}^{\infty}\frac{y^n}{n-1}$$

$$= \sum_{n=2}^{\infty}\left(\frac{1}{n-1} - \frac{1}{n}\right)y^n = \sum_{n=2}^{\infty}\frac{y^n}{(n-1)n} > 0.$$

Let's consider the second derivative:

$$\frac{\partial^2}{\partial x^2}G(x;y) = \frac{\partial}{\partial x}\{(1-y)ln(1-y) + (1-y)ln(1-x)\}$$

$$- \frac{\partial}{\partial x}\{(1-y)ln\left(1-x(1-y)\right) - y/(1-x)\}$$

$$= \frac{1-y}{1-x} + \frac{(1-y)^2}{1-x+xy} + \frac{y}{(1-x)^2} > 0.$$

The first derivative at the point $x=0$ is positive, and the second one is positive for $x \geq 0$, from which it follows that $G(x; y) > 0$ for $x > 0$, then $E[\Delta l^1(u)|H_\tau]$ is always above zero and monotonically grows with respect to γ.

The proof for $E[\Delta l^2(u)|H_\tau]$ is analogous.

Now then, in this case, all the average values $\Delta l^1(t)$, $\Delta l^2(t)$, $\Delta l(t)$ are positive for any γ, $\hat{\pi}_0$ and $\hat{\lambda}_0$ and monotonically increase with respect to γ, ($\Delta l_i^1(t)$, $\Delta l_i^2(t)$ and $\Delta l_i(t)$ analogously).

REFERENCES

Badinelli, R. 2010. A Stochastic Model of Resource Allocation for Service Systems. *Service Science* 2(1), 76–91.

Bartroff, J., Finkelman, J. and Lai, T. 2008. Modern Sequential Analysis and Its Applications to Computerized Adaptive Testing. *Psychometrika* 73(3), 473–486.

Becker, G. 1962. Investment in Human Capital: A Theoretical Analysis. *Journal of Political Economy* 70(5), 9–49.

Becker, G. 1975. *Human Capital: A Theoretical and Empirical Analysis with Special Reference to Education.* Chicago, IL: The University of Chicago Press.

Blackburn, K. and Varvarigos, D. 2008. Human Capital Accumulation and Output Growth in a Stochastic Environment. *Economic Theory* 36, 435–452.

Cao, H., Hu, Jianying, Jiang, Chen, Kumar, Tarun, Li, Ta-Hsin, Liu, Yang, lu, Yingdong, Mahatma, Shilpa, Mojsilovic, Aleksandra, Sharma, Mayank, Squillante, Mark, Yu, Yichong. 2011. On the Mark: Integrated Stochastic Resource Planning of Human Capital Supply Chains. *Interfaces.* 41 (5). 414–435.

Coase, R. 1937. The Nature of the Firm. *Economica* 4(16), 386–405.

De Smet, A., Lund, S. and Schaininger, W. 2016. Organizing for the Future. Platform-Based Talent Markets Help Put the Emphasis in Human-Capital Management Back Where it Belongs – On Humans. http://www.mckinsey.com/insights/organization/organizing for the future

Espinosa, E., Frausto, J. and Rivera, E. 2010. Markov Decision Processes for Optimizing Human Workflows. *Service Science* 2(4), 245–269.

Fan, X., Seshadr, A. and Taber, C. 2015. *Estimation of a Life-Cycle Model with Human Capital, Labor Supply and Retirement.* University of Chicago. Department of Economics. Workshops. April 15.

Flamholtz, E. 1999. *Human Resource Accounting: Advances in Concepts, Methods, and Applications.* New York: Springer.

Flamholtz, E., Bullen, M. and Hua, W. 2002. Human Resource Accounting: A Historical Perspective and Future Implications. *Management Decision* 40(10), 947–954.

Flamholtz, E., Geis, G. and Perle, R. 1984. A Markovian Model for the Valuation of Human Assets Acquired by an Organizational Purchase. *Interfaces* 14(6), 11–15.

Gans, N., Koole, G. and Mandelbaum, A. 2003. Telephone Call Centers: Tutorial, Review, and Research Prospects. *Manufacturing & Service Operations Management* 5(2), 160–171.

Gartner. Human Capital Management Definition. https://www.gartner.com/en/information-technology/glossary/hcm-human-capital-management [Accessed 2019-12-19].

Ibrahim, R., Armony, M. and Bassamboo, A. 2016. Does the Past Predict the Future? The Case of Delay Announcements in Service Systems. *Management Science.* Published Online in Articles in Advance 13 Jun 2016. doi: 10.1287/Mnsc.2016.2425.

Kahn, W. 1990. Psychological Conditions of Personal Engagement and Disengagement at Work. *Academy of Management Journal* 33(4), 692–724.

Kaplan, E. and Meier, P. 1958. Nonparametric Estimation from Incomplete Observations. *Journal of the American Statistical Association* 53(282), 457–481.

Lee, A. and Longton, P. 1959. Queueing Processes Associated with Airline Passenger Check-In. *Journal of the Operational Research Society* 10(1), 56–71.

Maister, D. 1993. *Managing the Professional Services Firm*. New York: Free Press.

Menard, C. 2000. *Institutions, Contracts and Organizations: Perspectives from New In-Stitutional Economics*. Northampton, MA: Edward Elgar Publishing.

Mincer, J. 1958. Investment in Human Capital and Personal Income Distribution. *Journal of Political Economy* 66(4), 281–302.

Nikiforov, I. 1983. *Sequential Detection of Changes in Time-Series*. Moscow: Sience (in Russian).

Nikiforov, I. 2016. Sequential Detection/Isolation of Abrupt Changes. *Sequential Analysis. Design Methods and Applications* 35(3), 268–301.

Palacios, M. 2013. Human Capital as an Asset Class: Implications from a General Equilibrium Model (April 19, 2013). Available at SSRN: https://ssrn.com/abstract=1307385 or http://dx.doi.org/10.2139/ssrn.1307385).

Rio, R. 2018. What is Enterprise Asset Management - EAM? www.ARCweb.com. Archived from the original on 13 April 2018. Retrieved 2020-06-03.

Shiryayev, A. 1977. *Optimal Stopping Rules*. New York: Springer.

Smith, D., Silverstone, Y. and Lajtha, A. 2013. A New Lens on Business Advantage: Human Capital Strategy and the Drive for High Performance. Retrieved from http://www.accenture.com/SiteCollectionDocuments/PDF/Accenture_A_New:Lens_on_Business_Advantage.pdf.

Thie, H. and Brown R. 1994. Future Career Management Systems for U.S. Military Officers – Rand Corp. https://www.rand.org/content/dam/rand/pubs/monograph_reports/2007/mr470.pdf.

van der Vaart, A.W. 1998. I. In *Asymptotic Statistics*. Cambridge: Cambridge University Press.

Wald, A. 1947. *Sequential Analysis*. New York: John Wiley & Sons.

Wu, Y. 2015. Organizational Structure and Product Choice in Knowledge-Intensive Firms. *Management Science* 61(8), 1830–1848.

7 Planning

Let's consider mathematical models and methods for Enterprise complex activity planning. *Planning* is, in a certain sense, the resultant step of the solution to the Enterprise Control Problem, since it is during planning that CA optimization as such is performed (see Enterprise Control Optimization Scheme (Section 3.4.3 and Figure 3.9)). Therefore, it would be appropriate to summarize the basic steps of setting and solving the Enterprise Control Problem and how it is reflected in previous sections of this book (Figure 7.1).

In Part I (Chapters 1 and 2), a systematic and methodological analysis of an Enterprise is carrie- out, and the Enterprise Control Problem is formalized as the control of the hierarchy of lifecycles of structural elements of activity (SEAs). Two major factors determining the success of an Enterprise are highlighted: (1) people, having the property of active choice and performing the role of CA subjects; (2) CA technologies, first of all, technological knowledge.

In Chapter 3, the Enterprise Control Problem is set up as a mathematical problem of find-ng optimal control actions in multi-element, multi-level, dynamic, active systems with constraints imposed on the constituents in the form of technological networks (m-DNAS). The optimization problem is stated in the form of expressions (3.11–3.19), reflecting several variants of the setting; a generalized plan to solve it is proposed in Section 3.4.3 in the form of a backward induction schema.

Chapter 4, based on the approaches of the theory of contracts and theory of control in organizations, sets out models of contracts, which are the main means of control within an Enterprise. The main result of Chapter 4 is Theorems 4.1 and 4.2 on the existence of optimal contracts (incentive systems) in m-DNASs, which play a significant role in solving the Enterprise Control Problem. The theorems determine ways to analytically solve the optimization problem (3.11–3.19) in practically important cases. The theorems ground the possibility, first, of proceeding from functional optimization – searching for functions – to parametric optimization, and second, of decomposing the problem by time periods and participants in an active system.

Chapters 5 and 6 set out mathematical models of technological knowledge and human capital as the main factors in Enterprise CA.

In this chapter, models of contracts (Chapter 4), technology (Chapter 5), and human capital (Chapter 6) are used to develop mathematical models of *optimal planning*, i.e., to complete the solution to the Enterprise Control Problem as an optimization problem (Chapter 3, Formulas 3.11–3.19).

The problem of optimal planning of the output of complex activity or actions (Section 3.4) reflects the specifics of each particular Enterprise and, as a result, does not have an analytical solution in general. Therefore, in Section 7.1, an algorithmic model of the planning process, reflecting the systemic characteristics of the problem and being applicable to solving the optimization problems of any

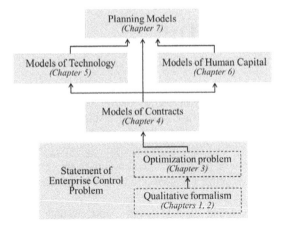

FIGURE 7.1 Enterprise Control Problem. Steps of the statement and the solution.

Enterprise, is proposed. In the following Sections 7.2–7.5, models and methods are presented, allowing one to solve analytically (completely or partially) optimization problems for such particular cases that are essential for the practice of Enterprise control.

7.1 ALGORITHMIC MODELS OF PLANNING PROCESS IN A HIERARCHICAL DYNAMIC MULTI-AGENT ACTIVE SYSTEM

7.1.1 AN ALGORITHM OF COMPATIBLE PLANNING IN A SEA HIERARCHY

A set of LCs" of SEA", representing the Enterprise and its activities (Chapter 1), is an entity with a complex internal structure and characteristics:

- complex technological connections between the elements and the hierarchy of control of SEA as subsystems;
- the autonomy of each of SEA as a constituent of the Enterprise;
- active choice, i.e. acting according to one's own interests and preferences, which is immanent for each of the complex actors of SEAs.

These traits of a controlled entity determine the particular importance of the holism of the whole plan and compatibility of the constituents' plans and dictate the generalized structure of the planning algorithm (Figure 7.2), which should be recursively executed by each of the actors of SEA hierarchy (the i-principal of a subsystem):

- collects necessary information about subordinate elements (SEAs and elementary operations);

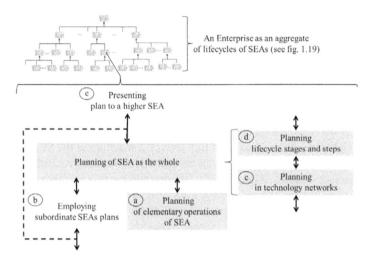

FIGURE 7.2   The general structure of the planning algorithm.

- develops (according to the SEA technology) SEA plan employing plans of subordinates;
- coordinates plans with the actors of subordinate SEAs and superior SEAs;
- translates the outputs to the superior SEA actor, following the logical model and hierarchy Γ (see the definitions in Sections 3.4 and 4.3).

At that, information is transmitted following the hierarchy of SEAs' subordination, i.e. the logical model and hierarchy Γ, and the planning process (information integration, and processing) is carried out according to the cause-effect model/network G.

A control model and an algorithm for compatible planning of implementation of an Enterprise's CA LCs must adequately take into account the following systemic factors.

The model should describe the practical control issues of products, systems, and enterprises lifecycles (Martin et al. 2012). Lifecycles control in practice, as a rule, is implemented in the form of projects or production programs, which are structured in the form of phases and stages, as well as of gates, separating phases and stages. Each stage consists of projects and actions/work executed sequentially and/or in parallel. Gates reflect conditions, imposed on the outputs of the corresponding elements of CA, to move from one stage to another, for example, completion of a frontend engineering design, control of characteristics, achievement of a certain maturity level, completion of integration, etc.

In the case of successfully passing a gate, program plans (including stages, projects, actions/work) do not change; otherwise, one returns to the previous stages within the given LC and/or escalates problems to a higher level (superior SEA actor), and/or changes the program plans. A significant share of repeats in stages of production programs is noted, for example, in Braha and Yaneer (2007), which leads to significant overrun budgets and time delays in programs of complex products and systems development (Report 2005).

Such a structure, consisting of a chain of stages, having a complicated structure, allowing for returns and repeats, generalizes the SEA process model (Section 1.4.2) and the models described above to reflect various particular features of CA implementation. Figure 7.3 illustrates a generalized model for implementation of the LC of such SEA that describes a complex *project program*.

On the right side of the figure, in a free format, a structure of the SEA, describing a project/product program as a whole, is presented, taking into account its particular features discussed above. This SEA is decomposed (within the framework of the generalized process model) into stages 1, 2, ..., M, which in turn (within the framework of the cause-effect model) are decomposed into SEAs and elementary operations of a next, subordinate level, by forming parallel-sequential structures. SEAs of the subordinate level, in turn, can also be decomposed, forming a hierarchical fractal structure.

On the left side of Figure 7.3, CA models (Chapter 1) are shown; the arrows reflect information flows between the models: the output data of some models are the input ones to others. The flow directions also illustrate the recursiveness of interconnections of the models and the fractal structure of SEAs.

Practical considerations allow us to formulate an assumption "On the statistical independence of implementation of CA elements (stages of lifecycles, projects, actions/works)":

Assumption A7	Unscheduled, a priori uncertain deviations from prescribed time terms, planned actions and output can be considered statistically independent.

The assumption is supported by the following consideration. If regularities of such deviations are revealed, the actors of CA (the management) will adjust the relevant standards and plans, after which the deviations from the new standards will again

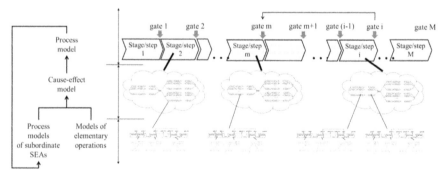

FIGURE 7.3 The generalized structure of the implementation models of LC of SEA.

become independent. The need for such corrective actions arises from the actors' (managers') interest in *eliminating the uncertainty* of CA (of their business) as much as possible. The possibilities (probabilities) to successfully pass various gates and the final characteristics of actions and outputs are independent for the same reason.

In the majority of practically important cases regarding a set of CA elements, assumption A5 (introduced in Section 3.4.1) is also adequate, which implies the "smallness"* of values of uncertain deviations in the characteristics of states of CA elements, with respect to the known average values. Then the behavior of a CA element can be described by the sum of the known vector of average values and a "small" random vector, reflecting the uncertainty of CA. In this case, constructive results can be obtained by operating with average values of state vectors of CA elements, which is similar to ideas of the well-known system dynamics method (for example, Forrester (1971)). Let us expand this method by a scenario approach (for example, Dewar (2002)), which is widely used for decision-making in business, in particular, forecasting and planning in areas where true uncertainty is most significant, i.e. in the economy, in the social and political sphere. The approach is based on an expert definition of scenarios for the behavior of the system of interest and their use for calculations and forecasts. The scenario approach is essentially a subjective, heuristic way for knowledge generation with all its inherent drawbacks. However, in conditions when an instrumental objective research is impossible, in practice, this particular approach is applied.

Due to the specifics of complex activity, almost every element of CA, in one case, can be adequately represented as an elementary and not-structurizable one, and in the other – the same can and should be considered as a complex one – SEA, having a complicated internal hierarchical structure. Therefore, we use the principle of *generalization and abstraction,*† which is one of the main principles in the study of CA (Belov and Novikov, 2020b). According to this principle, in some cases, a plan or forecast of the state of the particular CA element and/or its outputs can be formulated as the expert opinion (of the CA actor); in other cases, they can be formed based on plans/forecasts of the subordinate elements of CA, following the structure of the algorithm (Figure 7.2), as a compatible plan of implementation of the hierarchical set of CA elements.

The solution of an Enterprise's CA planning problem consists in creating a tool for sequential reasoned integration of heterogeneous – actual deterministic, uncertain, and subjective – data on a significant quantity (up to several tens of thousands) of hierarchically interconnected elements of CA, having a varying structure and composition, in

---

* The concept of "smallness" can easily be formalized by definition of a criterion with respect to the boundary values for the elements of vectors of known average values and random vectors; and this will be done if it is necessary to obtain rigorous statements. In this context, the intuitively clear definition is sufficient.

† The principle of generalization and abstraction consists in using a detailed or, conversely, aggregated description and consideration of phenomena and processes under research. Abstracting from some details or, conversely, placing them in the focus of analysis depends, in any scientific research, on the specific goals of the researcher (on the subjectmatter of the research).

order to predict the output and effect of CA (operations of modern large enterprises cover cooperation of tens of thousands of relatively autonomous business entities, which, in turn, are enterprises, i.e. corporations, firms, divisions, working groups).

With a view of solving the planning problem, the state of each α-th element of CA (an SEA and/or an elementary operation) is modeled by a vector $x_\alpha(t) = (j_\alpha(t); r_\alpha(t); z_\alpha(t); l_\alpha(t))^\mathrm{T}$, where $j_\alpha(t)$ is labor consumption realized up to the end of period t; $r_\alpha(t)$ is resource consumption (of all other resources except labor) incurred up to the end of period t. We believe the created output $z_\alpha(t)$ or the volume of utility to be scalar and additive (which corresponds in practice to the often used *earned value* concept in the same-name method of project management, discussed in Section 8.4.6, as well as to the measurement of manufactured products or delivered services in labor hours or monetary measures); $l_\alpha(t)$ is the duration of time (number of periods) from the start of implementation of the CA element. We assume that each stage of the LC is implemented during several time periods, after which either transition to the next stage or the repeat of this one or return to the previous stage occurs (according to the process model, Section 1.4.2). The completion of implementation of the α-th CA element means the achievement of the element's goal; therefore, let us formalize the moment (end of period) of the time t_α of the CA element completion as a moment when the characteristics of the output for the first time reach a certain a priori defined set of target values $z(t_\alpha) \in Z_\alpha^*$; subsequently, at this moment the state of the element is equal to $x_\alpha(t_\alpha)$. The impossibility to complete the CA element by achieving the goal ($z(t_\alpha) \in Z_\alpha^*$) is associated with the need for modernization in the technology or refusal to complete the CA.

This set of vector $x_\alpha(t)$ elements is not the only possible one and can be changed depending on the specifics of the CA under consideration; however, the basic principles of operating with the state vector, discussed below, is also applicable (in particular, an example of the practical application of the implementation models, which has required an extension of the set of elements of the state vector of CA elements, is described in Section 8.4.1).

The behavior of CA elements (the state evolution over time) is uncertain, which is expressed in the indefinite moments t_α of CA elements' completion and stages of their LCs and, as a result, in the uncertain values of resources and labor expenses, required to obtain the target outputs $z_\alpha(t_\alpha) \in Z_\alpha^*$.

CA elements parameters, used in the planning algorithm, are prominent in heterogeneity and varying degrees of objectivity and certainty. In practice, a priori data can be received as normative, statistical data or expert estimates in the form of point values, admissible intervals or probability distributions (parameterized or tabular), in a particular case, deterministic values. Planning, normative, or guiding documents, as well as statistical estimates based on historical data and subjective expert (managers) estimates serve as data sources. That is, most of the initial data of the algorithmic model are formed (or at least verified) by people; therefore, developing the model, we must consider that the generated initial data should have "reasonable" volume. At the same time, firstly, a large number of CA elements, and secondly, a variety of characteristics of actions and outputs make the dimensionality of the problem very significant.

Due to the CA uncertainty, the significant impact of individuals and their active choice on the outputs of CA, it is necessary to use methods and approaches that are robust to probability distributions and other details of probabilistic models.

Let us define a scenario of implementation of the α-th element of CA as an entity of the form $\Sigma_\alpha = \{<\mu_{\alpha f}; m_{\alpha f}>; f = 1, 2, ..., F\}$, a set of twos $<\mu_{\alpha f}; m_{\alpha f}>$, where $m_{\alpha f}$ are the variants of implementation of the CA element, i.e. its state at the completion time $x_\alpha(t_\alpha)$, and $\mu_{\alpha f}$ are their weights for which $\displaystyle\sum_{f=1}^{F} \mu_{\alpha f} = 1$. The vectors $m_{\alpha f}$ have the same dimensionality and semantics as $x_\alpha(t)$ and are interpreted as some "stable" groups of feasible CA implementation trajectories. In the framework of the theoretical-probabilistic approach, the values of the state vector of the α-th element of CA are represented as the implementation of the random variable $x_\alpha(t_\alpha)$, and the vector $m_{\alpha f}$ corresponds to the conditional average value of the random vector $x_\alpha(t_\alpha)$, given the random number of the variant taking the value f, i.e., $m_{\alpha f} = E[x_\alpha(t_\alpha)|f]$.

Scenarios in the proposed format, on the one hand, can be interpreted as approximations of the probability distribution of random integers $f \in F$, each of which generates the unique implementation $x_\alpha(t_\alpha) = m_{\alpha f}$. As the number of variants F increases, the "accuracy" of approximation increases and can be made arbitrarily high. On the other hand, the constraint on the quantity of variants F to be considered allows the dimensionality of the problem to be adjusted and, thus, a compromise of "accuracy-dimensionality" to be achieved. In practice, as a rule, scenarios consisting of the only variant are used, because the problem of forecasting the implementation of the LCs of CA elements has the nature of coordination of plans, and the implementable plan cannot be multiple (backup variants can be developed, but the plan selected by some criteria is implemented at any time). Therefore, quantitative algorithms are presented just for this case.

7.1.2   QUANTITATIVE PLANNING IN THE HIERARCHY OF STRUCTURAL ELEMENTS OF ACTIVITY

Elementary operations planning (Step a, Figure 7.2). An adequate plan for the elementary operation output in many practical cases is expertly formed scenario Σ_β, in which the average values of the characteristics $m_{\beta f}$ and their weight μ_f are directly given (and which most often consists of one variant $F = 1$). The development of such a plan is a heuristic operation, not requiring and not allowing for formalization. In other cases, a plan must be developed based on the analysis of labor and other resource expenses. This is also important to obtain requirements for resource pools, i.e. the initial data for the problems of compatible control of active resources, used for CA lifecycles implementation (Chapter 6 and Section 7.4).

Let's consider from these positions the elementary operation implementation process (we omit the index β, the identifier of the operation, when it does not lead to ambiguous understanding).

The dynamics of implementation of an elementary operation, in the general case, is described by a system of equations:

$$\begin{cases} j(t) = j(t-1) + Q_j\left(r(t); \ x(t-1); \ D(t); \ t-t_s\right); \\ r(t) = r(t-1) + Q_r\left(j(t); \ x(t-1); \ D(t); \ t-t_s\right); \\ z(t) = z(t-1) + Q_z\left(j(t); \ r(t); \ x(t-1); \ D(t); \ t-t_s\right); \\ l(t) = l(t-1) + 1 = t - t_s; \\ j\left(t_s\right) = 0; \quad r\left(t_s\right) = r_0; \quad z\left(t_s\right) = 0; \quad l\left(t_s\right) = 0; \end{cases} \qquad (7.1)$$

System (7.1) reflects the technological function of the operation $Q(\cdot)$ and the vector-function $D(t) = (d_j(t); \ d_r(t))^{\mathrm{T}}$ of the current availability (and/or assignment) of the resources necessary for the operation (specialists of the required qualifications, equipment, materials, components, etc.). The elementary operation is implemented from the beginning moment t_s until the a priori unknown moment t_β of achievement of the desired result $z(t_\beta) > Z_\beta^*$ (the scalar equivalent of the general condition $z(t_\beta) \in Z_\beta^*$). In the general case, the initial resource expenses r_0 are necessary to start an operation.

The components of the technological function $Q_j(\cdot)$, $Q_r(\cdot)$ and $Q_z(\cdot)$ depend on the current state of the operation $x(t)$ and on $D(t)$; the functions $Q_j(\cdot)$, $Q_r(\cdot)$ and $Q_z(\cdot)$ are either known (from regulatory documents, for example, job cards, worksheets, etc.) for standard works, or are defined expertly for rarely implemented work.

The availability of resources $D(t)$ for various works is modeled by functions of various kinds, for example:

a) the function $D(t)$ is binary and takes values {1; 0}, reflecting the cases "resources are available in the required volume, the operation can be implemented" or "resources are not available, the operation cannot be implemented";

b) the function $D(t)$ takes values of the percentage of resource availability and the operation is implemented with proportional productivity.

Section 7.4 is devoted to issues of resource planning and control; in this section, we assume the schedule of the resource availability $D(t)$ to be a known function of t.

In most cases, the components of the technological function can be (piecewise) linearized, for example, in the following form:

- $Q_j(r(t); \ x(t-1); \ D(t); \ t-t_s) = a_j d_j(t)$, where a_j makes sense of the standard number of required staff, $d_j(t)$ can admit any of the above interpretations, "a" or "b," and $a_j \, d_j(t)$ as a whole is labor consumption realized during the period t;
- $Q_r(j(t); \ x(t-1); \ D(t); \ t-t_s) = a_r d_r(t)$, where a_r are norms for resource utilization, $d_r(t)$ can admit any of the above interpretations, "a" or "b," and $a_r \, d_r(t)$ is resource consumption realized during the period t;

- $Q_z(j(t); r(t); x(t-1); D(t); t-t_s)=a_{jz}a_jd_j(t) + a_{rz}r(t)+\xi_t$, where a_{jz} and a_{rz} are norms of labor and other resource productivity, ξ_t is a random process reflecting the uncertainty of a technology during each period t, having zero average value and such a standard deviation that $\sigma_\xi \ll a_{jz}; a_{rz}$ (according to assumption A5).

Then expressions (7.1) take the form:

$$j(t) = a_j h \tilde{d}_j(t);$$

$$r(t) = r_0 + a_r \tilde{d}_r(t);$$

$$z(t) = a_r r_0 + a_{zj}a_j \tilde{d}_j(t) + a_{zr}a_r \tilde{d}_r(t) + \tilde{\xi}_t;$$

$$l(t) = t - t_s;$$

where $\tilde{d}_j(t) = \sum\limits_{i=t_s}^{t} d_j(i)$ and $\tilde{d}_r(t) = \sum\limits_{i=t_s}^{t} d_r(i)$ are known functions of time, and

$\tilde{\xi}_t = \sum\limits_{i=t_s}^{t} \xi_i$ is a random variable with zero average value and the dispersion

$\sigma_\xi^2(t - t_s + 1)$.

Given the conditions of assumption A5, the duration t_β for implementation of an elementary operation can be found as a minimal integer solution with respect to t of the inequality $Z_\beta^* \le a_r r_0 + a_{zj}a_j \tilde{d}_j(t) + a_{zr}a_r \tilde{d}_r(t)$ (it is easy to show that this inequality has a unique solution: all coefficients a_*, Z_β^*, r_0 are positive, and both functions $\tilde{d}_j(\cdot)$ and $\tilde{d}_r(\cdot)$ monotonically increase). Then the scenario variant (the characteristics of the operation at the time of its completion) takes the value:

$$m_{\beta f} = \left(a_j \tilde{d}_j(t_\beta); \ r_0 + a_r \tilde{d}_r(t_\beta); \ Z_\beta^*; \ t_\beta \right)^T \tag{7.2}$$

Expression (7.2) can be used, firstly, to calculate values of the scenario variants for implementation of elementary operations, and secondly, to obtain values of the required volumes of resource pools for solving problems of their control.

Obtaining plans from the subordinate SEAs actors and coordinating them (Step b/e, Figure 7.2) is an organizational and control action; therefore it does not need to be formalized.

Planning in technological networks (Step c, Figure 7.2). Let's consider a procedure to form a plan in technological networks, i.e. parallel-sequential structures, based on plans of constituent elements (optimization in networks is studied in Sections 7.1.3, 7.1.4 below).

A combined estimate m_a of a composition of several ($i=1, 2, ..., I_a$) CA elements can be obtained in the following form:

- A sequential composition, i.e. the sum of the element estimates:

$$m_\alpha = \sum_{i=1}^{l_\alpha} m_i. \tag{7.3}$$

- A parallel alternative composition (if exactly one of I_a of CA elements is implemented with the probability π_i), i.e. the weighted sum of the element estimates:

$$m_\alpha = \sum_{i=1}^{l_a} \pi_i m_i. \tag{7.4}$$

- A parallel unopposed composition (all I_a elements of CA are implemented):

$$j(t_\alpha) = \sum_{i=1}^{l_a} j(t_i), r(t_\alpha) = \sum_{i=1}^{l_a} r(t_i), z(t_\alpha) = \sum_{i=1}^{l_a} z(t_i), t_\alpha = \max_{i=1,...,l_\alpha} \{t_i\}. \tag{7.5}$$

Planning the transition through lifecycle phases (Step d, Figure 7.2).

Let's consider planning for transition through phases of LCs as a problem of searching the weight of a way in the graph from the zero node to the terminal one.

Let's renumber all the gates and phases, denote the set of phases and gates as {0, 1, 2, ..., M} (Figure 7.4).

Uncertainty of a SEA implementation appears in:

- the a priori indefinite moments t_i of the completion of the phases and transition gates,
- the a priori indefinite completion dates of each of the projects, works/ actions included in the phases (the subordinate elements of CA),
- the a priori indefinite transition gates, i.e. the indefinite transition function $s(t) \rightarrow s(t+1)$; as a result, in the indefinite spending of the resources needed to obtain the required outputs of the phases $z(t_i) \in Z_\beta^*$.

The process starts from state 0. Having transited to the state $i-1$, the process stays the same for several periods of time τ; at the same time, actions are implemented as long as either the desired output is achieved or the impossibility to achieve the goal becomes clear. After that, the process transits into the state i (successful transition through the i-th gate) or returns to the state $i-1$ and re-implementation of the current phase i occurs or returns by j stages and their re-implementation occur. In the

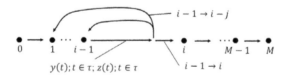

FIGURE 7.4   The behavior of the process s(t) – transition through the LC phases.

terminal state, M, the process remains forever. Let us denote the implementation completion moment of the terminal stage M and the LC of an SEA by t_a.

According to the semantics of a lifecycle, the arch from the $(i-1)$th node into the i-th have weight, which we interpret as phase plans. The weights of the other arches corresponding to returns to the previous LC phases (from the i-th node to the $i-j$-th one, where $0 \le j < i$) are equal to zero.

Let Π_i be the weight of way from the i-th node to terminal n-th node that has the same dimensionality as m_i. Π_i means a plan for implementation of all phases, starting from the $(i+1)$th one to the final n-th one, inclusive. Then for Π_i the system of equations is satisfied:

$$
\begin{cases}
\Pi_i = m_i + \displaystyle\sum_{j=-i}^{0} k(i, j)\Pi_{i+j}; & \text{for } 0 \le i < n \\
\Pi_n = 0.
\end{cases}
\tag{7.6}
$$

Wherefrom it follows that the weights Π_i are linear combinations of the LC phase plans m_i. Let us obtain expressions for Π_i. The existence of a solution is quite simply proved by the mathematical induction method through the possibility to eliminate, from system of equations (7.6), all unknown Π_i except Π_0, by sequentially expressing Π_i through Π_0 and m_i.

It is also easy to show that the solution for Π_0 has the form $\Pi_0 = \displaystyle\sum_{i=1}^{n} v_{0,i} m_i$, where

$v_{i,j}$ is the element of the i-th row of the j-th column of the matrix $(E-K)^{-1}$, E is the unity matrix, and the matrix K has the form:

$$
K =
\begin{pmatrix}
k(0,\,0) & k(0,\,1) & 0 & & 0 \\
k(1,\,-1) & k(1,\,0) & k(1,\,1) & 0 & \\
k(m,\,-m) & k(m,\,i) & k(m,\,0) & k(m,\,1) & 0 \\
\cdots & \cdots & \cdots & \cdots & \cdots \\
& & & & k(M-2,\,1) \\
k(M-1,\,1-M) & & & & k(M-1,\,0)
\end{pmatrix}.
$$

The expression for Π_0 ensures the plan estimate m_a of the output of the LC of SEA as a whole is obtained through the phase plan estimates m_i:

$$
m_\alpha = \Pi_0 = \sum_{i=1}^{n} v_{0,i} m_i
\tag{7.7}
$$

Thus, expression (7.2) for an elementary operation planning, expressions for parallel–sequential compositions of plans of several elements of CA (7.3–7.5), expressions (7.6–7.7) for plan of the characteristics of LC of SEA make up the computational basis for CA lifecycles modelling and, together with the structure of the algorithm (Figure 7.2), provide the possibility of compatible planning of the implementation of an interconnected set of CA elements.

7.1.3 OPTIMAL PLANNING OF CA EXECUTION ACCORDING TO THE NETWORKED TECHNOLOGY

Consider the optimization task of CA execution according to the *networked technology*, which is a typical constituent process of any CA.

The technology of any SEA is considered (see previous Sections 3.4, 4.3, and others) as an organized set of technologies of elementary operations and/or subordinate SEAs and cause–effect models that combine partial components into an integrated networked technology.

Suppose a *principal*, an actor that manages the execution of SEA, knows (a) the cause–effect model of SEA – graph G;* (b) the technological functions $\{Q_i(\cdot)\}$ and cost functions $\{c_i\}$ of all i-th CA elements executed by subordinate *agents*. Then the principal can implement for each node i of the graph G the following algorithm, which leads to the optimal SEA execution plan (in the sense of minimal feasible principal's expenses):

1. Find the function $Q_i(y_{W(i)})$ determining the relation between the result z_i of agent i and the actions vector $y_{W(i)}$ of all predecessors. (This function can be treated as *the aggregate technology of agent i*. Suppose, agent n, executes the final element of technology of the entire SEA.)
2. Find the set

$$A_i = \left\{ (y_{W(i)}) \in \{0;1\}^{|W(i)|} \middle| Q^i(y_{W(i)}) = 1 \right\} \tag{7.8}$$

   of the actions vectors for achieving the result of agent i.
3. Find the set of optimal plans $y_{W(i)}$

$$A_n^* = \operatorname*{Arg\,min}_{(y_{W(i)}) \in A_i} \sum_{j \in W(i)} c_j \tag{7.9}$$

   of the actions vectors for achieving the result of agent i with the minimum total cost

$$C_i = c_i + \min_{(y_{W(i)}) \in A_i} \sum_{j \in W(i)} c_j \tag{7.10}$$

---

* Hereinafter, it's assumed, unless otherwise stated, that the technological graph, technological functions, and other elements of task statement satisfy the assumptions introduced above in Sections 3.4, 4.3, and others.

The feasibility and optimality (minimal cost plan) of each plan $y_{W(i)} \in A_n{}^*$ follow from the definition of Steps 2 and 3 of the algorithm.

The methods of graph theory, network scheduling, planning, and control can be used in the general case to find the set $A_n{}^*$.

For the conjunctive technological functions, sets (7.8) and (7.9) coincide with $A_n{}^* = A_n = N$. For the disjunctive technological functions, $A_n{}^*$ is the set of all nodes of the graph G that lie on the shortest path (in terms of the total cost) from any of its inputs to the output; the value C_n equals the length of this path.

7.1.4 OPTIMAL DESIGN PROCESS OF NETWORKED TECHNOLOGY

The CA execution models considered in Section 7.1.3 are based on the assumption that the managing actors are fully aware of the network G and of all constituents' technological functions. However, the technology should be initially created. The technology design often consists in the development of a sequence of actions under a priori external uncertainty and also with a shortage or even lack of knowledge about the possible methods for achieving a goal (the result of a corresponding activity), i.e., a priori uncertainty in the cause–effect and/or logical relations between different possible technology elements.

The technology evolution/design process (Chapter 5) consists, in general, in

a) elimination of all kinds of uncertainty (considering the expenses) by means of the actor's purposeful "learning by doing" actions following the networked technology structure;

b) synthesis of *optimal technology* – for achieving the required goal with the minimum design and implementation cost (along the whole technology lifecycle).

Consider the optimization problem in a DNAS (see Section 3.4 and 4.3.1 for details) developing a *networked technology*. Let one principal and n agents constitute an active system (complex actor of the SEA); they design networked technology (future SEA technology). The agents design partial technological elements (technologies of subordinated SEAs and elementary operations) and the principal has a priori defined some technological graph* G (cause–effect structure) integrating partial technological elements. The technology models of Chapter 5 describe the design process. For a given technological graph during one time period any agent can design a partial technological element for as many states of the environment as many resources are allocated by the principal. Assume each state of the environment requires the same amount of resources to be analyzed.

Then the principal can execute the following algorithm to realize the optimal process of the technology design (with minimal cost):

---

* Obviously, a technology graph development is a special case of partial technological element development and, if necessary, it can also be included in the consideration.

1. Construct a technological graph.
2. Partition the set of possible environment states into a finite set of non-inter-secting subsets and then estimate the probabilities of each subset (in accor-dance with Section 5.5.1, the uniform partition is the best one) for each node – each technological element of subordinate CA element.
3. Fix the relation between the learning/maturity characteristics of the nodes (agents) and the resources.
4. Find the relation between the characteristics of the entire technological graph and the resources (in particular, see Sections 5.4.1 and 7.1.3).
5. Solve the optimal control problem – allocate the resources among the net-work nodes.

Consider a series of models implementing the last step – optimization. Denote by $u \leq 1$ the resource volume, which drives the share of the states of the environment that are tested per one time period. For the uniform distribution (see (5.1)) of the environment states, the learning/maturity level depends on the time and resource volume as $L(t) = 1 - \exp(-ut)$.

In accordance with the aforesaid, for a "large number" of the states of the envi-ronment the expected time τ of reaching a required learning level $L_{req} \in [0, 1)$ can be approximated as: $\tau(u) = -\ln(1 - L_{req})/u$ (see Section 5.3.3).

Due to the convexity of function $\tau(u)$ by u, the following result can be easily estab-lished (similarly to the proof of Proposition 5.1).

Proposition 7.1. For any relation between the resource volume and learning time, there exists a constant value of the resource volume under which a required maturity/learning level is reached in the same or smaller expected time.

Assume the technology design process incurs some cost $c(uK)$. Let the cost func-tion be a strictly monotonically increasing and convex function of K – the number of states of the environment tested per period (K can be interpreted as the efficiency of allocated resources, analogous to cost function definition employed in Chapter 4).

Let's study two special cases: sequential and parallel technology design (see also Section 5.4.1).

Sequential technology design. Consider n technological elements with num-bers $i \in \overline{1,n}$ that are designed sequentially (in accordance with their numbers) and required learning/maturity level is just the same L_{req} for all of them. Then the design time for the entire complex of these technologies is the sum of the design times of partial technologies:

$$T_{max}\left(u_1, \ldots, u_n\right) = -\ln\left(1 - L_{req}\right)\sum_{i=1}^{n} \frac{1}{u_i} \tag{7.11}$$

Thus, the minimum design cost in such case is

$$c_{min}\left(u_1, \ldots, u_n\right) = c\left(\max_{i \in \overline{1,n}}\left\{u_i K_i\right\}\right) \tag{7.12}$$

The minimization problem of the design time (7.11) subject to the total resource volume C available for allocation among agents has the solution:

$$u_i = \frac{c^{-1}(C)}{\max_{i \in \overline{1,n}}\{K_i\}} = \text{const} \tag{7.13}$$

In other words, the same resource quantity is allocated for the optimal design of each technology. It follows from (7.11) and (7.13) that the complex of sequential technologies can be represented as an *aggregate technology* with the design time as a function of resource volume:

$$T(C) = -\ln\left(1 - L_{\text{req}}\right) n \frac{\max_{i \in \overline{1,n}}\{K_i\}}{c^{-1}(C)} \tag{7.14}$$

The inverse problem, which is to find the minimum cost $C_{\min}$ of the design process of the complex sequential technology in a given expected time T, has the solution

$$C_{\min} = c\left(-T^{-1}\ln\left(1 - L_{\text{req}}\right) n \max_{i \in \overline{1,n}}\{K\}\right) \tag{7.15}$$

Parallel technologies design. Consider n technological elements with numbers $i \in \overline{1,n}$ that are designed in parallel with the same learning/maturity level L_{req} for all of them. Then the design time for the entire complex of these technologies is the maximum of the design times of partial technologies:

$$T_{\min}\left(u_1, \ldots, u_n\right) = -\ln\left(1 - L_{\text{req}}\right) / \min_{i \in \overline{1,n}}\{u_i\} \tag{7.16}$$

In this case, the minimum design cost is

$$c_{\max}\left(u_1, \ldots, u_n\right) = \sum_{i=1}^{n} c\left(u_i K_i\right) \tag{7.17}$$

The minimization problem of the design time (7.16) subject to the total resource volume C available for allocation among agents has the solution:

$$u_i = -T_{\min}^* \ln\left(1 - L_{\text{req}}\right), \tag{7.18}$$

where $T_{\min}^*$ satisfies the equation

$$\sum_{i=1}^{n} c\left(-\ln(1 - L_{\text{req}})\, T_{\min}^* K_i\right) = C. \tag{7.19}$$

Note that the same resource amount is allocated for the optimal design (7.18) of each technology, and the design processes of all technologies are completed simultaneously in the time $T_{\min}^*$.

The inverse problem, which is to find the minimum upper bound C_{min} for the cost of designing the complex of parallel technologies in a given expected time T, has the solution defined by (7.19) with $T^*_{min} = T$.

It follows from (7.16) and (7.18) that the complex of parallel technologies can be represented as an *aggregate technology*. For the linear cost function $c()$, the analytic relation between the design time and resource quantity of this aggregate technology is given by

$$T(C) = -\ln\left(1 - L_{req}\right)C^{-1}\sum_{i=1}^{n} K_i. \tag{7.20}$$

In some cases, a sequential-parallel network structure of technology design process can be first decomposed into the sequential and parallel groups with the above optimal resource allocations and equivalent aggregate representations (expressions (7.14) and (7.20)). As a result, such networks can be researched in a simple analytic aggregate form.*

7.2   PLANNING OF TRANSITION FROM DESIGN PHASE TO EXECUTION PHASE IN DYNAMIC ACTIVE SYSTEM

7.2.1   OPTIMAL TRANSITION FROM DESIGN TO EXECUTION UNDER KNOWN EXTERNAL ENVIRONMENT

Based on the characteristics of the technology control processes, described in Chapter 5, let's consider a problem of decision-making so as to complete the technology creation (block 2 in Figure 5.1) and move on to the productive phase execution in the LC of CA (cycle b-3-c in Figure 5.1) and from Design phase to Execution phase, see Figure 1.12.

Let's use an SEA" model introduced in Chapter 5 in the form of a dynamic system with probabilistic uncertainty, in which during each period the environment takes one of K values, regardless of other periods, with the probabilities $\{p_k\}$. A controlling actor during each period can implement one of the two strategies[†] $u(\cdot)$: 0) to implement the creation of a CA technology ($u(t)=0$) or 1) to execute CA using the technology that has reached the current maturity level ($u(t)=1$). We assume the actor's objective function $\varphi(t; u(t); \cdot)$ to depend on the chosen strategy and on the state taken up by the environment during this period, as follows:

a) If the actor decides to design the technology and invests in the creation of the CA technology in order to obtain future benefits from its use during execution; then the effect for the actor is deterministic and negative: actor spends c_d regardless of the state taken up by the environment.

---

* Such representation of sequentialparallel networks is called aggregated. In accordance with the well-known aggregability criterion (see references in Belov and Novikov (2020a)), a network is aggregable if it does not contain bridges. Any network can be transformed into an aggregable one by splitting a series of nodes into new nodes; in this case, the optimal solution of the minimum design time (or cost) problem for the resulting aggregable network will be a lower bound of the corresponding solution for the initial network.

[†] In a general case, the actor manages subordinate agents to implement any strategy.

b) If the actor decides to execute CA and receive benefits from the use of technology, then the value of the objective function depends on the environment state.

If the environment takes up one of the known states, for which the technology has already
been mastered (we denote such an outcome as $\xi_t = 1$), then the actor receives the profit v.
   If the environment takes up an unknown state ($\xi_t = 0$), which requires technology
modernization, then the actor incurs the costs c_p, without receiving any profit (obviously, it makes sense to consider only the case $c_p > c_d$; if this is not so, the design
phase does not make economic sense).
   Let's combine all three cases:

$$\varphi(t; 1; \xi_t) = \left[v\xi_t - c_p\left(1 - \xi_t\right)\right]u(t) + c_d\left(1 - u(t)\right).$$

Turning to the expected values (taking into account $E[\xi_t] = L_{t-1}$), let's write the objective function $\Phi(t_1; t_2)$ of the actor during a time interval from t_1 to t_2 covering the
design and execution phases of LC of CA:

$$\Phi(t_1, t_2) = \sum_{t=t_1}^{t_2} \left[(v L_{t-1} - c_p (1 - L_{t-1}))u(t) - c_d(1 - u(t))\right]$$

Then the technological decision problem on the completion of the design phase and
transition to the execution phase of the CA lifecycle is to find the decision strategy
$\{u(t)\}$ maximizing the expected effect

$$\Phi(t_1, t_2) = \sum_{t=t_1}^{t_2} \left[(v L_{t-1} - c_p (1 - L_{t-1}))u(t) - c_d (1 - u(t))\right] \rightarrow \max_{u(t)} .$$

Assume the actor makes sequential decisions at each period $t = \overline{1, T}$ independently
of decisions at earlier periods; in such case all $\{u(t)\}$ are independent of each other.
Then at the current period t the decision strategy has to maximize $\Phi(t, T)$:

$$\max_{\{u(\tau)\}} \Phi(t, T) = \max_{\{u(\tau)\}} \left\{\sum_{\tau=t}^{T} (v L_{\tau-1} - c_p (1 - L_{\tau-1})) \, u(\tau) - c_d (1 - u(\tau))\right\} \quad (7.21)$$

Due to the independence of $\{u(t)\}$ for different periods, the maximum of the sum of
the expected effects is the sum of the maximum effects:

$$\max_{\{u(\tau)\}} \Phi(t, T) = \max_{\{u(\tau)\}} \left\{\sum_{\tau=t}^{T} (v L_{\tau-1} - c_p (1 - L_{\tau-1})) \, u(\tau) - c_d (1 - u(\tau))\right\} =$$

$$= \max_{\{u(\tau)\}} (v L_{t-1} - c_p (1 - L_{t-1})) \, u(t) - c_d (1 - u(t)) + \max_{\{u(\tau)\}} \Phi(t+1, T)$$

Making trivial transformations and denoting

$$L_{\text{thres}} = \frac{c_p - c_d}{c_p + v} \qquad (7.22)$$

we finally get $\max_{\{u(\tau)\}} \Phi(t, T) = (v + c_p) \max_{u(t)} \{(L_{t-1} - L_{\text{thres}}) u(t)\} - c_d + \max_{\{u(\tau)\}} \Phi(t+1, T)$;

the following result is immediate:

Proposition 7.2 The optimal decision strategy that yields the maximum total effect is given by

$$u(t) = \begin{cases} 0, & \text{if } L_{t-1} < L_{\text{thres}}, \\ 1, & \text{if } L_{t-1} \geq L_{\text{thres}}. \end{cases} \quad \text{where} \quad L_{\text{thres}} = \frac{c_p - c_d}{c_p + v} \qquad (7.23)$$

In other words, the optimal strategy (7.23) has a single switch from 0 to 1 (from the design phase to the execution phase), and the transition condition is determined by the technology's maturity level as follows. While this level is not exceeding the threshold ($L_{t1} < L_{\text{thres}}$), the actor benefits from technology design through investments; starting from the time t_{reach} of reaching the maturity level L_{thres}, the actor chooses the productive use of the technology (for gaining the payoffs from activity execution), further improving the maturity level in parallel. First, the actor just designs the technology and then redesigns (improves) it in the course of activity execution.

Using expressions (7.21) and (7.23) in combination with the Wald's lemma, we derive an explicit expression of the prior maximum expected effect

$$\Phi^*(1, T) = (v + c_p) \sum_{\tau = t_{\text{reach}} + 1}^{T} L_{\tau - 1} - c_d \, t_{\text{reach}} - c_p \, (T - t_{\text{reach}}) \qquad (7.24)$$

where t_{reach} is the expected time of reaching the maturity level L_{thres}. Substituting the expected maturity level $L_{\tau 1}$ into (7.24) produces:

$$\Phi^*(1, T) = (v + c_p) \sum_{\tau = t_{\text{reach}}}^{T-1} \left(1 - \sum_{k=1}^{K} p_k (1 - p_k)^{\tau} \right) - c_d t_{\text{reach}} - c_p (T - t_{\text{reach}}).$$

And finally

$$\Phi^*(1, T) = vT - (v + c_d) t_{\text{reach}} - (v + c_p) \left[1 + \sum_{k=1}^{K} \left[(1 - p_k)^{t_{\text{reach}}} - (1 - p_k)^{T} \right] \right]$$

Interestingly, the optimal strategy is independent of the interval length T, which actually drives the resulting effect $\Phi^*(\cdot)$ only.

The following conclusion is immediate from (7.23) and the monotonic increase of the process L_t (see Proposition 5.2 and its extensions to different integration processes in Section 5.4): for any arbitrarily large costs c_d and c_p such that $c_d < c_p$ and any arbitrarily small nonzero payoff v, there exists a time T_{payb} from which the agent's activity will yield a positive effect. In other words, T_{payb} determines the break-even point of the CA life cycle. This time can be found from the equation

$$a_1 t + \sum_{k=1}^{K}(1-p_k)^t = a_2\, t_{reach} + 1 + \sum_{k=1}^{K}(1-p_k)^{t_{reach}} \quad \text{in} \quad t, \quad \text{where} \quad 0 < a_1 = v/$$

$(v+c_p) < a_2 = (v+c_d)/(v+c_p) < 1$. The monotonic increase of the technology's maturity level allows proof that the sequential single-switch strategy is optimal among all sequential decision strategies $\{u(t)\}$ (not just among the strategies with independent decisions at each time). On the other hand, the optimal sequential decision strategy is no worse than any a priori strategy. This leads to another important result as follows.

Proposition 7.3. The sequential single-switch strategy (7.23) is optimal among all admissible ones. The resulting effect (7.24) is maximum achievable while the payback time T_{payb} is minimum possible.

It makes sense to expand the results obtained for the case when decisions on transition from technology development to its productive use can be made not after any period t, but only after a group of several n periods. Such conditions are typical, for example, for control of a technology for mass batch production, when decisions are made only after/before the release of a batch of products in a fixed known volume.

Let's suppose that during the design phase over each time period, the actor incurs the costs c_d and does not receive benefits regardless of the state of the environment. During the execution phase, if the environment takes up one of the known states (for which the technology has already been developed), the actor receives the benefit v; if the state of the environment was not met before (which required technology modernization), then actor incurs the costs c_p, without receiving benefits. After each group of periods (we refer to a group of periods as a *batch*) the actor

a) analyzes the states of the environment, encountered for the first time, and increases the maturity/learning level of the technology;
b) makes the choice of the LC phase for the next batch, the design or execution one.

Let us obtain an expression for effect on N time periods, divided into M batches, each having a size of n periods ($0 < n$). The m-th batch ($1 \le m \le M$) consists of periods with such indices t that $n(m-1)+1 \le t \le n\,m$ and $N = n\,M$.

The effect obtained during periods from 1 to N, as the difference in profits and costs, equals to $\sum_{m=1}^{M}[u(m) \sum_{\theta=n(m-1)+1}^{nm}(v\xi_\theta - c_p(1-\xi_\theta)) - (1-u(m))nc_d]$, where ξ_θ are random variables, characterizing the environment conditions: $\xi_\theta = 1$, if the state is known and $\xi_\theta = 0$ if such is new, $u(m)$ is the decision rule taking values 1, if the execution phase is chosen for the m-th batch, and 0 if the design one.

Let's carry out transformations in the analogous way as was already done in this section; by passing to mathematical expectations, we obtain the optimization problem (see (7.21)):

$$\Phi(t,T) = \sum_{m=1}^{M} \left(n\left(vL_{n(m-1)} - c_p \left(1 - L_{n(m-1)}\right) \right) u(m) - \left(1 - u(m)\right) nc_d \right) \to \max_{\{u(m)\}}$$

By denoting (see 7.22)) $L_{\text{thres}}^* = \dfrac{c_p - c_d}{c_p + v}$, we obtain

$$\max_{\{u(\mu)\}} \Phi(t,T) = (v + c_p) n \max_{u(m)} \left\{ (L_{n(m-1)} - L_{\text{thres}}^*) u(m) \right\}$$

$$- c_d n + \max_{\{u(\mu)\}} \Phi(t+1,T)$$

Wherefrom the optimal strategy follows:

$$u\left(m; L_{n(m-1)}\right) = \begin{cases} 0, & \text{if } L_{n(m-1)} < L_{\text{thres}}^*, \\ 1, & \text{if } L_{n(m-1)} \geq L_{\text{thres}}^*. \end{cases}$$

That is to say that, for the "batch" setting too, the optimal strategy is a sequential one-time switch strategy with the switch at the point, when a learning/maturity L_{thres}^* is reached that coincides with the level of the basic problem (7.22).

7.2.2 Transition from the Design Phase to Execution One under Unknown External Environment

Now, consider the problem of decision-making on the transition from the design phase to the execution phase under the unknown but fixed characteristics of the environment – the dimension K and the probabilities $\{p_k\}$ are constant but unknown. In this case, the technology's maturity level cannot be calculated and hence the decision strategy (7.22–7.23) (see Proposition 7.2) becomes inapplicable.

But anyway, the expected effect can be written as

$$\max_{\{u(\tau)\}} \Phi(t,T) = -c_d + \left(v + c_p\right) \max_{\{u(\tau)\}} \left\{ \left(\Pr\left(\xi_t = 1\right) - L_{\text{thres}} \right) u(t) \right\}$$

$$+ \max_{\{u(\tau)\}} \Phi(t+1,T). \tag{7.25}$$

Therefore, the sequential strategy optimizing the expected effect $E[\Phi(t,T)]$ consists in $(\Pr(\xi_t = 1) - L_{\text{thres}}) u(t) \to \max_{\{u(\tau)\}}$, which is achieved by $u(t) = 1$ if $\Pr(\xi_t = 1) > L_{\text{thres}}$ and $u(t) = 0$

otherwise. In other words, $u(t)$ must be the result of the sequential testing of the composite main hypothesis $L_t < L_{\text{thres}}$ against its composite alternative $L_t \geq L_{\text{thres}}$ (whether the value of the unobserved process L_t is exceeding the threshold L_{thres} or not).

Under the unknown characteristics of the environment, all available information for decision-making is whether a current environment state has been observed before or not. Denote by θ_k the numbers of periods when the environment takes a new state never observed before. These numbers form an increasing finite sequence $0=\theta_1<\theta_2<...<\theta_k<...<\theta_K$ observed by the actor. By definition, at each number θ_k the process L_t has an unknown increment p_k and takes the value $L_{\theta_k}=\sum_{i=1}^{k}p_i$, which is constant till the next period number θ_{k+1}. Consider the series lengths $\psi_k=(\theta_{k+1}-\theta_k-1)$ for $k=\overline{1,K-1}$. The values ψ_k are independent random variables, each obeying the geo-metric distribution parameterized by the current partial sum $L_{\theta_k}=\sum_{i=1}^{k}p_i$ of the probabilities of all realized states of the environment (note that this parameter is unknown and unobservable to the actor). In other words, $\Pr(\psi_k=n)=(1-L_{\theta_k})L_{\theta_k}^{n-1}$, and the expected values and variances are $L_{\theta_k}/(1-L_{\theta_k})$ and $L_{\theta_k}/(1-L_{\theta_k})^2$, respec-tively. The actor does not a priori know the dimension K and the distribution $\{p_k\}$; hence, the length of the sequence $\{\psi_k\}$ cannot be defined and this sequence should be considered a priori infinite.

Let s be the number of the last new state observed by the current period t, i.e., $0=\theta_1<\theta_2<...<\theta_s\leq t$; also denote $\psi_s=t-\theta_s$.

Thus, at each period t the actor has the following information as the base for decision:

- the series lengths $\psi_1, \psi_2, ..., \psi_{s-1}, \psi_s$ (further denoted by $\{\psi\}$);
- the knowledge that each of ψ_k is generated by the geometric distribution with an unknown increasing parameter $L_{\theta_k}<L_{\theta_{k+1}}$.

Under the unknown characteristics of the environment, the problem is to synthesize a *sequential criterion* $u(t, \{\psi\})$ for the composite main hypothesis H_0: $L_t<L_{\text{thres}}$ (the value L_{θ_s} does not exceed the threshold L_{thres} before the end of period t) against the set of composite alternatives $\{H_i$: $L_t\geq L_{\text{thres}}\}$ (the value L_{θ_s} exceeds the threshold L_{thres} before the end of period t) by maximizing the expected effect $E[\Phi(0, T)]$. We choose likelihood method as the basics for the decision strategy $u(t, \{\psi\})$, while the criterion parameters should be adjusted by optimizing the expected effect $E[\Phi(0, T)]$.

The relative likelihood ratio of the series lengths $\{\psi\}$ generated by the geometric distribution has the form

$$l(i,t)=\ln\frac{\Pr(\{\psi\}|H_i)}{\Pr(\{\psi\}|H_0)}=\sum_{k=i}^{s}\ln\frac{L_k^i}{L_k^0}\psi_k+\sum_{k=i}^{s-1}\ln\frac{1-L_k^i}{1-L_k^0},$$

where L_k^0 and L_k^i give the values of the process L_t at the times θ_k when the main $L_k^0<L_{\text{thres}}$ and alternative $L_k^i\geq L_{\text{thres}}$ hypotheses are true, respectively, and i ($i=1, 2,$

...s) means the number of the most likelihood alternative hypothesis (actually, the serial number of the new i-th state of the environment).

There is no available information on the properties of the environment, except the only constructive considerations about the values L_k^0 and L_k^i are the inequalities $L_k^0 < L_{thres}$ and $L_k^i \geq L_{thres}$. We assume $L_k^0 = L_{thres} - \Delta L$ and $L_k^i \geq L_{thres} + \Delta L$ and use this assumption to construct the likelihood criterion (as a matter of fact, this assumption seems neither better nor worse than any other): at the current period t, the main hypothesis is rejected for its alternative if at least one of the functions $l(i, t)$ exceeds some threshold l_{thres}, i.e., $\max\limits_i l(i, t) \geq l_{thres}$.

Denote $l(t) = \max\limits_i l(i, t)$ and study how $l(t)$ evolves with the course of time. If at the current period t a known state of the environment is observed, then each of the likelihoods $l(i, t)$, $1 \leq i \leq s$, increase by $a_1 = \ln\left(\dfrac{L_{thres} + \Delta L}{L_{thres} - \Delta L}\right) > 0$. As a result, $l(t)$ increases by the same value: $l(t+1) = l(t) + a_1$. If a new state is observed, then each of $l(i, t)$, $1 \leq i \leq s$ decreases by $a_2 = \ln\left(\dfrac{1 - L_{thres} - \Delta L}{1 - L_{thres} + \Delta L}\right) < 0$. Also the new $(s+1)$th function $l(s+1, t+1) = 0$ is formed. Therefore, in this case $l(t+1) = \max\{0;\ l(t) + a_2\}$.

The resulting value of the likelihood function $l(t)$ is compared to the threshold l_{thres} to make a decision.

All three constants of criteria a_1, a_2 and l_{thres} have to be chosen; so without loss of generality, assume $a_1 = 1$ and denote $a_2 = -a$.

Thus, the sequential likelihood-based criterion is constructed to be used under the unknown properties of the environment. This criterion includes the iterative calculation of the likelihood function $l(t)$ and the corresponding decision strategy $u(t, \{\psi\})$ given by

$$l(t+1) = \begin{cases} l(0) = 0; \\ l(t) + 1; \text{ if known environment state is observed;} \\ \max\{0;\ l(t) - a\}; \text{ if unknown environment state is observed;} \end{cases}$$

(7.26)

$$u(t; \{\psi\}) = \begin{cases} 0 \text{ if } u(t-1; \{\psi\}) = 0 \text{ and } l(t) < l_{thres}; \\ 1 \text{ if } u(t-1; \{\psi\}) = 1 \text{ or } l(t) \geq l_{thres}. \end{cases}$$

It is necessary to find values of the constants a and l_{thres} to complete the synthesis of the criterion. We make the choice based on the optimization of the expected effect $E[\Phi(\cdot)]$ for some selected scenario of the behavior of the environment; an algorithm of optimal choice of a and l_{thres} is given in Appendix A7.1. In such a way, the following statement is valid.

Proposition 7.4. The procedure (7.26) is the best in the class of sequential likelihood-based procedures for planning the transition from the design phase to the execution one under unknown external environment characteristics. In such case, the optimal

choice of the parameters a and l_{thres} is carried out according to the criterion $\min$
$\{\Phi(\{p_k\}, T, a, l_{\text{thres}})\} \to \max\limits_{a>0;\, l_{\text{hres}}>0}$ employing the algorithm given in Appendix A7.1.$^{\{p_k\}}$

The criterion (7.26) with the optimally chosen parameters a and l_{thres} is simulated
and numerically researched in Appendix A7.2.

Let's expand the results to the "batch production" case.

The optimal strategy obtained at the end of Section 7.2.1 defines the rule of transition from the design phase to the execution phase when the maturity/learning level
exceeds a certain threshold L^*_{thres}. In the case of unknown characteristics of the
environment, the maturity/learning level cannot be calculated; therefore, the actor
should synthesize a criterion based on observations of the numbers ς_m of cases in the
m-th batch, when the environment has taken up already known states. The values
ς_m form a sequence of random binomially distributed values with the parameters n
(the batch size) and L_m (maturity/learning level, being unknown to the actor). The
batch size n in practice is of the order of tens of thousands, therefore, the binomial
distribution of the values ς_m can be adequately approximated by the normal one,
with the mathematical expectations nL_m and dispersions $nL_m(1-L_m)<n/2$. Thus, an
actor needs a criterion for the optimal detection of the element of the sequence ς_m/n,
starting from which the mathematical expectation of the normally distributed value
ς_m/n exceeds the given boundary L^*_{thres}. According to the known results (Nikiforov
2016) and (Shiryaev 1977) and the above-mentioned considerations, the criterion has
a form analogous to (7.26):

$$l(m+1) = \begin{cases} l(0) = 0 \\ \max\{0;\, l(m)+\varsigma_m\,/\,n - a\} \end{cases}$$

$$u(m;\{\varsigma\}) = \begin{cases} 0 \text{ if } u(m-1;\{\varsigma\}) = 0 \text{ and } l(m) < l_{\text{thres}}; \\ 1 \text{ if } u(m-1;\{\varsigma\}) = 1 \text{ or } l(m) \geq l_{\text{thres}}. \end{cases}$$

(7.27)

where a and l_{thres} are parameters, for which the values are chosen so as to optimize
the expected effect $E[\Phi(\cdot)]$ for certain environmental characteristics (a simulation
algorithm for choice of a and l_{thres} is considered in Appendix A7.3.)

7.3 PLANNING AND CONTROL IN DYNAMIC MULTI-AGENT ACTIVE SYSTEM WITH CHANGING CHARACTERISTICS

Controlling problem solutions under possible changes in external and internal factors
is essential for solving the Enterprise Control Problem: firstly, an Enterprise, being a
complex system, is distinguished by the characteristic of evolution in time, and secondly, the environment also changes in time. Such changes on both sides, sooner or
later, lead to the fact that the Enterprise's CA technology becomes inadequate to the
environment, which manifests itself in the form of the occurrence of true uncertainty
events (Chapter 1, Section 2.3).

In this section, we introduce a classification of control problems under the conditions when, during a time interval under consideration, one or several Enterprise or/

and environment characteristics can change once (at the moment in time t_d); we refer to this event as *"disorder"*. Thereafter the problem is solved as a special case of implementation of the Enterprise Control Optimization Scheme (Section 3.4.3, Figure 3.9).

7.3.1 Classes of Optimization Problem in an Active System with Changing Characteristics

As in the previous sections, we consider an Enterprise as a multi-element dynamic active system with a constraint in the form of a technology imposed on joint activity, in general cases characterized by formulation (3.11–3.17). Let us use the notations introduced in Section 3.4 and consider the assumptions made as satisfied. We assume that change in characteristics can concern a principal's income functions, agent's costs and CA technology. Let us admit the following model of CA technology, taking into account environment factors. Both before and after a disorder, a technology satisfies one of the assumptions A2/A2' or A3/A3' (Section 3.4.1–3.4.2). The output $z_w(y_A[1^*t])$ of the Enterprise's CA (such of the root ω_w-principal) is considered as a random variable with known distribution; at that, the values $z_w(y_A[1^*t])$ also belong to known target areas, see Sections 2.3 and 3.4.1. This stochastic model reflects the effect of measurable uncertainty of CA before and after disorder, and disorder itself is considered as the occurrence of a true uncertainty event that causes inadequacy of the technology and requires technology modernization.

Let us analyze possible variants of the problem using Table 7.1, which lists all the possible options for the principal's and agent's awareness about the elements of the optimization problem statement: the principal's income function, agent cost functions and the probability distribution of the CA output before and after the disorder (we denote all functions after the disorder using symbol "+" as a superscript). Under the conditions of compliance with A2/A2' or A3/A3', the problem allows decomposition by periods and by agents; therefore, when analyzing the Table 7.1, we suppose a contractual interaction of the principal with each of the agents separately as well as for any period separately. Moreover, we assume that before making a decision for the period t regarding the "game history," the principal knows the output of CA during previous periods, and each of the agents knows both the output and the action. Awareness of the agent and the principal is reflected in the third and fourth columns of Table 7.1.

1–2. Change in the principal's income function $h(\cdot) \rightarrow h^+(\cdot)$ is considered in rows 1 and 2 of Table 4.3. If a new income function $h^+(\cdot)$ and *the disorder moment t_d* are known to the principal (the first line of Table 7.1), then the formulation is reduced to a set of *typical* – discussed above in Section 4.1 – static incentive problems, solved separately for each period.

If the principal's new income function $h^+(\cdot)$ is unknown to the principal, then this statement does not make sense, since the principal does not have enough information for making decisions: does not know income.

3–9. Change in the agent's cost function $c(\cdot) \rightarrow c^+(\cdot)$ is considered in rows 3–9 of Table 7.1. If the disorder moment and a new cost function are known to both the agent and the principal (line 3), then the formulation is reduced to a set of typical tasks that are sequentially and independently solved at different time periods.

TABLE 7.1

Classification of Dynamic Incentive Problems

№	Subject–Matter of Disorder	The Agent Knows	The Principal Knows	Problems
1	$h(\cdot) \rightarrow h^+(\cdot)$	Does not matter	$t_d; h^+(\cdot)$	Typical problem
2			Nothing or t_d	Does not make sense
3			$t_d; c^+(\cdot)$	Typical problem
4		$t_d; c^+(\cdot)$	$c^+(\cdot)$	Screening
5			Nothing	Has no solution
6	$c(\cdot) \rightarrow c^+(\cdot)$		$t_d; c^+(\cdot)$	Typical problem
7		$c^+(\cdot)$	$c^+(\cdot)$	Typical problem
8			Nothing	Has no solution
9		Nothing	Does not matter	Has no solution
10			$t_d; F_\theta^+(\cdot)$	Typical problem
11		$t_d; F_\theta^+(\cdot)$	$F_\theta^+(\cdot)$	Screening
12			Nothing	Has no solution
13	$F_\theta(\cdot) \rightarrow F_\theta^+(\cdot)$		$t_d; F_\theta^+(\cdot)$	Typical problem
14		$F_\theta^+(\cdot)$	$F_\theta^+(\cdot)$	Statement D1
15			Nothing	Has no solution
16		Nothing	Does not matter	Has no solution

If the principal knows the agent's new cost function, but doesn't know the moment of its change (line 4), then it's the rationale for him to offer the agent at any time a menu of such contracts, that are optimal for a set of cost function variants, i.e. the known *screening* approach used in conditions of *asymmetric awareness* (see Novikov (2013), Bolton and Dewatripont (2005)).

If the agent knows both the new cost function and the disorder moment, and the principal knows none of this (line 5), then the problem has no solution for the following reasons. In order to get a gain greater than zero, the principal must incentivize the agent to act at least in some way. So a contract that provides a gain of not less than zero should be offered to the agent. But when the agent's cost function is unknown, the principal cannot form such a contract. For analogous reasons, the problems in rows 8, 12, and 15 of the table, when the principal does not know the new cost functions or the output distribution, have no solution.

If the principal knows both the agent's new cost function and the disorder moment, and the agent knows only the cost function (line 6), then this case comes down to a typical problem: the principal, possessing *complete information*, offers a contract corresponding to $c(\cdot)$ until the disorder moment, and thereafter the principal offers $c^+(\cdot)$; the agent can identify the moment of disorder by the moment of changing in the principal's offer and respond optimally. That is, in this case one has a set of typical problems.

Let's consider the case when the principal and agent know a new cost function, but do not know the disorder moment (line 7). Above, we assumed that the agent's cost function is continuously differentiable and strictly monotonic, and this means that, by observing actual costs, the agent can identify the fact of disorder (if the latter has taken place). Moreover, the cost function disorder is reliably detected by the agent immediately after the period, which comes after a disorder and in which the agent chooses some action y for which $c(y; \cdot) \neq c^+(y; \cdot)$. However, during this one period (when choosing the action) the agent is guaranteed not to know the cost functions. Therefore, in the context of the agent's shortsightedness, the principal always has to offer a contract, accounting for the worst variant of the cost function for the agent, i.e. on the function max $\{c(\cdot); c^+(\cdot)\}$, with this happening both before and after the occurrence of disorder and its detection by the agent. Thus, in this case a typical problem arises with the principal's additional costs, the value of which can be estimated by both players (the principal and the agent).

If the agent does not know the new cost function, the problem also has no solution, regardless of the principal's awareness (line 9): in this case, the agent cannot estimate possible losses during the periods, lasting until the agent identifies the new cost function, and therefore the agent always prefers refusal from action.

10–16. Change in the activity output distribution $F_\theta(\cdot) \rightarrow F_\theta^+(\cdot)$ is considered in lines 10–16. The function $F_\theta(z_w(t); y_A[1*t])$ characterizes the distribution of an Enterprise's CA output values $z_w(t)$ at the current time period t from the agents' actions during the current and previous periods $y_A[1*t]$.

If the principal knows both the new probability distribution function $F_\theta^+(\cdot)$ and the moment of disorder, and the agent knows at least the new function $F_\theta^+(\cdot)$, then a set of typical problems arises (lines 10 and 13).

If the agent knows the new probability distribution function $F_\theta^+(\cdot)$ and the moment of disorder, and the principal knows only the new function $F_\theta^+(\cdot)$, then a sequential screening problem arises (line 11).

If the agent does not know the probability distribution function $F_\theta^+(\cdot)$, the problem also has no solution in this setting, regardless of the principal's awareness (line 16): in this case, the agent cannot estimate possible expected gains and losses during the periods until the agent identifies the new function $F_\theta^+(\cdot)$, and therefore the agent prefers refusal from any actions.

Statement D1 (line 14) is a multi-period model of contracts with a change in the distribution $F_\theta(\cdot)$ at some a priori unknown time moment. In this model, both the principal and the agents know the new function $F_\theta^+(\cdot)$ and know that it can change no more than once, but a priori they do not know the disorder moment (we denote by $p_\theta(\cdot)$ and $p_\theta^+(\cdot)$ the corresponding distributions probability density functions), the functions $c(\cdot)$, $h(\cdot)$ being also common knowledge. This statement is the only one among all variants (lines 1–16) requiring specific methods to be solved and it is studied in detail in the next section.

7.3.2 PLANNING AND CONTROL PROCEDURE IN AN ACTIVE SYSTEM WITH CHANGING CHARACTERISTICS

Let's point out systemic conditions of the problem by considering it in relation to implementation of an Enterprise CA in practically significant cases.

1. Assumptions A7 (Section 7.1.1) are valid, stating that the rational behavior of CA actors (the Enterprise's management) includes regularization of activity, as one of the directions, which in turn leads to statistical independence in the appearance of CA measurable uncertainty.
2. The economic nature of the costs $c(\cdot)$ and the income $h(\cdot)$ allows us to assume their additivity and consider the objective functions of each of the agents $f(\cdot)$ and principal $\Phi(\cdot)$ during several periods as the sum of objective functions on each of the periods.
3. Theses 1 and 2 above, assumptions A2/A2', A3/A3' and Theorem 4.2 imply the probabilistic independence of time periods and the correctness of the solution to the problem in the setting with independent periods (Novikov and Shokhina 2003).
4. It is feasible to assume the principal's and agents' "full awareness" about the conditions of the problem; that is, they know not only the functions $c(\cdot)$, $h(\cdot)$, $F_\theta(\cdot)$, but also have complete knowledge about each other's knowledge. "Full awareness" in practice arises, in particular, as a consequence of "the fair and open market effect": For example, a customer (principal) knows the "market conditions" for the production of a typical, standard, common product/service, when both the executor (agent) is an individual and a firm. In this case, the customer (principal) does not care what the technology and costs of the particular executor are. This allows the principal (generally speaking, regardless of the knowledge and even manipulation of the agent!) to form an incentive system, relying on the "fair and open market" characteristics of the activity.
5. It is feasible to assume agents' shortsightedness, i.e. the opportunity for each of them at any time to terminate participating in the active system and CA execution. This means that the principal should always offer a contract, taking into account the worst variant for the agent. Because if the principal does not do this, the agent refuses the contract, and therefore neither the agent nor the principal receives any new information about the environment state, and their further interaction loses the sense.
6. It follows from Theses 4 and 5 that if the principal forms such a contract and the agents are rational, then the principal can predict the agents' action. The CA output is observed by the principal, so the principal a posteriori possesses the same information as the agent. This fact can be generalized in the form of a *principle of "incentive contract transparency"*: if the awareness allows the principal to form an incentive contract, the agent is rational and does not manipulate, then the principal can reliably predict the actions of the agent and, therefore, has the same completeness of awareness as the agent.

7. In the general case, it is possible to distinguish several strategies of partici-
pants depending on the type of the functions $c(\cdot)$, $h(\cdot)$, $F_\theta(\cdot)$ and $F_\theta^+(\cdot)$. The
principal has the options:

   (a) to form an incentive system based on $F_\theta(\cdot)$ up to a certain point, detect
disorder and after detection to form an incentive system based on $F_\theta^+(\cdot)$;
   (b) to form always an incentive system based on $F_\theta^+(\cdot)$ or $F_\theta(\cdot)$.
        Each agent has the options:
   (c) if the agent knows that the expected losses after disorder before the
principal detects them are so great that the activity does not make sense
to the agent at all;
   (d) if the execution of the activity is feasible from the agent's point of view.
        The current conditions for the arising of variants (a)–(d) are specific
(depending on the form of the functions $c(\cdot)$, $h(\cdot)$, $F_\theta(\cdot)$, and $F_\theta^+(\cdot)$); therefore, their analysis is beyond the scope of this research. The only combina-
tion of interest to study is <(a)+(d)>, and only that is further considered.

8. In practice, the principal, as a rule, has no external constraints on changes
in the incentive system.

9. As a rule, there are no considerations that allow one to reasonably suppose
the possibility of disorder occurrence at certain moments in time (to set out
an a priori probability distribution of the disorder moment).

So, let's consider a multi-agent dynamic active system, with one principal, with a
probabilistic model of uncertainty, with a disorder – change of the characteristics of
the Enterprise, consisting in change in the probability distributions function (density)
of the output of the agents' actions.

We assume the following *functioning order* of the active system.

Before the beginning of each period t, the principal, based on observations of the
Enterprise's CA output $z_w[1*t - 1]$ in previous periods and on a priori knowledge,
makes a decision whether disorder has occurred. Depending on this decision, the
principal offers the incentive functions $\{\sigma_i'\}$ to the agents. The agents make decisions
and act; uncertainty, driving the outputs, is implemented. Thereafter remuneration of
agents and transition to the next time period are carried out.

We assume the following *awareness* of the participants:

Both the principal and agents know: $c_i(y_i)$ – the agents' cost functions during one
period, $h(Z)$ – the principal's income function during one period, the Enterprise's CA
output distribution density $p_\theta(z_w(t); y_A[1*t])$ and $p_\theta^+(z_w(t); y_A[1*t])$ before and after the
disorder moment. The principal and agents do not know either the disorder moment
or even a priori distribution of the disorder moment.

Let us remember that, as a result of the above assumptions A2/A2' or A3/A3',
the principal can design a compatible optimal incentive system, that is optimal for
the principal, by decomposing the game of agents and by periods before and after
disorder (this is also possible, for example, in the case of unrelated periods and independent agents). Let $\sigma_i(z_w[1*t]; \chi_0; 0)$ be the optimal incentive function for the i-th
agent before disorder, given the density $p_\theta(\cdot; \cdot)$, and $\sigma_i(z_w[1*t]; \chi_1; 1)$ be the same after
disorder, given the density $p_\theta^+(\cdot; \cdot)$; χ_0 and χ_1 are the corresponding plans for action.
Such functions $\sigma_i(\cdot)$ satisfy the conditions:

$$\begin{cases} \min_{y \in P_q[\sigma(\cdot)]} \{E_{\theta|q}[H(\zeta) - \sum_i \sigma_i(\zeta; \chi_q; q)]\} \rightarrow \max_{\{\sigma_i(\cdot; \chi_q; q)\} \in M}; \\ \text{where } P_q[\sigma(\cdot; q)] = \prod_i \text{Arg} \max_{y \in A_i} \{E_{\theta|q}[\sigma_i(\zeta; y; q)] - c_i(y)\}; \qquad (7.28) \\ \min_{r=0,1} \{E_{\theta|r}[\sigma_i(\zeta; \chi_q; q)]\} \geq c_i(\chi_q). \end{cases}$$

Let us set the problem so as to build an incentive system in the class:

$$\sigma_i(z_w[1*t]; t) = \sigma_i(z_w[1*t]; \chi_0; 0)(1 - u(t)) + \sigma_i(z_w[1*t]; \chi_1; 1)u(t), \qquad (7.29)$$

where $u(t)$ is the principal's decision function about disorder detection – detection of the changes in the Enterprise's characteristics; so $u(t) = 0$ when the principal believes there is no disorder and $u(t) = 1$ after the principal detects the disorder.

Let's define the *control effectiveness criterion* over the interval $[1; T]$:

$$\Phi(u(\cdot); \tau; T) = \sum_{t=1}^{\tau-1} E_{\theta|0}[H(z) - \sum_i \sigma_i(z; t)] + \sum_{t=\tau}^{T} E_{\theta|1}[H(z) - \sum_i \sigma_i(z; t)],$$

where $E_{\theta|0}[\cdot]$ and $E_{\theta|1}[\cdot]$ mean averaging over the distributions $p_\theta(\cdot; \cdot)$ and $p_\theta^+(\cdot; \cdot)$ respectively.

The criterion $\Phi(\cdot)$ has the meaning of the average value of the difference between the principal's income and costs for a certain scenario, when the Enterprise and/or external characteristics change at the time $\tau \in (1; T)$. Then the problem consists of finding the principal's decision function $u(t)$ based on observations of the agents' outputs (and actions) such that

$$\Phi(u(\cdot); \tau; T) \rightarrow \max_{u(\cdot)}.$$

The problem in this setting belongs to the class of disorder problems (for example, Nikiforov (1983), Nikiforov (2016), and Shiryayev (1977)) in a sequential parametric setting with independent observations, known parameter values before and after disorder, and an unknown a priori distribution of the disorder moment. Traditionally (Nikiforov 2016, Shiryayev 1977), to solve such problems, the decision rules $u(t)$ based on the likelihood ratio are used, when at each moment in time $t > 0$ the value of the decision function S_t is calculated, which in our case takes the form:

$$S_0 = 0;$$

$$S_t = \max\left\{0; S_{t-1} + \sum_i \ln \frac{p_{i,1}(z_i(t); \chi_0)}{p_{i,0}(z_i(t); \chi_0)}\right\}; \qquad (7.30)$$

$$u(t) = \begin{cases} 0 & \text{if } S_t \leq \delta \\ 1 & \text{if } S_t > \delta \end{cases}.$$

The sequential statistics S_t is the logarithmic likelihood ratio of disorder versus its absence, written down in a form convenient for calculations in these conditions.

The decision threshold δ drives the characteristics of the decision-making procedure: the balance between *false positive* (the intensity of false decisions or the average time between two false decisions or the probability of false decision generation during a given time period) and *false negative* (the average time of detection delay or the detection probability during a given time interval after disorder) rates in sequential sense. It is known (for example, Nikiforov (1983), Nikiforov (2016), and Shiryayev (1977)) that the maximum likelihood statistics allows one to formulate the decision rule being most effective compared to other statistics with respect to a criterion when one of the error rates is fixed at a level not lower than the given one, and the second error rate is optimized.

Below, we choose the decision threshold δ by optimizing $\Phi(u(\cdot); \tau, T)$ for the same scenario(s).

Let's rewrite the control effectiveness criterion $\Phi(u(\cdot); \tau, T)$ in the equivalent form:

$$\Phi\left(u(\cdot);\tau,T\right) = \Phi^*(\tau;T) + (a_{00} - a_{10}) \sum_{t=1}^{\tau-1} \Pr\left(S_t \leq \delta\right)$$

$$-(a_{11} - a_{01}) \sum_{t=\tau+1}^{T} \Pr\left(S_t \leq \delta\right) \to \max;$$

where $\Phi^*(\tau,T)$ is a summand, being independent of the decision function; $a_{q|r} = E_{\theta|r}[H(Z) - \sum_i \sigma_i(z_i; \chi_q; q)]$ are coefficients being independent of the decision function; $\Pr(S_t > \delta)$ are the probabilities that the value of the decision function S_t does not exceed δ, if the disorder has not yet occurred (for $t < \tau$) and has occurred (for $t > \tau$).

Let's denote $\pi(x; d; t) = \Pr(S_t > x \mid \delta = d)$ – the probability that S_t exceeds x at period t if the decision-making threshold is set up to d. The probabilities $\pi(x; d; t)$ are defined at $x \in \mathfrak{R}^1; d \in \mathfrak{R}_+^1; t \in \{0; 1; 2; \ldots; T\}$ and evolve following the system of equations:

$$\begin{cases} \pi\left(x;d;0\right) = \begin{cases} 0 \text{ for } x < 0; \\ 1 \text{ for } x \geq 0; \end{cases} \\ \pi\left(x;d;t+1\right) = \int_0^d \pi\left(y;d;t\right)\rho_0\left(x-y;t\right)dy + \int_d^{+\infty} \pi\left(y;d;t\right)\rho_1\left(x-y;t\right)dy. \end{cases}$$

where $\rho_q(\cdot;t)$ is the p.d.f. of the increments $\sum_i (\ln(p_{i,1}(z_i(t);\chi_q)) - \ln(p_{i,0}(z_i(t);\chi_q)))$ of the decision function S_t before $t < \tau$ and after $t > \tau$ the disorder $p_\theta(\cdot; \cdot) \to p_\theta^+(\cdot; \cdot)$.

Then the optimal value of the threshold δ^* is obtained as a solution of the optimization problem:

$$\delta^* = \arg \max_{d>0} \left\{ (a_{0|0} - a_{1|0}) \sum_{t=1}^{\tau-1} \pi(d;d;t) - (a_{1|1} - a_{0|1}) \sum_{t=\tau+1}^{T} \pi(d;d;t) \right\}$$

The system of equations with respect to $\pi(x; d; t)$ in the general case cannot be analytically solved, although its numerical solution and the subsequent choice of the optimal value of the threshold δ^* is not difficult.

Thus, sequential decision rule (7.30) based on the likelihood ratio with the threshold δ^*, found by numerical methods based on $\Phi(u(\cdot);\tau;T) \rightarrow$ max, ensures an algorithmic solution to the interests' coordination problem in a dynamic active system with change in characteristics, by choosing the best one in the class incentive system (7.29).

In practice, various cumulative sum algorithms (Nikiforov 1983, Nikiforov 2016) are widely used, in which an increment of the decision function is formed as linear (or quadratic) functions of multidimensional differences between the actual observed values and their average values before disorder. The advantage of such algorithms is their simplicity, robustness to the type of distribution of the values being observed; in addition, these algorithms become the maximum likelihood algorithms when the values being observed are distributed normally, and disorder consists in change in the average ones (or dispersions).

An example of an Enterprise planning procedure consisting of one principal and one agent, following Example 4.4, is presented in Appendix A7.4.

7.4   PLANNING OF HUMAN CAPITAL

Let's move on to the solution of the optimal control problem as applied to human capital – to the headcount of active resource pools. For this purpose, we first summarize requirements to the pools headcount control models (see also Section 6.1.1) and analyze their main features, drivers, and influencing factors.

The models should integrate and reflect:

(a) employees grouped by their qualifications and motivation, AEs traffic (the numbers of AEs joining and leaving an Enterprise), and its uncertainty;
(b) all kinds of expenses associated with each employee (including their development and relocation, including temporarily attracted AEs);
(c) a demand for the active resources caused by CA implementation – resource pools headcount considering their capabilities; unevenness and uncertainty of CA and, therefore, those of the demand;
(d) assumptions about the characteristics of processes, describing AEs traffic and the demand uncertainty (for example, about stationarity or trends).

Models should allow an effect of the whole set of active resource pools to be estimated, depending on factors (a)–(d), and to choose optimal (effect maximizing) control actions.

In practice, all factors (a)–(c) usually become known in detail a posteriori, costs (b) are also known precisely both a posteriori and a priori (on a reasonable planning horizon). However, a priori information (a) and (c) about future states and characteristics of processes, as well as assumptions (d) are always uncertain; therefore control models should be robust to these uncertain factors.

In Section 7.4, as in Chapter 6, we use the term "an active element" or "AE," as an equivalent to a person, an individual, an employee, an active resource unit, agent, or/ and principal; and plural AEs – as equivalent to people, employees, active resources.

7.4.1 SOURCES OF UNCERTAINTY AND VARIANTS OF OPTIMIZATION TASK

Human capital control is hampered by uncertainty, generated by two sources: external demand to CA output unevenness and, therefore, unevenness of a demand for active resources from the CA implementation (process (a), above) and AEs' traffic (process (c) – joining and leaving). Traditionally, uncertainty is modeled by random processes; and we similarly use stochastic models to represent the uncertainty sources (processes (a) and (c)).

It is reasonable to employ all available information to choose optimal control actions. The solution of the considered problem is complicated by the lack of objective a priori information about processes (a) and (c); instead of such information the following are available and can be used:

i. assumptions and hypotheses stated by experts (managers) about the characteristics of processes (Enterprise and external environment parameters);
ii. expert estimates and forecasts of concrete variables;
iii. statistical estimates of parameters based on observations of processes during previous time periods.

When developing solution methods, it is necessary to take into account that information of types i and ii cannot be precise, accurate, and complete, since assumptions, admissions, expert estimates, and forecasts are always subjective. Statistical estimates (information of type iii), in turn, even being strongly consistent, are based on samples of a limited length, and therefore cannot be considered "accurate" enough (these specifics are discussed in detail in Section 6.3.1). However, even in conditions of the use of subjective and inaccurate a priori information, it makes sense to develop rigorous mathematical models, in order to build forecast models and make control decisions based on the same. This can be confirmed by the following reasons.

A CA actor (an Enterprise's management) can almost always make reasonable assumptions about the future implementation of such CA, for which this actor is responsible. If this is not so, then the actor–management is not experienced enough in the activity–business and should be fired and replaced.

Such assumptions can be formulated in the form of expert estimates of the parameters or characteristics of processes, describing the Enterprise CA (business) and its context in the form of CA scenarios (see also Section 7.1) or in some other form. If the assumptions cover all the most likely scenarios of CA implementation (business evolution), except for the occurrence of true uncertainty events (force majeures), and control actions are optimized for such scenarios, then these CA (business) control actions are optimal in all cases except force majeure. The force majeure exemption and liability waiver are fundamental business practice principles and should be reasonably employed to solve Enterprise Control Problems as well.

The following three groups of assumptions about the nature of CA implementation (business evolution) and its context can be considered practically significant:

I. The Enterprise CA actor (management) believes the external conditions to be stable (the characteristics of uncertainty sources to be constant) and the possibility of significant changes to be negligible within the framework of the forecasting and planning horizon. There is a reason to assume that the characteristics of uncertainty sources can be statistically estimated, and these estimates adequately describe the processes within the forecast and planning horizon. The problem solution in this case, i.e., a stationary process of the demand for active resources from the CA implementation (business) and active resources' (AEs') traffic, is studied and obtained in Section 7.4.3 in the form of Proposition 7.5.

II. The Enterprise CA actor (management) has reasonable assumptions about future external environment evolution leading to some trends of the CA implementation conditions (business and/or labor market): the characteristics of the active resources demand and their traffic. And the CA actor is going to make responsible control decisions based on the forecast and assumptions. This optimization problem in the general case does not have an analytical solution, but it can be easily solved numerically. Certain cases of option II allow analytical solutions, one of which is researched in Section 7.4.3 in the form of Proposition 7.6.

III. The Enterprise CA actor (management) believes a certain stationarity of the CA conditions, but the probabilistic model is not considered adequate. It is supposed that the boundaries of the intervals of admissible process values can be correctly set. This case of minimal a priori information about the active resources demand and their traffic is considered in Section 7.4.4; an analytical solution for the same is obtained in the form of Proposition 7.7.

In fact, options I and II correspond to cases when the actor (management) has enough information, allowing formulation of a reasoned future evolution scenario, a certain vision of the CA future implementation; i.e. stationary (option I) and non-stationary (option II) cases are solved. Option III reflects the case, when the actor has only minimal a priori information about the conditions of CA implementation.

7.4.2   KNOWN METHODS AND MODELS

The problem under consideration belongs to the field of dynamic or multi-step *resource control problems*. Starting with the work of R. Bellman (see, for example, the review by Smith (1999)), the *dynamic programming method* (DP) is used to control an Enterprise's resources. In recent years, such has also been used to solve human resource control problems. A number of papers (i.e. Rao (1990)) show that human capital control models are analogous to the "Wagner–Whitin" inventory control model.

In the paper by Chen et al (2014), the DP method is used to schedule and distribute personnel across a variety of projects according to the criterion of minimizing project completion time, given constraint imposed on available resources. In the paper by Silva and Costa (2013), one is considering the problem of employees' appointment using DP for a variety of information technology projects, with the complexity of each project and the availability of resources of relevant qualifications taken into account. In the paper by Elshafei and Alfares (2008), the DP method is used for work scheduling for employees in a specific case, when, during each week, work days must be alternated with rest days, and additional restrictions are imposed on the sequence of the alternation. As the optimality criterion, the minimization of cost for employees' remuneration (including for appointments for the weekend) is employed. The paper by Xiea et al (2015) presents the optimal management of researchers' movements within the institutions of the Chinese Academy of Sciences based on the DP methods. The authors of the paper by Si et al (2004) propose a computationally efficient DP algorithm for distribution of heterogeneous human and physical resources of an Enterprise for transportation and logistics tasks. The paper by Nirmala and Jeeva (2010) poses the problem of optimal hiring and promotion of employees between positions of two levels; theorems on the existence of solutions are formulated; the problem is solved numerically, and the solution is illustrated by examples. In Rao (1990), various types of costs for human capital are distinguished, a human resources planning model is developed to minimize costs, the approach applied is illustrated by numerical examples. In the work by Mehlmann (1980), a model of Markov behavior of each of their statistically equivalent employees of different grades is proposed. Using the DP method, templates for optimal hiring and promotion of employees are obtained. Optimality is understood as the minimum discrepancy between the goal and the current states. The paper by Berovic and Vinter (2004) is devoted to the solution of the inventory control problem using DP methods in a deterministic formulation with impulse control, terminal constraints, and a discontinuous objective function.

However, despite the large number of works, the overwhelming majority of them either use assumptions that simplify real business, or prove the existence theorems for solutions without obtaining an analytical solution to Bellman's equations, or solutions are obtained in the form of numerical algorithms to solve the problem.

The purpose of the model to be developed is to obtain an analytical solution to the DP problem in the statements, reflecting the practically interesting conditions of an Enterprise CA control.

7.4.3 PLANNING OF THE HEADCOUNT OF THE ACTIVE RESOURCE POOL

Let us model an Enterprise as a set of active resource pools (see Chapter 6), where each pool is represented and studied as a dynamic multi-element active system (AS) with uncertainty, consisting of one farsighted principal and multiple not farsighted agents. We solve the human capital control problem as an independent optimal head-count planning of each active resource pool.

We assume that the technology of AEs joint activity (and other factors) allows the problem to be decomposed by agents and periods (which is natural to real Enterprises, see Sections 3.4 and 4.3) or that there is not any constraint on AEs' joint activity and the active elements act independently.

It is supposed, that at any period each AE can stay in only one of two states: to participate in the pool (to be an employee of the Enterprise) or to remain outside the pool (to not be an employee of the Enterprise). The events of AEs' transitions from one state to another form the active resource (Enterprise stuff) traffic which is distin-guished by uncertainty: the headcount cannot be completely driven by a managing actor (the Enterprise's management). Indeed, all acts of offers acceptance, joining, and leaving an Enterprise are the result of an AEs' active choice, which cannot be directed by the managing actor. Practically in any cases (in any industry and in any jurisdiction), the Enterprise expenses caused by firing the AEs are very consider-able; therefore this approach (firing) is used in practice extremely seldom and is not considered further.

We suppose that at the initial moment of each period t, the principal generates $u(t) \geq 0$ *offers* to AEs, staying outside the pool (we call such AEs applicants and denote a set of applicants as $U(t)$), to join the pool. It's assumed there is an unlimited number of AEs outside the pool and so offers number $u(t)$ should not be bound from above.

The applicants implement binary actions $y_\eta(t) = 1$, accept the offers, and join the pool, or $y_\eta(t) = 0$, i.e., reject and remain outside the pool. The participants of the pool ($N(t)$ – their set), also implement an action to stay in the pool ($y_\eta(t) = 1$) or to leave the pool ($y_\eta(t) = 0$). Let us denote the pool headcount at the beginning of the t-th period as $n(t)$; then:

$$n(t) = n(t-1) + u(t) - \mu(t), \qquad (7.31)$$

where $\mu(t) = \displaystyle\sum_{\eta \in N(t-1) \cup U(t)} (1 - y_\eta(t))$, in the general case, we do not impose any con-straints on the characteristics of the sequence $\mu(t)$.

The sequence $u(t)$ is the control by which the principal influences the pool; and the optimization problem is solved with respect to the sequence $u(t)$.

Model of the demand for active resources generated by a CA implementation. The demand for active resources is driven by the flow of actions of various types that must be executed to implement the CA (see Section 6.2.1). Let's denote the demand for participants of the pool during the t-th period by $d(t)$ and consider it as a random variable reflecting the CA uncertainty, possibly depending on its own entire history $d([0*(t-1)])$; in the general case, we do not also make any special assumptions about the characteristics of the random sequence $d(t)$.

Model of Enterprise CA implementation. Resource pools are created to meet the demand from the CA; therefore, the effectiveness of pool management (6.4) over a period of time $[t; T]$ can be written down in the form:

$$\Phi(t;T) = \sum_{\tau=t}^{T} \delta(\tau;t)\phi(n(\tau);d(\tau);u(\tau);v(\tau);c^*(\tau);\tau) \qquad (7.32)$$

where $\delta(\cdot)$ is the distribution of the principal's farsightedness, $\phi(\cdot)$ is the function of the principal's gain over the period τ, depending on the pool headcount $n(\tau)$, the demand $d(\tau)$, offers $u(\tau)$, all kinds of costs $c^*(\tau)$, associated with the AEs and AEs' productivity $v(\tau)$.

As noted above, the excess of headcount over demand causes unproductive costs, and the headcount shortage causes CA under-implementation or the need for urgent replenishment of the pool which causes the use of more expensive resources (we assume, that in case of headcount shortage the principal can "immediately" replenish the pool, acquiring more expensive active resources in necessary volume). Let's introduce a *penalty function* – the excess of actual human capital costs over the minimal possible ones (in case of "perfect" control) for one period:

$$R(x) = \begin{cases} c_{reg}x & \text{if } x \geq 0, \\ (c_{ext} - c_{reg})|x| & \text{if } x < 0. \end{cases} \qquad (7.33)$$

where $x = n(t) - d(t)$; and c_{reg}, c_{ext} are labor costs to sustentation of one regular AE and one "external," more expensive, AE for one time period; at that, $0 < c_{reg} < c_{ext}$,* let us believe both of these quantities to be known and constant. Let us assume that more expensive "external" resources are guaranteed to be available (they can be acquired "immediately," in any volume and for any necessary period[†]). We assume one-time costs for acquiring an "external" AE to be small compared to the current sustentation, which is often consistent with practice. Objective function (7.32) over the interval $1 \leq t \leq T$, considering (7.33), takes the form:

$$\Phi(1;T) = \Phi^*(1;T) - \sum_{t=1}^{T} \delta(t;t_0) R(n(t) + u(t) - \mu(t) - d(t)) \qquad (7.34)$$

where $\Phi^*(\cdot)$ is a part of the objective function, being independent of the control $u(t)$ and having the meaning of the maximum possible value $\Phi(\cdot)$, if $n(t) \equiv d(t)$ throughout the whole interval $1 \leq t \leq T$.

In the future, let's assume $t_0 = 0$ and $\delta(t; t_0) = \gamma^t$ (where γ is some constant $0 < \gamma < 1$).

---

* If this is not so, then the obvious strategy is to abandon staff employees and use only temporarily attracted resources in exact accordance with the changing demand/need.

† In "any volume" is understood in the sense of the ability to provide any practically possible business need; "for any necessary period" is understood in the sense that the attraction can be instantly finished when the need disappears.

We seek the optimal control $u(t)$, which provides the maximum to the objective function $\Phi(\cdot)$, which, in turn, requires

$$\sum_{t=1}^{T} \gamma^{t} R\big(n(t)+u(t)-\mu(t)-d(t)\big) \rightarrow \min_{\{u(t);\, t=1,2,...,T\}} \qquad (7.35)$$

The posed problem is the classical optimization problem of multi-step decision-making; therefore it is quite natural to apply the dynamic programming method.

For option I (stationary problem statement) we use the stochastic sequences to model the demand $d(t)$ and traffic $\mu(t)$ of active resources. The conditions of Assumption A7 (Section 7.1.1) are valid in many practically interesting cases of a mature labor market and are often used to describe AEs' behavior (Gans 2003, Lee and Longton 1959). Given established and generally accepted requirements for competencies, free legislation, experience recognized by other companies, a rapid entry of new AEs into an Enterprise CA, the employee behavior model is well described by Markov processes. Therefore, let's assume that the following assumption is valid:

Assumption A8   The elements of active resources behave statistically independently from each other.

Under the conditions of assumptions A7 and A8, the sequences $\mu(t)$ and $d(t)$ can be considered as stationary, independent of each other and being Markov ones; let us denote the probability distributions of their states by $\Pr(d(t)=f)=Q_\delta(f)$ and $\Pr(\mu(t)=m)=P_\mu(m)$. Then problem (7.35) takes the form:

$$\sum_{t=1}^{T} \gamma^{t} E_{\mu;\delta}[R(n(t)+u(t)-\mu(t)-d(t))] \rightarrow \min_{\{u(t);\, t=1,2,...,T\}}$$

Taking into account (7.31, 7.33) we write the Bellman functional equations for this problem:

$$\begin{cases} F_T(n) = \min_u E_{\mu;\delta}[R(n+u-\mu-\delta)]; \\ F_t(n) = \min_u E_{\mu}[E_{\delta}[R(n+u-\mu-\delta)]+\gamma F_{t+1}(n+u-\mu)]. \end{cases} \qquad (7.36)$$

The solution of equations (7.36) is considered below in this section and in Appendix A7.5.

In the case of option II (considerable known trends in the characteristics of the demand and AEs traffic) let us use non-stationary models of $\mu(t)$ and $d(t)$ sequences with probabilistic uncertainty – the time-dependent distributions $Q_\delta(t)$ and $P_\mu(t)$. In this case, the Bellman functional equations do not have an analytical solution, but are easily solved numerically. Below (Proposition 7.6) we study a particular case when the analytical solution of the Bellman equations for version II can be found.

In the case of option III (minimum a priori knowledge about demand and AEs traffic) we use the interval model of uncertainty; then the functional equations take the form:

$$\begin{cases} F_T(n) = \min_{u} \max_{\mu \in [\tilde{\mu}_-; \tilde{\mu}_+]; \delta \in [\tilde{\delta}_-; \tilde{\delta}_+]} [R(n+u-\mu-\delta)]; \\ F_t(n) = \min_{u} \max_{\mu \in [\tilde{\mu}_-; \tilde{\mu}_+]; \delta \in [\tilde{\delta}_-; \tilde{\delta}_+]} [R(n+u-\mu-\delta) + \gamma F_{t+1}(n+u-\mu)]. \end{cases} \quad (7.37)$$

where $[\mu^-; \mu^-_+]$ and $[\delta^-; \delta^-_+]$ are sets of possible values of the sequences $\mu(t)$ and $d(t)$, defined by their borders. In this case, any assumptions about the characteristics of the sequences $\mu(t)$ and $d(t)$ are not necessary. The solution of equation (7.37) is presented in Appendix A7.6.

Let's consider version I of the human capital control problem when the sequences $d(t)$ and $\mu(t)$ and consequently $n(t)$ are stationary.

Problem (7.36) is a special case of a controlled Markov chain, which has been studied in sufficient detail in the literature on stochastic estimation and control; see, for example, Kumar and Varaiya (1986). In this work, the problem of estimate of the parameters of a Markov chain is considered in detail, the existence and uniqueness of optimal control over the same are proved, and it is shown that control actions also form a Markov chain. It is proved that the maximum likelihood estimates of the parameters of a controlled Markov chain are strongly consistent. In addition, the control built on the basis of such estimates is "self-optimizing," that is, converging, in Cesaro's sense, to the optimal control with respect to the minimum cost criterion (see Theorem 6.5, p. 272, Kumar and Varaiya (1986)). Empirical distributions, estimated based on the samples of $\mu(t)$ and $d(t)$, are the best estimates of the distributions P_μ and Q_f, i.e., those are the maximum likelihood estimates. Therefore, we use the corresponding empirical distributions as P_μ and Q_f.

The optimal control $u(t)$ is obtained in Appendix A7.5 as the solution of functional equations (7.36) under conditions (7.31)–(7.35) in the form $u(n) = \max\{0; x_{g\_opt} - n\}$, where the value x_{g_opt} is obtained in the process of the dynamic programming problem (7.36) solving.

In fact, the control is narrowed down to $u(t+1) = \max\{0; x_{g\_opt} - n(t)\}$, at the same time the value of the level x_{g_opt} depends on the convolution of probability distributions P_μ and Q_f and not on each of the distributions separately, and is obtained from rule (A7.20) defined in Appendix A7.5. Let us note that level x_{g_opt} obviously exceeds average headcount $x_{g\_opt} > E[n(t)]$. In addition, the obtained optimal control strategy does not depend on the discount coefficient γ; therefore, by repeating the calculations with the appropriate notations, it is easy to show that the solution does not depend on the principal's farsightedness. The result obtained allows one to formulate

Proposition 7.5. The optimal control of the headcount of an active resource pool, with respect to criterion (7.35), is the strategy* $u(t+1) = \max\{0; x_{g\_opt} - n(t)\}$ (being invariant to the distribution of the principal's farsightedness), where the value of the

---

* Actually, optimal is a control that aims to maintain a constant level of headcount.

constant parameter x_{g_opt} is obtained in the course of the solution of a dynamic programming problem (from rule (A7.20)) in the case when:

- sources of CA uncertainty $d(\cdot)$ and active resources' behavior $\mu(\cdot)$ allow a probabilistic description,
- their characteristics are known and constant in time.

Wherein $\Phi(1; T)=\Phi^*(1; T) - (1 - \gamma^{T+1})(1 - \gamma)^{-1}E_{\mu;d}[R(x_{g\_opt} - \mu - d)]$. ●

While obtaining the solution $u(t+1)=\max\{0; x_{g\_opt} - n(t)\}$ regarding the characteristics of the sequences $\mu(\cdot)$ and $d(\cdot)$, one made no assumptions, except for stationarity, i.e., the invariance of the probability distributions P_μ and Q_f by time. This feature of the solution has a significant practical importance, i.e., such that it ensures the stability of the solution with respect to the form of the distributions P_μ and Q_f, which is especially important in conditions of inaccurate knowledge of the characteristics of these probability distributions.

The solution formulated in Proposition 7.5, with appropriate adjustments, is also suitable for use in certain non-stationary cases. In particular, if there is a demand model in the form of:

$$d(t) = d_0(t) + \beta(t), \qquad\qquad (7.38)$$

where $d_0(t)$ is the known non-decreasing function of t and $\beta(t)$ is a random sequence of independent identically distributed variables, just as in variant I, one obtains the validity of

Proposition 7.6. The optimal control of the headcount of an active resource pool with respect to criterion (7.35), is the strategy

$$u(t+1) = \max\left\{0; x_{g\_opt} + d_0(t) - u(t)\right\},$$

(being invariant to the distribution of the principal's farsightedness), where the value of the parameter x_{g_opt} is obtained in the course of the solution of a dynamic programming problem (from rule (A7.20)) in the case when:

- the representation $d(t)=d_0(t)+\beta(t)$ is satisfied, where $d_0(t)$ is a known non-decreasing function of t, $\beta(t)$ is a random sequence,
- sources of CA uncertainty $\beta(\cdot)$ and such of active resources' behavior $\mu(\cdot)$ allow a probabilistic description,
- their characteristics are known and constant in time.

At the same time $\Phi(1; T)=\Phi^*(1; T) - (1 - \gamma^{T+1})(1 - \gamma)^{-1}E_{\mu;\beta}[R(x_{g\_opt} - \mu - \beta)]$. ●

The proof of Proposition 7.6 coincides with the proof of Proposition 7.5 with the corresponding adjustment related to the need to take into account the known additive component of the demand process $d_0(t)$.

Let us now consider option III of the setting, when in problem (7.35) only the boundary values of the intervals of possible values, reflecting the uncertainty of the activity $d(t)$ and AE traffic $\mu(t)$, are known. No assumptions are made regarding other characteristics of the processes.

Functional equations (7.37) corresponding to this case are solved in Appendix A7.6, and the best guaranteed strategy has the form $u_{opt}(n) = \max\{0, (x_{int} - n)\}$.

This strategy is similar to the optimal strategy of the dynamic probabilistic uncertainty model (option I), which allows us to formulate

Proposition 7.7. The best guaranteed (invariant to the distribution of the principal's farsightedness) strategy for control over the headcount of an active resource pool with respect to criterion (7.35), is:

$$u(t+1) = \max\{0; x_{int} - n(t)\}$$

where x_{int} is obtained in the course of the solution of an interval dynamic programming problem (rule (A7.26)) in the case of minimal a priori information about the conditions of CA implementation in the form of intervals of possible values $d(\cdot)$ and $\mu(\cdot)$. •

7.4.4   PLANNING CHARACTERISTICS OF ACTIVE RESOURCE LIFECYCLES

Let's now study problem (6.1–6.5) to consider the possibility to control the active resource headcount, by influencing the parameters of their lifecycles.

We consider an active resource pool model to be an active system (Section 7.4.3) in the stationary mode, when an AE's flow, leaving the pool is compensated by a flow of applicants joining the pool. We assume the AEs to behave statistically identically and independently of each other; we also use such productivity of an AE and the AE's associated costs per period, which are averaged by the entire time-in-the-pool. Then effect (6.4) generated by all AEs in the pool over the interval $[1; T]$ takes the form:

$$\Phi(1;T) = Tn^* \left\{ h - c_{st} - \left(c_{ad} + c_{att} \right) \lambda\left(c_{st} \right) - c_{off} \lambda\left(c_{st} \right) / \pi\left(c_{st} \right) \right\},$$

where

c_{st} is the average compensation package (salary, bonuses, and other financial benefits) and other operational costs associated with AE per one period of time,

c_{off} is the average costs of the search and preparation on offer,

c_{ad} is the average costs for admission and adaptation in the pool,

c_{att} is the average principal's expenses caused by unexpected leaving of one AE,

h is the average principal's income from the activity of one AE in the pool per one period,

$\lambda(c_{st})$ is the average share of AEs leaving the pool per one period $(y_\eta(t)=0)$,

$\pi(c_{st})$ is the average share of applicants joining the pool $(y_\eta(t)=1)$

n^* is the constant average headcount equal to the average demand $(n^* = d^*)$.

The functions $\lambda(c_{st})$ and $\pi(c_{st})$ reflect the dependence of AEs' preferences on the operational costs of various types, first of all, costs for wages, social benefits, training,

etc.; the preferences, in turn, drive the average percentages of AEs leaving and joining the pool.

The principal's averaged income h depends on the technology; technology control
is described in Chapter 5, so we take this parameter as a constant. The averaged
costs c_{off} of the search, offer preparation, c_{ad} of admittance and adaptation in the
pool, c_{att} of leaving the pool are transactional ones and are also accepted as constant.
The average headcount is determined by the average demand, being not subject to
control and being also considered constant. Then the problem $\Phi(1;T) = Tn^*\{h - c_{st} -
(c_{ad} + c_{att})\lambda(c_{st}) - c_{off}\lambda(c_{st})/\pi(c_{st})\} \to$ max reduces to the optimization problem:

$$C(c_{st}) = \{c_{st} + (c_{ad} + c_{att})\lambda(c_{st}) + c_{off}\lambda(c_{st})/\pi(c_{st})\} \to \min_{c_{st} > 0}, \qquad (7.39)$$

where $C(c_{st})$ is the average principal's expenses during one period normalized to one
AE in the pool.

The dependences of the average percentages $\lambda(c_{st})$ and $\pi(c_{st})$ of AEs leaving and
joining the pool on the costs c_{st} (see also assumption A4) should be introduced to
solve the optimal control problem (7.39). These dependencies are not measurable or
associated with any objective law; therefore, they can only be formalized as expert
assumptions and estimations of the management. However, the constructive expert
considerations allow one to formulate a number of characteristics of the functions
$\lambda(\cdot)$ and $\pi(\cdot)$:

a. for $c \gg c_{st0}$; $\lambda(c) \approx 0$ and $\pi(c) \approx 1$, where c_{st0} is the current level of costs, for
which the values $\lambda(c_{st0}) = \lambda_0$ and $\pi(c_{st0}) = \pi_0$ are known;
b. for $c \ll c_{st0}$; $\lambda(c) \approx 1$ and $\pi(c) \approx 0$;
c. $\lambda(\cdot)$ and $\pi(\cdot)$ do not have break points, are monotonic, $\lambda(\cdot)$ decreases, and $\pi(\cdot)$
increases with respect to c_{st}.
d. also the management, based on experience, can estimate the range of values
$c_{st0} - \Delta c_1 \leq c_{st} \leq c_{st0} + \Delta c_2$, going beyond which does not make sense for business reasons.

Conditions a–d are satisfied, for example, by a family of the logistic functions
$(1 + \exp(-z))^{-1}$; let's use it for approximation of $\lambda(\cdot)$ and $\pi(\cdot)$:

$$\lambda(c;x_1;x_2) = \frac{\lambda_0}{\lambda_0 + (1 - \lambda_0)\exp(x_1(c - c_{st0}))} \quad \text{and} \quad \pi(c;x_1;x_2)$$

$$= \frac{\pi_0}{\pi_0 + (1 - \pi_0)\exp(x_2(c_{st0} - c))},$$

where x_1 and x_2 are positive parameters, to be screened.

To screen the values of the parameters x_1 and x_2 let's expertly set the values $\lambda(c_{st0} -
\Delta c_1) = \lambda_1$ and $\pi(c_{st0} - \Delta c_1) = \pi_1$; then we obtain the parameters as the solutions to the
equations $\lambda(c_{st0} - \Delta c_1; x_1; x_2) = \lambda_1$ and $\pi(c_{st0} - \Delta c_1; x_1; x_2) = \pi_1$ with respect to x_1 and x_2.

Now optimization problem (7.39) can be written down in the form:

$$c+\left(c_{ad}+c_{att}\right)\frac{1}{1+\left(\lambda_0^{-1}-1\right)\exp\left(x_1\left(c-c_{st0}\right)\right)}+c_{off}\frac{1+\left(\pi_0^{-1}-1\right)\exp\left(x_2\left(c_{st0}-c\right)\right)}{1+\left(\lambda_0^{-1}-1\right)\exp\left(x_1\left(c-c_{st0}\right)\right)}\underset{c>0}{\rightarrow\min}$$

The obtained problem is easily solved with respect to c. Its advantage, which is important for practice, is the possibility to study the solution with respect to the parameters x_1 and x_2, and consequently, with respect to the expertly defined values $\lambda(\cdot)$ and $\pi(\cdot)$ for various c_{st}, including in a graphic way. An example of the practical use of this technique is given in Section 8.4.3.

CONCLUSION

Mathematical models and optimal planning methods are developed in Chapter 7. These models and methods ensure the direct search for optimal control actions, i.e., "Step 1" of the Enterprise Control Optimization Scheme (Section 3.4.3, Figure 3.9):

- First, planning algorithmic models are developed (Section 7.1), possessing maximum generality and therefore being applicable to any Enterprise. However, these models do not provide analytical results; accordingly, they do not support planning optimization.
- Second, optimization models are developed for several practically important cases of Enterprise operations, analytical results are obtained, and statements about the optimality of the planning methods are proved (Sections 7.2–7.4).

Planning models (introduced in Section 7.1) are algorithmic, i.e., represented by the algorithm structure (Figures 7.2–7.3) and a set of numerical models (expressions of Sections 7.1.2–7.1.3), which make up the computational basis of the algorithm. The models demonstrate the compatible planning procedure in a hierarchical interrelated set of relatively autonomous structural elements of an Enterprise's CA (which correspond to business units in terms of business practice). In Section 7.1.4, the optimal planning process for a networked technology development/learning process is investigated; Proposition 7.1 states the existence of a certain resource volume that ensures the achievement of the required level of maturity/learning.

The transition from the technology design to its productive use is practically important, and Section 7.2 is devoted to CA planning when the planning horizon includes such a transition. Firstly, Propositions 7.2 and 7.3 about the existence of an optimal sequential transition strategy among all possible ones are proved, and the characteristics of this strategy are obtained in an analytical form when the Enterprise and characteristics of the external environment are known (Section 5.3.1). Secondly, the sequential decision criterion (7.26) is synthesized (Proposition 7.4) when the Enterprise and external environment characteristics are unknown. A numerical algorithm to choose criterion parameters is developed (Appendix A7.1) that ensures the best solutions, given a certain Enterprise and its external environment characteristics. Thirdly, a simulation and analytical study of the characteristics of this algorithm are performed (Appendix A7.2). All results are extended to the case of "batch production."

Variability is a universal trait of any complex system, as well as of an Enterprise and its external environment, and is possibly one of its main features. Within the framework of the Enterprise Control Problem, such variability leads to CA technology inadequacy for the external environment and the need to modernize or develop new technology. In this regard, the problem of Enterprise CA planning in the face of the changing characteristics of CA implementation is very relevant. This problem is described in Section 7.3, which contains models and methods for coordinating CA actors' interests in a dynamic system with changing characteristics, and a set of dynamic problems to coordinate actors' interests is clustered and studied. An optimal incentive system in a chosen class is built, employing the sequential likelihood decision rule, and an algorithm for choosing the decision rule parameters is proposed.

The invariableness of the external conditions and the CA implementation stationarity throughout the entire planning interval are other important cases of the Enterprise Control Problem. These circumstances lead to the use of sound technology, and in such a case the problem comes down to resource optimization, primarily human capital. The corresponding models and methods are researched in Section 7.4.

Dynamic programming problems are stated and analytically solved for cases where CA implementation and active resource behavior characteristics are known and constant in time or follow known trends, and the uncertainty can be adequately described by probabilistic or interval models (Propositions 7.5–7.7).

A model is also developed (Section 7.4.4) to control a pool of active resources by adjusting the parameters of their lifecycle.

It is important to note from a practical point of view that the models and methods considered are based on management accounting concepts, without simplifying assumptions, and integrate all types of human capital costs traditionally considered. At the same time, at the formal level, the models and methods explore all the main aspects of CA implementation, primarily uncertainty in the demand for active resources and their traffic.

APPENDIXES

APPENDIX A7.1 OPTIMAL CHOICE OF THE DECISION-MAKING PROCEDURE PARAMETERS (7.26)

We use the optimization algorithm, ensuring the choice of the parameters a and l_{thres} for procedure (7.26), consisting of the following steps:

1. We define a technology design scenario: firstly, we set the duration T of a time interval (from 0 to T, at the beginning of which the maturity/learning level is $L_0 = 0$); secondly, we choose the expected characteristics of the environment and technology design process, i.e., the probability distribution $\{p_k\}$ and its dimension K.

2. We calculate the effect $\Phi(\{p_k\}, T, a, l_{\text{thres}})$ as a function of the parameters of the criteria a and l_{thres}, probability distribution $\{p_k\}$, its dimension K, and duration T.

3. After obtaining the function $\Phi(\{p_k\}, T, a, l_{\text{thres}})$ we choose the optimal values of a and l_{thres}, the guaranteed result method

$$\min_{\{p_k\}} \{\Phi(\{p_k\}, T, a, l_{\text{thres}})\} \rightarrow \max_{a>0;\, l_{\text{thres}}>0}$$

(or any other known method to eliminate uncertainty for similar optimization problems can be used).

Let's calculate the expected effect on some time interval between 0 and T (with the initial learning level $L_0=0$) as a function of the constants a and l_{thres} and also of the assumed characteristics of the environment – the distribution $\{p_k\}$ and its dimension K.

Hereinafter, a sequence of the numbers $\{k_1, k_2, \ldots, k_K\}$ of new states of the environment in the order of their observation during technology design is called a trajectory while the periods when the states k_i occur are denoted by θ_i. As a trajectory evolves, the learning level varies from 0 to 1, taking the values $L_{\theta_i} = \sum_{j=1}^{i} p_{k_i}$ at the periods θ_i. The probability of each trajectory $\{k_i\}$ equals $P(\{k_i\}) = \prod_{i=1}^{K} \left[p_{k_i} (1 - L_{\theta_i - 1})^{-1} \right]$.

First, let's calculate the value of the effect $\Phi(\{k_i\}, T, a, l_{\text{thres}})$ for each trajectory and then average the effects over the trajectories

$$\Phi(\{p_k\}, T, a, l_{\text{thres}}) = \sum_{\{k_i\}} V(\{k_i\}, T, a, l_{\text{thres}}) P(\{k_i\})$$

(A7.1)

$$= \sum_{\{k_i\}} V(\{k_i\}, T, a, l_{\text{thres}}) \prod_{i=1}^{K} \left[p_{k_i} (1 - L_{\theta_i - 1})^{-1} \right]$$

For calculating the effect $V(\{k_i\}, T, a, l_{\text{thres}})$, some trajectory $\{k_i\}$ is assumed to be fixed. Hence, for the sake of simplicity let's denote $k_i=i$, and accordingly $p_i = p_{k_i}$ and $L_i = L_{\theta_i}$.

Introduce a two-dimensional discrete random process $(k(t); l(t))$, where

• $k(t)$ denotes the number of all unrealized trajectory states after period t; obviously, $k(0)=K-1$, and at the subsequent periods θ_i the function $k(t)$ gradually decreases by 1 down to 0;

• $l(t)$ denotes the values of the likelihood function ($l(0)=0$, and at the subsequent times $l(t)$ varies between 0 and l_{thres} inclusive, following the rule (7.26).

If at some period t the second component of the process $(k(t), l(t))$ reaches the value $l(t)=l_{\text{thres}}$, then the effect for this trajectory takes the value $v(T - t) - c_p k(t) - c_d t$. Therefore, the expected effect for the trajectory is

$$\Phi\left(\{k_i\},T,a,l_{\text{thres}}\right)=\sum_{t;k}\left(v\left(T-t\right)-c_d t-c_p k\right)\Pr\left(k;l_{\text{thres}};t\,\big|\{k_i\}\right)=$$

$$=vT-\left(c_d+v\right)\left\{\sum_{t;k}t\Pr\left(k;l_{\text{thres}};t\,\big|\{k_i\}\right)+\frac{c_p}{c_d+v}\sum_{t;k}k\Pr\left(k;l_{\text{thres}};t\,\big|\{k_i\}\right)\right\}.$$

Consider this expression in detail.

The first term vT does not depend on the characteristics of the environment, either on the trajectory or the parameters of the criterion; hence, it is omitted for the sake of simplicity.

The second term describes the learning cost: the constant $(v+c_d)$ is multiplied by the sum of the expected time of reaching the required learning level (the first sum) and the expected number of unrealized states of the environment (the second sum) with the factor $\mu=c_p\,(v+c_d)^{-1}$.

Thus, the optimal effect can be calculated by minimizing the cost

$$C\left(\{k_i\},T,a,l_{\text{thres}}\right)=\sum_{t;k}t\Pr\left(k;l_{\text{thres}};t\,\big|\{k_i\}\right)+\mu\sum_{t;k}k\Pr\left(k;l_{\text{thres}};t\,\big|\{k_i\}\right)\qquad\text{(A7.2)}$$

In view of (A7.2), effect (A7.1) takes the form

$$\Phi\left(T,a,l_{\text{nop}}\right)=vT-\left(c_d+v\right)\sum_{\{k_i\}}C\left(\{k_i\},T,a,l_{\text{nop}}\right)P\left(\{k_i\}\right)=$$

$$=vT-\left(c_d+v\right)\sum_{\{k_i\}}C\left(\{k_i\},T,a,l_{\text{thres}}\right)\prod_{i=1}^{K}\left[p_{k_i}\left(1-L_{\theta_i-1}\right)^{-1}\right]$$

This means that the effect optimization problem $\Phi(T,a,l_{\text{thres}})\to\max$ is equivalent to the expected cost minimization problem $C(T,a,l_{\text{thres}})\to\min$, where

$$C\left(T,a,l_{\text{thres}}\right)=\sum_{\{k_i\}}C\left(\{k_i\},T,a,l_{\text{thres}}\right)\prod_{i=1}^{K}\left[p_{k_i}\left(1-L_{\theta_i-1}\right)^{-1}\right]=$$

$$=\sum_{\{k_i\}}\left(\sum_{t;k}(t+\mu\,k)\Pr\left(k;l_{\text{thres}};t\,|\,\{k_i\}\right)\right)\prod_{i=1}^{K}\left[p_{k_i}\left(1-L_{\theta_i-1}\right)^{-1}\right]$$

For solving this problem, we have to find the probability distribution $\Pr(k(t);l_{\text{thres}};t)$. Also note that the expected cost can be written as

$$C\left(T;a;l_{\text{thres}}\right)=\sum_{\{k_i\}}C\left(\{k_i\};T;a;l_{\text{thres}}\right)P\left(\{k_i\}\right)$$

$$=\sum_{\{k_i\}}\left[\sum_{t;k}(t+\mu\,k)\Pr\left(k;l_{\text{thres}};t\,|\,\{k_i\}\right)\right]P\left(\{k_i\}\right)=$$

$$= \sum_{\{k_i\}} \sum_{t;\, k} t \, \Pr\left(k; l_{\text{thres}}; t \mid \{k_i\}\right) P\left(\{k_i\}\right) + \mu \sum_{\{k_i\}} \sum_{t;\, k} k \, \Pr\left(k; l_{\text{thres}}; t \mid \{k_i\}\right) P\left(\{k_i\}\right).$$

Consequently

$$C\left(T; a; l_{\text{thres}}\right) = \bar{t}\left(K; \{p_k\}; a; l_{\text{thres}}\right) + \mu \bar{k}\left(K; \{p_k\}; a; l_{\text{thres}}\right) \qquad \text{(A7.3)}$$

where $\bar{t}$ $(K;\ \{p_k\};\ a;\ l_{\text{thres}})$ gives the expected time of reaching the level l_{thres} by the process $l(t)$; $\bar{k}$ $(K;\ \{p_k\};\ a;\ l_{\text{thres}})$ is the expected number of unrealized states of the environment by the time when the process $l(t)$ reaches the level l_{thres}; finally, the known parameter $\mu = c_p\, (v + c_d)^{-1}$ characterizes the general impact of the payoff v and costs c_p and c_d.

Formula (A7.3) can be used for the analytical study of the expected cost dynamics under different values of the parameters. Obviously, the function $\bar{t}(\cdot)$ is monotonically increasing in a and l_{thres} while the function $\bar{k}(\cdot)$ is monotonically decreasing in a and l_{thres} for any probability distributions of the states of the environment. For $l_{\text{thres}} = 0$ (obviously, $a \leq l_{\text{thres}}$), the criterion is satisfied immediately at time 1; the functions $\bar{t}(\cdot)$ and $\bar{k}(\cdot)$ equal to 1 and $K - 1$, respectively, and the expected cost becomes $C(T, 0, 0) = 1 + \mu\, (K - 1)$.

Conversely, for "very large" values of l_{thres}, the criterion cannot be satisfied on the entire interval to T, the functions $\bar{t}(\cdot)$ and $\bar{k}(\cdot)$ equal to T and 0, respectively, and the expected cost becomes $C(T, a, \infty) = T$ (for any a).

Hence, the expected cost $C(T, a, l_{\text{thres}})$ has an optimum that depends on K, $\{p_i\}$, μ, a, and l_{thres} (in a special case, the optimum corresponds to one of the boundary values, $1 + \mu\, (K - 1)$ or T).

Let's return to obtaining the probabilities $\Pr(k;\ l_{\text{thres}};\ t \mid \{k_i\})$ for a fixed trajectory $\{k_i\}$.

By definition, the process $(k(t),\ l(t))$ evolves in accordance with the following rules.

- At the initial time $t = 1$, the process has the deterministic value $(k(0);\ l(0)) = (K - 1;\ 0)$.
- At each time $t > 0$ when a known state of the environment is realized again, $(k(t);\ l(t)) = (k(t - 1);\ l(t - 1) + 1)$. If also $l(t - 1) \geq l_{\text{thres}}$, then $(k(t);\ l(t)) = (k(t - 1);\ l_{\text{thres}})$. The probability of this event is $L_{k(t)}$.
- At each time $t > 0$ when an unknown state of the environment is realized, $(k(t);\ l(t)) = (k(t - 1) + 1;\ \max\{0;\ l(t - 1) - a\})$. If also $l(t - 1) \geq l_{\text{thres}}$, then $(k(t);\ l(t)) = (k(t - 1) + 1;\ l_{\text{thres}})$. The probability of this event is $1 - L_{k(t)}$.

For $0 \le k < K$ and $0 < l < l_{\text{thres}}$, the evolution of the probability function $P(k; l; t)$ of the process $(k(t), l(t))$ with the discrete time $t > 0$ can be therefore described by the system of difference equations:

$$P(k;l;t) = L_k P(k;l-1;t-1) + (1-L_{k+1}) P(k+1;l+a;t-1);$$

$$P(K-1;0;0) = 1 \text{ and } P(k;l;0) = 0 \quad \forall k < K-1 \text{ or } \forall l > 0$$

$$P(k;l_{\text{thres}};t) = L_k \left(P(k;l_{\text{thres}}-1;t-1) + P(k;l_{\text{thres}};t-1) \right)$$

$$\hspace{4cm} + (1-L_{k+1}) P(k+1;l_{\text{thres}};t-1); \hspace{2cm} \text{(A7.4)}$$

$$P(k;0;t) = \sum_{l=1}^{a} (1-L_{k+1}) P(k+1;l;t-1);$$

$$P(k;l;t) \equiv 0 \quad \text{if } l_{\text{thres}} < l \quad \text{or} \quad l < 0 \quad \forall k, \forall t.$$

Using the system of difference equations (A7.4), we can iteratively calculate the probabilities of the process $(k(t); l(t))$ states (see Appendix A7.2). In turn, the probabilities of the times of reaching the threshold level l_{thres} and the number of the unrealized trajectory states can be obtained as $\Pr(k(t); l_{\text{thres}}; t) = L_k P(k; l_{\text{thres}} - 1; t - 1)$. This gives the expected cost, and hence the cost $C(T, a, l_{\text{thres}})$ can be optimized numerically by choosing the optimal values of the parameters a and l_{thres} so that $C(T, a, l_{\text{thres}}) \to \min$ for the expected characteristics of the environment – the probability distribution $\{p_k\}$ and its dimension K and $\min_{\{p_k\}} \{ \Phi(\{p_k\}, T, a, l_{\text{thres}}) \} \to \max_{a>0; l_{\text{thres}}>0}$.

Let's note that for an excessive dimensionality of the problem (K and T), obtaining the function $\Phi(\{p_k\}, T, a, l_{\text{thres}})$ based on equations (A7.1 – A7.4) can be replaced by the Monte Carlo simulation modeling method.

APPENDIX A7.2 SIMULATION-BASED STUDY OF THE DECISION-MAKING PROCEDURE (7.26)

The characteristics of the decision-making procedure (7.26) are studied by simulation of the difference equations (A7.4) numerical solution, the iterative calculation of the probability function $\Pr(k(t); l_{\text{thres}}; t)$ and the expected cost $C(T, a, l_{\text{thres}})$. The optimal values of the parameters a and l_{thres} are chosen by the exhaustive search with a given step depending on the expected characteristics of the environment and technology – the distribution $\{p_k\}$ and its dimension K.

Different scenarios are considered as follows: the uniformly distributed probabilities $\{p_k\}$ of the environment states of the dimension $K=5$, ..., 80 varied with Step 5 and the parameter $\mu = 3$, ..., 30 varied with step 3.

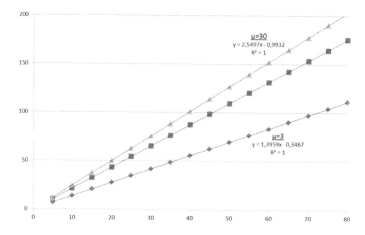

FIGURE A7.1   The dependence of $C_{opt}(K; \mu)$ on dimensionality K under different fixed μ.

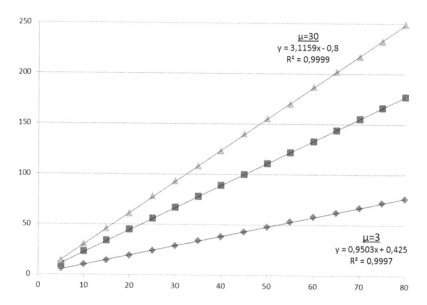

FIGURE A7.2   The dependence of $l_{opt}(K; \mu)$ on dimensionality K under different fixed μ.

Figure A7.1 presents the plot of optimized costs $C_{opt}(K, \mu) = \min\limits_{a>0;\, l_{thres}>0} \{C(K, \mu, a,$

$l_{thres})\}$ and Figure A7.2 demonstrates the plot of optimal threshold $l_{opt}(K; \mu)$ obtained by the simulations.

The simulation results led to the following conclusions.

Firstly, for all the values K and μ considered, the least expected cost is achieved for $a=0$. This result is interpreted below.

Secondly, the following functions were constructed in tabular form:

- the minimum in l_{thres} expected cost $C_{opt}(K; \mu)$ for different K and μ, $a=0$;
- the optimal value $l_{opt}(K; \mu)$ of parameter l_{thres} for different K and μ under which the minimum cost $C_{opt}(K; \mu)$ is achieved.

In accordance with Figures A7.1 and A7.2, for any fixed μ both functions $C_{opt}(K; \mu)$ and $l_{opt}(K; \mu)$ can be considered linear in K with a high accuracy for engineering applications ($R^2 \geq 0.99$). Their linear approximations have the form

$$C_{opt}(K;\mu) = K \cdot (0,5 \cdot \ln(\mu) + 0,85) - 0,33 \cdot \ln(\mu) + 0,13;$$
$$l_{opt}(K;\mu) = K \cdot (0,95 \cdot \ln(\mu) - 0,12) - 0,05 \cdot \mu + 0,56. \tag{A7.5}$$

Expressions (A7.5) can be used to perform preliminary estimations and also to choose the initial values of the parameter l_{thres} in simulations.

Approximations (A7.5) well match the results of numerical experiments and, at the same time, have a high accuracy (see the values R^2 for the graphs in Figures A7.1 and A7.2). Such a high accuracy of the linear approximations of experimental data should be thoroughly analyzed for explaining trends (A7.5). Let's do this.

For the optimal parameter value $a=0$, the likelihood function $l(t)$ of criterion (7.26) takes the form:

$$l(0) = 0$$

$$l(t+1) = \begin{cases} l(t); \text{ if new environment state is observed;} \\ l(t) + 1; \text{ if known environment state is observed.} \end{cases} \tag{A7.6}$$

Consequently, at each time (in particular, when the criterion is satisfied – the likelihood function $l(t)$ reaches the threshold l_{thres}) we have the equality $l(t) = t - (K - k(t))$, where t is the total number of observations and $(K - k(t))$ is the number of observations with newly realized states of the environment never occurring before. As a result,

$$t = l(t) + K - k(t). \tag{A7.7}$$

The expected value of $(K - k(t))$ is the learning level multiplied by K, i.e., K $(1 - (1 - 1/K)^t)$. On the other hand, the expected value of $k(t)$ (the number of all unrealized states) is $E[k(t)] = K(1 - 1/K)^t$. Hence, it follows that the expected time $\bar{t}$ $(K; \{p_k\}; a; l_{thres})$ of reaching the level l_{thres} by the process $l(t)$ and the expected number $\bar{k}$ $(K; \{p_k\}; a; l_{thres})$ of the unrealized states of the environment by this time satisfy the equation

$$\bar{k}(K;l_{thres}) = K(1 - 1/K)^{\bar{t}(K;l_{thres})}. \tag{A7.8}$$

Hereinafter, $\bar{t}(K; l) = \bar{t}(K; \{p_k\}; a; l)$ and $\bar{k}(K; l) = \bar{k}(K; \{p_k\}; a; l)$ for the case $a=0$.

Since $\bar{t}(K; l)$ monotonically increases and $\bar{k}(K; l)$ monotonically decreases in l, the expected cost (A7.3) are minimized by choosing a value l_{thres} such that

$$\frac{\partial}{\partial l}C(T; a; l) = \frac{\partial}{\partial l}\bar{t}(K; l) + \mu\frac{\partial}{\partial l}\bar{k}(K; l) = 0. \tag{A7.9}$$

Substituting (A7.8) into (A7.9) gives the equation (A7.10). From this equation, find the expected time $\bar{t}(K; l_{opt})$ corresponding to the optimal expected cost and then, using $\bar{t}(K; l_{opt})$, calculate the optimal threshold l_{opt}.

$$\left(1+\mu\ln\left(1-1/K\right)K\left(1-1/K\right)^{\bar{t}(K;l_{opt})}\right)\frac{\partial}{\partial l}\bar{t}(K; l) = 0. \tag{A7.10}$$

The derivative $\frac{\partial}{\partial l}\bar{t}(K; l)$ is positive for any l because the expected time is monotonically increasing in l. Therefore, the desired value $\bar{t}(K; l_{opt})$ can be obtained from

$$1+\mu\ln\left(1-1/K\right)K\left(1-1/K\right)^{\bar{t}(K;l_{opt})} = 0.$$

Solve this equation in $\bar{t}(\cdot)$, taking into account $ln(1-1/K) \approx -1/K$. Then the value $\bar{t}(K; l_{opt})$ corresponding to the optimal expected cost is

$$\bar{t}\left(K; l_{opt}\right) \approx K\ln(\mu). \tag{A7.11}$$

Using (A7.7) and (A7.8), we find the approximate relation of $\bar{t}(K; l)$, $\bar{k}(K; l)$ and l_{opt}. Applying the expectation operator to (A7.7) we get: $E[t] = E[l(t)] + K - E[k(t)]$. In view of (A7.8), we can write $E[t] = E[l(t)] + K - K\left(1-1/K\right)^{E[t]}$.

Since $E\left[l\left(\bar{t}(K; l)\right)\right] = l$, then $\bar{t}(K; l) \approx l + K - K\left(1-1/K\right)^{\bar{t}(K;l)}$, or, in an equivalent form:

$$l \approx \bar{t}\left(K; l\right) - K + K\left(1-1/K\right)^{\bar{t}(K;l)}. \tag{A7.12}$$

Finally, we substitute (A7.11) into (A7.12) to get

$$l_{opt} \approx \bar{t}\left(K; l\right) - K + K\left(1-1/K\right)^{\bar{t}(K;l)} = K\ln(\mu) - K + K\left(1-1/K\right)^{K\ln(\mu)}$$

$$= K\ln(\mu) - K + Ke^{K\ln(1-1/K)\ln(\mu)} \approx K\ln(\mu) - K + Ke^{-\ln(\mu)}$$

$$= K\ln(\mu) - K + K/\mu$$

Finally, the approximate value of the optimal threshold is

$$l_{opt} \approx K\ln(\mu) - K + K/\mu. \tag{A7.13}$$

Due to the linear relation of $\bar{t}(K; l)$, $\bar{k}(K; l)$ and l_{thres} (see expression (A7.7)), the optimal expected cost has a similar trend:

$$C\left(T;\ a=0;\ l_{opt}\right) \sim K\ln(\mu) + K. \tag{A7.14}$$

Thus, the analytic approximations of the optimal threshold (A7.13) and expected cost (A7.14) well express the main trends of the simulation experiments of (A7.5).

APPENDIX A7.3 OPTIMISATION IN "BATCH PRODUCTION" CASE (7.27)

The values of the effect $\Phi(\cdot)$ in a "batch production" case are not analytically expressed through the parameters of the criteria a and l_{thres}; therefore, let's point out a simulation algorithm for the parameters choice.

Let's choose a certain set of environmental characteristics, for which an optimal decision rule should be constructed; in turn, the environmental characteristics drive the learning/maturity curve L_{nm}. Considering this curve we calculate the effect values for various combinations of the parameters a and l_{thres} and choose the best combination.

The decision to switch from the design phase to the implementation phase, on the basis of the fact that the decision function $l(m)$ reaches the threshold l_{thres}, can be made after m various batches. The effect value also depends on the batch number m, after which transition between the LC phases is performed. Let's calculate the probability of decision-making after the m-th batch for different m and average the effect by m for various combinations of the parameters a and l_{thres}.

By virtue of the procedure (7.27) definition and the characteristics of the values ς_m, the values of the decision function $l(m)$ form a sequence of random variables, i.e. random walk between the "reflecting" (point 0) and "absorbing" (point l_{thres}) boundaries. Let us denote by $P_m(x)$ the distribution function of the values $l(m)$, by $F_m(x)$ the normal distribution function of the values $(\varsigma_m/n - a)$ (of course, $F_m(x)$ depends on $L_{n(m-1)}$ and a, but these dependences are not shown, in order to not burden the denotations). System of equations (A7.15) describing the evolution $P_m(x)$ for $m = 0, 1, \ldots, M$ and $0 \leq x \leq l_{thres}$ include the initial conditions for $m = 0$, the condition on the upper "absorbing" boundary (in point l_{thres}) for all $x \in [0; l_{thres})$ and $m \geq 0$:

$$P_0(x) = \begin{cases} 0 & \text{for } x < 0 \\ 1 & \text{for } x \geq 0 \end{cases}$$

$$P_{m+1}(x) = \int_0^{l_{thres}-} F_m\left(x-y\right) dP_m(y); \tag{A7.15}$$

$$P_{m+1}\left(l_{thres}\right) = 1 - \int_0^{l_{thres}-} F_m\left(l_{thres} - y\right) dP_m(y);$$

System of equations (A7.15) allows one to calculate $P_m(l_{\text{thres}})$, and on their basis the probability of decision-making after exactly m batches as $(P_m(l_{\text{thres}}) - P_{m-1}(l_{\text{thres}}))$. In this case, the value of the parameter l_{thres} is taken into account explicitly; the value of the parameter a and the environmental characteristics (through $L_{n(m-1)}$) determine the math expectation and dispersion of the normal distributions $F_m(\cdot)$.

The effect in the case of decision-making after the m-th batch is (similarly to 7.24):

$$\Phi_m(1; M) = (v + c_p) n \sum_{i=m+1}^{M} L_{n(i-1)} + nm(c_p - c_d) - nMc_p \qquad (A7.16)$$

The subtrahend nMc_p in (A7.16) is constant and can be omitted; the effect can also be normalized by the positive constant $(v + c_p) n$. After that, (A7.16) takes a more compact form: $\Phi_m(1; M) = \sum_{i=m+1}^{M} L_{n(i-1)} + mL_{\text{thres}}$; and as a result, the effect averaged by m derives in the form

$$\Phi^*(1; M) = \sum_{m=1}^{M} \left[mL_{\text{thres}} + \sum_{i=m+1}^{M} L_{n(i-1)} \right] \left(P_m(l_{\text{thres}}) - P_{m-1}(l_{\text{thres}}) \right) \qquad (A7.17)$$

Expressions (A7.15–A7.17) allow the effect values for the given environmental characteristics (defining the introduction curve) and various combinations of the parameters a and l_{thres} to be obtained numerically and their optimal values to be chosen. It is easy to show that the probabilities $P_m(l_{\text{thres}})$ for any m and any environmental characteristics monotonically increase with respect to a and decrease with respect to l_{thres}; at the same time, $\Phi_m(1; M)$ for any environmental characteristics and $L_{\text{thres}} \in (0; 1)$ has the only maximum with respect to $m \in \{1, 2, \ldots M\}$. Therefore, the problem of choosing values a and l_{thres} has a unique solution.

Appendix A7.4 Example of "Simple Agent" Model Planning with Disorder of Technology Function

Let's consider the simplest Enterprise (one principal and one agent according to Example 4.4); we assume the disorder in the distribution function from $G(z) = z/(\beta_0 + z)$ to $G^+(z) = z/(\beta_1 + z)$. Then, the output distribution density, depending on the action of the agent y before ($i = 0$) and after ($i = 1$) disorder, has the form:

$$p_z(z; y \mid i) = \begin{cases} \dfrac{\beta_i}{\beta_i + y} \delta(z - y) + \dfrac{\beta_i}{(\beta_i + z)^2} & \text{for } z \le y \\ 0 & \text{for } z > y \end{cases},$$

and the output average value: $E[z(y) \mid i] = \beta_i \ln(1 + y/\beta_i)$.

Before ($i=0$) and after ($i=1$) decision-making about disorder detection, the principal constructs such plan, desirable for him, for the AE's action, that $x_i^* = (\sqrt{\beta_i^2 + 4\gamma r \beta_i} - \beta_i)/2$.

However, taking into account the need to compensate AE's costs in the worst case (when disorder occurred, but the principal does not detect it and offers a contract in the expectation of no disorder, or vice versa), the incentive system should look like:

$$\sigma_C(x_i^*, z | i) = \begin{cases} \dfrac{(x_i^*)^2(x_i^* + \beta_i)}{2r\beta_i} + a_i, & z \geq x_i^*, \\ 0, & z < x_i^*. \end{cases}$$

where the value of the compensating additive a_i is determined by the condition:

$$\min_{i=0;1} \left\{ \int_0^{+\infty} \sigma_C(x_i^*, s | i) p_z(s, x^* | i) ds; \int_0^{+\infty} \sigma_C(x_i^*, s | i) p_z(s, x^* | 1-i) ds \right\} \geq c(x_i^*).$$

In the case of a simple agent $a_i = \min_{i=0;1} \left\{ 0; \dfrac{(x_i^*)^2}{2r} \dfrac{x_i^* (\beta_{1-i} - \beta_i)}{\beta_i (\beta_{1-i} + x_i^*)} \right\}.$

The likelihood ratio l_t, forming the decision function S_t, takes the form:

$$l_t = \ln(\beta_1 / \beta_0) + \begin{cases} 2\ln\big((\beta_0 + z_t)/(\beta_1 + z_t)\big) & \text{if } z_t \in [0, x_0^*), \\ \ln\big((\beta_0 + z_t)/(\beta_1 + z_t)\big) & \text{if } z_t = x_0^*. \end{cases}$$

Also the disorder detection statistics $S_t^1 = \sum_{\tau=1}^{t} (z_\tau - E[z(x^*)])$,

$S_t^2 = \sum_{\tau=1}^{t} (\sigma_C(x^*, z_\tau) - c(x^*, r))$, $S_t^3 = \max_{1 \leq \theta < t} \left\{ \sum_{\tau = t - \theta + 1}^{t} z_\tau - \theta\, E[z(x^*)] \right\}$ or

$S_t^4 = \max_{1 \leq \theta < t} \left\{ \sum_{\tau = t - \theta + 1}^{t} \sigma_C(x^*, z^\tau) - \theta c(x^*, r) \right\}$ can be used within the framework of the

cumulative sum method.

In this case, it is necessary to use the values of the principal's objective function before and after disorder, as well as in the case of erroneous decisions; for illustration purposes, these values are given as Table A7.1.

Let's consider a numerical example. Let $T=500$, $T_d=200$, $r=1$, $\gamma=10$, $\beta_0=100$, $\beta_1=60$. The expected (in the sense of mathematical expectation) and actual trajectory (cumulative sum of the AE's activity output) are shown in Figure A7.3 (the dashed lines show the curves corresponding to non-detection of disorder). Sketches of the dynamics of the AE's cumulative costs and the principal's incentive costs

TABLE A7.1

Values of the Principal's Objective Function $\Phi(\cdot)$ Depending on the Presence of Disorder and its Detection by the Principal

Disorder (j)	Solution (i)	$\Phi(\sigma(\cdot \mid i), z \mid j)$
0	0	$\gamma\beta_0 \ln\left(1 + x_0^* / \beta_0\right) - c\left(x_0^*\right) - a_0$
1	0	$\gamma\beta_1 \ln\left(1 + x_0^* / \beta_1\right) - c\left(x_0^*\right) - a_0$
0	1	$\gamma\beta_0 \ln\left(1 + x_1^* / \beta_0\right) - c\left(x_1^*\right) - a_1$
1	1	$\gamma\beta_1 \ln\left(1 + x_1^* / \beta_1\right) - c\left(x_1^*\right) - a_1$

are shown in Figure A7.4 (the dashed lines show the curves corresponding to non-detection of disorder).

The average values of the statistics l_t before and after disorder are -0.04 and $+0.04$, respectively, and the standard deviations are 0.29 and 0.27. Moreover, before disorder, the statistics l_t take value $\ln\dfrac{\beta_1}{\beta_0} + \ln\dfrac{\beta_0 + x^*}{\beta_1 + x^*} = -0.29$ with the probability $\dfrac{\beta_0}{\beta_0 + x^*} = 0.5$, and after the disorder, with probability $\dfrac{\beta_1}{\beta_1 + x^*} = 0.38$.

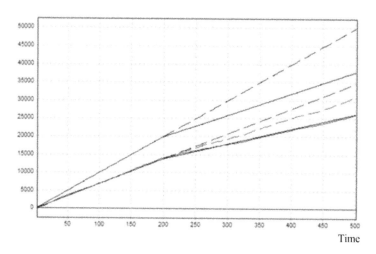

Time

FIGURE A7.3 Dynamics of the AE's activity cumulative outputs (planned, expected, and actual).

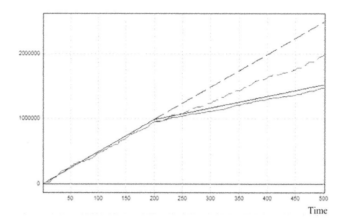

FIGURE A7.4 Dynamics of the AE's and the principal's cumulative expenses.

The dynamics of the values of the statistics S_1 and S_2 and decision function (7.30) are shown in Figures A7.5 and A7.6.

In the retrieval samples under consideration, given $\delta = 2$, disorder is detected 10 periods after such occurs.

The decision threshold δ can be chosen not only with respect to the criterion, when one of the errors is fixed at a level not higher than the specified one, and the second is optimized, but also with respect to a criterion of optimization of the principal's objective function $\Phi(\cdot)$ along with fixed time interval.

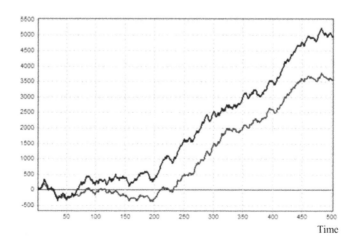

FIGURE A7.5 Dynamics of the statistics S_1 and S_2.

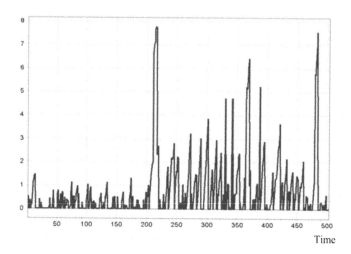

FIGURE A7.6 Dynamics of the statistics l_t.

APPENDIX A7.5 BELLMAN EQUATIONS SOLUTION FOR PROBABILISTIC CASE (7.36)

Let's solve the Bellman equations for dynamic programming problem (7.36).

Let's define a random sequence $\varepsilon(t)$ as the sum of the sequences $\mu(t)$ and $d(t)$; the probability distribution $\hat{Q}_\varepsilon$ of the values $\varepsilon(\cdot)$ is the convolution of P_μ and Q_f. The process $\varepsilon(\cdot)$ makes sense of the sum of the leaving AEs, AEs rejecting the offer ($\mu(t)$), and the demand ($d(t)$). Let's introduce a function

$$g(x) = E\big[R(x)\big] = c_{reg}\sum_{\varepsilon=d_{\min}}^{x}(x-\varepsilon)\hat{Q}_\varepsilon + (c_{out}-c_{reg})\sum_{\varepsilon=x}^{\hat{d}_{\min}}(\varepsilon-x)\hat{Q}_\varepsilon,$$

having the meaning of conditional expectation for the objective function for the next period, provided that the sum of the headcount of regular AEs $n(t)$ and issued offers $u(t)$ is equal to x. Then for the stationary case, the functional equations take the form:

$$F_T(n) = \min_{u\geq 0}\big\{g(n+u)\big\}, \qquad\qquad (A7.18)$$

$$F_{t-1}(n) = \min_{u\geq 0}\Big\{g(n+u)+\gamma\sum_{\mu}F_t(n+u-\mu)P_\mu\Big\}, \qquad (A7.19)$$

In (A7.19) and below, the summing over μ supposes always the same range of change in μ; therefore, to simplify the record, the limits of the sum are omitted.

Let's denote $\bar{d} = E\big[d(t)\big]$ and $\bar{\mu} = E\big[\mu(t)\big]$.

From the definition of $g(x)$, one can get:

$$g(x) = \begin{cases} (c_{out} - c_{st})(\bar{d} + \bar{\mu} - x) & \text{for } x < \hat{d}_{min}, \\ (c_{out} - c_{st})(\bar{d} + \bar{\mu} - x) + c_{out}\sum_{\varepsilon=\hat{d}_{min}}^{x}(x-\varepsilon)\hat{Q}_{\varepsilon} & \text{for } \hat{d}_{min} \leq x < \hat{d}_{max}, \\ c_{st}(x - \bar{d} - \bar{\mu}) & \text{for } x \geq \hat{d}_{max}. \end{cases}$$

The first differences $g(x)$ have the form $\Delta g(x) = -(c_{out} - c_{st}) + c_{out}\sum_{\varepsilon=\hat{d}_{min}}^{x}\hat{Q}_{\varepsilon}$, the first

differences are negative (equal to $-(c_{out} - c_{st})$) for $x \leq \hat{d}_{min}$ and positive (equal to c_{st}) for $x \geq \hat{d}_{max}$.

Over the interval $\hat{d}_{min} \leq x \leq \hat{d}_{max}$ the second differences $\Delta^2 g(x) = c_{out}\hat{Q}_x$ are non-negative since $\hat{Q}_x \geq 0$ (outside the interval those are equal to 0); therefore $\Delta g(x)$ monotonically increases and changes the sign once; therefore $g(x)$ has the single minimum. Let's find the minimum point x_{g_opt} of the function $g(x)$ (where $\Delta g(x)$ changes the sign) using the following rule.

By sequentially increasing x by one, starting from $\hat{d}_{min}$, let's find x_1 such that

$$\sum_{\varepsilon=\hat{d}_{min}}^{x_1}\hat{Q}_{\varepsilon} \geq \alpha_{st\_out} = 1 - c_{st}/c_{out}, \text{ and } \sum_{\varepsilon=\hat{d}_{min}}^{x_1-1}\hat{Q}_{\varepsilon} \leq \alpha_{st\_out}, \text{ then}$$

$$x_{g\_opt} = \arg\min\{g(x_1); g(x_1 - 1)\} \qquad (A7.20)$$

Let's consider equation (A7.18); due to the characteristics of $g(x)$

$$F_T(n) = \begin{cases} g(x_{g\_opt}) = \text{const} & \text{for } n \leq x_{g\_opt}, \ u = x_{g\_opt} - n, \\ g(n) & \text{for } n > x_{g\_opt}, \ u = 0. \end{cases} \qquad (A7.21)$$

Let's consider equation (A7.19) for $T-1$: $F_{T-1}(n) = \min_{u \geq 0}\{g(n+u) + \gamma\sum_{\mu}F_T(n+u-\mu)P_{\mu}\}$.

Let's define function $h_T(x) = \sum_{\mu}F_T(x-\mu)P_{\mu}$, then

$F_{T-1}(n) = \min_{u \geq 0}\{g(n+u) + \gamma h_T(n+u)\}$.
Let us analyze the behavior of $h_T(x)$ over different intervals of the set of definition
For $x \leq x_{g\_opt}$ $h_T(x) = g(x_{g\_opt}) = \text{const}$.
Let's estimate the first differences $\Delta h_T(x)$ for $x > x_{g\_opt}$:

$$\Delta h_T(x) = \sum_{\mu}F_T(x-\mu)P_{\mu} - \sum_{\mu}F_T(x-1-\mu)P_{\mu}$$

$$= \sum_{\mu}\Delta F_T(x-\mu)P_{\mu}.$$

Due to the characteristics of the function $g(x)$ and expressions (A7.21), the first differences $\Delta F_T(\cdot)$ are always non-negative; therefore the differences $\Delta h_T(\cdot)$ are also non-negative; therefore the function $h_T(\cdot)$ is monotonically non-decreasing for $x > x_{g\_opt}$:

$$h_T(x) = \begin{cases} g(x_{g\_opt}) = \text{const} & \text{for } x - x_{g\_opt}, \\ g(x) - f(x) & \text{for } x_{g\_opt} < x < \hat{d}_{\max}, \\ \hat{c}_{st}(x - \bar{d} - 2\bar{\mu}) & \text{for } x \geq \hat{d}_{\max}. \end{cases}$$

where $f(\cdot)$ is some function monotonically increasing over $[x_{g\_opt}; \hat{d}_{\max}]$ from 0 to $c_{st}\bar{\mu}$.

Then

$$g(x) + \gamma\, h_T(x) = \begin{cases} g(x) + \gamma g(x_{g\_opt}) & \text{for } x \leq x_{g\_opt}, \\ (1+g)g(x) - \gamma f(x) & \text{for } x_{g\_opt} < x < \hat{d}_{\max}, \\ (1+\gamma)g(x) - \gamma c_{st}\bar{\mu} & \text{for } x \geq \hat{d}_{\max}. \end{cases}$$

i.e. the sum $g(x) + \gamma h_T(x)$ is monotonically decreasing for $x \leq x_{g\_opt}$ and monotonically increasing for $x > x_{g\_opt}$, then

$$F_{T-1}(x) = \begin{cases} (1+\gamma)g(x_{g\_opt}) = \text{const} & \text{for } x \leq x_{g\_opt}, \quad u = x_{g\_opt} - n \\ g(x) + \gamma h_T(x) & \text{for } x > x_{g\_opt}, \quad u = 0 \end{cases}$$

and

$$F_{T-1}(x) = \begin{cases} (1+\gamma)g(x_{g\_opt}) & \text{for } x \leq x_{g\_opt}, \\ (1+\gamma)g(x) - \gamma f(x) & \text{for } x_{g\_opt} < x < \hat{d}_{\max}, \\ (1+\gamma)g(x) - \gamma c_{st}\bar{\mu} & \text{for } x \geq \hat{d}_{\max}. \end{cases}$$

Statements about the characteristics of the functions $F_t(\cdot)$ and $h_t(\cdot)$ can be successively proved using the mathematical induction method for any $t < T$, by decreasing t, by passing $t+1 \rightarrow t$.

For the function $h_{T-1}(x) = \sum_\mu F_{T-1}(x - \mu)P_\mu$ the considerations expressed for $h_T(x)$ are valid; therefore:

$$h_{T-1}(x) = \begin{cases} (1+\gamma)g(x_{g\_opt}) & \text{for } x \leq x_{g\_opt}, \\ (1+\gamma)g(x) - \tilde{f}(x) & \text{for } x_{g\_opt} < x < \hat{d}_{\max}, \\ (1+\gamma)g(x) - (1+2\gamma)c_{st}\bar{\mu} & \text{for } x \geq \hat{d}_{\max}. \end{cases}$$

where $\tilde{f}(x)$ is some function monotonically increasing over $[x_{g\_opt}; \hat{d}_{\max}]$ from 0 to $(1+2\gamma)c_{st}\bar{\mu}$.

Now

$$g(x)+\gamma h_{T-1}(x)=\begin{cases} g(x)+\gamma(1+\gamma)g(x_{g\_opt}) & \text{for } x\leq x_{g\_opt}, \\ (1+\gamma+\gamma^2)g(x)-\gamma\tilde{f}(x) & \text{for } x_{g\_opt}<x<\hat{d}_{max}, \\ (1+\gamma+\gamma^2)g(x)-\gamma(1+2\gamma)c_{st}\bar{\mu} & \text{for } x\geq\hat{d}_{max}. \end{cases}$$

Let's denote $\Gamma_k=\sum_{i=0}^{k}\gamma^i=(1-\gamma^{k+1})/(1-\gamma)$ and

$$\Delta_k=\sum_{i=0}^{k}i\gamma^{i+1}=\gamma^{k-1}+(1-\gamma^{k-1})/(1-\gamma)^2-(1-k)\gamma^k/(1-\gamma),$$

Then

$$F_{T-2}(x)=\begin{cases} \Gamma_2 g(x_{g\_opt}) & \text{for } x\leq x_{g\_opt}, \\ \Gamma_2 g(x)-\gamma\tilde{f}(x) & \text{for } x_{g\_opt}<x<\hat{d}_{max}, \\ \Gamma_2 g(x)-\gamma\Delta_2 c_{st}\bar{\mu} & \text{for } x\geq\hat{d}_{max}. \end{cases}$$

Let:

$$F_{T-n}(x)=\begin{cases} \Gamma_n g(x_{g\_opt}) & \text{for } x\leq x_{g\_opt}, \\ \Gamma_n g(x)-g\tilde{f}(x) & \text{for } x_{g\_opt}<x<\hat{d}_{max}, \\ \Gamma_n g(x)-\gamma\Delta_n c_{st}\bar{\mu} & \text{for } x\geq\hat{d}_{max}. \end{cases} \tag{A7.22}$$

where $\tilde{f}(x)$ is some function monotonically increasing over $[x_{g\_opt}; \hat{d}_{max}]$ from 0 to $\Delta_2 c_{st}\bar{\mu}$.

Since $h_{T-n}(x)=\sum_{\mu}F_{T-n}(x-\mu)P_{\mu}$, then

$$h_{T-n}(x)=\begin{cases} \Gamma_n g(x_{g\_opt}) & \text{for } x\leq x_{g\_opt}, \\ \Gamma_n g(x)-\tilde{f}(x) & \text{for } x_{g\_opt}<x<\hat{d}_{max}, \\ \Gamma_n g(x)-(\gamma\Delta_n+\Gamma_n)c_{st}\bar{\mu} & \text{for } x\geq\hat{d}_{max}. \end{cases}$$

It is easy to show that $\gamma\Delta_n+\Gamma_n=\Delta_{n+1}$, then

$$g(x)+\gamma h_{T-n}(x)=\begin{cases} g(x)+g G_n g(x_{g\_opt}) & \text{for } x\leq x_{g\_opt}, \\ (1+\gamma G_n)g(x)-\gamma\tilde{f}(x) & \text{for } x_{g\_opt}<x<\hat{d}_{max}, \\ (1+\gamma\Gamma_n)g(x)-\gamma\Delta_{n+1}c_{st}\bar{\mu} & \text{for } x\geq\hat{d}_{max}. \end{cases}$$

As a result, we get:

$$F_{T-(n+1)}(x) = \begin{cases} \Gamma_{n+1}g(x_{g\_opt}) & \text{for } x \leq x_{g\_opt}, \\ \Gamma_{n+1}g(x) - g\tilde{f}(x) & \text{for } x_{g\_opt} < x < \hat{d}_{max}, \\ \Gamma_{n+1}g(x) - \gamma\Delta_{n+1}c_{st}\bar{\mu} & \text{for } x \geq \hat{d}_{max}. \end{cases} \tag{A7.23}$$

Then it follows from the principle of mathematical induction and (A7.22–A7.23) that for any $t \leq T$ it is valid that:

$$F_t(x) = \begin{cases} \Gamma_{T-t}g(x_{g\_opt}) & \text{for } x \leq x_{g\_opt}, \\ \Gamma_{T-t}g(x) - \gamma\hat{f}(x) & \text{for } x_{g\_opt} < x < \hat{d}_{max}, \\ \Gamma_{T-t}g(x) - \gamma\Delta_{T-t}c_{st}\bar{\mu} & \text{for } x \geq \hat{d}_{max}. \end{cases} \tag{A7.24}$$

From expression (A7.24), it is easy to obtain the optimal value for the objective function $F_t(x_{g\_opt})$ (those are not of independent interest); however, expressions (A7.24) allow the optimal control strategy for the stationary case to be formulated:

$$u(n) = \max\left\{0; x_{g\_opt} - n\right\},$$

where the value x_{g_opt} is obtained from rule (A7.20).

Appendix A7.6 Bellman Equations Solution for Interval Case (7.37)

Let's solve the Bellman functional equations of interval statement (7.37); let's consider the first of the equations.

Let's introduce $\varepsilon(t) = \mu(t) + d(t)$, $e^-_- = \mu^-_- + \delta^-_-$, $e^-_+ = \mu^-_+ + \delta^-_+$. Let's denote $R_{<\mu\delta>}(x) = \max_{z \in [\tilde{e}_-; \tilde{e}_+]} \{R(x - z)\}$. Since $R(\cdot)$ is piecewise linear, the function $R_{<\mu\delta>}(\cdot)$ is also piecewise linear. For some

$$x_s = \left(1 - \alpha_{st\_out}\right)e^-_+ + \alpha_{st\_out}e^-_-, \tag{A7.25}$$

the value for which is found as the solution $c_{st}(x - \tilde{e}_-) = (c_{st} - c_{out})(x - \tilde{e}_+)$; and for any $x \geq x_s$ inequality $R(x - \tilde{e}_-) \geq R(x - \tilde{e}_+)$ is satisfied, and therefore $R_{<\mu\delta>}(x) = R(x - \tilde{e}_-) = c_{st}(x - \tilde{e}_-)$. In its turn, $R(x - \tilde{e}_+) \geq R(x - \tilde{e}_-)$ is satisfied for $x \leq x_s$; therefore $R_{<\mu\delta>}(x) = R(x - \tilde{e}_+) = (c_{st} - c_{out})(x - \tilde{e}_-)$.

Combining both cases, we get:

$$R_{<\mu\delta>}(x) = \begin{cases} c_{st}(x - \tilde{e}_-) & \text{for } x > x_s, \\ (c_{st} - c_{out})(x - \tilde{e}_+) & \text{for } x \leq x_s. \end{cases}$$

Then, considering $F_T(n) = \min_{u \geq 0} \{R_{<\mu\delta>}(n + u)\}$, we get

$$F_T(x) = \begin{cases} c_{st}(x - \tilde{e}_-) & \text{for } x > x_s, \\ R_s = (c_{st} - c_{out})(\tilde{e}_+ - \tilde{e}_-) = \text{const} & \text{for } x \leq x_s. \end{cases}$$

Now let's consider the second of equations (7.37) for $t=T-1$

$$F_{T-1}(n) = \min_{u \geq 0} \max_{\mu;\delta} \left\{ R(n+u-\mu-\delta) + \gamma F_T(n+u-\mu) \right\} =$$

$$= \min_{u \geq 0} \max_{\mu} \max_{\delta} \left\{ R(n+u-\mu-\delta) + \gamma F_T(n+u-\mu) \right\}.$$

Let's introduce a function $R_{<\delta>}(x) = \max_{z \in [\delta_-;\delta_+]} \{R(x-z)\}$, then

$$F_{T-1}(n) = \min_{u \geq 0} \max_{\mu} \left\{ R_{<\delta>}(n+u-\mu) + \gamma F_T(n+u-\mu) \right\}.$$

For $R_{<\delta>}(x)$ all comments regarding the function $R_{<\mu\delta>}(x)$ are true; therefore (herewith $x_\delta = (1-\alpha_{st\_out})\tilde{\delta}_+ + \alpha_{st\_out}\tilde{\delta}_-$):

$$R_{<\delta>}(x) = \begin{cases} c_{st}(x-\tilde{\delta}_-) & \text{for } x > x_\delta, \\ (c_{st}-c_{out})(x-\tilde{\delta}_+) & \text{for } x \leq x_\delta. \end{cases}$$

Since the boundary values μ and d are not negative, then $x_s \geq x_\delta \geq 0$.

Let's denote $A_T(x) = R_{<\delta>}(x) + \gamma F_T(x)$ and we get:

$$A_T(x) = \begin{cases} (c_{st}-c_{out})(x-\tilde{\delta}_+)+\gamma R_s & \text{for } x < x_\delta. \\ c_{st}(x-\tilde{\delta}_-)+\gamma R_s & \text{for } x_\delta \leq x \leq x_s, \\ c_{st}(x-\tilde{\delta}_-)+\gamma c_{st}(x-\tilde{e}_-) & \text{for } x > x_s. \end{cases}$$

Then the equation for $F_{T-1}(n)$ takes the form: $F_{T-1}(n) = \min_{u \geq 0} \max_{\mu \in [\tilde{\mu}_-;\tilde{\mu}_+]} \{A_T(n+u-\mu)\}$.

Thus we get:

$$\max_{\mu \in [\tilde{\mu}_-;\tilde{\mu}_+]} \{A_T(x-\mu)\} = \begin{cases} (c_{st}-c_{out})(x-\tilde{e}_+)+\gamma R_s & \text{for } x < x_1. \\ c_{st}(x-\tilde{e}_-)+\gamma R_s & \text{for } x_1 \leq x \leq x_2, \\ c_{st}(x-\tilde{e}_-)+\gamma c_{st}(x-\tilde{e}_- - \tilde{\mu}_-) & \text{for } x > x_2. \end{cases}$$

Since this function over the half-intervals $x \leq x_1$ and $x_1 < x$ completely coincides with the function $R_{<\mu\delta>}(x)$, then the point x_1 coincides with the point x_s (A7.25). Further,

$$\max_{\mu \in [\tilde{\mu}_-;\tilde{\mu}_+]} \{A_T(x-\mu)\} = \begin{cases} (c_{st}-c_{out})(x-\tilde{e}_+)+\gamma R_s & \text{for } x < x_s. \\ c_{st}(x-\tilde{e}_-)+\gamma R_s & \text{for } x_s \leq x \leq x_2, \\ (1+\gamma)c_{st}(x-\tilde{e}_-)-\gamma c_{st}\tilde{\mu}_- & \text{for } x > x_2. \end{cases}$$

This function reaches at x_s its minimum, being equal to $(1+\gamma)R_s$.

From the equation $c_{st}(x - \tilde{e}_-) + \gamma R_s = (1+\gamma)c_{st}(x - \tilde{e}_-) - \gamma c_{st}\mu\tilde{\ }_-$ we find the point $x_2 = \mu\tilde{\ }_- + x_s$.

Then

$$F_{T-1}(x) = \begin{cases} (1+\gamma)R_s & \text{for } x < x_s, \\ c_{st}(x - \tilde{e}_-) + \gamma R_s & \text{for } x_s \le x \le x_s + \tilde{\mu}_-, \\ (1+\gamma)c_{st}(x - \tilde{e}_-) - \gamma c_{st}\tilde{\mu}_- & \text{for } x > x_s + \tilde{\mu}_-. \end{cases}$$

Let's consider:

$$F_{T-2}(n) = \min_{u \ge 0} \max_{\mu} \max_{\delta} \left\{ R\left(n + u - \mu - \delta\right) + \gamma F_{T-1}\left(n + u - \mu\right)\right\} =$$

$$= \min_{u \ge 0} \max_{\mu} \left\{ R_{<\delta>}\left(n + u - \mu\right) + \gamma F_{T-1}\left(n + u - \mu\right)\right\}.$$

Let's denote $A_{T-1}(x) = R_{<\delta>}(x) + \gamma F_{T-1}(x)$ and get:

$$A_{T-1}(x) = \begin{cases} (c_{st} - c_{out})(x - \tilde{\delta}_+) + \gamma(1+\gamma)R_s & \text{for } x < x_\delta, \\ c_{st}(x - \tilde{\delta}_-) + \gamma(1+\gamma)R_s & \text{for } x_\delta \le x < x_s, \\ c_{st}(x - \tilde{\delta}_-) + \gamma c_{st}(x - \tilde{e}_-) + \gamma^2 R_s & \text{for } x_s \le x < x_s + \tilde{\mu}_-, \\ c_{st}(x - \tilde{\delta}_-) + \gamma(1+\gamma)c_{st}(x - \tilde{e}_-) - \gamma^2 c_{st}\tilde{\mu}_- & \text{for } x_s + \tilde{\mu}_- < x. \end{cases}$$

Then $A_{T-1}(x) = A_T(x) + \gamma^2 R_s$ for $\mu\tilde{\ }_- + x_s < x$.

Let us show, using the mathematical induction method, that for all $0 < i \le T$ it is valid that $A_{T-i}(x) = A_T(x) + \Omega(i)$ for $\mu\tilde{\ }_- + x_s < x$, where $\Omega(i)$ is some function depending on γ, R_s and i, but being independent of x.

For $i = 1$, the relationship is obtained above.

Let for some $1 < i \le T$

$$A_{T-i}(x) = \begin{cases} (c_{st} - c_{out})(x - \tilde{\delta}_+) + \gamma R_s + \Omega(i) & \text{for } x < x_\delta, \\ c_{st}(x - \tilde{\delta}_-) + \gamma R_s + \Omega(i) & \text{for } x_\delta \le x < x_s, \\ c_{st}(x - \tilde{\delta}_-) + \gamma c_{st}(x - \tilde{e}_-) + \Omega(i) & \text{for } x_s \le x < x_s + \tilde{\mu}_-, \\ c_{st}(x - \tilde{\delta}_-) + \gamma(1+\gamma)c_{st}(x - \tilde{e}_-) - \gamma^2 c_{st}\tilde{\mu}_- & \text{for } x_s + \tilde{\mu}_- < x. \end{cases}$$

Then:

a. $\max\limits_{\mu} A_{T-i}(x - \mu) = (c_{st} - c_{out})(x - \tilde{e}_+) + \gamma R_s + \Omega(i)$ is fulfilled for $x < x_s$;

b. $\max\limits_{\mu} A_{T-i}(x - \mu) = c_{st}(x - \tilde{e}_+) + \gamma R_s + \Omega(i)$ is fulfilled for $x_s \le x < x_s + \mu\tilde{\ }_-$;

c. $\max\limits_{\mu} A_{T-i}(x - \mu) = (1+\gamma)c_{st}(x - \tilde{e}_+) - \gamma c_{st}\mu\tilde{\ }_- + \Omega(i)$ is fulfilled for

$x_s + \mu\tilde{\ }_- \le x < x_s + 2\mu\tilde{\ }_-$;

d. $\max\limits_{\mu} A_{T-i}(x - \mu) = (1+\gamma+\gamma^2)c_{st}(x - \tilde{e}_+) - \gamma(1+2\gamma)c_{st}\mu_-$ is fulfilled for

$x_s + 2\mu_- \leq x$.

Since $F_{T-(i+1)}(x) = \min\limits_{u \geq 0} \{A_{T-i}(n+u)\}$, then

$$F_{T-(i+1)}(x) = \begin{cases} (1+\gamma)R_s + \Omega(i) & \text{for } x < x_s, \\ c_{st}(x-\tilde{e}_-) + \gamma R_s + \Omega(i) & \text{for } x \in [x_s; x_s + \tilde{\mu}_-), \\ (1+\gamma)c_{st}(x-\tilde{e}_-) - \gamma c_{st}\tilde{\mu}_- + \Omega(i) & \text{for } x \in [x_s + \tilde{\mu}_-; x_s + 2\tilde{\mu}_-), \\ (1+\gamma+\gamma^2)c_{st}(x-\tilde{e}_-) - \gamma(1+2\gamma)c_{st}\tilde{\mu}_- & \text{for } x_s + 2\tilde{\mu}_- \leq x. \end{cases}$$

and $A_{T-(i+1)}(x) = R_{<\delta>}(x) + \gamma F_{T-(i+1)}(x)$.
In such a way, we finally obtain

$$A_{T-(i+1)}(x) = \begin{cases} (c_{st} - c_{out})(x - \tilde{\delta}_+) + \gamma[(1+\gamma)R_s + \Omega(i)] & \text{for } x < x_\delta, \\ c_{st}(x - \tilde{\delta}_-) + \gamma[(1+\gamma)R_s + \Omega(i)] & \text{for } x \in [x_\delta; x_s), \\ c_{st}(x - \tilde{\delta}_-) + \gamma c_{st}(x - \tilde{e}_-) + \Omega(i) & \text{for } x \in [x_s; x_s + \tilde{\mu}_-), \\ c_{st}(x - \tilde{\delta}_-) + \gamma(1+\gamma)c_{st}(x - \tilde{e}_-) - \gamma^2 c_{st}\tilde{\mu}_- & \text{for } x_s + \tilde{\mu}_- \leq x. \end{cases}$$

Let's define the function $\Omega(i)$ so that the equality $\gamma[(1+\gamma)R_s + \Omega(i)] = \gamma R_s + \Omega(i+1)$ to be fulfilled, which is equivalent to $\Omega(i+1) = \gamma^2 R_s + \gamma\Omega(i)$, wherefrom $\Omega(i) = \gamma^2 R_s (1 - \gamma^{i+1})(1 - \gamma)^{-1}$.

This expression allows to obtain the minimax value of the objective function $F_t(x_s) = (1+\gamma+\gamma^2(1 - \gamma^{T-t+1})(1 - \gamma)^{-1})R_s$ or for a stationary case $F_t(x_s) = (1 - \gamma)^{-1}R_s$.

The expressions for $A_t(\cdot)$ and $F_t(\cdot)$ allow the best guaranteed control strategy under interval uncertainty conditions to be obtained; let's formulate the strategy.

Values n, u, d, μ are integers and the value $x_s = (1 - \alpha_{st\_out})e_+^{\sim} + \alpha_{st\_out}e_-^{\sim}$ may not be integers. Therefore, let's find an integer x_{int}, ensuring the minimum value $A_t(x)$ on the set of the integer x for all t as follows:

$$x_{int} = \arg\min\left\{A_t\left(\left[x_{<\mu,\delta>}\right]\right), A_t\left(\left[x_{<\mu,\delta>}\right]+1\right)\right\}. \tag{A7.26}$$

Then the best guaranteed strategy has the form: $u_{opt}(n) = \max\{0, (x_{int} - n)\}$.

REFERENCES

Arts, J., Basten, R. and van Houtum, G. 2016. Repairable Stocking and Expediting in a Fluctuating Demand Environment: Optimal Policy and Heuristics. *Operations Research*. Published online in articles in advance 01 Jun 2016.

Belov, M. and Novikov, D. 2020. *Models of Technologies*. Heidelberg: Springer.

Belov, M. and Novikov, D. 2020a. *Methodology of Complex Activity - Foundations of Understanding and Modelling*. Heidelberg: Springer.

Berovic, D. and Vinter, R. 2004. The Application of Dynamic Programming to Optimal Inventory Control. *IEEE Transactions on Automatic Control* 49(5), 676–685.

Bolton, P. and Dewatripont, M. 2005. *Contract Theory.* Cambridge: MIT Press.

Braha, D. and Yaneer, B. 2007. The Statistical Mechanics of Complex Product Development: Empirical and Analytical Results. *Management Science* 53(7), 1127–1145.

Chen, J., Zhu, J. and Zhang D. 2014. Multi-Project Scheduling Problem with Human Resources Based on Dynamic Programming and Staff Time Coefficient. In *International Conference on Management Science and Engineering Management,* Helsinki, 1012–1018.

Dewar, J. 2002. *Assumption Based Planning a Tool for Reducing Avoidable Surprises.* Cambridge: Cambridge University Press.

Elshafei, M. and Alfares, H. 2008. A Dynamic Programming Algorithm for Days-Off Scheduling with Sequence Dependent Labor Cost. *Journal of Scheduling* 11(2), 85–93.

Forrester, J. 1971. Counterintuitive Behavior of Social Systems. *Technology Review* 73(3), 52–68.

Gans, N., Koole, G. and Mandelbaum, A. 2003. Telephone Call Centers: Tutorial, Review, and Research Prospects. *Manufacturing & Service Operations Management* 5(2), 79–88.

Kumar, P. and Varaiya, P. 1986. *Stochastic Systems: Estimation, Identification and Adaptive Control.* Englewood Cliffs, NJ: Prentice Hall Inc.

Lee, A. and Longton, P. 1959. Queueing Processes Associated with Airline Passenger Check-In. *Journal of the Operational Research Society* 10(1), 56–71.

Martin, J., Fairley, D., Lawson, B. 2012. Enterprise systems engineering. http://www.sebo kwiki.org/1.0.1/index.php?title = Enterprise_Systems_Engineering. In A. Pyster, et al. (eds.), *Guide to the Systems Engineering Body of Knowledge (SEBoK),* v. 1.0.1. http:// www.sebokwiki.org/1.0.1/index.php?title=Main_Page [Accessed September 19, 2019].

Mehlmann, A. 1980. An Approach to Optimal Recruitment and Transition Strategies for Manpower Systems Using Dynamic Programming. *The Journal of the Operational Research Society* 31(11), 1009–1015.

Nikiforov, I. 1983. *Sequential Detection of Changes in Time-Series.* Moscow: Sience (in Russian).

Nikiforov, I. 2016. Sequential Detection/Isolation of Abrupt. *Sequential Analysis. Design Methods and Applications* 35(3), 268–301.

Nirmala, S. and Jeeva, M. 2010. Dynamic Programming Approach to Optimal Manpower Recruitment and Promotion Policies for the Two Grade System. *African Journal of Mathematics and Computer Science Research* 3(12), 297–301.

Novikov, D. and Shokhina, T. 2003. Incentive Mechanisms in Dynamic Active Systems. *Autom. Remote Control* 64(12), 1912–1921.

Novikov, D. 2013. *Theory of Control in Organizations.* New York: Nova Science Publishers.

Rao, P. 1990. A Dynamic Programming Approach to Determine Optimal Manpower Recruitment Policies. *The Journal of the Operational Research Society* 41(10), 983–988.

Report to the Subcommittee on Readiness and Management Support, Committee on Armed Services. 2005. U.S. Senate. DEFENSE ACQUISITIONS. GAO-06-66. https://www .gao.gov/new.items/d0666.pdf, assessed 20-01-2020.

Shiryayev, A. 1977. *Optimal Stopping Rules.* New York: Springer.

Si, J., Barto, A., Powell, W. and Wunsch, D. 2004. *Handbook of Learning and Approximate Dynamic Programming,.* Hoboken, NJ: John Wiley & Sons, Inc.

Silva, L. and Costa, A. 2013. Decision Model for Allocating Human Resources in Information System Projects. *International Journal of Project Management* 31, 100–108.

Smith, D. 1999. Dynamic Programming and Inventory Management: What Has Been Learnt in the Last Generation? In *Proceedings of the 1999 ISIR Workshop on Inventory Management.* Exeter, UK, August.

von Neumann, J. and Morgenstern, O. 1953. *Theory of Games and Economic Behavior.* Third edition. Princeton, NJ: Princeton University Press.

Xieab, Y., Liuab, C., Wua, D., Chenc, Y., Lia, J. 2015. Dynamic Programming Based Research Position Planning: Empirical Analysis from the Chinese Academy of Sciences. *Procedia Computer Science* 55, 35–42.

Zermelo, E. 1913. Über eine Anwendung der Mengenlehre auf die Theorie des Schachspiels. In *Proceedings of the Fifth International Congress of Mathematicians, II*, Cambridge, 501–504.

Part III

Practice
Business Tools and Applications

8 Optimal Enterprise Control Framework and Practical Implementation

The structural, process, and mathematical models of an Enterprise's complex activity presented in the previous chapters of the book constitute the fundamentals or the system of ideas, conditions, and assumptions ensuring the solution to the Enterprise Control Problem; that is, they actually form a certain *framework** as an instrument to control the Enterprise (of any scale: from a working team or a working group containing several employees to an international corporation with multiple supply chains and contractors forming an "extended enterprise").

From a practical point of view, such a framework (we call it an *Optimal Enterprise Control Framework*, abbreviated OEC Framework) defines the "*universal algorithm* of Optimal Enterprise Control" (mentioned in Section 1.5). The *universal algorithm* uses the structural and process models of CA (Chapter 1) and includes implementation of the Enterprise Control Optimization Scheme (Section 3.4.3), which, in turn, integrates the mathematical models described in Chapters 4–7.

The concept of frameworks is very popular: since the 1980s, it has been widely used in system engineering and related industries (for example, Zachman, DoDAF, TOGAF) and is fixed in international standards. The proposed OEC Framework complies with modern approaches and meets the requirements of the ISO 42010 standard, fixing a system of interconnected viewpoints and model types, by means of which complex activity is specified and studied as a complex system.

This chapter is devoted to the practical use of the models and methods developed in Part I and Part II to solve business problems; its structure is as follows:

- Section 8.1 describes the generalized OEC Framework as "the universal algorithm of Optimal Enterprise Control"; the necessary conditions involved in the possibility of optimizing an Enterprise's activity are also formulated; and the generalizing capabilities of the OEC Framework are analyzed. Integration models are presented, demonstrating at what phases/stages of CA LCs well-known business models, approaches, and mathematical methods can be employed.
- Sections 8.2–8.4 contain examples of practical applications of the mathematical models and methods developed in Chapters 4–7 to control real

---

* Framework: a basic conceptional structure (as of ideas); a set of ideas, conditions, or assumptions that determine how something will be approached, perceived, or understood (Merriam-Webster's Collegiate Dictionary).

firms from various industries, i.e., manufacturing, professional services, and retail.

8.1   OPTIMAL ENTERPRISE CONTROL FRAMEWORK

8.1.1   OEC Framework as the Universal Algorithm of Optimal Enterprise Control

In Chapter 3 (preamble), methodological foundations of Enterprise control are formulated in the form of a system of theses and a plan of action (Figure 3.1). Based on these foundations, we illustrate the implementation of the OEC Framework in the generalized business case: the use of the Enterprise Control Optimization scheme to manage a "generalized Enterprise."

Following the terminology accepted in management and business, we use the concept of a "business unit" (BU) as an equivalent to the Enterprise and an actor of structural element of complex activity (SEA) (Figure 8.1 and Table 8.1). Let's formulate the set of concepts employed: in the left column of Table 8.1, each concept is described in business terms, and, in the right column, the equivalent concept is specified in terms of the methodology of complex activity (Chapter 1).

We consider a BU in the broadest possible sense: from a team or a working group of several people to an international corporation with multiple chains of suppliers and contractors, forming an "extended Enterprise."

According to the methodological foundations (Chapters 1–2), the "Universal algorithm" implements a process model which is unified for any BU of any scale (any SEA) and which reflects the lifecycle of CA, while concrete logical and cause–effect models – being specific to each concrete BU (of a concrete SEA) – are incorporated into this unified process model. The *"Universal algorithm"* generalizes the actions of

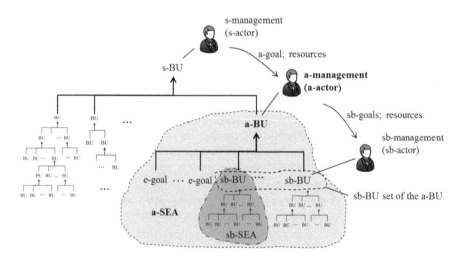

FIGURE 8.1   Structure of the concepts employed (BUs, SEAs, etc.).

TABLE 8.1
Set of Concepts Employed

Business Terms	Methodological Terms
a-BU – a BU to which the universal algorithm is applied	a-SEA – an SEA to which the universal algorithm is applied
s-BU – an a-BU which is superior to the a-BU or owners of the a-BU	s-SEA – an SEA which is superior to an a-SEA and which includes an a-SEA
a-management – a group of managers (in particular, one) managing an a-BU	a-actor – the complex actor of an a-SEA
a-goal – the goal of a-management which is realized by a-management implementing the a-BU's complex activity	a-goal – the goal of the a-actor which is realized by the a-actor implementing an a-SEA
sb-BU – a BU which is subordinated to an a-BU	sb-SEA – an SEA which is subordinated to an a-SEA, the constituent of the a-SEA
sb-management – a group of managers (in particular, one) managing an sb-BU	sb-actor – a complex actor of an sb-SEA
sb-goals – sub-goals into which the a-goal is decomposed and which are realized by sb-BUs	sb-goals – sub-goals into which an a-goal is decomposed and which are realized by sb-SEAs
e-goals – sub-goals into which an a-goal is decomposed and which are realized by the a-BU itself	e-goals – sub-goals into which an a-goal is decomposed and which are realized by elementary operations of a-SEA

a-management (an a-actor) during implementation of the lifecycle of a-BU's complex activity (LC of an a-SEA).

According to the conclusions in Section 2.1, each a-goal is set by the actor of the s-BU (the s-SEA), which is an external and superior entity in relation to the a-BU (a-SEA); therefore, the goal of the activity that a-management should implement together with the entire a-BU staff and sb-BUs (a complex a-actor and sb-SEAs) is the input for the "Universal algorithm." The resources provided to the a-management (a-actor) to achieve the goal posed by the s-BU (s-SEA) also constitute the input of the algorithm. The output of the a-BU's and sb-BU's (a-SEA, including sb-SEAs) complex activity forms the "Universal algorithm" output.

As complex activity is fractal (the a-BU's activity integrates, in turn, the activity of various types of sb-BUs, and the a-SEA consists of sb-SEAs), the universal algorithm includes multiple recursive calls to itself to implement the activity of sb-BUs (sb-SEAs), subordinated according to the hierarchy.

The application of the algorithm to an a-BU implies that the a-goal during a time period under consideration and the resources provided constitute the input of the algorithm (the a-goal is set and the resources are provided by the s-BU). Due to recursive calls to itself, the algorithm generates a hierarchical set of sb-BUs, subordinated to the a-BU (sb-SEAs and sb-actors). Thus, the algorithm demonstrates an important trait of an Enterprise as a complex system: an Enterprise almost constantly changes itself, following the needs to change its constituents and structure to meet the requirements of a changing CA goals and technologies.

The execution of the "Universal algorithm" is illustrated in Figure 8.2. It is developed based on two models: Lifecycle of CA: phases, stages, steps (Section 1.4.1, Figure 1.12), and Actions of the SEA actor during the CA lifecycle (Section 2.4, Figure 2.4), also including the Enterprise Control Optimization Scheme (Figure 3.9) and all mathematical models and methods presented in Chapters 4–7.

Arrows, as usual, reflect the control flow, and rectangles reflect aggregated instructions, actually being stages of the LC of CA (discussed in detail in Sections 1.4 and 2.4, Table 1.1, Figure 1.12, Figure 2.4).

The column (left part of Figure 8.2), representing the phases and steps of the lifecycle of complex activity, illustrates the place of the algorithm in the structure of the LC of CA.

Design phase

Instruction 1 (Steps 1–2 of the lifecycle of CA): Based on the a-goal (set by s-management), the a-management establishes the set of subordinate sub-goals (sb-goal and e-goal). Sub-goals can be defined as the result of a system analysis of the CA subject matter (utility–functions–elements; LC of CA and its stages), its place in the value chain of a potential consumer, and the technological readiness of a-management and the a-BU to achieve the set a-goal. In this regard, it is feasible to use practical experience in business processes development, reengineering, and improvement, fixed in the set of international standards and widely used models and approaches like ISO15288, ISO9000, ISO55000, ISO16085, and CMMI.

In practice, an Enterprise CA is focused on the creation of a valuable output as a necessary condition for obtaining a positive economic effect. Therefore, when establishing goals, it makes sense to use a value creation concept, for which one should determine and, along with the LC of CA execution, monitor the characteristics of the output value, the process of output creation, and potential and known stakeholders.

Also, for each of those sub-goals whose achievement seems risky, it is feasible to form alternative sub-goals that are added to the set of sub-goals, thus implementing the common risk mitigation and management practice (ISO16085, COSO).

For each of the sub-goals, a-management makes a decision as to whether this sub-goal should be implemented within the framework of the a-BU (as an elementary operation, the actor of which is the a-actor itself; we call such sub-goals e-goals) or it is necessary to organize subordinate BUs (and assign the sb-management) to implement such sub-goals; we call them sb-goals. A particular case of an sb-BU organization is, obviously, establishing a contract with an existing firm for the delivery of products and/or services.

Instruction 2 (Step 3 of the CA lifecycle): For each sb-goal and e-goal, a-management checks for the readiness of a known technology to achieve the goal by CA execution. If any technology (to achieve the a-goal) is not available or is not ready enough, a-management defines the goals of new CA aimed at creating/maturing such technology and organizes new sb-BUs (Steps 4–6 of the CA lifecycle). This case is

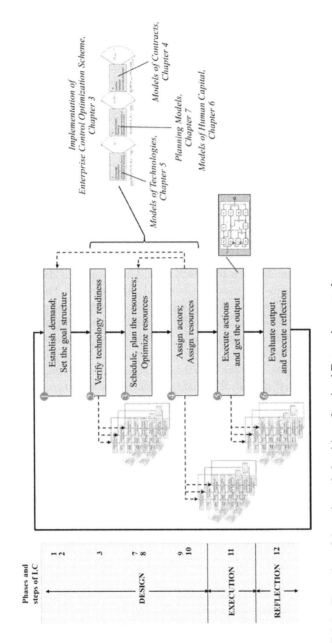

FIGURE 8.2 Execution of the universal algorithm of optimal Enterprise control.

presented in Figure 8.2 by dashed arrows going to the left from Instruction 2, which show, possibly, multiple recursive calls of the "Universal algorithm" with the corresponding sb-goals (from which emerges the fractal hierarchy of SEAs). Therefore, it is not necessary to separately include aggregated instructions describing the creation of new technology into the "Universal algorithm." In the presence of the required technology, the a-management acquires the technology and uses it to execute further Instructions 3–6 of the "Universal algorithm" (a special case of technology acquisition is the acquisition of an entity, a BU, that owns such technology).

Instruction 3 (Steps 7–8 of the CA lifecycle): Any actions are always executed following a time schedule and considering specific evolving conditions (the external environment, the outputs of previous actions, available resources, etc.). Therefore, a-management, based on the structure of goals and technologies, develops action plans – *work breakdown structures* – to achieve the goals, ensuring compatibility with the time schedule. The work (related to different goals) is grouped by calendar periods; respectively, the goals that should be achieved by different calendar dates are grouped. Resource planning is performed according to the algorithm described in Sections 7.1, 7.4. The a-management optimizes resources and the CA execution process using the methods and models described in Chapters 4–7.

In addition, the management for each employee of each BU designs incentive systems for such a time horizon for which the CA technology is determined using the models and methods proposed in Chapter 4. According to Theorems 4.1 and 4.2, incentives should depend on the outputs and/or actions of only this employee, independently of the outputs of the others, and in volumes, compensating "market determined" expenses of this employee in order to obtain the planned CA outputs using a certain technology.

Instruction 4 (Steps 9–10 of the CA lifecycle): To achieve each sb-goal, a-management organizes/establishes an sb-BU (a department/company and its leader) from the resources supplied to the a-actor along with the set a-goal. If there are no resources suitable for the creation of a BU, the a-actor sets goals and organizes the CA (SEAs and elementary operations) aimed at creating the resources from which the sb-BU can be formed (Step 6 of the CA lifecycle). The dashed arrows that go to the left of Instruction 4 show, possibly, multiple recursive calls of the "Universal algorithm" with the corresponding sb-goals.

The a-actor supplies each of the sb-actors with methods, ways, and means to achieve the sb-goal and allocates the necessary resources.

If necessary, Instructions 1–3 can be repeated cyclically, which are reflected by the dashed arrows coming out of Instruction 4 to the right and up.

Execution phase

Instruction 5 (Step 11 of the CA lifecycle): The a-management and a-BU employees carry out the actions, i.e., implement a-BU business processes (cause–effect model of an a-SEA) and, in parallel, a-management controls execution of a-BU and sb-BU actions.

The implementation is accompanied by "on-line" detection of actual and/or possible deviations from plans: the impossibility of achieving the goals and/or deadline delays and/or exceeding resource limits due to the occurrence of uncertainty events.

Having ascertained such deviations, a-management promptly escalates the problems to s-management and takes corrective actions, also by means of multiple recursive calls of the "Universal algorithm" with the corresponding sb-goals (dashed arrows passing to the left from Instruction 5).

Reflection phase

Instruction 6 (Step 12 of the lifecycle of CA): The a-management analyzes the outputs of CA implementation, time terms, and resource expenditures and makes the necessary adjustments (both in the current parameters and, if necessary, in the principles of organization and technology of activity).

Upon completion of all phases, the CA cycle is repeated.

Thus, the initial a-goal can generate a hierarchical set of interconnected sub-goals and actions that must be executed by the management and the staff of subordinate BUs in order to achieve the initial a-goal according to known technologies. This is realized through the "Universal algorithm" by multiple recursive calls of itself with various goals and resources.

8.1.2   INTEGRATION AND GENERALIZATION CAPABILITIES OF THE OEC FRAMEWORK

One of the motivating factors for the authors to write this book is a combination of two contradictory factors. On the one hand, there are a huge number of well-known and widely used management approaches and methods (for example, the site Value Based Management.net 2020 provides a list of more than 300 titles). On the other hand, there is a lack of generally accepted formal foundations allowing these approaches and methods to be matched up in some way, the most suitable ones to be chosen, and management efforts to be optimized.

The Optimal Enterprise Control Framework (including the models and methods developed in Chapters 4–7) positions, generalizes, and constructively concretizes almost all common approaches of management theory and practice, in particular (Figure 8.3):

- the value chain (Porter 1985) and other value-based approaches,
- management by the objectives approach – from the foundation (Druker 1954) to contemporary studies (for example, Gotteiner 2016),
- PDCA (Tague 2005), Fayol (Fayol 1917), and other managerial cycles,
- lifecycle concepts (Adizes 1999),
- business process reengineering (Hammer and Champy 1993),
- leadership concepts (Cole 2018, Northouse 2015, White 2015),
- project management (PMBOK 2017),
- quality management, process approach, and continual improvement processes (ISO 9004:2018),
- risk management (ISO 31000:2018),
- concepts of the theory of the firm (Coase 1937, Foss et al. 2000), industrial economy (Williamson 2009), business economics (Moschandreas 2000), managerial economics (Allen et al. 2009, Png and Lehman 2007).

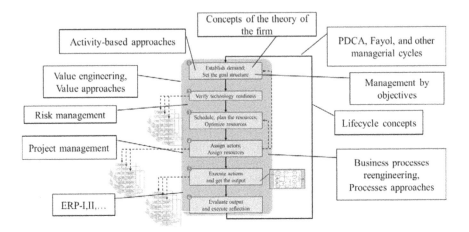

FIGURE 8.3 Optimal Enterprise Control Framework and managerial concepts and approaches.

In addition, due to the generality of approaches, the Optimal Enterprise Control Framework integrates formal models and methods of operations research and other fields of applied mathematics, as well as related disciplines. Table 8.2 provides a list of mathematical models and methods that are used or can be used, along with various phases and steps of the lifecycle of an Enterprise's complex activity.

Thus, Figure 8.3 and Table 8.2 play the roles of integration models: they represent the capabilities of the Optimal Enterprise Control Framework of summarizing widely used management approaches and concepts and using well-known mathematical models and methods.

The integration models demonstrate, on the one hand, the variety of management approaches and concepts and the mathematical models and methods used in practice and, on the other hand, a certain limitation of each of the approaches and methods, their focus on solving local (as opposed to the entire LC of CA) problems. This implies the fundamental impossibility of solving the Enterprise Control Problem using only one or more of these approaches and methods. That is, none of the approaches and methods (or even their combination) has a formal completeness in terms of solving the Enterprise Control Problem.

In contrast, the qualitative and mathematical models and methods developed and proposed in Chapters 4–7 allow the search for optimal control and constitute an integrated system, possessing methodological completeness from the point of view of solving the Enterprise Control Problem.

Furthermore, the developed models and methods allow hierarchical composition to be implemented, allow the principle of decomposition and aggregation of CA elements to be naturally realized, and, based on all the above, ensure that the partial tasks within the entire Enterprise Control Problem are correctly stated. In turn, any of the known approaches and methods can be used to solve partial problems, being integrated by the "Universal algorithm" within the OEC Framework.

TABLE 8.2

Main Classes of Models and Methods Employed Along with Various Stages of the LC of CA

Phase	Step		Models and Methods
DESIGN	1	Establishing demand and recognizing needs	• Strategic planning • Analysis (including scenario) and forecast of the environment • Data analysis • Marketing • Queuing theory
	2	Synthesis of a logical model	• Classification • Complex estimation • Decomposition/aggregation • Expert technology • Multi-criterion decision-making • Financial analysis • Optimization (in cases where it is possible to choose actors, outputs, and technologies) • Mathematical logic
	3	Technology readiness verification	• Methods of resource distribution • Mathematical logic • System optimization (if resources can be chosen)
	4	Synthesis of the cause-effect model	• Graph theory • Finite automations • Markov chains • Differential equations • Logistics • Complex estimation • Data analysis • Scenario analysis • Theory of reliability • Probability theory • Fuzzy sets • Interval analysis • Theory of decision-making
	5	Synthesis of the technologies of subordinate elements	See Steps 2–4
	6	Synthesis/modernization of resources	• Network scheduling and management • Decomposition/aggregation • Methods of modeling business processes • Discrete optimization • Schedule theory • Queuing theory • Game theory • Theory of decision-making

(Continued)

TABLE 8.2 (CONTINUED)

Main Classes of Models and Methods Employed Along with Various Stages of the LC of CA

Phase		Step	Models and Methods
	7	Scheduling and resource planning	See Steps 4 and 6
	8	Optimization of resource use	• Continuous and discrete optimization • Multi-criterion decision-making
	9	Assigning actors and defining responsibilities	• Decomposition/aggregation • Methods of modeling business processes • Discrete optimization
	10	Assigning resources	• Game theory • Schedule theory • Queuing theory
EXECUTION	11	Executing actions and forming the output	
REFLECTION	12	Evaluation of the output and reflection	• Strategic planning • Financial analysis • Decomposition/aggregation • Complex estimation • Data analysis • Expert technology • Theory of decision-making

8.1.3 PERFECT ENTERPRISE CONCEPT AND CHECKLISTS

The application of formal mathematical models and methods to any real-world entities always requires the introduction of certain assumptions, admissions, and conditions that these entities should meet in order for results to be correct. So, when creating mathematical models and methods (Chapters 4–7), a number of assumptions are made regarding the Enterprises under consideration: a set of conditions is defined which ensures a correct application of the developed models and methods for calculating optimal control constituents. These conditions and assumptions naturally distinguish a subset of Enterprises that allow subsequent optimization; we call such an Enterprise a *perfect Enterprise*. If, in turn, optimal control (calculated using models and methods developed in Chapters 4–7) is applied to a perfect Enterprise, we can say that its performance is optimal, and such an Enterprise can be called optimal. Thus, we can say that the conditions that perfect Enterprises satisfy in a certain sense play the role of necessary optimality conditions, and the conditions that are met by *optimal Enterprises* are sufficient.

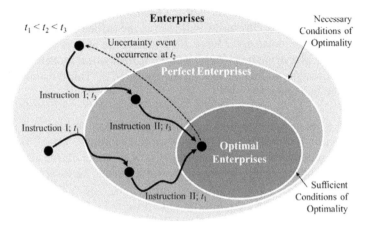

FIGURE 8.4 Concept of perfect and optimal Enterprise

Figure 8.4 illustrates the relations among the set of all possible Enterprises and the subsets of perfect and optimal Enterprises, as well as necessary and sufficient conditions.

The above considerations allow one to formulate a general algorithmic framework for optimizing an Enterprise's activity, consisting of the following aggregated instructions (Figure 8.4):

Instruction I. Lead the Enterprise to the form of a "perfect Enterprise," allowing optimization methods to be applied. Such a reduction is carried out not by mathematical methods but by organizational ones, since they actually ensure the fulfillment of preconditions for the correct application of formal optimization models.

Instruction II. Apply mathematical models and methods to find optimal control variants for various a priori chosen scenarios of the evolution of external conditions in which CA is implemented – for chosen planning condition variants.

This algorithmic framework naturally correlates with the *"Universal algorithm"* studied in Section 8.1.1 (Figure 8.2):

- Bringing the Enterprise to a perfect form (Instruction I) should be initiated during goal-setting (Instruction 1 of the "Universal algorithm") by setting the appropriate goal structure. The goals, in turn, during the next Instruction 2, lead to a hierarchy of new BUs, those that achieve the goal and bring an Enterprise to a perfect form.
- If one manages to bring the Enterprise to a perfect form, then optimal controls could be obtained (Instruction II) during the execution of Instruction 3 of the "Universal algorithm" – planning and optimization.

It should be noted that the evolution of an Enterprise and the environment sooner or later leads to the fact that the CA technology becomes inadequate to the external conditions, which appears in the form of the occurrence of true uncertainty events (see Sections 2.3 and 7.3). Obviously, in this case, the sufficient and necessary optimality conditions are violated; therefore, the maintenance of these conditions should be implemented as a dynamic process, and the mathematical models and methods developed in Chapters 4–7 allow such an implementation. This dynamic process is also illustrated by Figure 8.4:

- before some moment in time t_1, the Enterprise was brought to a perfect (Instruction I; t_1) and optimal (Instruction II; t_1) form;
- at some subsequent moment in time t_2 $(t_1 < t_2)$, an event of true uncertainty occurred, indicating the violation of the sufficient and necessary optimality conditions;
- true uncertainty events require the Enterprise to be brought again to the perfect (Instruction I; t_3) and optimal (Instruction II; t_3) form at some later time moment t_3 $(t_1 < t_2 < t_3)$.

Obviously, the execution of Instructions I–II of the algorithmic framework (as well as Instructions 1–6 of the "Universal algorithm") is in itself a complex activity. At the same time, bringing a perfect Enterprise to the optimal form (execution of Instruction II) consists of implementing formal models and methods; therefore, it is a regular activity following a known technology. At the same time, activity aimed at bringing the Enterprise to a *perfect form* (execution of Instruction I) is, for the most part, creative (the concepts of regular and creative activity are introduced and discussed in Section 1.3). The goal structure of this CA is defined by "conditions of Enterprise perfection," i.e., the necessary optimality conditions. Let us summarize all these conditions into a single list for the convenience of practical application.

Mathematical models and methods are developed to solve the Enterprise Control Problem based on the models of complex activity (Chapters 1–2) which describe an Enterprise and its activity in the most general case without any constraints. At the same time, a set of assumptions A1–A8 is introduced in Chapters 3–7, which limit the set of Enterprises to which the created models and methods can be applied. Thus, Assumptions A1–A8 play the role of the conditions which a perfect enterprise must satisfy, i.e., the necessary optimality conditions. Let's combine these conditions in Table 8.3. The assumption code (A1–A8), the section number in which the assumption is formulated, and the name of the assumption are indicated in the left column. The assumptions and comments are presented in the right column.

One of the most important characteristics of a perfect Enterprise is the continuous improvement in business processes, i.e., CA technologies, and such improvement is impossible without fixing business processes in the formal information models (not necessarily in computer systems). Therefore, an exemplar of the *maturity checklist* is formed to verify the existence and relevance of business process models to Enterprise operations (Table 8.4).

TABLE 8.3
Constraints on the Perfect Enterprise

Code (Section), Title	Definition and Comments
A1 (3.3.2) "On the validity of the rational behavior hypothesis"	The validity of the *hypothesis of rational behavior* (possibly taking into account limited rationality) is assumed: an actor, taking into account all the information available to them, chooses actions that lead to an output of that activity that the actor most prefers.
A2/A3 (3.4.1) "On the technological transparency/*observability* of an Enterprise"	A2: During each period, a principal observes only the network output, and the technological functions are biunique with respect to the agent's actions and the predecessors' outputs during the current period. A3: At each period, the principal observes the actual agents' actions during this period. When CA technology is mature and well tested, it is "transparent" to the principal.
A4 (3.4.1) "On a principal's awareness of the agents' cost function and reserve utility"	The principal's *awareness* of the "average market" cost function and reserve utility of all agents is assumed: the principal has complete information about the labor market values of agents' cost functions and reserve utility. The assumption is true in a developed labor market.
A5 (3.4.1) "On the *maturity of CA technology*"	The maturity of the CA technology is assumed (a. true uncertainty events requiring changes to the technology occur extremely rarely; b. upcoming events of measurable uncertainty do not lead to the non-achievement of the CA goal; their consequence is uncertainty in the values of the vector of CA output characteristics, this being within the objective area, as well as in the duration of the CA actor's actions and costs, whence it follows that the uncertain variation in the action duration does not exceed one discrete time period. As a consequence: 1. the CA output is considered to be binary: the goal is achieved or not achieved; 2. the measurable uncertainty impact appears in a priori unknown costs and characteristics of the CA output within the goal set; 3. All this allows the management to relatively accurately forecast the characteristics of the output, the time periods, and the costs within "small deviations."
A6 (3.4.2) "On the *tree-like structure* of SEAs"	The structure of SEAs (and the goal structure of an Enterprise) has the form of a single tree (with a single root node).
A7 (7.1.1) "On the statistical independence of implementation of complex activity elements (LC stages, projects, actions/work)"	Unscheduled, a priori uncertain deviations from prescribed time terms, planned actions, and output can be considered *statistically independent*. If management carries out continuous improvement of the Enterprise processes, if any dependences and patterns are detected, the management adjusts the relevant regulations and plans, after which deviations from the new regulations become independent again.
A8 (7.4.3) "On the statistical independence of actors' behavior"	The elements of active resources behave statistically independently from each other. Given established and generally accepted requirements for competencies, free legislation, experience recognized by other companies, and new employees' rapid entry into an Enterprise' activity, the employees' behavior model is described well by Markov processes.

TABLE 8.4

Maturity of Organization and Management Processes Checklist

Information Model of the Business Unit Operations

1   Does a BU core activity technology model exist,[55] including models …
   - of each kind of CA implemented by the BU's employees?
   - of each kind of CA being planned/or possible in the future?
   - of the employees' competencies required for each kind of executed and planned CA?
   - of other resources required for each kind of executed and planned CA?

2   Does a BU resource demand model exist, including models …
   - of the concrete actor (manager) activity forming the demand?
   - of the historical data on the demand?
   - of the demand forecast?
   - of the demand structure (time periods, resource characteristics, etc.)?

3   Does a BU active resource management model exist, including models …
   - of search and hiring?
   - of adaptation and training?
   - of firing and resignations?

4   Does a BU active resource use model exist, including models …
   - of active resource allocation?
   - of job assignments?
   - of performance control?

5   Does a business process management model exist, including a model for updating the elements of information models 1–4?

6   Do the actual processes comply in practice with models 1–5?

7   How often are models 1–5 updated?

Business Unit Operations

8   How can the following be fixed and obtained, and how relevant is the operational information on …
   - the current composition of the unit (resource pool)?
   - employees appointed to working groups or assigned for work execution?
   - plans for the appointment of employees to working groups and their assignment for work execution?
   - what time horizon and what breakdowns?
   - the current estimates of employees' competencies in comparison to those fixed in line 1 of the table?
   - estimates for the outputs of work executed by employees?
   - plans for hiring, training and preparation, and dismissals?

It also makes sense to note that the existence of a formal, relevant, up-to-date, verified, substantive, and structured specification recorded in electronic form and employed in the course of activity implementation and shared by all participants "degenerates" the problem of information control in TCOr.

8.2 SOME APPLICATIONS OF CONTRACTS

The coordination of CA actors' interests is carried out in practice in various cases, in particular, when hiring and regularly (usually, annually) negotiating employees' compensation packages between employees and management.*

We study the application of the models of actors' interests coordination considering the example of a system integrator company (we call it "the Integrator"), conducting project business (Belov 2015) and delivering professional services. The Integrator incorporates several specialized branches; the total headcount of all companies in the group exceeds 3,000 people – system architects, analysts, consultants, engineers, and programmers. The headquarters is located in Moscow; development and customer service offices are located in five cities in Russia.

The Integrator's current business is structured and managed in the form of projects which constitute the core type of business unit. Following reporting and control purposes all projects are grouped by types of services, by industries and clients; also, various types of projects are identified:

- commercial project – activity, carried out in order to meet a contract with a customer with the purpose of obtaining a financial output;
- presale project – organized sales activity, aimed at establishing an agreement with concrete potential customer;
- marketing project – organized activity in order to develop business relations with a customer or promote the Integrator's services or products;
- investment project – activity, aimed at developing new services, products or technological artefacts to be used in future commercial projects.

Business units of various types and lifecycle duration are established as the autonomous constituents of the Integrator, being considered as complex systems – Enterprises. The main types of BU, are listed in Table 8.5; the BUs' lifecycle structures are represented in Table 8.6.

BUs not only meet the definition of an Enterprise, but also correspond to SEAs, being structured in the form of subordinate SEAs (for example, disciplinary subsystems as constituents of the system being created and corresponding subprojects of disciplinary working groups within the project working group as a whole); an illustrative example is presented in Figure 8.5.

The Integrator simultaneously implements several hundred commercial projects (for example, in April 2014, there were about 750, and, in January 2020, more than 900); respectively, day-by-day control should be executed over several thousands of BUs, and each of them is controlled by a manager who is responsible for the business results of the corresponding BU. At the same time, BUs are in the complex hierarchical dependences on each other, which makes the problem of compatible control

---

* In practice, negotiation and definition of compensation packages is usually regulated by special policy. Such regulations and policies are part of "expanded CA technology" (Section 1.4); they are developed, improved, and regularly approved during the stage of the "Technology Design" of a CA lifecycle (Section 2.1).

TABLE 8.5

The Main Types of Business Units

Abbreviation	Content
Pr	Projects of all above-listed types
PCP	A sequence of tied presale projects and corresponding commercial projects
BU-S	Service of a certain kind consist of a set of investment projects and a set of $PCP_1, ..., PCP_N = <$Investment projects$+PCP_1, ..., PCP_N>$
BL	Business line – groups of technologically related services: $<$Investment projects$+PCP_1, ..., PCP_M>$
LC	Groups of projects, related to concrete large client: $<$Marketing projects$+PCP_1, ..., PCP_L>$

TABLE 8.6

Stages of BUs' Lifecycles

Stage Name		
In Business Terms	**In Terms of MCA**	**Stage Goal**
Preliminary	Establishing demand and recognizing needs	To define business prospects of BU
Preparation and business launch	Goal-setting and structuring of goals and tasks. Developing the technology	To create the BU's infrastructure, trained employees, work technologies, resources, etc.
Commercial	Executing actions and forming the output	To realize business opportunities in the form of commercial projects and get positive financial output
Closing	Evaluation of the output and reflection	To accumulate and retain knowledge and experience.

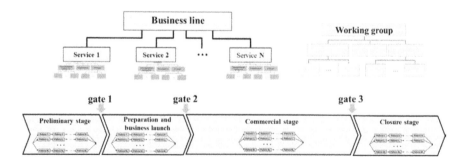

FIGURE 8.5 Example of SEAs, corresponding to a business unites.

over them extremely important for the Integrator's success. Moreover, it is necessary not only to ensure coordination to the BUs' activity with each other, but also to harmonize the operational activity with the sales efforts. And due to the existence of a large number of reflexive interconnections, this should be carried out in the form of a single process of optimizing corporate resources simultaneously as aligning them with sales volumes and prices on the whole set of multiple BUs.

Let us formalize the coordination of compensation packages of employees and BU managers according to the structure of the Integrator's complex activity – SEAs/BUs.

Each employee is involved, as a constituent of a complex actor, in several SEAs – BUs, so multiple coordination of employees' interests should be realized. As a result, the compensation package (CP) of each employee consists of several elements, each of which is associated with different BUs. An employee's CP and procedures for its approval are governed by the motivation regulation, which is one of the most important components in a Company's control system.

The CP of each employee $\sigma_i^*(\{x_l, y_{il}\}, t)$ during each period of time t can be represented as the sum of a conditionally constant part $\sigma_{i0}^*(x_0, y_{i0}, t)$ (monthly salary, medical insurance, and similar benefits) and a bonus part, including bonus elements $\sigma_{il}^*(x_l, y_{il}, t)$: for individual outputs in projects, for group outputs of project teams, for group outputs of a business line.

$$\sigma_i^*\left(\{x_l, y_{il}\}, t\right) = \sigma_{i0}^*\left(x_0, y_{io}, t\right) + \sum_{l \in L_{i,t}} \sigma_{il}^*\left(x_l, y_{il}, t\right),$$

where i is an employee's identifier; l is the BU identifier, in which the employee participates; $L_{i,t}$ is a set of such BUs; optimal plans for action x_l are determined by means of the solution of corresponding planning problems of form (3.17).

Therefore, the coordination of interests of employees as CA actors, in the form of coordination of the CP elements, is carried out regularly and repeatedly. The conditionally constant part $\sigma_{i0}^*(x_0, y_{i0}, t)$ and some "average value" of the total bonus for the outputs $\sum_{l \in L_i} \sigma_{il}^*\left(x_l, y_{il}, t\right)$ is negotiated and coordinated when hiring and annually when specifying the parameters of the annual bonus; the specific elements of bonuses for individual and group outputs in projects $\sigma_{il}^*(x_l, y_{il}, t)$ are determined when the i-th employee is appointed in a working group of the l-th BU (project).

The simultaneous engagement of each employee in several interconnected SEAs/BUs (employees in the role of agents and managers in the roles of both agents and principals) can potentially create serious methodological difficulties in dynamic coordination of the interests of many interconnected entities.

However, the situation is resolved due to the need to follow one of the basic principles of practical management: an incentive system must be understandable to all participants and unambiguously interpreted by them. The motivation regulation of Integrator determines conditions and a sequence of coordination of CP elements (by eliminating the factors of hierarchy, distributed control, and dynamics) in such a way that at the formal level decomposes the problem of coordination of all employees' CPs into many independent networked multi-element active systems, i.e., BUs, Enterprises.

Without adopting additional constraints, Theorems 4.1 and 4.2 can be applied to these BUs, which ultimately allows ones to determine, for each employee in each BU, the optimal compensatory incentive system $\sigma_{il}^{*}(x_l, y_{il}, t)$ of form (4.52–4.53), implementing the agents' actions vector as an equilibrium in the dominant strategies of their game with the principal's minimal total cost for incentive; the gains of all agents in this equilibrium are identically equal to their reserve utilities.

The incentive system of form (4.52–4.53) is not only optimal, but also (a) decentralizes the agents' game; (b) makes the agents' behavior independent of the CA technology, i.e., the network structure and the aggregate of agents' technological functions; (c) expands the solution to the case of constrained sets of each agent's possible actions.

In business terms, this means that it is beneficial for a rational employee to strictly fulfill job assignment, generally speaking, regardless of the actions of colleagues.

The optimal incentive system of form (4.52–4.53) is quite simple from a formal point of view; all "complexity" is concentrated in the problem of finding a plan for action and solving problem (3.20).

The above considerations once again confirm the important practical principle that at the meaningful level, an incentive system should be, firstly, targeted, i.e., to stimulate the employee to achieve each of the goals posed, and secondly, individual, i.e., to stimulate the achievement of precisely those goals for which the employee is responsible.

At the formal level, this means that the optimal incentive system can be designed using the following simple two-step algorithm independently for each of the Integrator's employees (i is the employee's identifier/number):

1. Optimal plans for actions x_l are determined by means of the independent solution of the corresponding problems of form (3.20).
2. An additive–compensatory incentive system is formed:

$$\sigma_i^{*}\left(\{x_l, y_{il}\}, t\right) = \sigma_{i0}^{*}\left(x_0, y_{io}, t\right) + \sum_{l \in L_i} \sigma_{il}^{*}\left(x_l, y_{il}, t\right)$$

$$\sigma_{il}^{*}\left(x_l, y_{il}, t\right) = \begin{cases} c_{il}^{t}\left(y_{Nl}\left(z_{nl}[1*t]\right)\right) + u_{il} + \varepsilon_{il}, & z_{nl}(t) \in Z_{il}^{t}\left(y_{il}^{\Pi}(t)\right); \\ 0, & z_{nl}(t) \notin Z_{il}^{t}\left(y_{il}^{\Pi}(t)\right); \end{cases} \quad l \in L_i.$$

The application of the additive–compensatory incentive system in practice is hampered by the fact that both the cost functions $c_{il}(\cdot)$ and the reserve utilities u_i are not based on objective laws known to the Integrator's management (to the principal), but are actually subjective estimates of employees (agents), who implement an active choice. However, the mass character and repeatability of multiple choices by many employees and the factual data recorded in the corporate accounting systems allow empirical data to be used as estimates of unknown functions. If necessary, historical data can be combined with expert estimates to formulate forecasts of the cost function $c_{il}(\cdot)$ and reserve utilities u_i in the future (a similar procedure is presented in the example of Section 8.3.3).

The presented example of a model of actors' interests coordination, formed on the basis of Theorem 4.2 is used in the Integrator and is the basis for solving practical problems of human capital management.

8.3   PRACTICAL TECHNOLOGY DEVELOPMENT OPTIMIZATION

Technology design and management have extremely wide practical application in all areas of human activity, primarily economic. This class of problems includes, for example, creating methods and means of manufacturing of any new product or service, methods and means of delivering it to the end user (sales and support), opening and developing new markets for existing or new products (sales and business development), and the CA technologies learning by individuals and organized groups of individuals of any scale (employee training, the new technologies implementation, innovations in the broadest sense). However, perhaps due to wide distribution and the enormous diversity of these issues, the formalization of such problems and the use of mathematically rigorous methods for their solution are difficult.

8.3.1   OPTIMAL TECHNOLOGY DEVELOPMENT IN BATCH MANUFACTURING

Let's consider an example of implementation of optimization models for transition from technology development to its productive use (Section 7.2.2) in the mass production case of the manufacturing company (we call it the Manufacturer) producing mass series of large-sized plastic pressed products.

The Manufacturer is one of the European market leaders in the large-sized plastic products segment; the range of its products includes several dozen units, among which the main share is industrial packaging and garbage containers for commercial, household, and industrial use.

The Manufacturer has a head office in the Volga region and several plants in Russia and other countries; the company factories ship to customers several batches of products daily; while headquarters officers execute sales and marketing, new products development, supply chain management, financial, HR and administrative functions.

The production is quite homogeneous and highly automated, it actually consists of only one processing stage – the final product molding; and each kind of product is manufactured by an automatic pressing machine in batches of fixed volume.

The product lifecycle includes: (i) product concept development; (ii) product design; (iii) machine-tool (transfer mold) manufacturing; (iv) pressing machine retooling and tuning; (v) regular production and delivery to customers. The costs of new product concept development and design (i–ii) are not considerable to be optimized. The machine-tool is produced by machine vendor; therefore associated cost (iii) is an external factor, being uncontrollable for the Manufacturer management (it also isn't a subject of optimization). Machine retooling and tuning are executed as the production of a series of test batches and settings adjustment (both machine parameters and plastic composition) after each test batch to increase the percentage of good products yield. So, the costs of machine retooling and tuning, firstly, can reach comparatively significant values, and secondly, are controlled and therefore should be optimized.

Upon retooling and tuning completion, the product is regularly manufactured in batches. The size of the test batch n is equal to the size of the regular one and cannot be changed. Normally a business plan assumes the output of at least M product batches to overcome breakeven point.

The occurrence of defective products can be described by the technology maturity/learning model (Section 5.3): the production of each product item is determined by some, a priori unknown, number of combinations of uncertain conditions (environmental states) and the likelihood of their occurrence. When the combination of conditions appears for the first time, the product item turns out to be defective, which requires adjustment of the machine parameters and plastic composition. If the same combinations arise after adjustment, a good product is obtained. Combinations of uncertain conditions appear independently for various product items. While tuning before the first test batch, a certain initial level of the percentage of good products yield is achieved, i.e., technology maturity/learning level, which, as a rule, roughly equals to 0.75 ($L_0 \approx 0.75$).

After each batch, a decision is made to continue tuning (to produce the next test batch), or to transit to regular production.

Each good product item from a regular batch brings benefits v; direct production cost of the item is c. The test batch items are not suitable for sale; the cost for producing one test batch as a whole equals to C_0. In regular production, each defect requires analysis and adjustment of the technological process; the cost for these operations is c_r for each defective item.

The approach used by the Manufacturer management "by default" consisted in transition from tuning to regular production only after reducing the number of defective products in the test batch to a level of not more than one item. The optimization problem was formulated as checking out the feasibility to follow the admitted practice or to find optimal transition rule.

The transition process is characterized by an initial level L_0, dimension K and probabilities $\{p_k\}$, these parameters are "implicit," since they are not available for instrumental measurement, and can only be set expertly.

The problem was solved on the example of a specific product, for which: batch size $n = 50$ items; minimum volume of output $M \geq 300$ batches (totally not less than 15 thousand items); cost–benefit ratios $C_0 \approx 1.5nv$, $c \approx 0.2v$ and $c_r \geq 10v$. The parameters n, M, C_0, v, c, and c_r are conventionally called "accounting" because their values are known precisely: they are taken from accounting systems or are specified by Manufacturer regulations.

The values of the accounting parameters made it possible to calculate the threshold level (see 7.22) $L^*_{thres} = 0.746$, after achievement of which, according to the results of Section (7.2.1), it is feasible to transit to the productive use of the technology, i.e., regular production. This means that the initial adjustment of the technology

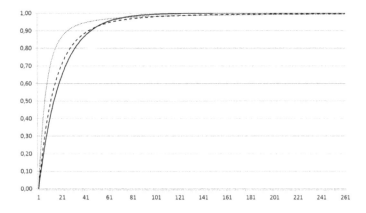

FIGURE 8.6 Maturity/learning curves for three types of distribution of environmental states.

parameters, ensuring a level of $L_0 \approx 0.75$, is sufficient for the transition to regular production, that there is no need to bear the costs and spend time on the production of test batches. The recommendation to start regular mass production with a defective item share of about 25% (12.5 pieces in a batch on average) is quite unusual, so, additional reasoning is absolutely necessary.

For this purpose, a simulation of economic effect was carried out based on the model of Section 7.2.2 and Appendix A7.3; a simulation study is described in Appendix A8.1. Due to the lack of a priori information that would make it possible to uniquely set the external environment model, and therefore, the technology maturity/learning curve, modeling was carried out for various combinations of the implicit parameters $(K, \{p_k\}$ and $L_0)$.

The distribution $\{p_k\}$ was assumed in three versions: even $p_k = 1/K$, binomial $p_k = C_K^k \, 2^{-k}$ (with the success probability equaling to 1/2) and "linearly growing" $p_k = 2 \, K^{-1}(K+1)^{-1} \, k$. Figure 8.6 shows the technology maturity/learning curves corresponding to these distributions at $K = 20$, the solid line corresponds to an even distribution, the dashed line corresponds to a "linearly growing" one, and the dotted line corresponds to the binomial one (the horizontal axis is the number of the tuning periods and the vertical axis is the maturity/learning level).

Some results for modeling the effect $\Phi_m(1, M)$ are presented as illustrations in Tables A8.1 and A8.2 and in Figures A8.1 and A8.2 in Appendix A8.1.

An analysis of the modeling results illustrates the conclusion that the values of accounting parameters, regardless of the values of implicit parameters, determine a significant trend: the effect $\Phi_m(1, M)$ (A7.16) monotonically decreases (a) with increase in the batch number m, after which transition to regular production is performed (b) with increase in the dimensionality of the set of possible environmental states K. The identified trend confirmed the recommendation to switch to mass production immediately after the initial adjustment of the technology parameters.

A comparison of the approach being recommended with the accepted practice was carried out in the course of another series of simulation experiments; their results are shown in Tables A8.3–A8.4 in Appendix A8.1.

An analysis of the results allows one to conclude that the recommended approach never impair the production efficiency, compared with the accepted practice, and depending on the combination of implicit parameter values may significantly increase the efficiency.

Important factors are, firstly, the decrease (by the amount of test batches cost) of the investments needed into the technology tuning, and secondly, a gain in time until the first delivery that would not have to be spent on the test batches production, which together leads to a significant reduction in the pay-back period for each new product.

The production efficiency also substantially depends on such an implicit parameter as the initial technology maturity/learning level L_0. Accordingly, another series of model experiments was performed, in the course of which the sensitivity of the recommendation fulfillment results to L_0 was investigated; the results of these experiments are presented in Tables A8.5 and A8.6. The content of Tables A8.5–A8.6 allows one to conclude that even in the case of lower initial technology maturity/learning level (even 40% of defective items in the first batch), it is feasible to follow new recommendation. Because traditional practice demonstrates bigger effect only in some cases and the gain is no more 1%.

Thus, the conclusions based on the modeling directly confirmed the recommendation on the feasibility to skip the test batches production and to start regular production immediately after the initial adjustment of the technological process. Empirical results of applying the recommendation while tuning the technology and producing the first 100 batches are shown in Table A8.7 and Figure A8.4.

The results show that in the case of the accepted practice, regular production would begin after the 26th batch (see Table A8.7 and Figure A8.4); by this time, costs for mastering would be −728 items (see Figure 8.7).

The implementation of the recommendation (to skip the test batches), firstly, reduced the maximum level of accumulated costs to −450 items, secondly, reduced the pay-back period (the 30th batch instead of the 41st, see Figure 8.7), and thirdly, provided approximately 14% increase in the financial result for the first 100 batches of the products (3387 instead of 2972 points).

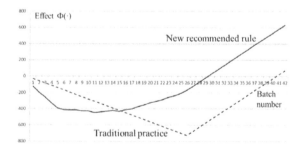

FIGURE 8.7   Costs of tuning of a test batches.

8.3.2 Optimal Learning in Customer Service Center

Let's consider the use of the technology control models applied to a certain Company; let's call it Customer Service Center (CSC). CSC provides mass services to third-party organizations – clients – and thus implements the outsourcing* of the HR documentary function (in electronic and paper form).

The CSC workload is generated by the requests flow, each of which should be processed at one of the work places occupied by ordinary employees of the CSC.

Customer service level agreements (SLA) establish the requests' intensity, characteristics of the work being performed, and the acceptable deadlines for completing the processing of each request from the moment such is received.

The flow intensity and request types are constant (about $N = 500$ requests per day). Despite the variety of the types of requests, the working hours to process any request is known and is considered constant (approximately one working day of one ordinary employee per request). The headcount of ordinary employees is maintained by the management in accordance with the flow intensity and labor law (taking into account adaptation periods, holidays, and absences, the headcount considerably exceeds N). On the one hand, this implies an acceptable labor rhythm, and on the other, the work quality fixed in SLA.

Ordinary employees, as a rule, fulfill the requests independently; however, if the features of the request are new for them, they involve "supervisors," tutors, who conduct training-by-working. As a result of the supervisor's help, the employee masters the technology and, with the next same combination of request parameters, performs the work independently. During a day, each supervisor can support the processing of up to five problematic requests (and train five employees) in this way.

The CSC is distinct in a noticeable labor turnover, voluntary resignations occur quite often. Figure 8.8 shows the empirical distribution of the share of ordinary employees depending on the time before leaving (the bar graph) along with an exponential trend line.

However, the relatively low job requirements for the ordinary employees make it possible to quickly replace the leavings from the labor market and adopt newcomers at the workplace. The work technology learning by an employee includes an initial training course on admission, which takes several days, and further training-by-working with supervisors' support.

The practical optimization problem was formulated as follows: to analyze the CSC operations and formulate recommendations on optimizing the learning process of ordinary employees to minimize labor costs of both ordinary employees and supervisors. The number of requests involving supervisors varied from 75 to 260 (averaging approximately at 150–160 requests) per day; ordinary employees headcount was maintained at the level of 546–550, and supervisors about 50.

---

* Outsourcing (Wikipedia) is an agreement in which one company hires another company to be responsible for a planned or existing activity that is or could be done internally, and sometimes involves transferring employees and assets from one firm to another.

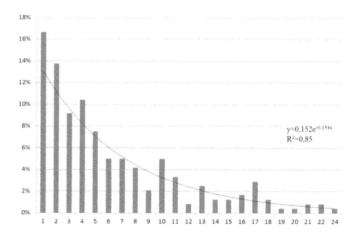

FIGURE 8.8 The empirical distribution of the share of employees depending on the time (in periods) before leaving with an exponential trend line.

The problem is formalized based on the CA technology control models (Chapter 5) and the active resource lifecycle models (Chapter 6). The discrete time period was admitted equal to one working day.

The external conditions under which the problem was solved were assumed to be stationary due to the constancy of the requests flow. Therefore, the labor costs of all employees were considered in a time-averaged form (and normalized by an ordinary employee cost), that is, the objective function – total labor cost – of the optimization problem was admitted as follows:

$$C(N_n; M) = N_n + Mc, \qquad (8.1)$$

where N_n is the time-averaged headcount of the ordinary employees' pool, M is the time-averaged headcount of supervisors, c is the ratio of the supervisor labor cost to the ordinary employee labor cost during a certain time interval ($c \approx 2.5$).

A model was designed (Appendix A8.2) to simulate the dependence of normalized averaged costs (8.1) on the essential parameters

t_{ad} – the duration of the initial training – adaptation period;

K_{ext} – the number of different typical requests;

k_s – the number of typical requests studied by an employee per one working day during the adaptation period.

The modeling demonstrates the following total labor cost $C(t_{ad}; k_s; K_{ext})$ characteristics:

A. when at least three typical requests per day are studied ($k_s \geq 3$) the costs $C(t_{ad}; k_s; K_{ext})$ monotonically decrease with respect to the initial training duration t_{ad} for any values $40 \leq K_{ext} \leq 100$;

B. for $k_s=2$, the costs $C(t_{ad}; k_s; K_{ext})$ monotonically decrease by t_{ad} for all values $40 \le K_{ext} \le 80$ and increase for $100 \le K_{ext}$;

C. for $k_s=1$, the csts $C(t_{ad}; k_s; K_{ext})$ monotonically increase by t_{ad} for all values $40 \le K_{ext}$;

D. the costs $C(t_{ad}; k_s; K_{ext})$ monotonically increase by K_{ext} for any t_{ad} and k_s;

E. the costs $C(t_{ad}; k_s; K_{ext})$ monotonically decrease by k_s for any t_{ad} and K_{ext}.

From these properties, it follows that the lowest level of costs is achieved at the highest possible rates of initial education ($k_s \ge 3$) and their durations.

Following this conclusion, recommendations were formulated to improve the learning strategy: to develop and implement a two-week entry training program focused on mastering the most common typical requests (50 such requests were identified).

The implementation of the recommendations increased the averaged technology maturity/learning level and reduced the total number of requests, requiring supervisors' involvement in an average of 85 requests (maximum 105 requests) per day, which allowed 29 supervisors (with an increase of regular employees headcount about 27) to be disengaged.

8.4 OPTIMAL PLANNING IN PRACTICE

8.4.1 COMPATIBLE PLANNING IN HIERARCHICAL ENTERPRISE

Let's consider an example of practical implementation of algorithmic models of planning process in a hierarchical dynamic multi-agent active system (Section 7.1) realized in Integrator firm (Section 8.2).

The process model (Section 1.4.2), defining the "Universal algorithm" of CA elements control, is used as the basis for the control regulations of Integrators' business units. The process model is:

- a tool for the maximum feasible CA regularization, that is, the CA technology fixing;
- a template, reflecting all the most important systemic CA LC aspects (steps, stages, phases, their contents, and interconnections) and thereby guaranteeing that these aspects are taken into account in control regulations being developed;
- a criterion, allowing standardizing, typical, "regular" (Section 1.3) activity to be separated from other CA types.

Integrator, as any "large" system, is characterized by a natural inertia; therefore, the basic principle of BUs' control and Integrator as a whole is "forecast versus plan matching," which consists in the fact that decisions are made on the basis of comparison of the forecast for business results with a plan, which allows for truly proactive control to be conducted. Forecasting and estimating of the BU lifecycle's economic and temporal characteristics (costs and revenues, completion deadlines), as well as the coordination of the plans between the BU actors, are based on the algorithmic model pointed out in Section 7.1.

Actually, Integrator's control system implements the models ("Universal algorithm") presented in Section 8.1 of this chapter.

It is feasible to measure control effectiveness, in the case of many times repeated cycles of making managerial decisions, by characteristics formed on the basis of the share of cases of achieving set goals or some total/average accuracy of achieving goals. As such, a characteristic one can use is "forecast error," which, due to the reflectivity of the BU's control, characterizes not so much the forecasting method as such, but the consistency of the BU's control as a whole.

The Integrator control system can be evaluated a posteriori based on the available significant history of operations. The forecast accuracy/plans consistency is a posteriori analyzed: the forecasts of the economic characteristics of the BU are compared with the actual data depending on the forecast horizon, i.e., the economic output for the year for two business lines. Examples of the gaps between the forecast and the actual figures are shown in Figure 8.9 and 8.10 in the form of graphs, which represent the gap depending on the number of the month in which the forecast is made (in horizontal axes). At the beginning of the first month of the year, the forecast interval is 12 months and decreases to one month by the last month of the year. Each of the graphs shows the gap for three annual periods (dashed and dotted lines), the averaged graph (solid line) and the linear trend (thin solid line).

The economic output is calculated as the difference between the earnings received and the costs for all BUs (projects) related to this business line. The earnings and costs were forecasted and coordinated between the BU managers in accordance with ratios (7.1–7.5). To bring to a uniform scale, the discrepancies are normalized as $|\varphi_t - \varphi_{act}|/(\max \{|\varphi_t - \varphi_{act}|\})$, where φ_{act} is the actual figure of the economic output for the year, $\varphi_t^{'}$ is the forecast formed in the t-th month of the year.

For all BUs, the gap decreases with decrease in the forecast horizon and the forecasts/coordinated plans do not have systematic errors. From the equations of the trend lines in the graphs, one can see that the linear model of the gap decrease is adequate (high approximation reliability R^2). Further, the trend line crosses the time

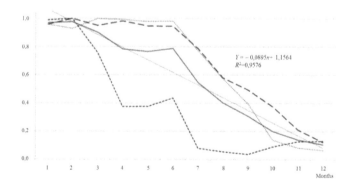

FIGURE 8.9   Sketch of the gap between forecast and actual figures ("business line 1").

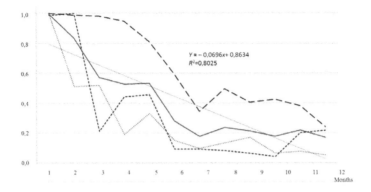

$Y = -0,0696x + 0,8634$
$R^2 = 0,8025$

FIGURE 8.10 Sketch of the gap between forecast and actual figures ("business line 2").

axis at points of months from 12.4 to 13, i.e., the average discrepancy becomes zero near point 13, which corresponds to the end of the twelfth month and to the forecast interval being equal to zero.

On the one hand, this is the expected conclusion: with decrease in the forecast horizon, uncertainty naturally decreases. On the other hand, this result alone confirms the absence of systematic errors in the algorithmic models. The BU managers' involvement in the information exchange loop makes the forecast and the BU control as a whole reflexive. Decrease in errors with decrease in the forecasting interval and the absence of systematic errors shows the models' robustness to reflection in the control loop <manager – controlled BU>. The relative forecast errors do not exceed 10 ... 12% on a three-month horizon and 40 ... 50% in a six-month period, which can be considered a good result. At the same time, the analyzed system is characterized by rather significant uncertainty, which is a natural feature of business and operations and is caused by the existence of separate transactions with high uncertainty.

In Figure 8.11, examples of economic output forecasts of several projects depending on time (by months) are given; the forecasts are normalized similarly to the graphs presented in Figure 8.9 and 8.10. The presence of volatile projects (Figure 8.11) accords well with the linear decrease in the discrepancy between the forecast

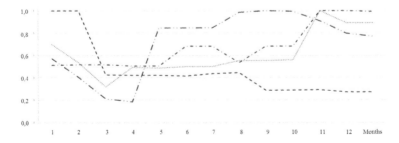

FIGURE 8.11 Example of change in forecasts of economic outputs of several projects.

and actual data: during each month, approximately the same number of projects are completed; for completed projects, the forecast values are close to the actual ones; uncertainty decreases in proportion to the remaining time (Figure 8.9 and 8.10).

The control system based on the considered algorithmic and numerical models involves the BU leaders and other employees of the Integrator in the information processing loop and requires certain labor costs from them; the total costs of the Integrator control system make up no more than 5% of the personnel costs, which seems to be a very adequate figure.

8.4.2 HEADCOUNT PLANNING AND OPTIMIZATION

Let's now consider the human capital control model applied to one of the business units of Integrator – active resource pool; Figure 8.12 shows one exemplar actual trajectory of the demand of the pool's employees (vertical axis) at different time periods (horizontal axis).

In this example, there is reason to assume the stability of the external and internal conditions, that is, to apply the optimal compatible strategy of active resources headcount control when the characteristics of the sources of CA uncertainty and the active resources' behavior are known and constant in time (Proposition 7.5 of Section 7.4.3).

The historical data availability makes it possible to construct an empirical probability distribution of the sum of uncertainty in demand for active resources and uncertainty in traffic (the results of the resources' active choice) – the convolution of the distributions P_μ and Q_δ (see Appendix A7.4).

From a business point of view, this optimization problem corresponds to the case when the management maintains the full-time employees' headcount at a certain constant M_f level, and covers the gap arising from the sales unevenness and exceeding this level, by acquiring external human resources (so-called freelancers and similar resources). The advantage of such external resources is their availability for "instant" hiring and the possibility to also refuse to use them at no additional cost, the disadvantage being in a higher operational price c_{out}, as compared to the full-time regular one c_{reg}. The idea of such strategy consists in the saving on paying for

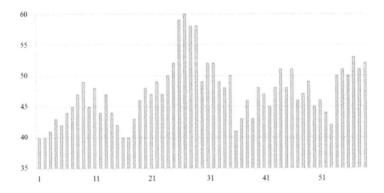

FIGURE 8.12 A sample of active resources demand.

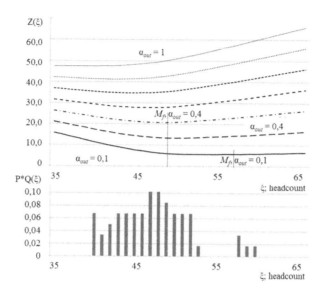

FIGURE 8.13   The cost $Z(\cdot)$ and the empirical distribution $P*Q(\cdot)$ as the functions of the headcount.

temporarily unused resources during low uneven demand periods, and formally such strategy corresponds to Proposition 7.5. As the model is relatively simple, the strategy is robust to inaccuracies in the parameters' values. The control strategy is illustrated in Figure 8.13: it is maintaining the headcount at the constant level $n(t)=x_{g\_opt}$, the value of the level x_{g_opt} itself is obtained from rule (A7.20), defined in Appendix A7.4. The upper part of Figure 8.13 presents the cost function $Z(\cdot)$ graphs for various ratios $\alpha_{out}=c_{reg}/c_{out}$, and the lower part demonstrates the empirical convolution of the distributions P_μ and Q_δ (we denote it by $P*Q(\xi)$), on the horizontal axis, that we are laying off the headcount ξ.

Given a low cost of external resources in comparison with the regular ones ($\alpha_{out} \cong 1$; $c_{reg} \cong c_{out}$), the cost function $Z(\cdot)$ does not have a minimum: it takes a value corresponding to the average demand.

Given a high cost of external resources ($\alpha_{out} \cong 0{,}1$; $c_{reg} \cong 0{,}1c_{out}$), the minimum point of the cost function lies closer to the upper boundary of the possible demand range; and the minimum is weakly expressed.

Given the presence of historical data and valid assumptions about the preservation of existing trends in the future, the use of empirical distribution is the most adequate and simplest approach to obtain the optimal headcount of full-time employees M_f.

Given the absence of such data, for example, when new businesses are being created or significant changes in external or internal factors are being expected, the convolution function of the distributions P_μ and Q_δ can be approximated by some known distributions, which allow obtaining of preliminary estimates of M_f. The numerical modeling demonstrates that in this example, the replacement of the empirical distribution by the binomial one with the equivalent two first moments leads to a difference of not more than one in the obtained values M_f for the two distributions. This suggests the feasibility of using the binomial distribution to obtain preliminary estimates for the headcount of full-time employees in the absence of historical data.

8.4.3 OPTIMIZATION OF ECONOMICAL CHARACTERISTICS OF HUMAN RESOURCE LIFECYCLES

Let's consider the application of the methods presented in Section 7.4.4 to control one Integrator's division (active resource pool).

Analysis of actual accounting data of the division (pool) shows that the headcount is stationary in the range of 40–60 people. The employees have a stable average workload and during the whole time-in-the-pool they generate the output that is much higher than their operational cost. The compensation package has the main share of the employee costs, the size of the CP varies slightly, depending on the calendar time or time-in-the-pool duration (at a fixed position), changes within 1–3% cannot be considered significant. This corresponds to the following assumptions about active resource lifecycle characteristics: $c_{st}(\theta) \approx \text{const} = c_{st0}$; $c_{src} = \alpha_{src}\, c_{st0}$; $c_{ad} = \alpha_{ad}\, c_{st0}$; $\alpha_{ad} = 0,3$; $c_{off} = \alpha_{off}\, c_{st0}$; $\alpha_{off} = 0,5$, $c_{trn} = c_{att} \approx 0$ where c_{st0} is the current compensation package (including all taxes, pensions, and other associated expenses).

The firing is small to negligible, and the dynamics of the employees' traffic follows the empirical distribution (Figure 8.14) of the share of the employees (vertical axis) depending on the time they worked in the company (horizontal axis, in nominal units).

On the one hand, the form of the empirical distribution witnesses that an employee's time-in-the-pool may be represented with good accuracy by a random exponentially distributed value; on the other hand, statement 6.2 of Section 6.3.2 constrains

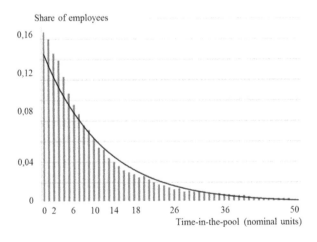

FIGURE 8.14 Empirical distribution of the share of employees by time-in-the-pool.

the feasibility to use the time-in-the-pool empirical distributions for practical conclusions.

Therefore, we characterize the employees' traffic by an indicator averaged by the time-in-the-pool, i.e., the leaving intensity during one period of time $\lambda(\cdot)$, assuming it does not depend on the time-in-the-pool θ; being estimated on the historical data, it is $\lambda(\cdot) = \lambda_0 \approx 1/13 \ldots 1/10$. The job offer acceptance probability, historically estimated, is $\pi(\cdot) = \pi_0 \approx 0.95$.

Let's assume each employee's perception of the value of working in Integrator, in comparison with other labor market alternatives, to be based on the size of the compensation package, as well as on some parameter X, reflecting the employee's active choice, so characteristics $\lambda(\cdot)$ and $\pi(\cdot)$ of the employees active choice depend on c_{st} and X.

In turn, the management tries to maintain a constant pool headcount (following statements 7.5 or 7.7), then the employees' traffic is balanced as $\lambda(c_{st0}; X)$ $M_{av} = \pi(c_{st0}; X) n_{off}$, where M_{av} is the average (by time) pool headcount, in fact, the management maintains the balance of employee traffic between the pool, i.e., the company, and the labor market, by setting an adequate level of the compensation package c_{st0}. Taking into account the remarks and notations made, the nominal pool costs optimization problem takes the form (using the expression from 7.4.4):

$$Z\left(c_{st}; x_1; x_2\right) \rightarrow \min_{c_{st} > 0},$$

where $Z(c_{st}; x_1; x_2) = c_{st} + \dfrac{c_{st}\alpha_{ad}}{1 + \left(\lambda_0^{-1} - 1\right)\exp\left(x_1\left(c_{st} - c_{st0}\right)\right)}$

$+ c_{st}\alpha_{off} \dfrac{1 + \left(\pi_0^{-1} - 1\right)\exp\left(x_2\left(c_{st0} - c_{st}\right)\right)}{1 + \left(\lambda_0^{-1} - 1\right)\exp\left(x_1\left(c_{st} - c_{st0}\right)\right)}$ for $x_1 > 0; x_2 > 0$ and $c_{st} \in [c_{st0} - \Delta c_1; c_{st0} + \Delta c_2]$.

Let's analyze the solution of the optimization problem $Z(c_{st}; x_1; x_2) \rightarrow \min$ using a graphical interpretation (Figure 8.15); let us use the nominal units $c = c_{st}/c_{st0} - 1$. The horizontal axis corresponds to the compensation package c (in nominal units), the zero point corresponds to c_{st0}. The families of curves represent the graphs of dependences of the costs $Z(\cdot)$ and the average shares $\lambda(\cdot)$ and $\pi(\cdot)$ for several values of the parameter $x_1; x_2 x_1, x_2$.

Curves 1 correspond to a weakly consolidated labor market; that is, when the range of compensation packages, being acceptable for employees (the zone in which the probability is significantly greater than 0 and less than 1) is quite large; on the contrary, curves 4 correspond to a highly consolidated labor market, i.e., a narrow spread of compensation packages. Having received the families of curves, the manager, based on his expert opinion, determines what kind of market the current situation belongs to.

If the labor market is consolidated (curves 4), then the potential cost reduction $Z(\cdot)$ is very insignificant: the minimum $Z(\cdot)$ of curve 4 is almost at point c_{st0}. Obviously,

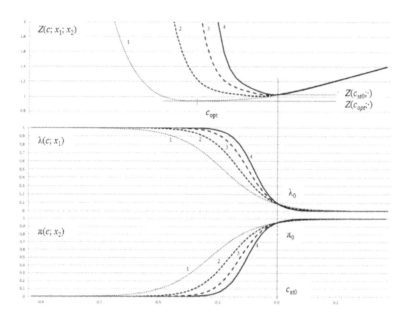

FIGURE 8.15 Graphs of dependences: $Z(\cdot)$, $\lambda(\cdot)$ and $\pi(\cdot)$.

in this case, the pool is in the optimal balance with the market and changes in the system being infeasible.

For the opposite case (curves 1), the minimum $Z(\cdot)$ can differ from $Z(0)$ by a significant amount, and the corresponding value c_{opt} can differ from c_{st0} (in our example, by 20%). In such case, management should study the feasibility to move to the optimum point by changing the compensation package size.

The most influential parameter in this case is the size of the "market averaged" compensation package size, the change which can significantly disrupt the balance of traffic. Therefore, this parameter requires not only monitoring, but also forecasting.

The analyzed example could be useful both for verifying the achievement of the optimal equilibrium area and for forecasting such areas in the cases of the external or internal conditions changes. After optimizing the cost parameters, several methods, to combine full-time employees with freelancers and out-staffers to meet the uneven resource demand, can be used based on the models in Section 7.4.3.

8.4.4 CONTRACTS IN CHANGING BUSINESS ENVIRONMENT

Let's study an example of the CA actors' interests' coordination models of Sections 6.3.2 and 7.3 applied to a national-wide food retailer company (we call it Retailer).

Let's illustrate the model's application to controlling the consistency of the store employees' interests with the Retailer's plans. A store is a basic element of the business network of Retailer, i.e., a core BU from a business point of view and an SEA from a formal point of view. In such a way, we are talking about compatibility of the

CA actors' interests within the SEA, i.e., the store, which is implemented by coordinating the incentive system (in the form of the compensation package, CP) of each employee in each reporting period $\sigma_i^*(\cdot, t)$. The CP is coordinated between employee and director, representing the interests of the Company's management (therefore, the shareholders of the company, since the management's interests are also compatible with the Company owners' interests). In such a way, the coordination of the ordinary employees' interests with the business owners' interests is realized. The coordination is implemented explicitly when hiring, when a candidate accepts an offer and signs a labor contract and later in implicit form periodically, when the employee decides to continue to work in Retailer or leave.

Then the coordination of the CA actor's (i.e., the employee's) interests is formalized by the model of a multi-element dynamic (with unrelated periods) active system with probabilistic uncertainty. In such a case, Theorems 4.1 and 4.2 are applicable.

The compatible compensation package size of each employee corresponds to the employee's specified qualifications and workload. The workload for each employee is determined, firstly, by the SEA technology (of the store and all employees working in it), and secondly, by the flow of customers and the purchase characteristics. If the first factor is known to the principal, then the second is determined by the uncertain environmental conditions: the socioeconomic situation in the country and the region, the peculiarities of the situation directly in the store vicinity, and, possibly, other factors. Possible changes in the environmental characteristics can cause workload changes and lead to a disorder of their interests' compatibility, which naturally requires a reaction from the superior actor to restore the interests' compatibility. Given short-term workload changes, the problem is solved by introducing various wages allowances; however, given a systematic external conditions change, an appropriate long-term reaction of the Retailer's management is necessary.

The compatibility restoration is carried out both by adjusting the incentive system of the existing staff and by changing their headcount (Section 7.4 is devoted to the consideration of such decisions).

The problem of consistency control is discussed in Section 7.3 and classified as the disorder detection problem given the probability distribution function of an agent's activity output and/or the probability distribution function of the environmental state $(F_\theta(\cdot) \rightarrow F_\theta^+(\cdot))$.

Let us measure the employee workload, i.e., the output of the action z_t, by the number of customers served during a shift; the total quantity of items of all purchases can also be used as z_t. Both indicators with reference to the calendar date and employee identifier are recorded by cash registers in electronic form; therefore they are convenient and accessible for accumulation, systematization, and analysis. Due to (a) the independence of the actions of individual buyers and (b) a significant number of customers serviced per shift (several tens to hundreds), each of the indicators can be considered as a sequence of independent random variables the distribution function of which is well approximated by a normal one. The indicators have seasonal and weekly trends, which is feasible to be reflected in the form of the known and time-dependent average values m_t, which at the moment of change in the environmental properties $(F_\theta(\cdot) \rightarrow F_\theta^+(\cdot))$ become other, but new values are a priori unknown.

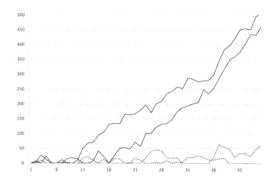

FIGURE 8.16 Examples of the dynamics of cumulative sums in the absence and presence of disorder.

In such conditions, the following decision rule is used to identify workload disorder for all store employees.

1. After each shift, the cumulative value of the workload z_t is calculated summarily for all store employees, serving the basis for calculation of the cumulative sums of the form

$$S^+(t) = \max_{1 \le \theta < t} \left\{ \sum_{\tau = t - \theta + 1}^{t} (z_\tau - m_\tau - \delta^+) \right\} \text{ and}$$

$$S^-(t) = \max_{1 \le \theta < t} \left\{ \sum_{\tau = t - \theta + 1}^{t} (m_\tau - z_\tau - \delta^-) \right\}.$$

2. A signal to detect changes in the external characteristics is being formed if $S^+(t) > \Delta^+$ (workload increase) or $S^-(t) > \Delta^-$ (decrease). If $S^+(t) \le \Delta^+$ and $S^-(t) \le \Delta-$, one believes the environment to be unchanged.

Figure 8.16 represents an illustrative example of changes in the cumulative sums $S^+(t)$.

The vertical axis represents $S^+(t)$, the horizontal axis represents time. The values of $S^+(t)$ in the absence of changes in the environmental properties are shown by the dashed line, and when changes occur at time $t = 10$, by the solid line, for two samples.

In the given example, the empirical values z_t vary from 750 to 850, the sample average $\hat{m}_t = 790$, and the dispersion $\hat{\sigma}_z^2 = 280$. We assume that after disorder the average increases by a fixed value $\Delta m = 20$, and the dispersion does not change. The constants δ^+, δ^-, Δ^+ and Δ define the characteristics of the disorder detection criterion and are selected, by following from the optimal detection of changes, corresponding to the expertly defined scenario (see Section 7.3.2).

The presented procedure implements the maximum likelihood criterion (Nikiforov 2016) of verification of the hypothesis about the increase of mathematical expectations by a fixed value $m_t \rightarrow m_t + \Delta m$ against the hypothesis about the absence of such a change, having the assumption of a normal distribution of the values being observed. In the example presented in Figure 8.16, the constant δ^+ is chosen to be equal to $\Delta m/2$. The signal generated in this way attracts the attention of the company's management and forces, if necessary, to conduct a more detailed analysis of the situation and take the necessary measures.

8.4.5   CONTROL OF CHARACTERISTICS OF HUMAN RESOURCE LIFECYCLES

Let's consider practical implementation of the active resource headcount control by regulating the parameters of their lifecycles applied to a food retail company, Retailer (see also Section 8.4.4). The models and methods described in Sections 6.2 and 7.4.4 are employed to analyze and forecast the economic output of various management initiatives. Let's consider one example of such analysis and forecast.

Figure 8.17 demonstrates that the empirical distribution of the share of employees depended on the time-in-the-pool (among those who already left), which shows a significant proportion of employees leaving during the early periods after joining.

A significant share of early attrition indicates possible problems in the hiring and adaptation procedures: entering the company, the employee discovers that the conditions do not suit the expectations, or adaptation ends unsuccessfully, in particular, the manager finds out that the employee does not match the required profile.

Using the active resource lifecycle model (Section 6.2), one performed an estimate of "potential losses" that the company might avoid if it solves the problems in the hiring and adaptation procedures. Model use allows the potential gains from improving procedures to be checked against the costs for implementing a procedure improvement project and a reasoned decision about launching or rejecting such a project to be made.

All employees are divided into groups according to the time-in-the-pool duration; Table 8.7 shows the shares of employees and the average time-in-the-pool within the groups. Despite the territorial distribution of the stores (thousands of the stores

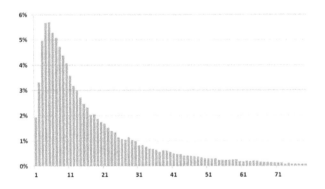

FIGURE 8.17 Empirical distribution of employees' shares in dependence on the time before resignation (among those who already left).

TABLE 8.7

Shares of Stuff by the Time-In-The-Pool Duration

		Average Time (of Nominal Periods)		
Groups:	Share	Actual	Option 1	Option 2
0–6 periods	27%	3.9	7.0	12.8
7–22 periods	46%	12.8	12.8	12.8
23 and more periods	27%	41.6	41.6	41.6
Total:	100%	18.5	19.3	20.9

are located in almost all regions of the Russian Federation), all employees of the category under consideration are assumed to belong to one resource pool, since it is not a territorial but only a functional factor that matters within the framework of this analysis.

The column "actual" shows the average time-in-the-pool based on actual data. The columns "Options" contain the expert estimates expected by the management of the possible average time after improving the hiring and adaptation procedures.

The effect of improving business processes on the company's economic output can be numerically estimated based on the expressions of the model (6.1–6.5). In this example, a change in the average time-in-the-pool for the first group (first row in the Table 8.7) from 3.9 periods to 7 leads to an increase in the average effect from one employee by 0.7%, and from 3.9 to 12.8 periods – by 2%. Given the headcount of employees of several tens of thousands, these insignificant relative changes entail significant cumulative effects. And, what is very important, these effects are achieved by improving the supporting business processes; that is to say that they do not require changes and expenses in the basic processes, which are always high.

Another example, sequential procedure for detecting changes in the characteristics of the active resource lifecycles was introduced in the same company for the operational control of traffic characteristics (the model of Section 6.3.2) of the largest mass category of employees – cashiers.

The existence of several (above ten) thousand geographically distributed stores requires automation for the operational control of the active resource characteristics. During each time period, it is necessary to quickly check against and analyze more than a thousand tuples of data, including: (a) the headcount N_τ; (b) the number of those who left ζ_τ^2; (c) the number of the current offers $n_{off,\tau}$; (d) the number of accepted proposals ζ_τ^1.

The posed problem is solved by employing the technique described in Section 6.3.2, which is applied in parallel to all pools in "scenario 3" (see Section 6.3.2). In this case, not just the functional, but also the territorial factor matters; so the employees of each store are considered as a separate pool of active resources.

The results of the detection serve the basis for a more detailed analysis of the situation in those entities, for which a decision about disorder detection was made.

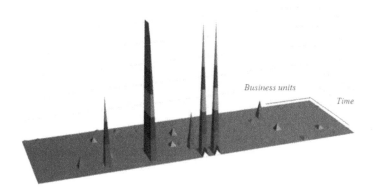

FIGURE 8.18   The detection decision function example.

For clarity, the results are displayed not only in numerical, but also in graphical form (Figure 8.18 shows an example of detection results).

In the vertical axis one lays off the relative likelihood of disorder presence against its absence; one of the horizontal axes corresponds to the pools, i.e., the stores, and the other corresponds to time. The peaks on the three-dimensional surface show a significant excess of the likelihood of disorder presence over its absence and serve as indicators for the management to review in detail the situation in the respective stores.

The introduction of these procedures and methods has led to an increase in the efficiency of the use of the basic resources – the cashiers – by 5–7%.

8.4.6   EARNED VALUE MANAGEMENT AND ACTIVITY PLANNING

The *Earned Value Method* (EVM) is very common and widely used in the theory and practice of firms and project management (for instance, see Reichel (2006) and the literature review in Marshall (2007)), so it makes sense to illustrate how the models and methods developed in the book, firstly, contracts and planning models, relate to Earned Value Method.

As in the earlier sections, we consider an Enterprise as a multi-element dynamic active system with a constraint in the form of a technology imposed on joint activity, in the general case characterized by formulation (3.11–3.17). We use the notations introduced in Section 3.4 and consider the assumptions made as satisfied. Let us admit that CA technology satisfies one of the assumptions A2/A2' or A3/A3' (Section 3.4.1–3.4.2). The output $z_w(y_A[1*t])$ of the Enterprise's CA (of the root ω_w-principal) is considered as a random variable with known distribution; at that, the values $z_w(y_A[1*t])$ also belong to known target areas, see Sections 2.3 and 3.4.1. This stochastic model reflects the effect of measurable uncertainty of CA. Under the conditions of compliance with A2/A2' or A3/A3', the problem allows decomposition by periods and by agents; therefore, we suppose a contractual interaction of the principal with each of the agents separately as well as for any period separately. Moreover, we assume that before making a decision for the period t regarding the "game history," the principal knows the output of CA during previous periods, and each of the agents knows both the output and the action.

Let the interaction of the principal and agents occur during the implementation of a *project*, i.e., of several consecutive periods of discrete time. By the end of the period T_0 (planned, called the *planned deadline for the completion of the project*), the principal needs to ensure a given total output $X_0 \geq 0$ of activity. Let the environment state values $\{\theta^t\}_{t=1, 2, \dots}$ during different periods be independent identically distributed random variables with the distribution function $F_\theta(\cdot)$, and let the principal conclude with the agent an optimal contract $\hat{\sigma}(z^t)$ determining the amount of the agent's remuneration during the period t, $t = 1, 2, \dots$.

Since the type and cost function of each agent are independent of the period number, for a given reliability α of each one-period contract, the principal should assign to the agent during each period the same plan, being equal to (compare with expression (4.31))

$$x_0 = X_0 / T_0 + F_\theta^{-1}(\alpha) \tag{8.2}$$

and, by virtue of (4.21), it is profitable for the agent to fulfill this plan.

The planned output (cumulative) of the agent's activity at the time point t is

$$X_0^t = t\,x_0 - t F_\theta^{-1}(\alpha) = t\,X_0 / T_0 \tag{8.3}$$

Sequence (8.3) in terms of *the earned value method* is called the *BQWS – Budgeted Quantity of Work Scheduled.*

Since the output $z^\tau = x_0 - \theta^\tau$ of the agent's activity during the period τ is a random variable, so the cumulative output X^t achieved by the period t is also a random variable:

$$X^t = t\,x_0 - \sum_{\tau=1}^{t} \theta^\tau = t\left(X_0 / T_0 + F_\theta^{-1}(\alpha)\right) - \sum_{\tau=1}^{t} \theta^\tau = X_0^t + t\,F_\theta^{-1}(\alpha) - \sum_{\tau=1}^{t} \theta^\tau \tag{8.4}$$

Sequence (8.4) in terms of the earned value method is the *AQWP – Actual Quantity of Work Performed.*

Let's define other indicators of earned value in terms of the uncertainty accounting additive model under consideration for ($t = 1, 2, \dots, T$):

- the principal's *budgeted expected* (in the sense of mathematical expectation) *costs* (*Budgeted Cost of Work Scheduled* – BCWS), a directive schedule:

$$c_0^t = t c\left(X_0 / T_0 + F_\theta^{-1}(\alpha), r\right) \tag{8.5}$$

- the principal's *actual costs* (*Actual Cost of Work Performed* – ACWP):

$$c^t = \sum_{\tau=1}^{t} \hat{\sigma}(x_0 - \theta^{\tau})$$ (8.6)

- a delay from the schedule (by time; such can be both positive and negative):

$$\delta(t) = \min\left\{\delta \mid X^{t-\delta} = X_0^t\right\}$$ (8.7)

- *earned value* (EV – Earned Value, Budgeted Cost of Work Performed – BCWP) as the budgeted cost of the work actually performed:

$$c_e^t = c_0^{t-\delta(t)}$$ (8.8)

- the current *forecast T(t) of the project completion time*:

$$T(t) = T_0 + \delta(t)$$ (8.9)

- *BAC – Budget at Completion* or BC – Budget Cost: C_0

$$C_0 = T_0\, c\left(X_0 / T_0 + F_\theta^{-1}(\alpha), r\right)$$ (8.10)

- the current linear *total cost estimate*:

$$C(t) = T(t)c^t / t$$ (8.11)

- *the actual time of the project completion*:

$$T' = \min\left\{t \geq 0 \mid X^t \geq X_0\right\}$$ (8.12)

- Cost Overrun:

$$\Delta c_e(t) = c^t - c_e^t$$ (8.13)

- *SPI – Schedule Performance Index*:

$$a^t = c_e^t / c_0^t$$ (8.14)

- CPI – Cost Performance Index:

$$b^t = c_e^t / c^t$$ (8.15)

Earned value indicators (8.2–8.15), which are usually divided into *primary* (8.2–8.6) and *derivative* ones (8.7–8.15), are an effective tool for planning of projects and operational control of their implementation.

Example 8.1. Let, under the conditions of Example 4.1, $r = 1$, $T_0 = 100$, $X_0 = 100$, $\Delta = 1$, $\alpha = 0,2$. The planned (8.3), actual (8.4), and expected ($X^t = X_0^t + t\,(F_\theta^{-1}(\alpha) - E\,\theta)$) trajectories are shown (from top to down) in the left part of Figure 8.19, the dynamics

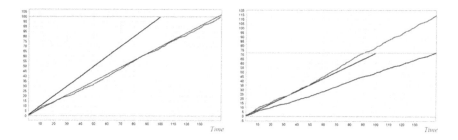

FIGURE 8.19   Sketches of the planned, expected and actual trajectories of EVM indicators.

of the budgeted and actual costs, as well as such of earned value, are shown in the right part of Figure 8.19.

We obtain the values of the indicators of earned value: $T' = 145$, $BAC = 72$, $\Delta c_e(T')$ $\approx 60\%$.

CONCLUSION

As a short conclusion to Chapter 8, let us note that

- the Optimal Enterprise Control Framework (Section 8.1) defines the "universal algorithm of the optimal Enterprise Control" and integrates all structural and process models (Chapter 1) and mathematical models described in Chapters 4–7, including the implementation of the Enterprise Control Optimization Scheme (Section 3.4.3).
- practical examples (Sections 8.2–8.4), first, illustrate the practical applicability of the developed models and methods, and second, confirm their importance for solving application problems to increase the efficiency of Enterprise control in various industries.

APPENDIXES

APPENDIX A8.1   SIMULATION OF THE OPTIMAL TECHNOLOGY DEVELOPMENT PROCESS IN BATCH MANUFACTURING

Various results of the nominal economic effect $\Phi_m(1, M)$ (c) simulation are illustrated in Tables A8.1 and A8.2 and in Figures A8.1 and A8.2. In the tables, the number m (batch number after which transition to regular production was made) changes by rows, K changes by columns, values of the effect are shown in the table cells; in the graphs, m is laid off on the horizontal axis, and the effect is laid off on the vertical axis, the level $L_0 = 0.75$.

Analysis of the simulation results illustrates the conclusion that the values of the accounting parameters, regardless of the values of the implicit parameters, determine a significant trend: the effect $\Phi_m(1,M)$ (A7.16) monotonically decreases (a) with

TABLE A8.1
The Effect $\Phi_m(1, M)$ with the Even Distribution $\{p_k\}$

$m\backslash K$	≤ 20	50	100	250	500
0	1382	1376	1364	1327	1264
1	1382	1376	1364	1327	1264
2	1370	1368	1359	1324	1263
3	1358	1357	1351	1320	1261
...	...	...	...	...	...
51	763	763	763	763	763
...	...	...	...	...	...

TABLE A8.2
The Effect $\Phi_m(1, M)$ with the Binomial and "Linearly Growing" Distributions $\{p_k\}$

$m\backslash K$	"Linearly Growing"			Binomial		
	10	20	30	10	20	30
0	1221	1034	877	1167	1066	1006
1	1221	1034	877	1168	1066	1006
2	1219	1034	877	1167	1065	1005
3	1216	1033	876	1164	1063	1003
...	...	...	...	...	...	
51	741	662	568	695	649	603
...	...	...	...	...	...	

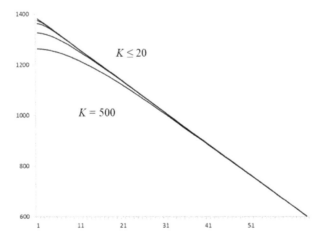

FIGURE A8.1 The effect $\Phi_m(1, M)$ dependence on the batch number m (the even distribution $\{p_k\}$).

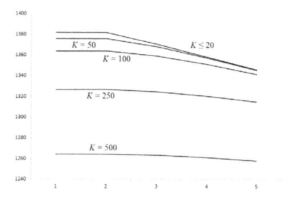

FIGURE A8.2 The effect $\Phi_m(1, M)$ dependence on m (the even distribution $\{p_k\}$; small *m*).

TABLE A8.3
Comparison of the Accepted Practice and the Recommended Approach

	Even Distribution				
K	≤20	50	100	250	500
Accepted practice	1379	1363	1339	1277	1182
Recommended approach	1382	1376	1364	1328	1264
Improvement percentage	100%	101%	102%	104%	107%
Number of batches	1	2	4	8	15

increase in the batch number *m*, after which transition to regular production is made (b) with increase in the dimensionality of the set of possible environmental states *K*. The identified trend confirmed the recommendation to switch to regular production immediately after the initial adjustment of the technology parameters.

Comparison of the recommended approach with the traditional practice was carried out in the other series of simulation experiments; their results are shown in Tables A8.3, A8.4.

In Tables A8.3, A8.4 the dimensionality of the set of the environmental states, i.e. potential sources of defect, changes by the columns. The first lines show the effect given implementation of the accepted practice; the second lines show those given the recommendations are followed; the third lines show the percentage of increase in the effect, and the fourth lines show the average number of test batches needed to transit to regular production given the accepted practice.

The analysis of the results allows one to make a conclusion that the recommended approach never impairs production efficiency, compared with the accepted practice, and, depending on the combination of the implicit parameter values, can significantly increase in efficiency.

TABLE A8.4

Comparison of the Accepted Practice and the Recommended Approach

	"Linearly Growing" Distribution			Binomial Distribution		
K	10	20	30	10	20	30
Accepted practice	1128	885	637	1077	950	872
Recommended approach	1221	1034	877	1167	1066	1006
Improvement percentage	108%	117%	138%	108%	112%	115%
Number of batches	16	28	33	15	20	23

The production efficiency also substantially depends on such an implicit parameter as the level of the initial technology maturity/learning level L_0. Therefore, another series of simulation experiments, during which the sensitivity of the results of the recommendation to L_0 was investigated, was performed; the results of these experiments are presented in Tables A8.5–A8.6, accomplished in the format of the previous tables.

The content of these tables allows one to conclude that, even in the case of low initial maturity/learning levels (40% of defect in the first batch), the feasibility to implement the recommendation preserves, because the traditional practice gives a greater economic effect only in certain cases, at which the gain is not more than 1%, while a loss in time (the need for test batches) preserves.

In such a way, the conclusions made on the basis of the simulation directly confirmed the recommendation on the feasibility to skip test production and start regular production immediately after the initial adjustment of the technological process.

Empirical results of application of the recommendation while tuning and manufacturing the first 100 batches are shown in Table A8.7 and Figure A8.3.

The results show that, in the case of the accepted practice, regular production would begin after the output of the 26th batch (see Table A8.7 and Figure A8.3). By this time costs for tuning would be −728 items (see Figure 8.7).

TABLE A8.5

Comparison of the Results of the Accepted Practice and the Recommended Approach with the Even Distribution and the Initial Level $L_0 = 0.6$.

K	≤20	50	100	250	500
Accepted practice	1376	1357	1328	1248	1124
Recommended approach	1374	1364	1345	1286	1185
Improvement percentage	99.8%	100.5%	101.3%	103.0%	105.5%
Number of batches	1	3	5	11	19

TABLE A8.6

Comparison of the Results of the Accepted Practice and the Recommended Approach with the Binomial and "Linearly Growing" Distributions and the Initial Level $L_0 = 0.6$.

	"Linearly Growing"			Binomial		
K	10	20	30	10	20	30
Accepted practice	220	353	361	214	390	519
Recommended approach	227	351	387	222	390	541
Improvement percentage	103%	99%	107%	104%	100%	104%
Number of batches	5	17	34	4	12	19

TABLE A8.7

The Numbers of the Defective Products in Batches

Batch number	1	2	3	4	5	6	7	8	9	...	25	26	27	...
Number of defects	17	12	11	12	11	7	5	5	6	...	2	1	0	...

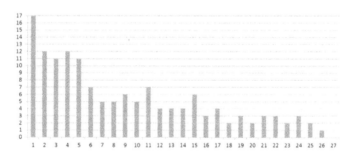

FIGURE A8.3   The numbers of the defective products in the batches.

APPENDIX A8.2   TECHNOLOGY LEARNING AT THE CUSTOMER SERVICE CENTER

Let's model the dependence of normalized averaged costs (8.1) on the duration of initial education – adaptation period (t_{ad}), the number of different typical requests (K_{ext}), and the number of typical requests (k_s) studied by an employee per one working day during the adaptation period.

The average headcount N_n of the ordinary employees' pool exceeds the number N required to fulfill all requests. This is due to the existence of periods when the employee does not proceed requests, firstly, during adaptation while being hired, and secondly, during regular vacations, illness, and other absences. In such case, the pool size is

$$N_n = N\left(1-\alpha_{abs}\right)^{-1}\left(1-t_{ad}/t_{avg}\right)^{-1} \approx N\left(1-\alpha_{abs}\right)^{-1}\left(1+t_{ad}/t_{avg}\right) \qquad (A8.1)$$

where α_{abs} is the average share of absence due to regular vacation, illness, and other similar cases; in practice, $\alpha_{abs} \approx 1/12...1/12,5$, t_{avg} is the average time-in-the-pool, in this case $t_{avg} \approx 155$, t_{ad} is time adaptation after entering, initial training etc. The value t_{ad}, among other factors influencing the technology learning/maturity level, was the subject–matter of analysis and optimization.

The expression for the feasible supervisors' headcount M is obtained based on the demand generated by ordinary employees (in cases when they don't have enough knowledge to process the requests).

An employee at each of N workplaces at the beginning of the time period t has individual technology learning level $L_{n,t}$, (n is the number of workplaces from 1 to N).

The number of requests x_t, the processing of which involves supervisors, is equal to the sum of such requests for all workplaces $n=1; 2; ... N$ – the sum of independent binary random variables, taking the value 0 or 1 with the probabilities $L_{n,t}$ and $(1 - L_{n,t})$, respectively.

Since N has an order of several hundred, the workload of supervisors is therefore approximated with good accuracy by a sequence of random independent normally distributed values. Given the constant conditions of the CSC's functioning, the time-averaged characteristics of these values were obtained and analyzed: the mathematical expectation and the dispersion accordingly $E[x_t]=N - \sum_{n=1}^{N} L_{n,t}$ and $\sigma^2[x_t]=\sum_{n=1}^{N} L_{n,t}\left(1-L_{n,t}\right)$. For this purpose, the learning process is approximated by the simplest model in the form of an exponential *learning curve* (5.2), and the attrition process is modeled by the stochastic flow with constant leaving intensity.

Learning/maturity level of an employee at the n-th workplace during the transition from period t to period $t+1$ changes as follows:

a) given the constant probability $\pi^- = 1/t_{avg}$ (where t_{avg} is the average time-in-the-pool) the employee leaves and is replaced by a new one, then $L_{n,t+1}=l_0$, where l_0 is the initial level of learning, $l_0=\kappa t_{ad}$ is assumed depending on the t_{ad} and on the "speed" κ of the initial training;
b) given the probability $(1-\pi^-)$ $L_{n,t}$ that the employee does not leave and processes a request all alone, then $L_{n,t+1}=L_{n,t}$;
c) given the probability $(1-\pi^-)$ $(1-L_{n,t})$ that the employee does not leave and involves a "supervisor" to process a request,* then $L_{n,t+1}=1-\gamma\left(1-L_{n,t}\right)$.

---

* For definiteness, we assume that an employee's leaving and replacement occurs "instantly" at the moment separating the t-th and $t+1$-th time periods. So during the first productive period after initial training, the employee works with the learning level l_0. The feasibility to use such an "averaged" model of resignations is examined in detail in Section 6.3.2, which is devoted to a practical analysis of the characteristics of employees' lifecycle.

$$L_{n,t+1} = \begin{cases} l_0 & \text{with the probability } \pi^-, \\ L_{n,t} & \text{with the probability } (1-\pi^-)L_{n,t}, \\ 1-\gamma+\gamma L_{n,t} & \text{with the probability } (1-\pi^-)(1-L_{n,t}). \end{cases}$$

If an employee at the workplace n (let us omit the number n to simplify expressions) begins working at a certain time point, then the learning level evolves as $L_t = 1-(1-l_0)\gamma^t$, where t is the number of periods.

The parameters l_0, κ, t_{ad}, γ of the technology learning/maturity model are the subject–matter of analysis and means to minimize the objective function, i.e., costs (8.1).

If an employee leaves after t periods, the time-averaged values L_t and $L_t(1-L_t)$ for his work time equal:

$$\bar{L}_t = \frac{1}{t}\sum_{i=0}^{t-1}\left(1-(1-l_0)\gamma^i\right) = 1 - \frac{1-l_0}{t}\sum_{i=0}^{t-1}\gamma^i = 1 - \frac{1-l_0}{1-\gamma}\frac{1-\gamma^t}{t},$$

$$\overline{L_t(1-L_t)} = \frac{1}{t}\sum_{i=0}^{t-1}\left(1-(1-l_0)\gamma^i\right)(1-l_0)\gamma^i = \frac{1-l_0}{t}\sum_{i=0}^{t-1}\gamma^i - \frac{(1-l_0)^2}{t}\sum_{i=0}^{t-1}\gamma^{2i}$$

$$= \frac{1-l_0}{1-\gamma}\frac{1-\gamma^t}{t} - \frac{(1-l_0)^2}{1-\gamma^2}\frac{1-\gamma^{2t}}{t}.$$

The probability of an employee's resignation exactly after t periods equals $\lambda(1-\lambda)^{t-1}$, then

$$\bar{L} = \sum_{n=1}^{\infty}\bar{L}_n\pi^-\left(1-\pi^-\right)^{n-1} = \sum_{n=0}^{\infty}\left(1-\frac{1-l_0}{n+1}\frac{1-\gamma^{n+1}}{1-\gamma}\right)\pi^-\left(1-\pi^-\right)^{n}$$

$$= 1-(1-l_0)\frac{\pi^-}{1-\pi^-}\frac{1}{1-\gamma}\left\{\sum_{n=0}^{\infty}\frac{(1-\pi^-)^{n+1}}{n+1} - \sum_{n=0}^{\infty}\frac{(\gamma(1-\pi^-))^{n+1}}{n+1}\right\}.$$

The representation $\ln(1-x) = -\sum_{n=1}^{\infty}n^{-1}x^n$ is valid $\forall\, x \in [0;\,1)$, then

$$\bar{L} = 1+(1-l_0)\frac{\pi^-}{1-\pi^-}\frac{1}{1-\gamma}\left(\ln(\pi^-) - \ln(1-\gamma(1-\pi^-))\right)$$

$$= 1+(1-l_0)\frac{\pi^-}{1-\pi^-}\frac{1}{1-\gamma}\ln\left(\frac{\pi^-}{1-\gamma(1-\pi^-)}\right).$$

The substitution $t_{avg} = 1/\pi^-$ allows getting:

$$\bar{L} = 1 - (1 - l_0) \frac{\ln\left(t_{avg}\left(1-\gamma\right)+\gamma\right)}{t_{avg}\left(1-\gamma\right)+\gamma-1}. \tag{A8.2}$$

The averaged dispersion $\overline{L(1-L)}$ is obtained similarly:

$$\overline{L(1-L)} = \pi^- \sum_{n=1}^{\infty} \overline{L_n(1-L_n)}\left(1-\pi^-\right)^{n-1}$$

$$= \frac{1-l_0}{1-\gamma}\frac{\pi^-}{1-\pi^-} \sum_{n=1}^{\infty} \frac{1-\gamma^n}{n}\left(1-\pi^-\right)^n - \frac{\left(1-l_0\right)^2}{1-\gamma^2}\frac{\pi^-}{1-\pi^-} \sum_{n=0}^{\infty} \frac{1-\left(\gamma^2\right)^n}{n}\left(1-\pi^-\right)^n$$

$$= \frac{1-l_0}{1-\gamma}\frac{\pi^-}{1-\pi^-} \ln\left(1/\pi^- - \gamma\left(1/\pi^- - 1\right)\right)$$

$$- \frac{\left(1-l_0\right)^2}{1-\gamma^2}\frac{\pi^-}{1-\pi^-} \ln\left(1/\pi^- - \gamma^2\left(1/\pi^- - 1\right)\right).$$

After substituting t_{avg} instead of $1/\pi^-$:

$$\overline{L(1-L)} = (1-l_0)\frac{\ln\left(t_{avg}\left(1-\gamma\right)+\gamma\right)}{t_{avg}\left(1-\gamma\right)+\gamma-1} - (1-l_0)^2 \frac{\ln\left(t_{avg}\left(1-\gamma^2\right)+\gamma^2\right)}{t_{avg}\left(1-\gamma^2\right)+\gamma^2-1}. \tag{A8.3}$$

Thus, the workload on supervisors during each time period is approximated by a sequence of normally distributed random variables with the mathematical expectation $N(1-\bar{L})$ and the dispersion $N\overline{L(1-L)}$ (A8.2) and (A8.3).

The required headcount of supervisors M, in addition to the characteristics of workload (A8.2) and (A8.3), depends on the admissible probability p_{ovl} that during a certain period the random workload exceeds the supervisors' capabilities and the request flows aren't fully processed – that is SLA conditions are violated:

$$M = \frac{1}{m_0}\left(N\left(1-\bar{L}\right) + \vartheta_{ovl}\sqrt{N\overline{L(1-L)}}\right) \tag{A8.4}$$

where m_0 is the number of problematic requests, the processing of which can be supported by a supervisor during one period ($m_0 = 5$), $\vartheta_{ovl} = \Phi^{-1}(p_{ovl})$, and $\Phi^{-1}(\cdot)$ is the inverse function of the standard normal distribution. The admissible level p_{ovl} is chosen by the management expertly. Business sense belongs to values from 1/100 to 1/1000 (which corresponds, by an average, to one case of SLA violation per 100 or 1000 working days, approximately once every four months or almost four years), then $2.3 \leq \vartheta_{ovl} \leq 3.1$. In the CSC, such violations are allowed once every six months, so $\vartheta_{ovl} = 2.44$.

Taking into account expressions (A8.1–A8.4), nominal costs (8.1) are equal to

$$C(N_n; M) = N(1 - \alpha_{abs})^{-1} \left(1 + t_{ad} / t_{avg} + c \frac{1}{m_0} \left(1 - \bar{L} + \vartheta_{ovl} \sqrt{N^{-1} L(1-L)} \right) \right).$$

After eliminating the constant summands and coefficients ($N(1 - \alpha_{abs})^{-1}$, t_{avg} and similar ones), the expression for nominal costs takes such form of the function of the technology learning/maturity parameters κ, t_{ad}, γ that is clear and convenient to the solution of the optimization problem:

$$C(t_{ad}; \kappa; \gamma) = (1 - \varepsilon \kappa f(\gamma)) t_{ad} + \vartheta \sqrt{(1 - \kappa t_{ad}) f(\gamma) - (1 - \kappa t_{ad})^2 f(\gamma^2)}, \qquad (A8.5)$$

where $\varepsilon = t_{avg} c / m_0 \approx 77.5$, $\vartheta = \varepsilon \vartheta_{ovl} N^{-1/2} \approx 8.5$, and
$f(x) = (t_{avg} - 1)^{-1} (1-x)^{-1} \ln[(t_{avg} - 1)(1-x) + 1]$ is a convex, smooth function, monotonically increasing for $x \in [0;1]$.

The parameters characterizing the "speed" of the technology learning during the initial training κ and learning-by-working γ are not caused by any physical laws and their "exact" values cannot be obtained by instrumental measurements. Therefore, it is necessary to involve experts to define their interval or point values. For the convenience of the experts, other parameters, directly tied to κ and γ, were introduced. Exponential learning model (5.2) assumes a uniform probability distribution of the possible environmental states, and the parameter γ depends on the number of possible states as $\gamma = 1 - 1/K_{ext}$; in this case K_{ext} corresponds to the number of possible typical combinations of the parameters of requests. The experts–supervisors classified all types of requests and determined typical combinations of the parameters; about 60 such types were obtained. The experts sought to distinguish typical combinations in such a way as to ensure a relative uniformity to the appearance of each of those in the flow of requests, which corresponds to a "disturbed uniform" distribution model (5.5–5.6). The "speed" of the technology learning during the initial education course κ is tied to K_{ext} as $\kappa = k_s / K_{ext}$, where k_s is the number of typical combinations of the parameters of requests (typical requests), being studied within one working day. The parameters K_{ext} and k_s are more intuitively comprehensible and more convenient for experts than γ and κ.

It was decided to search for optimal technology learning strategies within the range of K_{ext} from 40 to 100, and for k_s within the range from 1 to 8. For this purpose, on the basis of expression (A8.5), the dependencies of the nominal costs for the initial training time t_{ad} for various k_s and K_{ext} were analyzed. Figures A8.4–A8.7 illustrate the function evolutions $C(t_{ad}; k_s; K_{ext})$; those can be easily obtained analytically based on (A8.5).

In such a way, one can fix the following properties of the cost function $C(t_{ad}; k_s; K_{ext})$:

A. if learning "speed" of initial training isn't less than three typical requests per day $k_s \geq 3$, then the nominal costs $C(t_{ad}; k_s; K_{ext})$ monotonically decrease by the duration of initial education t_{ad} for all values $40 \leq K_{ext} \leq 100$;
B. if $k_s = 2$, then the nominal costs $C(t_{ad}; k_s; K_{ext})$ monotonically decrease by t_{ad} for all values $40 \leq K_{ext} \leq 80$ and increase, given $100 \leq K_{ext}$;

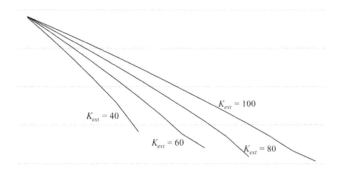

FIGURE A8.4 Sketch of the dependence of the costs $C(t_{ad}; k_s; K_{ext})$ on t_{ad} for $k_s = 8$.

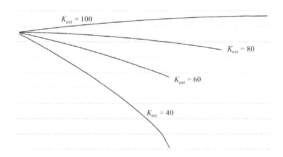

FIGURE A8.5 Sketch of the dependence of the costs $C(t_{ad}; k_s; K_{ext})$ on t_{ad} for $k_s = 3$.

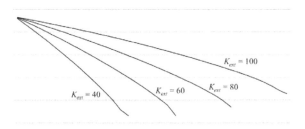

FIGURE A8.6 Sketch of the dependence of the costs $C(t_{ad}; k_s; K_{ext})$ on t_{ad} for $k_s = 2$.

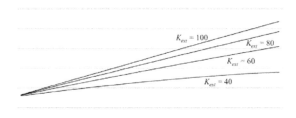

FIGURE A8.7 Sketch of the dependence of the costs $C(t_{ad}; k_s; K_{ext})$ on t_{ad} for $k_s = 1$.

C. given $k_s = 1$, the nominal costs $C(t_{ad}; k_s; K_{ext})$ monotonically increase by t_{ad} for all values $40 \leq K_{ext}$;

D. the nominal costs $C(t_{ad}; k_s; K_{ext})$ monotonically increase by K_{ext}, given any t_{ad} and k_s;

E. the nominal costs $C(t_{ad}; k_s; K_{ext})$ monotonically decrease by k_s, given any t_{ad} and K_{ext}.

REFERENCES

Adizes, I. 1999. *Managing Corporate Lifecycles: An updated and Expanded Look at the Corporate Lifecycles*. First edition. First printing. Paramus: Prentice Hall Press.

Allen, B., Weigelt, K., Doherty, N. and Mansfield, E. 2009. *Managerial Economics: Theory, Applications, and Cases*. Seventh Edition. New York: W. W. Norton & Company.

Belov, M. 2015. IBS Group, Eastern European ITS Services – Capability-Based Development for Business Transformation. In Gorod, A., White, B., et al. (eds.), *Case Studies in System of Systems, Enterprise Systems, and Complex Systems Engineering*. Boca Raton, FL: CRC Press, 129–164.

Coase, R. 1937. The Nature of the Firm. *Economica* 4(16), 386–405.

Cole, K. 2018. *Leadership and Management: Theory and Practice*. Seventh edition. Cengage Learning Sydney: Australia.

Drucker, P. 1954. *The Practice of Management*. New York : Harper & Row.

Fayol, H. 1917. *Administration industrielle et générale*. Paris: Dunod et Pinat.

Foss, N., Lando, H. and Thomsen, S. 2000. The Theory of the Firm. In B. Bouckaert and G. De Geest (eds.), *Encyclopedia of Law and Economics: Volume III. The Regulation of Contracts*. Cheltenham: Edward Elgar Publishing, 631–658.

Gotteiner, S. 2016. The OPTIMAL MBO. *European Accounting and Management Review* 2(2), 42–56.

Hammer and Champy. 1993. *Reengineering the Corporation: A Manifesto for Business Revolution*. New York: Harper Collins Publishers.

Marshall, R. 2007. The Contribution of Earned Value Management to Project Success of Contracted Efforts. *Journal of Contract Management* 47(9), 21–33.

Moschandreas, M. 2000. *Business Economics*. Second edition. London: Business Press.

Nikiforov, I. 2016. Sequential Detection/Isolation of Abrupt Changes. *Sequential Analysis. Design Methods and Applications* 35(3), 268–301.

Northouse, P. 2015. *Leadership: Theory and Practice*. New York: SAGE Publishing.

Png, I. and Lehman, D. 2007. *Managerial Economics*. London: Blackwell Pub.

Management Methods. Management Models. Management Theories. at . https://www.val uebasedmanagement.net/ Accessed September 27 2020.

PMBOK guide. 2017. *A Guide to the Project Management Body of Knowledge*. Sixth edition. Newtown Square: Project Management Institute.

Porter, M. 1985. *Competitive Advantage: Creating and Sustaining Superior Performance*. London: Collier Macmillan.

Reichel, C. 2006. Earned Value Management Systems (EVMS): "You Too Can Do Earned Value Management". *Paper presented at PMI® Global Congress 2006*, Seattle: Project Management Institute.

Tague, N. 2005. *Plan–Do–Study–Act Cycle. The Quality Toolbox*. Second edition. Milwaukee: ASQ Quality Press.

White, B. 2015. On Leadership in the Complex Adaptive Systems Engineering of Enterprise. *Transformation Journal of Enterprise Transformation* 5(3), 192–217.

Williamson, O. 2009. Transaction Cost Economics: The Natural Progression. *American Economic Review* 86(3), 215–226.

Afterword

The main results presented in the book and the prospects for applying them in practice are systematized in the conclusions to the chapters. Therefore, we do repeat them, but we discuss new prospects that have appeared in related sciences (see also Section 3.3), as well as new challenges posed to those related sciences.

Here is what we present in the book, in two sentences:

1. *the person as the core constituent of the complex system* is formalized and investigated;
2. *the optimization* and *control* problem of an Enterprise – *a complex system comprising people* – is formulated and solved.

And here we add a few more details:

a) we identify and study two fundamentally important human traits: (a) it is human complex activity that is the source of any value/utility in the world; (b) human behavior and, consequently, human complex activity are driven by human interests and preferences – the mental components of activity.
b) we develop an integrated system of structural and process models of *human complex activity*;
c) we state the mathematically rigorous *optimization problem* of *control* of a *complex system containing people*;
d) we solve this *control problem* mathematically rigorously using a system of integrated mathematical models and methods and get *optimal control* of a *complex system comprising people*.

Therefore, our book relates to various knowledge domains that study *complex systems* containing *people* and the *control* of such systems. Table AW.1 illustrates our contribution to each of the related knowledge domains.

TABLE AW.1

Contribution to the related knowledge domains

Related Science, Field of Knowledge	Our Contributions to the Knowledge Domain	Opportunities	Challenges
General Systems Theory	• We research the person as the core element of a Complex System (of a human-made system focused on value creation); human fundamental traits are researched: • human complex activity – the source of any kind of value; • human behavior driven by interests and preferences – human active choice • We formalize and research (as a set of structural and mathematical models) the complex activity and active factors of human behavior • We formalize and research the technology development processes • We state and solve the holistic formal Enterprise Control Problem and bridge the gap between systems engineering qualitative approaches and methods and mathematical models of operations research	• A unified apparatus to describe and optimize human-made complex systems, which include people • A unified organization and management view of such systems	Development of general theory of organization (as a property, process, and subject matter) of various kinds of natural and artificial systems
Systems Engineering; Systems of Systems; Complex Systems Engineering		• Description and analysis of the interrelated lifecycles of subject matters, actors, technologies, and resources of any complex activity • Quantitative description of the process and results of the design and development of Systems of Systems (including extended enterprises and large-scale design programs) and their effectiveness, integrated with the operations research apparatus • Description of the processes of design and implementation of new technologies	"Instrumentalization" of the proposed models, methods, and algorithms in the standards and managerial information and engineering systems of Complex Systems and Systems of Systems

(Continued)

TABLE AW.1 (CONTINUED)
Contribution to the related knowledge domains

Related Science, Field of Knowledge	Our Contributions to the Knowledge Domain	Opportunities	Challenges
Management theory and practice	• We develop an integrated set of formal models which generalizes all widely used managerial methods and approaches • We state and solve the holistic formal Enterprise Control Problem applicable to any business unit • We formalize and research the technology development processes applicable to the operations of any business unit	• Systematic generation of management decisions with an evaluation of their effectiveness • Analysis and synthesis of the optimal set of standard solutions • Transition from (qualitative) Management to (quantitative) Optimal Control • Quantitative knowledge management study • Quantitative human capital research	Mass implementation of templates and methods for the quantitative description of control systems based on uniform regulatory procedures for scenario modeling and performance evaluation
Theory of Control in Organizations & Mechanism Design (including Theory of Contracts)	• We develop the methodological foundation of the Theory of Control in Organizations – structural and process models of complex activity • We formulate and prove theorems of incentive problem decomposition in a hierarchical multi-agent dynamic active system with uncertainty	• Decomposition of socio-technical systems management tasks by actors, hierarchy levels, time periods, and technology stages	Decision-making methods under true uncertainty; models and methods for integrating typical control mechanisms; research on cooperative behavior of complex entities
Operations Research	• We state the holistic formal Enterprise Control Problem and develop a mathematically rigorous problem solution • This problem statement integrates and positions known operations research models and methods within the problem solution	• Application of well-known models and methods to a wide range of new applied problems: technology management, human capital management, etc.	Optimization models and methods of multilevel dynamic socio-technical systems comprising people

(Continued)

TABLE AW.1 (CONTINUED)
Contribution to the related knowledge domains

Related Science, Field of Knowledge	Our Contributions to the Knowledge Domain	Opportunities	Challenges
Psychology of Personality	• We introduce formal models of individual and group activity supported by advanced models of applied mathematics • We develop unified probabilistic models of the learning process and state and solve optimization and control problems of individual and group learning		Experimental identification of formal models of complex activity; their specification for typical practical situations
Methodology	• We study complex activity, develop an integrated set of structural and process models of complex activity • We introduce models of technology • All the abovementioned models are applicable to real practical cases and provide valuable output	• Constructive description of complex activity in the form of an integrated system of formal structural and process models • Introduction of formal models of activity technology – structural, process, and mathematical • Operations research apparatus to optimize activity use	Integrated study of the mental and behavioral components of activity, considering the individual characteristics of its actors; creative activity analysis

Index